Occasion Setting

Occasion Setting

ASSOCIATIVE LEARNING AND COGNITION IN ANIMALS

EDITED BY

Nestor A. Schmajuk
Peter C. Holland

AMERICAN PSYCHOLOGICAL ASSOCIATION • WASHINGTON, DC

Published by
American Psychological Association
750 First Street, NE
Washington, DC 20002

Copies may be ordered from
APA Order Department
P.O. Box 92984
Washington, DC 20090-2984

In the UK and Europe, copies may be ordered from
American Psychological Association
3 Henrietta Street
Covent Garden, London
WC2E 8LU England

Typeset in Minion by WorldComp, Sterling, VA
Printer: United Book Press, Inc., Baltimore, MD
Cover Designer: Berg Design, Albany, NY
Project Manager: Debbie K. Hardin, Reston, VA

Library of Congress Cataloging-in-Publication Data

Occasion setting : associative learning and cognition in animals / edited by Nestor Schmajuk, Peter C. Holland.
p. cm.
Includes bibliographical references and index.
ISBN 1-55798-490-5 (alk. paper)
1. Learning in animals. 2. Cognition in animals. 3. Classical conditioning. I. Schmajuk, Nestor. II. Holland, Peter C., 1951- III. American Psychological Association.
QL785.033 1998
156′.315—DC21 97-47677
CIP

British Library Cataloguing-in-Publication Data
A CIP record is available from the British Library.

Printed in the United States of America
First Edition

APA Science Volumes

Attribution and Social Interaction: The Legacy of Edward E. Jones
Best Methods for the Analysis of Change: Recent Advances, Unanswered Questions, Future Directions
Cardiovascular Reactivity to Psychological Stress and Disease
The Challenge in Mathematics and Science Education: Psychology's Response
Changing Employment Relations: Behavioral and Social Perspectives
Children Exposed to Marital Violence: Theory, Research, and Applied Issues
Cognition: Conceptual and Methodological Issues
Cognitive Bases of Musical Communication
Conceptualization and Measurement of Organism–Environment Interaction
Converging Operations in the Study of Visual Selective Attention
Creative Thought: An Investigation of Conceptual Structures and Processes
Developmental Psychoacoustics
Diversity in Work Teams: Research Paradigms for a Changing Workplace
Emotion and Culture: Empirical Studies of Mutual Influence
Emotion, Disclosure, and Health
Evolving Explanations of Development: Ecological Approaches to Organism–Environment Systems
Examining Lives in Context: Perspectives on the Ecology of Human Development
Global Prospects for Education: Development, Culture, and Schooling
Hostility, Coping, and Health

Measuring Patient Changes in Mood, Anxiety, and Personality Disorders: Toward a Core Battery

Occasion Setting: Associative Learning and Cognition in Animals

Organ Donation and Transplantation: Psychological and Behavioral Factors

The Perception of Structure

Perspectives on Socially Shared Cognition

Psychological Testing of Hispanics

Psychology of Women's Health: Progress and Challenges in Research and Application

Researching Community Psychology: Issues of Theory and Methods

Sleep and Cognition

Sleep Onset: Normal and Abnormal Processes

Stereotype Accuracy: Toward Appreciating Group Differences

Stereotyped Movements: Brain and Behavior Relationships

Studying Lives Through Time: Personality and Development

The Suggestibility of Children's Recollections: Implications for Eyewitness Testimony

Taste, Experience, and Feeding: Development and Learning

Temperament: Individual Differences at the Interface of Biology and Behavior

Through the Looking Glass: Issues of Psychological Well-Being in Captive Nonhuman Primates

Uniting Psychology and Biology: Integrative Perspectives on Human Development

Viewing Psychology as a Whole: The Integrative Science of William N. Dember

APA expects to publish volumes on the following conference topics:

Computational Modeling of Behavior Processes in Organizations

Dissonance Theory 40 Years Later: A Revival With Revisions and Controversies

Experimental Psychopathology and Pathogenesis of Schizophrenia

Intelligence on the Rise: Secular Changes in IQ and Related Measures
Marital and Family Therapy Outcome and Process Research
Models of Gender and Gender Differences: Then and Now
Psychosocial Interventions for Cancer

As part of its continuing and expanding commitment to enhance the dissemination of scientific psychological knowledge, the Science Directorate of the APA established a Scientific Conferences Program. A series of volumes resulting from these conferences is produced jointly by the Science Directorate and the Office of Communications. A call for proposals is issued twice annually by the Scientific Directorate, which, collaboratively with the APA Board of Scientific Affairs, evaluates the proposals and selects several conferences for funding. This important effort has resulted in an exceptional series of meetings and scholarly volumes, each of which has contributed to the dissemination of research and dialogue in these topical areas.

The APA Science Directorate's conferences funding program has supported 47 conferences since its inception in 1988. To date, 38 volumes resulting from conferences have been published.

William C. Howell, PhD
Executive Director

Virginia E. Holt
Assistant Executive Director

Contents

Contributors

Charlotte Bonardi, Department of Psychology, University of York
Mark E. Bouton, Department of Psychology, University of Vermont
Susan E. Brandon, Department of Psychology, Yale University
Catalin V. Buhusi, Department of Psychology, Duke University
June-Seek Choi, Department of Psychology, University of Massachusetts
T. L. Davidson, Department of Psychological Sciences, Purdue University
David N. George, Department of Psychology, University of Wales, College of Cardiff
Mark Gluck, Center for Molecular and Behavioral Neuroscience, Rutgers University
Murray J. Goddard, Department of Psychology, Duke University
Geoffrey Hall, Department of Psychology, University of York
Peter C. Holland, Department of Psychology, Duke University
Jeffrey Lamoureux, Department of Psychology, Duke University
Ralph R. Miller, Department of Psychology, SUNY at Binghamton
Esther Mondragón, Department of Psychology, University of York
John W. Moore, Department of Psychology, University of Massachusetts
Catherine Myers, Center for Molecular and Behavioral Neuroscience, Rutgers University
Sadahiko Nakajima, Psychology Department, University of Pennsylvania
James B. Nelson, Psychology Department, University of Vermont
Philippe Oberling, Louis Pasteur School of Medicine

John M. Pearce, Department of Psychology, University of Wales, College of Cardiff

Edward S. Redhead, Department of Psychology, University of Wales, College of Cardiff

Nestor A. Schmajuk, Department of Psychology, Duke University

Darlene M. Skinner, Department of Psychology, Duke University

Dale Swartzentruber, Department of Psychology, Ohio Wesleyan University

Allan R. Wagner, Department of Psychology, Yale University

James Zackheim, Center for Molecular and Behavioral Neuroscience, Rutgers University

Introduction

Sixty years ago, B. F. Skinner (1938) proposed that a discriminative stimulus in an operant conditioning paradigm does not elicit a response but simply "sets the occasion" for the response to occur. More recently, investigators have claimed that, whereas in many Pavlovian conditioning paradigms a conditioned stimulus (CS) elicits a conditioned response (CR) because it signals the occurrence of an unconditioned stimulus (US), in other paradigms a CS controls behavior because it "sets the occasion" for the responding produced by another CS. In the first case the CS is said to act as a "simple CS"; in the latter case the CS is said to act as an "occasion setter" (Holland, 1983, 1992) or "facilitator" (Rescorla, 1985).

Pavlovian occasion-setting data attracted attention for several reasons. First, occasion setters showed important differences in the effects of fairly basic conditioning operations, such as extinction and summation, which suggests the operation of a mechanism that is distinguishable from simple conditioning. Second, at least in some preparations, relatively minor variations in the temporal or sensory characteristics of compound stimuli resulted in a CS behaving as a simple CS or as an occasion setter. Third, early theoretical efforts implied that Pavlovian occasion setting was related to interesting problems in behavior theory, including discriminative

---

The conference on Occasion Setting: Theory and Data was sponsored by the Science Directorate of the American Psychological Association; and the Vice Provost for Academic and International Affairs, the Dean of Arts and Sciences, and the Department of Psychology: Experimental of Duke University. We wish to thank our sponsors and Martha Barbour and Jef Lamoureux for making local conference preparations at Duke.

stimulus function in operant conditioning, the influence of motivational variables on behavior, and the hierarchical organization of memory.

In the spring of 1997, a group of experimentalists and theoreticians gathered at Duke University to discuss the current state of data and theories of simple classical conditioning and occasion setting. This book provides an overview of the meeting.

Part I of the book compares the properties of simple stimuli and occasion setters, including an examination of the parallels between phenomena observed in simple conditioning and occasion setting, a study that supports the view that occasion setting is the result of a type of associative learning in which the occasion setter becomes associated with the CS–US association itself, a demonstration that feature-positive and feature-negative procedures may be logical but not psychological opposites, and a discussion of the generality of the properties of occasion setters.

In chapter 1, Ralph R. Miller and Philippe Oberling stress the parallels between phenomena observed in Pavlovian excitatory conditioning and phenomena observed in occasion setting. These analogies include extinction; evidence of temporal encoding; overshadowing; recovery from overshadowing by way of extinction of the overshadowing stimulus; blocking; dependence of blocking on the blocking and blocked stimuli encoding the same temporal information; latent inhibition; learned irrelevance; modulation by higher order stimuli; summation; asymptotic stimulus control being directly proportional to the intertrial–interstimulus interval in Pavlovian conditioning and the intertrial–feature-target interval in occasion setting; contexts being able to substitute for discrete stimuli as occasion setters, just as they can for Pavlovian CSs; and the relationships between Pavlovian conditioned excitation and inhibition and serial positive and serial negative occasion setting.

In chapter 2, Charlotte Bonardi proposes that, in contrast to the explanations that assume that occasion setting is the consequence of some special learning mechanism that is independent of simple associative learning, occasion setting is the result of a particular type of associative learning in which the occasion setter becomes associated with the CS–US association itself. She presents evidence that is consistent with this proposal—including the acquisition of occasion setting without specific discrimination training, blocking of the occasion setter in a serial–positive discrimination, and the specificity of an occasion setter to a given target-US association and suggests that an advantage of this analysis is that it provides a link with the instrumental analog of occasion setting—discriminative control—for which an associative explanation has been suggested.

In chapter 3, Mark E. Bouton and James B. Nelson report a number of experiments in which rats learned to discriminate trials that signaled a food US from those that did not. In feature-negative learning (A+, XA–), the feature (X) inhibited performance through two mechanisms: direct inhibition of the US representation and activation of a context-dependent inhibitory association that is learned between the target (A) and the US. The latter form of inhibition dominates serial feature-negative discrimination learning and may be a mechanism of negative occasion setting. Bouton and Nelson present recent experiments that are designed to extend this analysis to serial feature-positive discrimination learning (X→A+, A–). With their methods, the rat solves the discrimination by merely associating the feature with the US—that is, they find no evidence of positive occasion setting. Similar results such as these were obtained with several different feature-target intervals and with a serial procedure in which the feature remains on and overlaps the target. Bouton and Nelson also obtain similar results after other treatments thought to enhance positive occasion setting, including inhibitory preconditioning of the target and manipulations of feature and target salience. On the basis of their results, Bouton and Nelson suggest that feature-positive and feature-negative procedures may be logical, but not psychological, opposites.

In chapter 4, Darlene M. Skinner, Murray J. Goddard, and Peter C. Holland point out that the defining characteristics of occasion setters as originally defined by Holland (1983, 1992) might be more task-specific than originally thought. Although the notion of modulation is widely applicable, the details of these applications might differ from preparation to preparation.

Part II analyzes different paradigms in which the concept of occasion setting can be applied, including Pavlovian feature-ambiguous discriminations, operant matching-to-sample tasks, contextual control, motivational control of feeding behavior, and the role of attention in the solution of conditional discriminations.

In chapter 5, Sadahiko Nakajima points out that mastery of a feature-ambiguous discrimination task (A–, XA+, B+, XB–) troubles one major theory of hierarchical learning, the US–threshold modulation hypothesis proposed by Rescorla (1985), because X cannot both lower and raise the threshold of US representation at the same time. Another major theory, the occasion-setting hypothesis of Holland (1983, 1985), explains the mastery of this task by assuming that X acts positively on the A–US association and negatively on the B–US association. The task can also be solved through configural learning—that is, animals may treat XA and XB as single conditioned stimuli. These theoretical issues are addressed in autoshaping experiments that explore the temporal relationship between X and the targets, the effect of target reversal (A+, B–) on the original learning, and the transfer between concurrently trained feature-ambiguous tasks.

In chapter 6, Dale Swartzentruber suggests that insight into the mechanisms of occasion setting might be gained by considering the involvement of memory coding processes. For example, one possibility is that, upon presentation of the occasion setter, the subject prospectively processes the representation of a specific target CS or CS–US association. Another possibility is that, upon presentation of the target, the subject retrospectively processes the memory trace of the OS. Although a number of researchers have addressed the topic of memory codes in operant matching-to-sample and conditional discrimination tasks, it has received little attention in the Pavlovian occasion-setting literature. Swartzentruber therefore discusses the implications and utility of this perspective, using data from experiments on Pavlovian conditional discrimination learning and from a Pavlovian analog to one of Roitblat's (1980) experiments that investigated prospective and retrospective codes.

In chapter 7, Geoffrey Hall and Esther Mondragón indicate that training given in one context may fail to transfer to another. For instance, the latent inhibition effect is attenuated when preexposure and conditioning occur in different contexts, and the vigor of a conditioned response is sometimes found to decline when a conditioned stimulus trained in one context is presented in another. It has been suggested that this type of contextual control occurs because the contextual cues come to act as occasion setters that are capable of fostering the retrieval of information acquired in their presence. But although theoretically appealing, the parallel between occasion-setting and contextual control seems to be inexact. In particular, contextual control can be established without the explicit discrimination training (feature-positive training) usually employed in the standard procedure for establishing a discrete cue as an occasion setter. Hall and Mondragón report the results of a set of experiments that explore the source of this discrepancy. They present evidence that shows that the formation of direct excitatory associations between the target stimulus and the occasion setter (or context) in whose presence training occurs can obscure evidence for conditional control by an event trained as an occasion setter. Once this factor is taken into account, the essential identity between contextual control and occasion setting becomes apparent.

In chapter 8, T. L. Davidson indicates that a long-standing challenge for researchers of feeding behavior has been to explain how departures from homeostasis produce behavioral changes that serve to restore energy balance. Many accounts have addressed this question within drive, incentive, or other motivational frameworks. In this chapter, Davidson considers the possibility that the effects of energy need on feeding can be understood as an example of Pavlovian occasion setting. From this perspective, interoceptive cues produced by fasting and other sources of metabolic depletion (i.e., hunger signals) are seen as highly valid predictors of when conditioned food cues (e.g., taste, texture, aroma, and visual features of food) and cues related to food will be followed by particular types of postingestive USs. In this role, hunger signals augment feeding behavior by modulating the effectiveness of the food cue–postingestive US association.

Davidson's approach provides a nonmotivational account of the effects of energy need on feeding behavior and suggests new research strategies for investigating the neurohormonal controls of food intake.

In chapter 9, John M. Pearce, David N. George, and Edward S. Redhead present a series of experiments which used autoshaping with pigeons that examined the extent to which changes in attention can influence acquisition of a conditional discrimination. In one set of experiments, pigeons received a conditional discrimination in which some stimuli, but not others, were relevant to its solution. Subsequent transfer tests that involved a new conditional discrimination revealed more rapid learning with the previously relevant than irrelevant stimuli. In a second set of experiments, pigeons were trained with a negative patterning discrimination in which an irrelevant stimulus was present on every trial. The ease with which the discrimination was solved was influenced by manipulations that were designed to alter the attention that was paid to the irrelevant stimulus. Pearce and collaborators consider the implications of these results for certain elemental and configural theories of discrimination learning.

Part III introduces four formal models of classical conditioning that address occasion setting. In chapter 10, John W. Moore and June-Seek Choi offer the bold suggestion that the actual trigger for the CR is not the CS source, which is an occasion setter, but time-segmented features of the nominal CS that inform the actor that the US is imminent. Like contextual and intertrial stimuli, a nominal CS sets the occasion for the timed CR. According to Moore and Choi, this viewpoint is justified by behavioral data from human and animal classical eyeblink conditioning, which can be described by computational models that assume that nominal CS onsets and offsets produce cascades of activation within a neural network.

In chapter 11, James Zackheim, Catherine Myers, and Mark Gluck indicate that, although sensory-motor conditioning involves the pairing of CS and US, the CS may not always be a direct predictor of the US. Instead, an appropriately timed CS(X) that precedes a second CS(A) only on trials where CS(A) is paired with the US may act as an occasion setter.

The authors explain that the Gluck and Myers (1993) trial-level model of the hippocampal mediation of stimulus representation displayed contextual occasion setting. That is, the three-layer hippocampal network learned to predict the US from CS(A) only on trials where CS(X) was present as a contextual stimulus. The model achieved this by using appropriate compound representations of the stimuli in the hidden unit (internal) layer of the network. Holland (1986), however, has noted that true occasion setting is sensitive to the timing of CS(X) within the trial. In order to address this feature of occasion setting, the authors present a generalized form of the Gluck and Myers model that incorporates a recurrent-network architecture that shows temporal sensitivity to occasion setting.

In chapter 12, Susan E. Brandon and Allan R. Wagner describe how, in their treatments of occasion setting (Wagner, 1992; Wagner & Brandon, 1989), they have supposed that the distinguishing behavioral phenomena are produced by two separable processes: a modulation of otherwise-elicited conditioned responses by conditioned emotional responses and discriminative control by configural cues. In this chapter, Brandon and Wagner summarize, with the aid of computer simulations, how these processes are incorporated within a relatively conventional associative structure (Wagner, 1981) and present the results of several studies that support their views. Brandon and Wagner suggest that the multiple-determination view of occasion setting may be useful in explaining the variations in occasion setting that are observed with different conditioning preparations and in different laboratories.

In chapter 13, Jeffrey A. Lamoureux, Catalin V. Buhusi, and Nestor A. Schmajuk apply a network model of classical conditioning presented by Schmajuk and DiCarlo (1992) to the description of occasion setting. The Schmajuk–DiCarlo model is a real-time network in which CS inputs are connected to the CR output both directly and indirectly through a hidden-unit layer that codes configural stimuli. In the network, a CS acts as a simple CS through its direct connections with the output units and as an occasion setter through its indirect configural connections by way of the hidden units. Computer simulations demonstrate that the network accounts for a large part of the data on occasion setting. The model also seems useful for explaining the apparently conflicting results in occasion setting that are reported in the literature.

REFERENCES

Gluck, M. A., and Myers, C. E. (1993). Hippocampal mediation of stimulus representation: A computational theory. *Hippocampus, 3,* 491–516.

Holland, P. C. (1983). Occasion-setting in Pavlovian feature positive discriminations. In M. L. Commons, R. J. Herrnstein, & A. R. Wagner (Eds.), *Quantitative analyses of behavior: Discrimination processes* (Vol. 4, pp. 183–206). New York: Ballinger.

Holland, P. C. (1985). The nature of conditioned inhibition in serial and simultaneous feature negative discriminations. In R. R. Miller & N. E. Spear (Eds.), *Information processing in animals: Conditioned inhibition* (pp. 267–297). Hillsdale, NJ: Erlbaum.

Holland, P. C. (1986). Transfer after serial feature-positive discrimination training. *Learning and Motivation, 17,* 243–268.

Holland, P. C. (1992). Occasion setting in Pavlovian conditioning. In D. Medin (Ed.), *The psychology of learning and motivation* (Vol. 28, pp. 69–125). San Diego, CA: Academic Press.

Rescorla, R. A. (1985). Inhibition and facilitation. *Information processing in animals: Conditioned inhibition* (pp. 299–326). Hillsdale, NJ: Erlbaum.

Roitblat, H. L. (1980). Codes and coding processes in pigeon short-term memory. *Animal Learning and Behavior, 8,* 341–351.

Schmajuk, N. A., & DiCarlo, J. J. (1992). Stimulus configuration, classical conditioning, and the hippocampus. *Psychological Review, 99,* 268–305.

Skinner, B. F. (1938). *The behavior of organisms.* New York: Appleton-Century-Crofts.

Wagner, A. R. (1981). SOP: A model of automatic memory processing in animal behavior. In N. E. Spear & R. R. Miller (Eds.), *Information processing in animals: Memory mechanisms* (pp. 5–47). Hillsdale, NJ: Erlbaum.

Wagner, A. R. (1992). Some complexities anticipated by AESOP and other dual-representation theories. In H. Kimmel (Chair), *Pavlovian conditioning with com-*

plex stimuli. Symposium conducted at the XXV International Congress of Psychology, Brussels, Belgium.

Wagner, A. R., & Brandon, S. E. (1989). Evolution of a structured connectionist model of Pavlovian conditioning (AESOP). In S. B. Klein & R. R. Mowrer (Eds.), *Contemporary learning theories: Pavlovian conditioning and the status of traditional learning theory* (pp. 149–189). Hillsdale, NJ: Erlbaum.

PART I

Properties of Occasion Setters

1

Analogies Between Occasion Setting and Pavlovian Conditioning

Ralph R. Miller and Philippe Oberling

Occasion setting refers to the potential of a stimulus to clarify the predictive value of an ambiguous cue. More technically speaking, occasion setting refers to the ability of a punctate stimulus (or diffuse context), sometimes called an *occasion setter* or *feature*, to modulate responding to a partially reinforced conditioned stimulus (CS) when the occasion setter and the target CS are presented in close temporal proximity. In other words, the occasion setter (X) "sets the occasion" for responding (or not responding) to the CS (A). Specifically, positive occasion setters signal that a CS will be reinforced, and negative occasion setters signal that a CS will not be reinforced (see Exhibit 1). The term *occasion setter* originated with Skinner (1938), who applied it to operant situations (see Bonardi, 1988, 1989; Colwill & Rescorla, 1990; Davidson, Aparicio, & Rescorla, 1988; for contemporary examples of occasion setting in instru-

Support for this research was provided by National Institute of Mental Health Grant 33881, Université Louis Pasteur-Strasbourg, Fondation Bettencourt-Schueller, Sandoz Laboratories (France), and Fondation Guy Weisweiller. The authors would like to thank Moore Arnold, Robert Barnet, Aaron Blaisdell, Daniel Burger, Robert Cole, James Denniston, Lisa Gunther, James Esposito, Haney Mallemat, Hernan Savastano, and Russell Wishtart for their assistance in gathering the data from our laboratory that we present here and for their comments on an early version of this chapter.

Exhibit 1

Defining Occasion Setting

	Train	Test	Result
No occasion setting	A→US/A	A	CR
Positive occasion setting	X→A→US/A	X→A	CR
		A	—
		X	—
Negative occasion setting	A→US/X→A	A	CR
		X→A	—
		X	—

NOTE: Partial reinforcement without an occasion setter is ambiguous. Occasion setters can remove this ambiguity. X and A represent initially neutral punctate stimuli, which as a consequence of training has resulted in A becoming an excitatory conditioned stimulus and X becoming an occasion setter. → denotes "followed by"; different trial types that were given interspersed are separated by / ; the approximate magnitude of the observed conditioned responding is indicated by the presence or absence of a conditioned response (CR) in the result column.

mental situations with a discriminative stimulus playing the role of an occasion setter).

Although interest in occasion setting was dormant for several decades, there has been a recent resurgence of interest in the topic, particularly in Pavlovian situations. This resurgence is a result in large part to the fact that occasion setters have been found to modulate simple associations, an unexpected phenomenon in the framework of reflexive Pavlovian responding in which the acquired potential of a stimulus is limited to being able to directly elicit a conditioned response (see Pavlov, 1927). This finding encourages the use of occasion-setting principles to augment associative theory in providing explanations of complex acquired behavior, particularly choice behavior. It should be emphasized that this renewed interest in occasion setting relies mainly on the monumental work of Peter Holland (e.g., 1992) and colleagues in illuminating the nature of occasion setting. Central to our understanding of occasion setting are two early findings: First, a single stimulus can simultaneously possess both excitatory (i.e., Pavlovian) and modulatory (i.e., occasion-setting) properties, and these two properties are (almost) independent of each other (e.g., Holland,

1983, 1985; Rescorla, 1985, 1986, 1987; Ross, 1983). In actuality, positive occasion-setting training often gives the occasion-setting stimulus both occasion-setting properties and Pavlovian excitatory properties. Nonreinforced presentations of the occasion setter alone during or after training, however, commonly eliminate (i.e., extinguish) the Pavlovian excitatory properties of the stimulus without influencing its occasion-setting properties (see "Extinction," later in this chapter). Second, Holland and other researchers have determined that occasion setters affect behavior through some means other than their associations to the unconditioned stimulus (US) summating with CS–US associations (e.g., Holland, 1983, 1985, 1989). These two important findings themselves do not illuminate the way in which occasion setters act to modulate Pavlovian responding or the conditions under which a stimulus will come or not come to serve as an occasion setter. This chapter primarily addresses the latter question.

Like many researchers, our interest in occasion setting was kindled primarily by its potential use as a means of accounting for complex learning phenomena within the framework of the simple and relatively well understood principles of Pavlovian conditioning. Our presentation in this chapter will be relatively nontheoretical. In our view, models at the associative or cognitive levels rarely reflect actual psychological mechanisms (which potentially provide explanations of behavior at a more molecular level of explanation), but instead serve primarily as heuristic devices to guide us toward discovering important new behavioral phenomena. Our heuristic with respect to this chapter is the potential analogy between serial occasion-setting phenomena and the phenomena discovered during 80 years of research in Pavlovian conditioning.

EXTINCTION

The earliest phenomenon that led us to think about a set of analogies between serial occasion setting and excitatory Pavlovian conditioning was extinction. In Pavlovian conditioning, *extinction* is often described operationally as repeated nonreinforced presentations of the CS, which results in a decrement in conditioned responding (see top part of Exhibit 2).

Exhibit 2

Extinction

Group	Train	Extinguish	Test	Result
	Extinction in Pavlovian conditioning (Pavlov, 1927)			
Extinction	A→US	A	A	cr
Control	A→US	B	A	**CR**
	Extinction in occasion setting (Rescorla, 1986; see also Ross, 1983)			
OSing	X→A→US/A/Y→B→US/B	Context only	X→B	**CR**
			B	cr
Exp. 1	X→A→US/A/Y→B→US/B	X	X→B	**CR**
			B	cr
Exp. 2	X→A→US/A/Y→B→US/B	X→A/A→US	X→B	cr
			B	cr
Exp. 3	X→A→US/A/Y→B→US/B	X→A	X→B	cr
			B	cr

NOTE: X, Y, A, and B were initially neutral stimuli. → denotes "followed by"; different trial types that were given interspersed are separated by / ; the approximate magnitude of the observed conditioned responding is indicated by the case, size, and boldness of the font used in the result column. Only select groups are represented here.

Seeking an analogy to Pavlovian extinction within occasion setting, Rescorla (1986; see also Ross, 1983) initially examined the effects of presenting the occasion setter alone (i.e., group Exp. 1 in the bottom part of Exhibit 2). (Note that throughout this chapter, we ignore procedural details and the fine grain of the data of individual studies. For this information, readers should consult the primary sources.) As indicated in Exhibit 2, Rescorla found that simple, nonreinforced presentation of occasion setter X did not attenuate occasion setting by X (group Exp. 1). However, duplication of the training treatment with the reinforcement contingencies reversed from those of training did attenuate occasion setting. That is, reinforcement on trial types that lacked reinforcement during initial occasion-setting training and nonreinforcement on trial types that were reinforced during initial training sufficed to degrade the initial occasion-setting value of a stimulus. Moreover, this outcome was observed with or without

A→US trials (groups Exp. 2 and Exp. 3, respectively). Thus, with regard to behavioral consequences, presentation of X alone is actually a poor analogy to Pavlovian extinction. If extinction treatment is operationalized as exposure to the training conditions (either for all trials or only for those trials involving the feature) with the trial-by-trial reinforcement contingencies reversed, however, then a good analogy of the extinction of Pavlovian excitation exists within occasion setting. This analogy follows the same operational rule for decrementing stimulus control by an occasion setter as by a Pavlovian excitor (i.e., training conditions with reversal of the reinforcement contingencies).[1]

TEMPORAL CODING

In recent years, considerable attention in Pavlovian conditioning has been directed toward the role of timing, beyond the long-recognized benefits for behavioral control of close temporal proximity. Those espousing the traditional view assume that temporal proximity is a catalyst for Pavlovian conditioning. In contrast, recent research has suggested that (a) Pavlovian associations include information about the temporal relationship of the paired events, and (b) this temporal information is used by subjects in determining the form and timing of conditioned responding (see Miller & Barnet, 1993, for a brief review).

One example of such a demonstration is provided by Barnet, Cole, and Miller (1997). In this study (see Exhibit 3), group 1st-ORDER dis-

---

[1] Although it is a digression from occasion setting, consider for a moment the implications of this finding for our conceptualization of extinction in general—that is, rather than defining extinction in the abstract as nonreinforced presentation of a stimulus that previously had acquired control over behavior, extinction might be viewed more generally as duplication of the conditions of training with the trial-by-trial reinforcement contingencies reversed. Thus, our seeking analogies to Pavlovian conditioning in order to better understand occasion setting not only might tell us something about occasion setting but also about the real essence of the phenomenon in question (e.g., extinction) in a variety of situations, thereby freeing us from conceptualizations that are specific to a single situation, such as simple Pavlovian excitatory conditioning. This approach immediately gives greater generality to the phenomenon of extinction. For example, *extinction*, operationally defined simply as nonreinforced exposure to a stimulus, is not applicable to a stimulus following Pavlovian inhibition training (i.e., A→US/AB), because this treatment does not yield a loss of inhibitory control by stimulus B. However, extinction, operationally defined as a reversal of the reinforcement conditions of Pavlovian inhibition training (i.e., A/AB→US treatment following A→US/AB training), does degrade B's inhibitory value. Thus, in this framework, the conclusion that inhibition is not subject to extinction is incorrect.

Exhibit 3

Temporal Coding in Pavlovian Conditioning

(As Demonstrated in Sensory Preconditioning, Barnet, Cole, & Miller, 1997)

Group	Phase 1	Phase 2	Test	Result
EXP	S3→S1/S4→S2	S1→US/US→S2	S3	CR
			S4	**CR**
CONTROL	S1/S2/S3/S4	S1→US/US→S2	S3	—
			S4	—
1st-ORDER	S3→S1/S4→S2	S1→US/US→S2	S1	**CR**
			S2	cr

NOTE: S1, S2, S3, and S4 were initially neutral stimuli. → denotes "followed by"; different trial types that were given interspersed are separated by / ; the approximate magnitude of the observed conditioned responding (CR) is indicated by the case, size, and boldness of the font used in the result column.

played the well-known superiority of forward (S1) over backward (S2) CSs with regard to subsequent behavioral control. But when second-order cues were paired with the first-order forward and backward CSs (i.e., group EXP), stronger excitatory responding to the second-order CS (S4), which had been paired with the backward first-order CS (S2), was seen than to the second-order CS (S3), which had been paired with the forward first-order CS (S1). This observation is surprising in light of the prevailing view that responding to the second-order CS is mediated by the first-order CS. In that framework, more vigorous responding to a first-order CS (in this case the forward paired CS) should produce more vigorous responding to the second-order CS that had been paired with it. Barnet et al. explained the observed data in terms of an integration of temporal maps from each of the two phases of training, so that, in the integrated maps, onset of S4 had better temporal contiguity with onset of the US than did onset of S3. This and many other studies (e.g., Matzel, Held, & Miller, 1988) strongly indicate that CS–US temporal relationships are an inexorable part of the content of Pavlovian associations.

Now consider a recent demonstration of temporal encoding in occasion setting reported in a study by Holland, Hamlin, and Parsons (1997).

Exhibit 4

Temporal Coding in Occasion Setting

(Holland, Hamlin, & Parsons, 1997)

Train	Test	Result
OS.L⟶CS.L→US/CS.L/OS.S→CS.S→US/CS.S	OS.L⟶CS.L	**CR**
	CS.L	cr
	OS.S→CS.S	**CR**
	CS.S	cr
	OS.L→CS.L	CR
	CS.L	cr
	OS.S⟶CS.S	CR
	CS.S	cr
	OS.L⟶CS.S	**CR**
	CS.S	cr
	OS.S→CS.L	**CR**
	CS.L	cr
	OS.L→CS.S	CR
	CS.S	cr
	OS.S⟶CS.L	CR
	CS.L	cr

NOTE: OS.S was the occasion setter (OS) trained with a short (S) occasion setter onset to CS onset interval; OS.L was the occasion setter (OS) trained with a long (L) occasion setter onset to CS onset interval; → denotes "followed by" with a short interval; ⟶ denotes "followed by" with a long interval; CS.S was the CS trained with a short (S) occasion setter to CS interval; CS.L was the CS trained with a long (L) occasion setter to CS interval; different trial types that were given interspersed are separated by /; the approximate magnitude of the observed conditioned responding (CR) is indicated by the case, size, and boldness of the font used in the result column.

In this study, occasion setters were trained with short or long intervals between their onset and that of their accompanying target CSs. Each feature was then tested for transfer to both its own training target CS and the target CS used in training the other occasion setter. Moreover, at test, intervals between termination of the feature and onset of the test CS included both the short and long intervals of training for all combinations of features and target CSs (see Exhibit 4). Holland and his colleagues

Exhibit 5

Overshadowing in Pavlovian Excitation

(Kaufman & Bolles, 1981; Matzel, Schachtman, & Miller, 1985)

Group	Train	Extinguish A	Test	Result
OV	BA→US	Context only	A	cr
CONTROL	A→US	Context only	A	**CR**
RECOV	BA→US	B	A	**CR**

NOTE: B and A were initially neutral stimuli, with B being more salient than A. The approximate magnitude of the observed conditioned responding (CR) is indicated by the case, size, and boldness of the font used in the result column. Only select groups are represented here.

found that occasion setters retained their modulatory potential best on these transfer tests when they were conducted with an interval between their onset and the onset of the test target CS that was the same as the interval that prevailed during training of the feature. However, the modulatory potential of the occasion setter was unaffected by the occasion setter–target CS interval that prevailed during training of the target CS. Thus, the information encoded about a stimulus that allows it to serve as an occasion setter appears to include the interval from the onset of the occasion setter to the onset of a target CS—that is, feature–target intervals—are encoded as part of the content of occasion setting. This property of occasion setters is analogous to the previously discussed propensity of conventional CS representations to be encoded to include information concerning the interval between CS and US onset.

OVERSHADOWING

Let us consider overshadowing. When two stimuli are presented in compound and reinforced (e.g., BA→US), each cue (particularly the less salient cue) accrues less potential to elicit conditioned responding than does the same cue when reinforced alone (i.e., A→US). Exhibit 5 illustrates overshadowing of CS A by CS B in group OV relative to group CONTROL. Notably, Kaufman and Bolles (1981) and Matzel, Schachtman, and Miller (1985) found that recovery of responding to overshadowed cue (A) can be obtained through massive posttraining extinction of the overshadowing cue (B, see group RECOV in Exhibit 5). This recovery from overshadowing without further training strongly suggests that overshadowing is a result at least in part of a failure to express an A–US association that was acquired during training, rather than a failure to acquire the A–US association as assumed by most models of learning (e.g., Rescorla & Wagner, 1972).

We recently conducted a series of studies that examined overshadowing of potential occasion setters (Gunther, Cole, & Miller, 1997). In this and all subsequent studies from our laboratory that we will describe, the basic procedure was conditioned suppression of licking by water-deprived rats. Lights, tones, and clicks served as the controlling stimuli, and a brief, mild foot shock served as the unconditioned stimulus. Duration of conditioned suppression of ongoing drinking behavior was our basic dependent variable. In this first series of studies, the occasion setters were local context cues that cycled 5 min on, then 5 min off. More specifically, the overshadowing occasion setter was a bright flashing light, and the overshadowed occasion setter was a soft click train. The three positive occasion-setting studies of this series are represented in Exhibit 6. Experiment 1 merely documented in our preparation occasion setting by stimulus X (as opposed to the possibility that X came to simply serve as another excitatory Pavlovian CS that associatively summated with A). This was done by taking advantage of the knowledge that occasion setters do not transfer their modulation to unambiguous CSs (e.g., Holland, 1985; Rescorla, 1985) such as CS B, which was reinforced during training both in the presence and absence of X. As can be seen in Exhibit 6, X modulated responding to A but not to B. Notably, responding to B was not at ceiling, so if X had had Pavlovian excitatory potential, it would have been expected to augment responding to CS B as well as CS A. The modulation of conditioned responding of CS A, but not CS B, indicates that our preparation established X as an occasion setter when no competing occasion setter was present.

In Experiment 2 (see Exhibit 6), group CONTROL was trained with stimulus X as an occasion setter for target CS A using exactly the same parameters as in Experiment 1. For group OV, however, X was com-

Exhibit 6

Overshadowing in Occasion Setting

(Gunther, Cole, & Miller, 1997)

	Group	Train	Extinction	Test	Result
Exp. 1		X→A→US/A/X→B→US/B→US		X→A	**CR**
				A	cr
				X→B	**CR**
				B	**CR**
Exp. 2	OV	YX→A→US/A		X→A	CR
				A	cr
	CONTROL	X→A→US/A		Y→A	**CR**
				X→A	**CR**
				A	cr
Exp. 3	OV	XY→A→US/A	Context	X→A	CR
				A	cr
	EXTINCTION	XY→A→US/A	Y→A	X→A	**CR**
				A	cr

NOTE: X, Y, A, and B were initially neutral stimuli. X→A→US denotes X onsetting before the A→US trial with X staying on for some time after the completion of the trial (i.e., X was a local context that served as an occasion setter); different trial types that were given interspersed are separated by /; the approximate magnitude of the observed conditioned responding (CR) is indicated by the case, size, and boldness of the font used in the result columns.

pounded (simultaneous onset, simultaneous termination) with the more salient stimulus Y. As indicated in Exhibit 6, responding to A in the presence of X was greater for group CONTROL than for group OV. This demonstrates overshadowing of X as an occasion setter by Y. In Exp. 3, group OV received the same treatment as group OV in Exp. 2 and yielded similar weak occasion setting. However, group EXTINCTION had the occasion-setting value of Y degraded following overshadowing treatment. Enhanced modulatory control of responding to A by X was observed as a result of this degradation of Y. In fact, X exhibited modulatory control in group EXTINCTION comparable to that observed in group CONTROL of Exp. 2. Thus, we see that, analogous to Pavlovian conditioned excitation, both overshadowing and recovery from overshadowing as a result of de-

Exhibit 7

Blocking

Group	Phase 1	Phase 2	Test	Result
	Blocking in Pavlovian conditioning (Kamin, 1968)			
Block	B→US	BA→US	A	cr
Control	C→US	BA→US	A	**CR**
	Blocking in occasion setting (Bonardi, 1991; see also Swartzentruber, 1991)			
Block	Y→A→US/X	YX→A→US/A	X→A	cr
			A	cr
Control	Z→X→US/X	YX→US/A	X→A	**CR**
			A	cr

NOTE: A, B, C, X, Y, and Z were initially neutral stimuli. → denotes "followed by"; different trial types that were given interspersed are separated by /; the approximate magnitude of the observed conditioned responding (CR) is indicated by the case, size, and boldness of the font used in the result column. Only select groups are represented here.

grading the behavioral control of the overshadowing stimulus can be obtained in occasion setting.

BLOCKING

Blocking of Pavlovian excitation is depicted in the top portion of Exhibit 7. Simply put, training a target CS (A) in the presence of another CS (B) that has previously been trained with the same US interferes with behavior control by the target CS (Kamin, 1968). The analogous phenomenon—blocking of a potential occasion setter—has been reported by several different laboratories. For example, as illustrated in the bottom portion of Exhibit 7, Swartzentruber (1991) has obtained blocking of occasion setting with a context as the blocked feature (X) and a punctate stimulus as the blocking feature (Y), and Bonardi (1991) has obtained the same outcome with a punctate stimulus serving as the blocked feature. In essence, both studies found that if X was trained as an occasion setter in the presence of Y, and Y had been pretrained as an occasion setter in its own right, the presence of Y during training of X interfered with X becoming an occasion setter. (Notably, Y was not more salient than X, thereby minimizing any possible attenuation of X as an occasion setter because of overshadowing of X by Y.) Thus, in occasion setting there is a clear analogy to blocking of Pavlovian excitation.

DEPENDENCE OF CUE COMPETITION ON TEMPORAL RELATIONSHIPS

In our own laboratory, we have demonstrated that blocking of Pavlovian excitation depends on the blocking and blocked CSs having the same temporal relationship to the US (Barnet, Grahame, & Miller, 1993). This is depicted in Exhibit 8. Second-order conditioning was used in all cases in order to reveal otherwise latent simultaneous and backward associations (Matzel, Held, & Miller, 1988). In Phase 1, groups in the block condition received CS A in a forward (i.e., serial) relationship to the US, and CS B in a simultaneous relationship with the US. Control participants received the same treatment except that the blocking CS (A or B, respectively, for even- and odd-numbered pairs of groups) had CS E substituted for the blocking CS. In Phase 2, CS C was compounded with the blocking CS (A or B) and was followed immediately with the US. For groups Block F–F and S–S (numbers 1 and 2 in Exhibit 8), the temporal relationships between the blocking stimulus and the US in Phase 1 (A or B, respectively) and between the added element (C) and the US in Phase 2 was the same, and blocking was observed in both cases. For groups Block F–S and S–F (numbers 3 and 4), these two temporal relationships differed, and blocking was not observed in either case.

Although we explained these findings in terms of blocking depending on the need to equate the temporal relationship between the blocking CS and the US in Phase 1 with the temporal relationship of the blocked CS and the US in Phase 2, there was an alternative interpretation of these results: Possibly the critical factor was maintaining the same temporal relationship between the blocking CS and the US in Phases 1 and 2. This relationship was changed between Phases 1 and 2 for groups Block F–S and S–F (numbers 3 and 4) in which no blocking was observed, but was

Exhibit 8

Dependence of Pavlovian Blocking on Common Temporal Relationships to the US Between the Blocking CS and Blocked CS

(Tested Within Second-Order Conditioning, Barnet, Grahame, & Miller, 1993)

Group	Phase 1	Phase 2	Phase 3	Test	Result
Block F-F	A→US/B.US	AC→US	D→C	D	cr
Control F-F	E→US/B.US	AC→US	D→C	D	**CR**
Block S-S	A→US/B.US	BC.US	D→C	D	cr
Control S-S	A→US/E.US	BC.US	D→C	D	**CR**
Block F-S	A→US/B.US	AC.US	D→C	D	**CR**
Control F-S	E→US/B.US	AC.US	D→C	D	**CR**
Block S-F	A→US/B.US	BC→US	D→C	D	**CR**
Control S-F	A→US/E.US	BC→US	D→C	D	**CR**
Block F-S*	A→US/B.US	A→C.US	D→C	D	**CR**
Control F-S*	E→US/B.US	A→C.US	D→C	D	**CR**
Block S-F*	A→US/B.US	C→B.US	D→C	D	**CR**
Control S-F*	A→US/E.US	C→B.US	D→C	D	**CR**

NOTE: A, B, C, D, and E were initially neutral stimuli. → denotes "followed by"; the "." as in "B.US" denotes that stimulus B and the US were simultaneous in onset and termination; different trial types that were given interspersed are separated by /; the approximate magnitude of the observed conditioned responding (CR) is indicated by the case, size, and boldness of the font used in the result column.

unchanged for groups Block F–F and S–S (numbers 1 and 2) in which blocking was observed. Groups Block F–S* and S–F* (numbers 5 and 6) allowed us to examine and reject this possibility. No blocking was observed in these groups even when the temporal relationship of the blocking CS and the US was maintained between Phases 1 and 2.

For present purposes, the question is whether there is an analogy within occasion setting to this requirement for blocking of Pavlovian excitation. In Exhibit 9, we depict a series of experiments that identified an analogous requirement within occasion setting (Hallam, Grahame, Barnet, & Miller, 1997). In this series, we used a punctate negative occasion setter.

Exhibit 9

Dependence of Blocking of Occasion Setting on Common Temporal Relationships to the Conditioned Stimulus Between the Blocking and Blocked Occasion Setters

(Hallam, Grahame, Barnet, & Miller, 1997)

Group	Phase 1	Phase 2	Test	Result
1. Block F-F	Y→A/A→US	YX→A/A→US	X→A	**CR**
			A	**CR**
Control F-F	Z→A/A→US	YX→A/A→US	X→A	cr
			A	**CR**
2. Block S-S	YA/A→US	YXA/A→US	XA	**CR**
			A	**CR**
Control S-S	ZA/A→US	YXA/A→US	XA	cr
			A	**CR**
3. Block F-S	Y→A/A→US	YXA/A→US	XA	cr
			A	**CR**
Control F-S	Z→A/A→US	YXA/A→US	XA	cr
			A	**CR**
4. Block S-F	YA/A→US	YX→A/A→US	X→A	cr
			A	**CR**
Control S-F	ZA/A→US	YX→A/A→US	X→A	cr
			A	**CR**

NOTE: X, Y, Z, and A were initially neutral stimuli. → denotes "followed by"; different trial types that were given interspersed are separated by /; the approximate magnitude of the observed conditioned responding (CR) is indicated by the case, size, and boldness of the font used in the result column.

There was either a 5-sec gap between the termination of the occasion setter and the onset of the target CS (forward condition [F]), or the occasion setter and the target CS were presented simultaneously (simultaneous condition [S]). For the block condition, Y was established as a negative occasion setter during Phase 1, serially (i.e., forward) with respect to the target CS (X) for groups Block F–F and F–S and simultaneously with respect to X for groups Block S–S and S–F. The subjects in the control condition received identical treatment but with an irrelevant stimulus (Z) rather than with Y, thereby controlling for nonassociative factors. In Phase 2, we attempted to establish X as a serial or simultaneous occasion setter in the presence of Y. We found that, relative to their appropriate control groups, groups Block F–F and S–S exhibited blocking of X from becoming an effective negative occasion setter (i.e., responding to A was as strong in the presence of X as in the absence of X). In groups Block F–S and S–F, however, for which the temporal relationship of Y to the target CS (A) in Phase 2 was different from the temporal relationship of Y to the target CS in Phase 1, X came to act, respectively, as a simultaneous and serial occasion setter.

Thus, we see that blocking of occasion setting is enhanced when the temporal relationships between the blocking feature and the target CS and between the blocked feature and the target CS are the same. This is analogous to the finding that blocking of Pavlovian excitation is greatest when the temporal relationships to the US of the blocking and blocked CSs are the same. Notably, the procedure for simultaneous negative occasion setting is identical to that for Pavlovian conditioned inhibition. Hence, the results of this series suggest that serial negative occasion setting and Pavlovian conditioned inhibition (i.e., simultaneous negative occasion setting) are supported by different types of knowledge that do not interact with each other. Such a conclusion is in full agreement with Holland's (1985) view that simultaneous negative occasion setting (i.e., Pavlovian conditioned inhibition) and serial negative occasion setting ("true occasion setting," in Holland's terminology) are fundamentally different. In this framework, these results are to be expected.

LATENT INHIBITION

The well-known latent inhibition effect of Pavlovian conditioning (Lubow & Moore, 1959) is depicted in the top portion of Exhibit 10. The basic phenomenon is that nonreinforced exposure to a CS (A) before CS–US training trials retards behavior control by that CS during training. Hence, more training trials are required to obtain a degree of behavioral control comparable to that of subjects not preexposed to the CS.

Exhibit 10

Latent Inhibition

	Group	Phase 1	Phase 2	Test	Result
	Latent inhibition in Pavlovian conditioning (Lubow & Moore, 1959)				
	EXP	A	A→US	A	cr
	CONTROL	—	A→US	A	**CR**
	Latent inhibition in occasion setting (Oberling, Gunther, & Miller, 1997)				
Exp. 1		X→A→US/		X→A	**CR**
		A/X→B→US/B→US		A	cr
				X→B	**CR**
				B	**CR**
Exp. 2	EXP	X	X→A→US/A	X→A	**CR**
				A	cr
	CONTROL	Y	X→A→US/A	X→A	**CR**
				A	cr
Exp. 3	EXP	X→A/A→US	X→A→US/A	X→A	**CR**
				A	cr
	CONTROL	Y→A/A→US	X→A→US/A	X→A	**CR**
				A	cr

NOTE: A, B, X, and Y were initially neutral stimuli. → denotes "followed by"; different trial types that were given interspersed are separated by / ; the approximate magnitude of the observed conditioned responding (CR) is indicated by the case, size, and boldness of the font used in the result column.

Oberling, Gunther, and Miller (1997) examined possible analogies within occasion setting of latent inhibition in Pavlovian conditioning (see the bottom portion of Exhibit 10). A serial punctate positive occasion setter was used, with a 10-sec gap between termination of the occasion setter (X) and onset of the target CS (A). Exp. 1 was designed simply to document acquisition of positive occasion setting with our specific task (rather than associative summation of the target CS and any Pavlovian excitatory value that the occasion setter might have acquired). Stimulus X preceded target CS A when A was reinforced, but not when A was not reinforced; thus, X was a potential occasion setter of A. CS B, however, was reinforced consistently in both the presence and absence of X; as a consequence, B was an unambiguous CS. At test, presentation of X failed to enhance responding to B, but did enhance responding to A. Notably, responding to B was not asymptotic, so a ceiling effect did not mask any potential associative summation effect between X and B. Hence, X appears to have become an occasion setter for A.

Exp. 2 sought an analogy within occasion setting to the latent inhibition effect of excitatory Pavlovian conditioning. We initially examined the effects of massively presenting the intended occasion setter alone during Phase 1 (i.e., group EXP in Exp. 2). In Phase 2, we gave both groups EXP and CONTROL serial positive occasion-setting training with stimulus X as the occasion setter. As indicated in Exhibit 10, we found that nonreinforced pretraining presentations of stimulus X alone did not retard acquisition of occasion setting by X.

There is an alternative interpretation of these results, however. In Pavlovian excitatory conditioning, CS preexposure retards behavioral control by the CS, but, with a sufficient number of CS–US trials, behavioral control is established (Lubow & Moore, 1959). Because we did not record behavior during occasion-setting training, one might wonder whether we simply failed to observe a retardation effect in group EXP because we gave too many training trials. Preliminary parametric research had established, however, that the amount of occasion-setting training that we gave both groups in Phase 2 was the minimum amount of training necessary to obtain occasion setting by X in group CONTROL. Thus, the lack of retardation in group EXP was not the result of excessive occasion-setting training.[2]

In Experiment 3, we examined another possible occasion-setting

[2]The lack of retardation in this experiment suggests that the conventional view of latent inhibition of a Pavlovian excitor needs to be reconsidered. The retardation that constitutes the latent inhibition effect in Pavlovian conditioning is commonly viewed as arising from a loss of attention to the preexposed CS (e.g., Rescorla, 1971). However, if one assumes that attention is required for the acquisition of occasion-setting as well as Pavlovian excitatory potential, latent inhibition of occasion setting should have been observed in this study. Our failure to observe latent inhibition with simple nonreinforced preexposure to the intended occasion setter suggests (to the extent that null results can suggest anything) that attentional explanations of latent inhibition are not correct. This is not the place to review alternative views of latent inhibition in Pavlovian conditioning, but the reader may consult Grahame, Barnet, Gunther, and Miller (1994) and Wagner (1978) for a discussion of these alternatives.

analogy to latent inhibition in Pavlovian conditioning. We administered pretraining treatment identical to the subsequent occasion-setting treatment, except that the trial-by-trial reinforcement contingencies were reversed (i.e., the reinforced trials of subsequent occasion-setting training were not reinforced, and the nonreinforced trials of subsequent occasion-setting training were reinforced). We found that this pretraining treatment was highly effective in retarding the development of positive occasion setting. Thus, with respect to its behavioral consequences, presentation of stimulus X alone (in Exp. 2) is, in its outcome, a poor analogy to Pavlovian latent inhibition. As was the case with extinction, however (see Rescorla, 1986; Ross, 1983), if latent inhibition treatment is operationally defined as exposure to the training conditions with the trial-by-trial reinforcement contingencies reversed, then a good analogy of the latent inhibition of Pavlovian excitation exists within occasion setting.

One might well ask whether the present latent inhibition effect for occasion setting depended on X being presented with A during Phase 1 as opposed to X being presented with some other target CS during Phase 1. The data do not allow us to answer that question.

The results are congruent with the view that both pretraining and posttraining treatments that mirror the training treatment, except for the trial-by-trial reversal of reinforcement contingencies (i.e., latent inhibition and extinction, respectively), are effective means of attenuating not only excitatory Pavlovian conditioning but more generally the effects of any type of interstimulus relationship. Note that this view of latent inhibition and extinction in both Pavlovian excitation and occasion setting is similar to regarding latent inhibition and extinction as forms of interference, as suggested by Bouton and Nelson (chapter 3, this volume).

LEARNED IRRELEVANCE

Another well-established phenomenon in Pavlovian conditioning is the learned irrelevance effect (e.g., Baker, 1976; see top portion of Exhibit 11). The learned irrelevance effect refers to the retarded behavioral control by a CS during CS–US pairings that is observed as a result of previous

Exhibit 11

Learned Irrelevance

Group	Phase 1	Phase 2	Test	Result
	Learned irrelevance in Pavlovian conditioning (Baker, 1976)			
EXP	A→US/A/US	A→US	A	—
CONTROL	Context only	A→US	A	**CR**
	Learned irrelevance in occasion setting (Oberling, Gunther, & Miller, 1997)			
EXP	X→A→US/X→A/A→US/A	X→A→US/A	X→A	**CR**
			A	**CR**
CONTROL	Y→A→US/Y→A/A→US/A	X→A→US/A	X→A	**CR**
			A	cr

NOTE: A, X, and Y were initially neutral stimuli. → denotes "followed by"; different trial types that were given interspersed are separated by /; during Phase 1, A was reinforced on 50% of its presentations both in the presence and absence of X (or Y); the approximate magnitude of the observed conditioned responding (CR) is indicated by the case, size, and boldness of the font used in the result column. The parameters were identical to those used in the latent inhibition of occasion-setting studies depicted in Exhibit 10, in which the presence of occasion setting was documented.

uncorrelated exposure to the CS and US. We have examined an occasion-setting analogy to this effect in our laboratory (Oberling, Gunther, & Miller, 1997; see bottom portion of Exhibit 11). In Phase 1, subjects in group EXP experienced CS A on a partial reinforcement schedule, with A being reinforced as often when it was preceded by X as when it was not preceded by X, whereas group CONTROL received this treatment with another stimulus (Y). Thus, for group EXP, X was noninformative concerning whether A was going to be reinforced. In Phase 2, we trained both groups with X as a positive occasion setter for target CS A. As indicated, X was greatly retarded in coming to serve as an occasion setter for group EXP relative to group CONTROL. As in Pavlovian conditioning, the retardation of occasion setting produced by learned irrelevance treatment appeared greater than that produced by latent inhibition treatment with otherwise similar parameters.

One might ask (as in our demonstration of an occasion-setting analogy to Pavlovian latent inhibition) whether the present learned irrelevance effect for occasion setting depended on X being presented with A during Phase 1, as opposed to X being presented with some other target CS—that is, is the learned irrelevance for X as an occasion setter specific for X modulating responding to A, or would it transfer to target CSs other than the target CS that was used in learned irrelevance treatment? Our data do not speak to that question. The present retardation effect, however, certainly was not due to Pavlovian learned irrelevance with respect to A impeding A's becoming a Pavlovian excitor. This is clear both because the US was never administered in the absence of A during Phase 1 and because the control group received comparable A–US experience. This study indicates that within occasion setting there is a phenomenon analogous to learned irrelevance in Pavlovian conditioning.

THE POTENTIAL FOR A STIMULUS'S INFORMATIONAL VALUE TO BE MODULATED BY ANOTHER STIMULUS

Consider the potential of conditioned responding to a Pavlovian CS to be modulated by another stimulus that is present on the test trial. These other stimuli (X in the top portion of Exhibit 12) are of course what we have been calling occasion setters (Holland, 1985; Rescorla, 1985). For the moment, however, rather than focusing on occasion setters, let us focus on the potential of CSs to be modulated in the responding that they elicit. The potential to be modulated is a characteristic of Pavlovian CSs. The immediate question is whether there is an analog to this phenomenon in occasion setting—that is, can the occasion-setting properties of a stimulus be modulated by another stimulus? Or, in other words, can one stimulus set the occasion for another stimulus to serve as an occasion setter? Recent research indicates that this does occur. For example, Arnold, Grahame, and Miller (1991; see bottom portion of Exhibit 12; see also Nakajima, 1994) demonstrated what they called *higher order occasion setting.* Not only was A ambiguous as a CS, but X and Y were ambiguous occasion setters because they were not consistent positive or negative occasion setters. It was stimulus Z that disambiguated the occasion-setting functions of stimuli X and

Exhibit 12

Stimulus Modulation

Train	Test	Result
	Stimulus modulation of Pavlovian responding (i.e., first-order occasion setting, e.g., Holland, 1985; Rescorla, 1985)	
X→A→US/A/B→US	X→A	**CR**
	A	cr
	X→B	**CR**
	B	**CR**
	Modulation of occasion setting (i.e., higher order occasion setting; Arnold, Grahame, & Miller, 1991; see also Nakajima, 1994)[a]	
Z→X→A→US/	Z→X→A	**CR**
X→A/	X→A	cr
Z→Y→A/	Z→Y→A	cr
Y→A→US/	Y→A	**CR**
Z→X/	Z→X	cr
X/	X	cr
Z→Y/	Z→Y	cr
Y/	Y	cr

NOTE: X, Y, Z, and A were initially neutral stimuli. → denotes "followed by"; different trial types that were given interspersed are separated by / ; the approximate magnitude of the observed conditioned responding (CR) is indicated by the case, size, and boldness of the font used in the result column.

[a] All subjects received all of the listed trial types.

Y, thereby allowing X and Y in turn to disambiguate whether A would be reinforced. The discrimination could not have been solved on the basis of Z and A alone, nor on the basis of X, Y, and A alone—that is, neither Z without X and Y nor X and Y without Z provided sufficient information for participants to determine if A was going to be reinforced. Thus, we see that the potential to reduce ambiguity by an accompanying stimulus is a property of occasion setters as well as Pavlovian excitors.

This demonstration is consistent with previous studies of pigeons in delayed symbolic matching-to-sample, which could be interpreted as second-order occasion setting (e.g., Edwards, Miller, & Zentall, 1985; Maki, 1979). In addition, several examples of what could be viewed as higher order occasion setting using human research participants have been reported (e.g., Biederman, 1972; Gollin, 1966). Moreover, Sidman, Kirk, and Willson-Morris (1985) have demonstrated that humans can learn a "five-term contingency," which consists of stimulus Z modulating the meaning of stimulus Y, stimulus Y modulating the meaning of stimulus X, and stimulus X providing information concerning the immediately prevailing response–reinforcer association. This task is functionally equivalent to third-order occasion setting.

The Pavlovian excitatory properties of a stimulus appear to be largely independent of the occasion-setting properties of that stimulus. The occurrence of higher order occasion setting raises the question of whether the first-and second-order occasion setting attributes of a stimulus are also independent of each other. More research will be necessary to answer this question.

SUMMATION

Pavlov (1927) demonstrated response summation for independently trained Pavlovian CSs, a phenomenon that is currently regarded as evidence of associative summation because it can occur even when one of the contributing CSs was trained without coming to elicit the target response. Analogous to associative summation, Morrell and Holland (1993) have demonstrated the summation of the occasion-setting properties of two independently trained negative occasion setters when they are presented together immediately before a target CS. Thus, summation of potentials to elicit Pavlovian responding has a clear analog in occasion setting.

TEMPORAL RATIOS

Yet another parallel between Pavlovian excitatory conditioning and occasion setting can be seen in the dependence of stimulus control on the ratio of the occasion setter–target CS interval to the intertrial interval during occasion-setting training. Gibbon and Balsam's (1981) scalar expectancy theory of learning captures an analogous relationship in Pavlovian conditioning, and there are considerable data that support their view. Specifically, the ratio of C/T predicts the asymptote for Pavlovian excitatory responding, in which the cycle time (C) is the interval between presentations of the US, and waiting time (T) is the total duration of the CS between CS–US pairings. Analogous to this temporal relationship, Holland (1995) and Holland and Morrell (1996) have reported that the optimal interval between an occasion setter and its target CS is directly related to the intertrial interval. Thus, we see another analogy between the rules that govern occasion setting and those that govern Pavlovian excitatory conditioning.

CONTEXTS CAN SUBSTITUTE FOR PUNCTATE STIMULI

Under some conditions, a context can function as a Pavlovian excitor and directly elicit behavior like a punctate CS—that is, either a conditioned excitor or a conditioned inhibitor (e.g., Fanselow, 1986). Under other conditions, a context can serve as an occasion setter that provides clarifying information about an ambiguous target CS. For example, a CS trained in one context and extinguished in a second context will still elicit conditioned responding in the first context, but not in the second context. It is important to note that the modulatory role of the test context is not due to direct context–US associations because posttraining extinction of context–US associations fail to eliminate the effect. This phenomenon, in which the context comes to set the occasion for conditioned excitation, has been called *renewal* by Bouton (Bouton & King, 1983; Bouton & Swartzentruber, 1986; Grahame, Hallam, Geier, & Miller, 1990). Moreover, similar contextual modulation of Pavlovian inhibition has been demonstrated in our laboratory (Fiori, Barnet, & Miller, 1994).

Contexts in our laboratory have proven easier than punctate stimuli to establish as occasion setters under otherwise similar circumstances. In unpublished studies, we found that at least 20 sessions of training were necessary to establish positive occasion setting with a punctate stimulus as the occasion setter. In contrast, we have found that a single session of excitatory training in one context, followed by a single session of extinction in a different context, suffices to produce strong excitatory responding in the training context relative to the extinction context (i.e., the renewal effect). As stated earlier, Bouton and his colleagues have demonstrated that this effect need not arise from the excitatory value of the CS associatively summating with the Pavlovian excitatory value of the context that was used for the CS–US trials. We should add that there can be a midground between punctate stimuli and global contexts as occasion setters—that is, "temporally local contexts"—in which the CS trials are embedded in one local context when the CS is reinforced and in another when it is not reinforced. We used a temporally local context as an occasion setter in our demonstration of an occasion-setting analog to Pavlovian overshadowing. In our laboratory, temporally local contexts appear to yield occasion setting at rates between those of punctate and global contexts.

FACILITATION AND ATTENUATION

As yet another parallel between Pavlovian conditioning and at least serial occasion setting, one might view the relationship between Pavlovian conditioned excitation and conditioned inhibition as being analogous to that between serial-positive and serial-negative occasion setting. Just as Pavlovian inhibitors are in some sense opposites of Pavlovian excitors, some investigators regard serial-negative occasion setters as opposites of serial-positive occasion setters (e.g., Holland, 1985).

RELATIVE RATES OF ACQUISITION FOR POSITIVE AND NEGATIVE OCCASION SETTING

In unpublished work, we have observed, under otherwise comparable conditions, that serial-positive occasion setting is more readily acquired than serial-negative occasion setting. Specifically, we found that, with one of our preparations for serial-positive occasion setting, at least 20 sessions were required to obtain behavior clearly indicative of positive occasion setting. In contrast, with otherwise equivalent parameters, at least 30 sessions were required to establish negative occasion setting. This difference is analogous to the well-known finding that Pavlovian conditioned excitation is far more rapidly acquired than Pavlovian conditioned inhibition. Thus, we see another analogy between occasion setting and Pavlovian conditioning. This pair of effects is likely a result of some combination of two factors: First, greater attention is likely paid to reinforced trials than to nonreinforced trials; and second, knowledge of the absence of reinforcement is not possible until *after* knowledge of reinforcement has been acquired.

CONCLUSION

Thus, we see many well-established phenomena within Pavlovian conditioning that appear to have clear analogies within occasion setting. These are summarized in Exhibit 13. Looking specifically for such analogies in occasion setting has inspired research that otherwise might not have been considered. Thus, examining occasion setting by analogy to Pavlovian conditioning has proven to be a fruitful research strategy: Not only has it illuminated the conditions under which occasion setting occurs, it has also increased our knowledge concerning simple Pavlovian conditioning. As described earlier, this unexpected benefit is most evident regarding extinction and latent inhibition of Pavlovian excitatory conditioning. The search within occasion setting for analogs to these Pavlovian phenomena has suggested that the *trial-by-trial reversal of reinforcement contingencies* from that of target training might constitute better operational definitions of extinction and latent inhibition than "presentation of the CS alone."

Of course, there are other possible ways of structuring analogies within occasion setting for the same phenomena in Pavlovian conditioning that we have just considered. It is not clear that our versions of the analogous procedures were the optimal ones for obtaining analogous effects. Examining these alternatives is a task for the future, and comparing the magnitude

Exhibit 13

Summary

Parallels between Pavlovian excitation and occasion setting have been observed for the following phenomena:

- Extinction
- Evidence of temporal encoding
- Cue competition
  - Overshadowing
  - Recovery from overshadowing via extinction of the overshadowing stimulus
  - Blocking
  - Dependence of blocking on the blocking and blocked stimuli encoding the same temporal information
- Latent inhibition
- Learned irrelevance
- Modulation by higher order stimuli
- Summation
- Asymptotic stimulus control being directly proportional to the ratio of intertrial interval to interstimulus (ITI/ISI) in Pavlovian conditioning and ITI (feature–target interval) in occasion setting
- Contexts being able to substitute for discrete stimuli as occasion setters, just as they can for Pavlovian CSs

The relationship between Pavlovian conditioned excitation and inhibition appears in many ways analogous to serial-positive and serial-negative occasion setting. For example, acquisition of feature-positive discriminations is faster than acquisition of feature-negative discriminations, just as conditioned excitation is acquired in fewer trials than is conditioned inhibition.

of the effects obtained when different procedures are used as potential analogies is apt to be highly informative regarding the nature of occasion setting.

The present parallels between occasion setting and Pavlovian conditioning point toward future potentially illuminating studies of occasion setting. Moreover, they also raise the central question of whether the observed parallels reflect an analogy or a homology. Although the specific content of the information provided by an occasion setter and that provided by a Pavlovian conditioned stimulus may differ, the processes that operate on occasion-setting information and on Pavlovian conditioning information appear to be similar (analogous) if not identical (homologous). This invites a strategy of trying to identify phenomena in one domain (Pavlovian conditioning or occasion setting) that do not have an equivalent within the other domain. There should be a complete one-to-one relationship between Pavlovian and occasion-setting phenomena if common processes subserve both types of learning. In contrast, if different but similar processes govern the two types of learning, we would expect that some phenomena will be found for one type of learning with no counterpart in the other type of learning. One seeming discrepancy between Pavlovian conditioning and occasion setting is the greater potential of simultaneous negative features (i.e., Pavlovian conditioned inhibitors) to transfer their behavior modulation to unambiguous excitors relative to serial-negative features (i.e., occasion setters). This seeming difference, however, might be more appropriately attributed to a difference in the content of what each type of learning encodes rather than how the information is processed (see Bonardi, chapter 2, this volume).

Our analysis of occasion setting through analogy with Pavlovian conditioning speaks to the *processes* underlying acquisition and loss of effective occasion-setting information. However, our knowledge of the *content* of information underlying occasion setting itself is far from complete. Suggestions over the past 15 years have included viewing occasion setters as (a) stimuli that lower (or raise in the case of negative occasion setters) the activation thresholds necessary for US representations to produce conditioned responding (Rescorla, 1985), (b) retrieval cues for specific CS–US associations (Holland, 1983), (c) more generalized retrieval cues that possess hierarchical value relative to CSs (Holland, 1990), (d) configured cues (Schmajuk, Lamoureux, & Holland, 1998), and (e) cues that elicit affective responses that in turn modulate the retrieval of information about specific outcomes (Brandon & Wagner, 1991).

If occasion setters serve as cues for retrieving specific CS–US associations in a manner that is analogous to how CSs apparently act as retrieval cues for representations of specific USs (e.g., Holland, 1983), then occasion setters might be expected to obey the known rules of Pavlovian conditioning. The strong analogy between occasion setting and Pavlovian conditioning presented here is congruent with this view. Problematic, however, is the observed transfer of occasion-setting potential by a feature to previously occasion-set target CSs other than the one with which the feature was trained—that is, if an occasion setter simply facilitates retrieval of the specific CS–US association with which it was trained, no transfer to a different CS–US association should be observed. Thus, the finding of transfer between CSs under any conditions is problematic for this viewpoint (but see Bonardi, chapter 2, this volume, for a defense of this view).

None of the other conceptualizations of occasion setting is without problems of its own, however. For example, the conditions that best promote occasion setting appear to be those that are least apt to promote configuring (Thomas, Curran, & Russel, 1988). Specifically, occasion setting is most robust when the occasion setter and its target excitor are highly distinctive, such as when these stimuli are of different modalities and are separated by a temporal gap, or at least do not overlap in time (Holland, 1983, 1986). In contrast, the opposite conditions tend to promote configuring; configuring is most likely to occur when the two stimuli are of the same modality and are simultaneously presented. If an occasion-setting discrimination is solved through configuring, it should be easier to solve the problem under conditions that favor configuring than under those that mitigate against it. A further problem for a configural view of occasion setting is that preexposure to an intended occasion setter alone (see Exhibit 10) does not appear to retard development of occasion setting, despite the common view that preexposure to an element interferes with subsequent configuring of a compound stimulus that includes that element. In addition, occasion setting is seen to transfer from the ambiguous CS of occasion-setting training to other ambiguous (or at least previously occasion-set) CSs (e.g., Rescorla, 1985). This last observation is also problematic to a configural view of occasion setting. For the time being, which conceptualization of occasion-setting content is most accurate remains to be determined. The other chapters in this book present, in much greater detail, the cases for one or another of these theoretical views of occasion setting.

REFERENCES

Arnold, H. M., Grahame, N. J., & Miller, R. R. (1991). Higher-order occasion setting. *Animal Learning & Behavior, 19,* 58–64.

Baker, A. G. (1976). Learned irrelevance and learned helplessness: Rats learn that stimuli, reinforcers, and responses are uncorrelated. *Journal of Experimental Psychology: Animal Behavior Processes, 2,* 130–141.

Barnet, R. C., Cole, R. P., & Miller, R. R. (1997). Temporal coding differentiates forward and backward conditioning. *Animal Learning & Behavior, 25,* 221–233.

Barnet, R. C., Grahame, N. J., & Miller, R. R. (1993). Temporal encoding as a determinant of blocking. *Journal of Experimental Psychology: Animal Behavior Processes, 19,* 327–341.

Biederman, I. (1972). Human performance in contingent information-processing tasks. *Journal of Experimental Analysis of Behavior, 26,* 301–314.

Bonardi, C. (1988). Associative explanations of discriminative inhibition effects. *Quarterly Journal of Experimental Psychology, 40B,* 63–82.

Bonardi, C. (1989). Inhibitory discriminative control is specific to both the response and the reinforcer. *Quarterly Journal of Experimental Psychology, 41B,* 225–242.

Bonardi, C. (1991). Blocking of occasion setting in feature-positive discriminations. *Quarterly Journal of Experimental Psychology, 43B,* 431–448.

Bouton, M. E., & King, D. A. (1983). Contextual control of the extinction of conditioned fear: Tests for associative value of the context. *Journal of Experimental Psychology: Animal Behavior Processes, 9,* 248–265.

Bouton, M. E., & Swartzentruber, D. E. (1986). Analysis of the associative and occasion-setting properties of contexts participating in a Pavlovian discrimination. *Journal of Experimental Psychology: Animal Behavior Processes, 12,* 333–350.

Brandon, S. E., & Wagner, A. R. (1991). Modulation of a discrete Pavlovian conditioned reflex by a putative emotive Pavlovian conditioned stimulus. *Journal of Experimental Psychology: Animal Behavior Processes, 17,* 299–311.

Colwill, R. M., & Rescorla, R. A. (1990). Evidence for the hierarchical structure of instrumental learning. *Animal Learning & Behavior, 18,* 71–82.

Davidson, T. L., Aparicio, J., & Rescorla, R. A. (1988). Transfer between Pavlovian facilitator and instrumental discriminative stimuli. *Animal Learning & Behavior, 16,* 285–291.

Edwards, C. A., Miller, J. S., & Zentall, T. R. (1985). Control of pigeons matching and mismatching performance by instructional cues. *Animal Learning & Behavior, 13,* 383–391.

Fanselow, M. S. (1986). Associative vs. topological accounts of the immediate shock freezing deficit in rats: Implications for the response selection rules governing species-specific defensive reactions. *Learning and Motivation, 17,* 16–39.

Fiori, L. M., Barnet, R. C., & Miller, R. R. (1994). Renewal of Pavlovian conditioned inhibition. *Animal Learning & Behavior, 22,* 47–52.

Gibbon, J., & Balsam, P. (1981). Spreading association in time. In C. M. Locurto, H. S. Terrace, & J. Gibbon (Eds.), *Autoshaping and conditioning theory* (pp. 219–253). New York: Academic Press.

Gollin, E. S. (1966). Solution of conditional discriminations by young children. *Journal of Comparative and Physiological Psychology, 62,* 454–456.

Grahame, N. J., Barnet, R. C., Gunther, L. M., & Miller, R. R. (1994). Latent inhibition as a performance deficit resulting from CS-context associations. *Animal Learning & Behavior, 22,* 395–408.

Grahame, N. J., Hallam, S. C., Geier, L., & Miller, R. R. (1990). Context as an occasion setter following either CS acquisition and extinction or CS acquisition alone. *Learning and Motivation, 21,* 237–265.

Gunther, L. M., Cole, R. P., & Miller, R. R. (1997). *Overshadowing of an occasion setter.* Manuscript submitted for publication.

Hallam, S. C., Grahame, N. J., Barnet, R. C., & Miller, R. R. (1997). *Blocking between and within serial feature-negative discrimination and Pavlovian inhibition.* Manuscript in preparation.

Holland, P. C. (1983). Occasion setting in Pavlovian feature positive discriminations. In M. L. Commons, R. J. Herrnstein, & A. R. Wagner (Eds.), *Quantitative analyses of behavior: Discrimination processes* (pp. 183–206). Cambridge, MA: Ballinger.

Holland, P. C. (1985). The nature of conditioned inhibition in serial and simultaneous feature negative discriminations. In R. R. Miller & N. E. Spear (Eds.), *Information processing in animals: Conditioned inhibition* (pp. 267–297). Hillsdale, NJ: Erlbaum.

Holland, P. C. (1986). Temporal determinants of occasion setting in feature positive discriminations. *Animal Learning & Behavior, 14,* 111–120.

Holland, P. C. (1989). Transfer of negative occasion setting and conditioned inhibition across conditioned and unconditioned stimuli. *Journal of Experimental Psychology: Animal Behavior Processes, 15,* 311–328.

Holland, P. C. (1990). Forms of memory in Pavlovian conditioning. In J. L. McGaugh, N. M. Weinberger, & G. Lynch (Eds.), *Brain organization and memory: Cells, systems, and circuits* (pp. 78–105). New York: Oxford University Press.

Holland, P. C. (1992). Occasion setting in Pavlovian conditioning. In D. L. Medin (Ed.), *The psychology of learning and motivation, Vol. 28* (pp. 69–125). San Diego, CA: Academic Press.

Holland, P. C. (1995). The effects of intertrial and feature-target intervals on operant serial feature-positive discrimination learning. *Animal Learning & Behavior, 23,* 411–428.

Holland, P. C., Hamlin, P. A., & Parsons, J. P. (1997). Temporal specificity in serial feature positive discrimination learning. *Journal of Experimental Psychology: Animal Behavior Processes, 23,* 95–109.

Holland, P. C., & Morrell, J. R. (1996). The effects of intertrial and feature-target intervals on operant serial feature negative discrimination learning. *Learning and Motivation, 27,* 21–42.

Kamin, L. J. (1968). "Attention-like" processes in classical conditioning. In M. R. Jones (Ed.), *Miami symposium on the prediction of behavior: Aversive stimulation* (pp. 9–31). Miami, FL: University of Miami Press.

Kaufman, M. A., & Bolles, R. C. (1981). A nonassociative aspect of overshadowing. *Bulletin of the Psychonomic Society, 18,* 318–320.

Lubow, R. E., & Moore, A. V. (1959). Latent inhibition: The effect of nonreinforced exposure to the conditioned stimulus. *Journal of Comparative and Physiological Psychology, 52,* 415–419.

Maki, W. S. (1979). Pigeon's short-term memories for surprising vs. expected reinforcement and nonreinforcement. *Animal Learning & Behavior, 7,* 31–37.

Matzel, L. D., Held, F. P., & Miller, R. R. (1988). Information and expression of simultaneous and backward conditioning: Implications for contiguity theory. *Learning and Motivation, 19,* 317–344.

Matzel, L. D., Schachtman, T. R., & Miller, R. R. (1985). Recovery of an overshadowed association achieved by extinction of the overshadowing stimulus. *Learning and Motivation, 16,* 398–412.

Miller, R. R., & Barnet, R. C. (1993). The role of time in elementary associations. *Current Directions in Psychological Science, 2,* 106–111.

Morrell, J. A., & Holland, P. C. (1993). Summation and transfer of negative occasion setting. *Animal Learning & Behavior, 21,* 145–153.

Nakajima, S. (1994). Contextual control of Pavlovian feature-positive and feature-negative discriminations. *Animal Learning & Behavior, 22,* 34–46.

Oberling, P., Gunther, L. M., & Miller, R. R. (1997). *A search for an occasion setter preexposure effect.* Manuscript in preparation.

Pavlov, I. P. (1927). *Conditioned reflexes.* London: Oxford University Press.

Rescorla, R. A. (1971). Summation and retardation tests of latent inhibition. *Journal of Comparative and Physiological Psychology, 75,* 77–81.

Rescorla, R. A. (1985). Conditioned inhibition and facilitation. In R. R. Miller & N. E. Spear (Eds.), *Information processing in animals: Conditioned inhibition* (pp. 299–326). Hillsdale, NJ: Erlbaum.

Rescorla, R. A. (1986). Extinction of facilitation. *Journal of Experimental Psychology: Animal Behavior Processes, 12,* 16–24.

Rescorla, R. A. (1987). Facilitation and inhibition. *Journal of Experimental Psychology: Animal Behavior Processes, 13,* 250–259.

Rescorla, R. A., & Wagner, A. R. (1972). A theory of Pavlovian conditioning: Variations in the effectiveness of reinforcement and nonreinforcement. In A. H. Black & W. F. Prokasy (Eds.), *Classical conditioning II: Current research and theory* (pp. 64–99). New York: Appleton-Century-Crofts.

Ross, R. T. (1983). Relationships between the determinants of performance in serial feature-positive discriminations. *Journal of Experimental Psychology: Animal Behavior Processes, 9,* 349–373.

Schmajuk, N., Lamoureux, J. A., & Holland, P. C. (1998). Occasion setting: A neural network approach. *Psychological Review, 105,* 3–32.

Sidman, M., Kirk, B., & Willson-Morris, M. (1985). Six-member stimulus classes generated by conditional-discrimination procedures. *Journal of the Experimental Analysis of Behavior, 43,* 21–42.

Skinner, B. F. (1938). *The behavior of organisms.* New York: Appleton-Century-Crofts.

Swartzentruber, D. (1991). Blocking between occasion setters and contextual stimuli. *Journal of Experimental Psychology: Animal Behavior Processes, 17,* 163–173.

Thomas, D. R., Curran, P. J., & Russell, R. J. (1988). Factors affecting conditional discrimination learning by pigeons: II. Physical and temporal characteristics of stimuli. *Animal Learning & Behavior, 16,* 468–476.

Wagner, A. R. (1978). Expectancies and priming in STM. In S. H. Hulse, H. Fowler, & W. K. Honig (Eds.), *Cognitive processes in behavior* (pp. 177–209). Hillsdale, NJ: Erlbaum.

2

Conditional Learning: An Associative Analysis

Charlotte Bonardi

It is now well established that the ability of a conditioned stimulus (CS) to evoke its conditioned response (CR) may be controlled by the presence of certain stimuli. These modulatory stimuli, which have also been called *occasion setters,* appear to affect the degree to which the animal can retrieve or use the information in an associative link. Although this effect can sometimes be explained in terms of the simple associative properties of the controlling stimulus (see, e.g., Brandon & Wagner, chapter 12, this volume), at other times it cannot (see Hall & Mondragón, chapter 7, this volume; and Swartzentruber, 1995, for a review). This latter observation is of some importance, as it suggests that occasion setters acquire their properties through some learning process that is not associative in origin. Because many theories of occasion setting are relatively silent about the conditions under which occasion setters are formed, this has left open the possibility that some new, nonassociative learning mechanism is required to explain how occasion setters are established (e.g., Bouton,

This work was supported by grants from the Biotechnology and Biological Sciences Research Council. I would like to thank Geoffrey Hall, Rob Honey, Jasper Ward-Robinson, and other members of the lab for much helpful discussion, and Richard Dale, Iona Pinder, and Alan Willis for their care of the animals.

1990; Holland, 1983; Rescorla, 1985). In this chapter I reject this suggestion and develop the contrasting view that associative theory can be adapted to accommodate occasion setting, provided that special assumptions are made about the events that can enter into associations. It is typically assumed that associations may form between "simple" events, such as lights, tones, and food presentation; but it is possible that they can also form between more complex events. For example, in a standard positive occasion-setting discrimination (F t+, t–) the target, t, is reinforced (+) when it is signaled or accompanied by the feature, F. I will argue that this pairing of target and reinforcement is perceived by the animal as a complex event that can enter into associations in exactly the same way as a more simple event. The feature's occasion-setting properties arise because it becomes associated with this complex event, and this association then allows the feature to retrieve, or facilitate the degree to which the animal can use, the target–reinforcer association (e.g., Bonardi, 1988, 1991).

This approach has the advantage of making a clear set of predictions about the conditions under which occasion setters will form and about the way in which they operate on the target–reinforcer association. The rest of this chapter will evaluate these predictions.

CONDITIONS OF OCCASION-SETTER FORMATION

Nonexplicit Training

Most accounts of occasion setting say relatively little about the conditions under which occasion setters form; nevertheless, they do make some assumptions about the conditions required for occasion-setter formation, and one of these concerns the necessity for what has been called *explicit training.* In a standard feature-positive occasion-setting procedure, the target stimulus is reinforced when it is signaled by the feature and nonreinforced when it is presented alone. This means that the target stimulus is ambiguous, and the animal needs the feature to be able to predict the outcome of any trial. It has been argued that this informational role played by the feature is necessary for it to become an occasion setter (e.g., Bouton, 1993; Rescorla, 1985; see also Swartzentruber, 1995). The implication is that, if the nonreinforced target trials were omitted, the feature would no longer supply information and therefore would not become an occasion setter. The account being proposed here imposes no such constraint, because it assumes that occasion setting results from formation of an association between the feature and the target-US pairing and that formation of this association obeys standard associative rules. Associative theory stipulates, however, that for an association to form between two events, they must simply be paired[1]—which in this case means that the feature must simply accompany target-US pairings. Thus, according to this analysis, there is no need for trials on which the target is presented alone, and occasion setting would be obtained even if they were omitted, in what I call a *nonexplicit training procedure.* No other theories anticipate occasion setting after such a training regime, and therefore the first experiment I will describe was designed to test this unique prediction.

In Bonardi (1992, Experiment 3), which used rat subjects, the training procedure entailed presentations of an extended feature stimulus of 3 min in duration, during which varying numbers of brief (5-sec) target stimuli occurred at unpredictable intervals; these target presentations were followed by food reinforcement (cf. Kimmel & Ray, 1978; Wilson & Pearce, 1989, 1990). Feature presentations were separated by 6-min periods in which no stimuli were programmed to occur. Throughout the experiment animals were rewarded with food pellets for pressing a lever according to a variable interval (VI) schedule, so that the conditioned response, the magazine approach, to the target stimuli interfered with this lever-pressing response; the measure of conditioning was thus conditioned suppression of lever-pressing.

Animals were given training with two features, X and Y, and two targets, a and b; a was reinforced during presentations of feature X, and b during presentations of feature Y. Neither a nor b was presented without

[1] It is also necessary that the second event be surprising—not predicted by anything else. This will be taken up in the next section.

Exhibit 1

Design of Experiment 1

Group	Training	Test
Cond/Same	X (a+)	X (a)
	Y (b+)	Y (b)
Cond/Diff	X (a+)	X (b)
	Y (b+)	Y (a)
Hab/Same	X (a–)	X (a)
	Y (b–)	Y (b)
Hab/Diff	X (a–)	X (b)
	Y (b–)	Y (a)

NOTE: The features, X and Y, were 3-min presentations of a clicker and dark (offset of the houselight), respectively; the targets, a and b, were 5-sec presentations of a white noise or a pulsed jewel light that were counterbalanced. All animals received eight training sessions with each feature, each of which comprised four feature presentations separated by an intertrial interval (ITI) of 6 min. There were three target presentations during each feature, which in Groups Cond/Same and Cond/Diff were reinforced by the delivery of three food pellets. Groups Hab/Same and Hab/Diff received one test session with each feature, whereas Groups Cond/Same and Cond/Diff received two; each test session consisted of two feature presentations, and no target presentations were reinforced.

its respective feature. The question of interest was whether this nonexplicit training procedure would be sufficient to establish X and Y as occasion setters. In order to determine this, after training, the animals were divided into two groups, Group Cond/Same and Group Cond/Diff. Group Cond/Same received presentations of a in feature X, and b in feature Y, exactly as during training. Group Cond/Diff, on the other hand, received presentations of a in feature Y and b in feature X so that, for these animals, each target was presented in the alternative feature (see Exhibit 1).

If during training X and Y had become occasion setters, so that X controlled responding to a, and Y responding to b, then animals in Group Cond/Same, who experienced a in feature X at test, would be able to access the a–US association and hence show strong conditioned responding (strong suppression of lever-pressing). Group Cond/Diff experienced a in feature Y during the test, however, and would not be able to access the a–US association so readily; they would therefore show only attenuated conditioned responding. Therefore, if nonexplicit training were sufficient to produce occasion setting, one would expect more suppression in Group Cond/Same than in Group Cond/Diff. If nonexplicit training does not produce occasion setting, however, the animals would form only simple Pavlovian associations between each feature and the US and between each target and the US. Responding at test would therefore be determined by the sum of those two associations, and this sum would be the same for Group Cond/Same as for Group Cond/Diff; consequently, if nonexplicit training does not produce occasion setting, there would be no difference in responding between the two groups. The results from this experiment are shown in the top panel of Figure 1. It may be seen that, according to the predictions I have outlined, animals in Group Cond/Same showed more suppression than those in Group Cond/Diff. This result confirms the suggestion that nonexplicit training made X and Y into occasion setters.

There is, however, an alternative interpretation of these results. During the test phase, animals in Group Cond/Diff were presented with, for example, target a in feature Y for the first time. It is possible that this novel stimulus configuration produced some generalization decrement, so that the a at test was perceived as a slightly different stimulus from the a that had been reinforced during training. This would reduce responding to a in Group Cond/Diff and hence could explain the results observed. Although I made every attempt to choose stimuli that would minimize this likelihood, it seemed prudent to evaluate the possibility experimentally. Thus, the experiment included two further groups, Groups Hab/Same and Hab/Different, trained in exactly the same way as Groups Cond/Same and Cond/Diff, except that a and b were never followed by reinforcement. This means that X and Y would acquire no occasion-setting control over a and b for these animals. There was then a test phase in which Group Hab/Same experienced a in X and b in Y, exactly as in training, and Group Hab/Diff experienced the converse arrangement, a in Y and b in X.

If a were to suffer generalization decrement in Group Cond/Diff, it would also do so in Group Hab/Diff, and this would be manifest as a return of unconditioned responding to a, because it would be perceived as a partially novel stimulus. In the present procedure, unconditioned

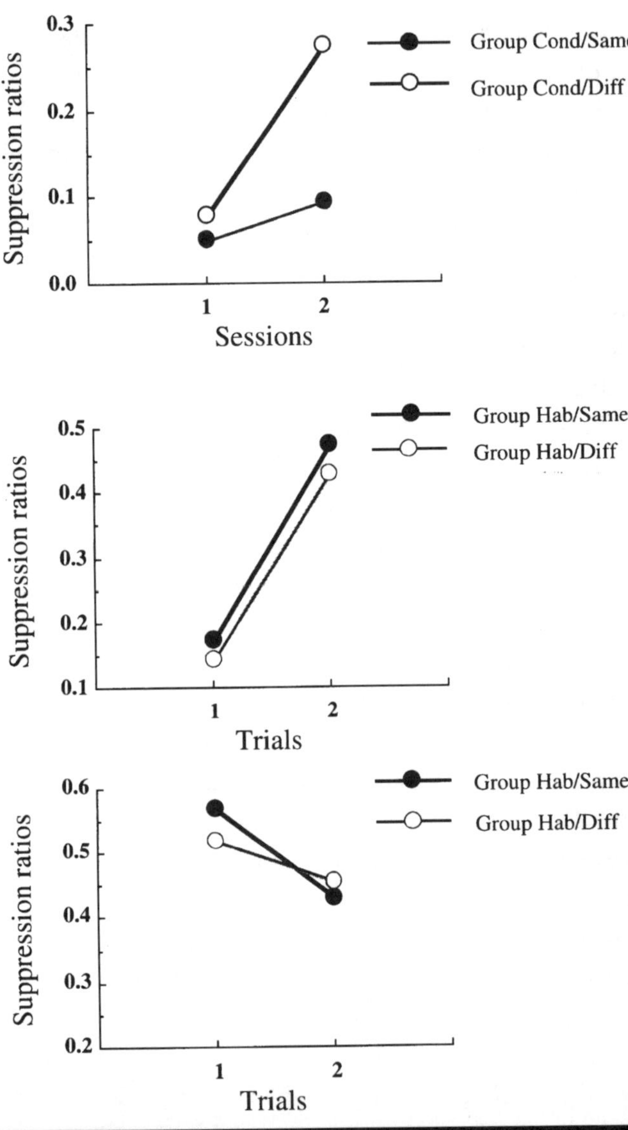

Figure 1

(Top panel) Group mean corrected suppression ratios for Groups Cond/Same and Cond/Diff during the test. *(Center panel)* Group mean suppression ratios for Groups Hab/Same and Hab/Diff during the first two trials of training. *(Lower panel)* Group mean suppression ratios for Groups Hab/Same and Hab/Diff during the test.

responding would be detectable in the same way as conditioned responding—as suppression of the lever-press response. Thus, if generalization decrement of the target stimuli were to occur in Groups Cond/Diff and Hab/Diff, then there would be more suppression in Group Hab/Diff than in Group Hab/Same at test.

The results from this second pair of groups are shown in the center and lower panels of Figure 1. The center panel shows responding during a and b at the very start of training, when they were completely novel; it is evident that they elicited substantial suppression but that this quickly habituated. The question of interest is whether there was any return of this unconditioned suppression in Group Hab/Diff during the test. The lower panel shows the results from the test; it is clear that there is no sign of such an effect—Group Hab/Diff appeared no more suppressed than Group Hab/Same. There is therefore no evidence for generalization decrement of the target stimuli by this measure, and hence no indication that the loss of conditioned responding in Group Cond/Diff could be attributable to such an effect—a finding that is consistent with the results of other experiments that have found occasion setting after nonexplicit training but use the experimental context as the controlling cue (e.g., Hall & Honey, 1989, 1990; see Hall & Mondragón, chapter 7, this volume). The entire pattern of results is therefore more consistent with the prediction of the account being suggested here—that the nonexplicit training given to Groups Cond/Same and Cond/Diff was sufficient to establish X and Y as occasion setters.[2]

[2]The fact that an occasion setter's properties are not affected by presenting it alone could be seen as a problem for this analysis, because such treatment will eliminate the properties of an excitatory CS. Presenting a stimulus alone does not necessarily eliminate associative information, however—it will not affect the properties of a conditioned inhibitor, for example, which must be paired with the US to lose its inhibitory properties. Perhaps the correct analysis of extinction in simple Pavlovian conditioning is to argue that an association will be extinguished only by superimposition of a second association that conveys contradictory information. Applying this analysis to the case of occasion setting yields the prediction that, to reduce the ability of an occasion setter to signal reinforcement of a target CS, that occasion setter must be paired with contradictory information—*nonreinforcement* of that target CS. This, of course, is exactly what has been observed (e.g., Rescorla, 1986; but see, e.g., Holland & Gory, 1986).

Blocking

The proposal that occasion setting might result from a form of classical conditioning suggests another prediction about the conditions under which occasion setters will form, and this concerns the phenomenon of blocking. One of the basic principles of associative learning is that, in order to create an association between two events, it is not enough to present them together; the second of the two events must be surprising—not predicted by anything else. This principle is the source of blocking, in which the pairing of two events results in only a poor association between them, because the second event is already well-predicted by some other as a result of previous training. It follows, then, that if formation of an occasion setter is the result of association formation, it should also be subject to blocking. If occasion-setter formation is the result of some unspecified learning process that is not associative in origin, however, there is no particular reason for blocking to be evident in this way. The next experiment was therefore designed to look for blocking of occasion-setter formation (Bonardi, 1991, Experiment 2).

The procedure in this experiment was very similar to that in the previous experiment, with the following exceptions: First, a standard occasion-setting procedure was used throughout—that is, target stimuli were not only presented and reinforced during the feature but also occurred with the same frequency, nonreinforced, in the feature's absence. Second, no lever was present in this experiment; the conditioned response was therefore indexed by the number of entries into the food magazine made during the target stimuli.

In the first phase of training, a single group of animals received occasion-setting training with a feature stimulus, X, and a target stimulus, a. Once the animals had learned this discrimination, they were given a further phase of training with the original target stimulus, a, and a second, novel target stimulus, b. Target a was reinforced in the presence of a simultaneous compound of the pretrained feature, X, and a second, novel feature, Z. Target b was also reinforced in the presence of feature Z, but Z was

Exhibit 2

Design of Experiment 2

Phase 1	Phase 2	Test
X (a+) a–	XZ (a+) a–	Z (a) a
	YZ (b+) b–	Z (b) b

NOTE: Features X and Y were 3-min presentations of a clicker and a tone that were counterbalanced; Z was offset of the houselight for all subjects. The targets, a and b, were 5-sec presentations of a white noise or a pulsed jewel light that were counterbalanced. Each training session consisted of four feature presentations; all animals received 12 training sessions in Phase 1 and 10 sessions with each feature compound in Phase 2. There were six target presentations during each feature, each reinforced by delivery of a food pellet; targets occurred at the same rate during the 6-min period preceding each feature presentation, but these target presentations were nonreinforced. Test sessions were identical to those of compound training except that only feature Z was presented, no food was delivered, and a was the target during half the feature presentations and b during the other half.

presented in compound with a second, novel feature, Y. Finally, the effect of Z alone on responding to both a and b was examined (see Exhibit 2).

In the first phase of training, X would be established as an occasion setter for a, which, according to the account being suggested here, results from formation of an association between X and a-reinforcer pairings. This means that, in the second stage of training, when the compound of X and Z signals reinforcement of a, the a-reinforcer pairings cannot be surprising because they are well predicted by X; Z therefore cannot become associated with them and as a result cannot become an occasion setter for a. Feature Z also accompanies b-reinforcer pairings in this stage and thus also has the opportunity to become an occasion setter for this stimulus. Pairings of b and the reinforcer have never occurred before and consequently are surprising; thus Z can become associated with them and therefore become an occasion setter for b. In other words, if occasion setting were subject to blocking, at test Z would have a greater effect over responding to b than over responding to a.

The results from this experiment are shown in Figure 2—responding to a is shown on the left, and responding to b on the right. Neither a nor

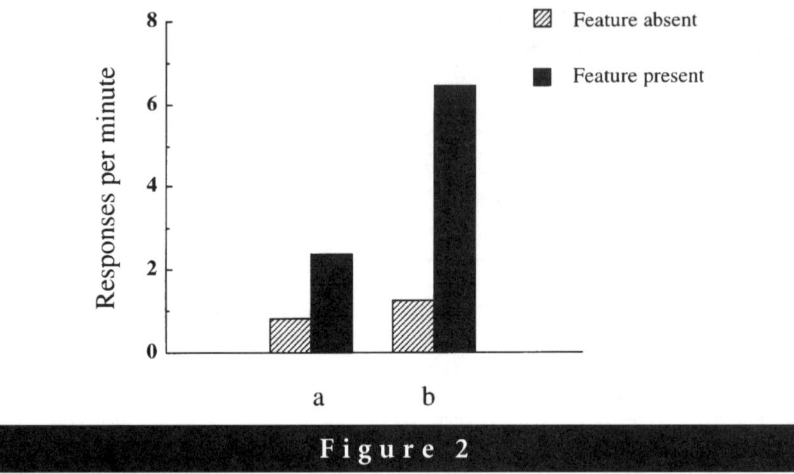

Figure 2

Mean response rates during the target CSs a and b in the presence and absence of feature Z during the test.

b elicited much responding when presented alone, and the presence of feature Z enhanced responding to both of these stimuli. The critical finding, however, is that this enhancement was significantly greater for b than for a. This is exactly what was predicted and is consistent with the suggestion that the ability of Z to act as an occasion setter for a was blocked by the presence of the pretrained feature, X.

TARGET OF OCCASION-SETTER ACTION

The second class of predictions I shall consider concerns the site of occasion-setter action, or where on the target–US association the occasion setter operates. The predictions of the account being proposed here are quite clear on this point: Because the basic assumption of the theory is that an occasion setter's properties arise through its association with pairings of the target and the reinforcer, the implication is that its action will be directed at this particular target–reinforcer association. Holland's (1983) theory makes the same prediction.

There have been other suggestions. For example, Rescorla (1985) suggested that occasion setters operate solely on the US representation by changing its threshold of activation. An alternative theory is that the occasion setter could affect the activation threshold of the target CS representation in the same way. Another possibility is that it could independently affect both the CS and the US thresholds, thus acting independently on both components of the association, but not being specific to their combination.

These different accounts have different implications for the degree to which an occasion setter is specific to the original target–US association, that is, for the degree to which it will show transfer to some other association. The ability of an occasion setter for one target–US association to show transfer to another can be examined in a number of ways. First, one can look at the degree to which it is target-specific by examining its effect on a different target stimulus associated with the original US; if it acts on the target representation, there should be no transfer. Second, one can look at the degree to which it is US-specific by examining its effect on the same CS associated with a different US; if it acts on the US representation, there should be no transfer. Finally, one can take an occasion setter that signals two different target–US associations and examine its effects on recombinations of these targets and USs, thus examining the degree to which it is specific to a particular association. If the occasion setter acts on the association as a whole rather than on the target and US representations separately, there should be no transfer in this case (cf. Jenkins, 1985). Experiments in each of these categories can help discriminate among the various theories of occasion setting outlined earlier; I will consider each in turn.

Target Specificity

The earliest theories of occasion-setter action made opposing predictions about whether occasion setters would transfer to other CSs—Rescorla (e.g., 1985) predicted that they would, and Holland (e.g., 1983) that they would not. For this reason, many experiments have examined the target-specificity of occasion setters; their results unfortunately have been difficult to characterize in a simple way. Nevertheless, it is possible to draw a few generalizations about when transfer will be observed and when it will not (see Swartzentruber, 1995, for a review). First, occasion setters tend to transfer better to cues that have also been involved in occasion-setting discriminations than to those that have not. Second, when transfer does occur to occasion-set cues, it tends to be incomplete; the occasion setter tends to be less effective with the transfer target than with the original training target. At first sight it is difficult to see how these observations can be easily reconciled with any of the theories I have outlined, but closer consideration reveals that this apparent inconsistency may be illusory. I shall take each point in turn.

Selective Transfer to Occasion-Set Cues

It is now relatively well established that occasion setters tend to transfer better to targets from other occasion-setting discriminations than to other types of target stimuli; many types of transfer targets have been tried, although one of the most common is a cue that has simply been conditioned and then extinguished.[3] This effect has been replicated in our laboratory (Bonardi & Hall, 1994, Experiment 1); the main features of this study are summarized next.

Using the general procedures outlined in the previous experiment, rats were given training on two occasion-setting discriminations, in which feature X signaled reinforcement of target a and feature Y signaled reinforcement of target b; the animals were also given training with a third target stimulus, c (see Exhibit 3). Stimulus c was never presented in the presence of either X or Y; in the first phase of training it was consistently followed by reinforcement, but in the second phase this reinforcement was omitted so that responding to c dropped to a level similar to that of b when it was presented without its feature, Y. For half the animals, stimulus b was a clicker and c a white noise, whereas for the remaining animals this arrangement was reversed. Thus, b and c could be regarded as being equally similar, in physical terms, to a, which was a tone for all animals. Finally, the degree to which feature X transferred its occasion-setting pow-

[3]This is probably because such a stimulus is similar to an occasion-set cue, in that it has been both reinforced and nonreinforced and also would command a low rate of conditioned responding, as would an occasion-set cue without its occasion setter.

Exhibit 3

Design of Experiment 3

Stage 1	Stage 2	Test
X(a+) a–	X(a+) a–	X(b–) b–
Y(b+) b–	Y(b+) b–	X(c–) c–
c+	c–	

NOTE: Features X and Y were 3-min presentations of a striplight and dark (offset of the houselight) that were counterbalanced. Target stimuli were of 10-sec duration; a was a tone for all animals; b and c were a click and a noise that were counterbalanced. Each training session consisted of four feature presentations, two of each; there were three target presentations during each feature, each reinforced by delivery of a food pellet. The target presented during a particular feature occurred at the same rate during the 6-min period preceding each presentation of that feature, but these target presentations were nonreinforced; the feature and the preceding 6-min period constituted a feature trial. Trials with stimulus c, of which there was one per session, comprised a six-minute period in which six 10-sec c presentations occurred; these were reinforced in the 16 sessions of Stage 1 and were nonreinforced in the six sessions of Stage 2. The test session (which followed a preliminary test and two reminder sessions of Stage 2 training) was conducted in extinction and consisted of four trials with feature X, two with b and two with c.

ers to b and c was examined. We anticipated that we would replicate the result found by others: that X would have more of an effect on responding to b, which had been the target of an occasion-setting discrimination, than on responding to c, which had not. The results of this test are shown in Figure 3, which shows that these anticipations were realized. Stimulus c, if anything, elicited slightly more responding than b when presented alone; X, however, had virtually no effect on responding to c but a sizable and significant effect on responding to b. The implication is that transfer of occasion setting depends on the training history of the transfer target.

Observations of this type appear difficult to reconcile with the original theories of occasion setting proposed by Rescorla (1985) and Holland (1983); Rescorla's account predicted that transfer would be obtained and Holland's that it would not; in addition, neither of these predictions depended on the transfer target's previous treatment.[4] This type of argument

[4] Rescorla (e.g., 1985) has argued that transfer will only occur to a cue that has a component of inhibitory associative strength; because both occasion-set and trained and extinguished cues have such an inhibitory component, however, his theory would not anticipate differential transfer in this example.

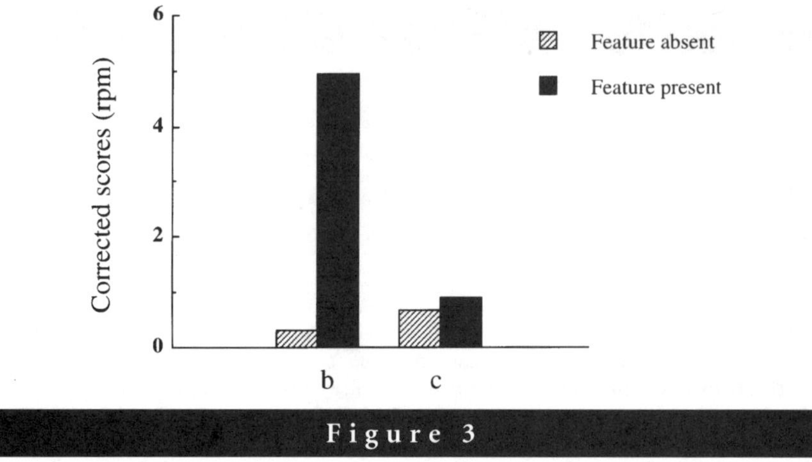

Figure 3

Group mean corrected response rates during b and c in the presence and absence of feature X during the test.

prompted Holland to reject his original proposal that occasion setters were association-specific (e.g., 1989a). He instead suggested that an occasion setter would act on any target–US association, even one with which it had not been trained; the only requirement was that, in order for the occasion setter to be effective, both elements of the association had to have been subject to occasion setting in the past. Such theoretical revision may be premature, however, because the basic observation might be interpretable in other, simpler ways. First, comparing transfer to target CSs with different training histories is problematic because these previous treatments may affect the ease with which responding to the stimuli can be changed, regardless of how that change is produced; perhaps responding to an occasion-set cue would be differentially enhanced even if that enhancement were produced not by an occasion setter, but, for example, by a Pavlovian CS or a generally arousing stimulus. This might produce a result that looks like differential transfer of occasion setting even though it has nothing specifically to do with the occasion setter. On these grounds alone one could legitimately argue that, in order to evaluate transfer of occasion setting, the only appropriate transfer target is one that has a training history that is essentially identical to that of the original target—in other words, a target that has also been involved in an occasion-setting discrimination.

A second problem in interpreting this type of differential transfer effect arises when one takes account of stimulus generalization. Predictions about transfer typically assume that the animal can perfectly discriminate all stimuli that are involved; in practice, this assumption is unlikely. This is a problem because consideration of stimulus generalization can also provide alternative explanations of the apparently selective transfer to occasion-set cues. For example, even if the occasion setter were specific to the training target, the animal might show some generalization between the two occasion setters. This clearly could provide a source of transfer to an occasion-set target that would not be available to a target that had never been involved in an occasion-setting discrimination.

Generalization among the target stimuli can also, with the appropriate assumptions, produce this type of result. Even an account that predicts that occasion setters are target-specific would predict transfer to the degree that there is generalization between training and transfer targets. This in itself cannot explain selective transfer of the type in the experiment just described, because the physical identities of the two transfer targets were counterbalanced; there are, however, other possible sources of generalization apart from the physical characteristics of the stimulus. For example, there is now a considerable body of evidence to suggest that stimuli can become more similar as a result of sharing a common training history—what has been called an *acquired equivalence effect* (Honey & Hall, 1989; for a recent discussion of possible mechanisms, see Hall, 1996). If acquired equivalence occurs between stimuli that have both been targets of occasion-setting discriminations, this could explain the selective transfer we have been considering (cf. Lamarre & Holland, 1987; Wilson & Pearce, 1990). For example, consider the experiment just described. The counterbalancing ensured that a, on the basis of its physical characteristics, was equally similar to b and c. The fact that feature X, which had been trained with target a, had more of an effect on b than on c therefore cannot be, because the animals showed more generalization from a to b than from a to c. If one makes the additional assumption, however, that the common

Exhibit 4

Design of Experiment 4

Group	Stage 1	Stage 2	Revaluation	Test
OS	X(a+) a–	X(a+) a–		
	Y(b+) b–	Y(b+) b–	a+ d–	b versus c
	c+	c–		
	d+	d–		
C	X(a+) a–	X(a+) a–		
	Y(b+) b–	Y(b+) b–	d+ a–	b versus c
	c+	c–		
	d+	d–		

NOTE: Features X and Y were 3-min presentations of a striplight and dark (offset of the houselight) that were counterbalanced. Target stimuli were of 10-sec duration; a and d were a steady tone and a pulsed tone that were counterbalanced; b and c were a click and a noise that were counterbalanced. Each training session consisted of four feature presentations, two of each; there were three target presentations during each feature, each reinforced by the delivery of food; the target presented in a particular feature occurred at the same rate during the 6-min period preceding presentation of that feature, but these target presentations were nonreinforced. The feature and the preceding 6-min period constituted a feature trial. Trials with d and c, of which there was one each per session, each comprised a 6-min period in which six 10-sec presentations of one of these targets occurred; these were reinforced in the 24 sessions of Stage 1 and were nonreinforced in the 6 sessions of Stage 2. In each of the 16 sessions of the revaluation stage, animals in Group OS received 12 reinforced a trials and 6 nonreinforced d trials; for Group C the roles of a and d were reversed. The four test sessions, conducted in extinction, each consisted of four presentations of b and four of c.

training history shared by a and b, as the targets of occasion-setting discriminations, made them more similar through some type of acquired equivalence, the animals would be expected to show more generalization between a and b than between a and c, and this could explain the selective transfer effect that we observed. Is there any evidence for this assumption? The next experiment was designed to examine this question.

The design of this experiment (Bonardi & Hall, 1994, Experiment 2) was very similar to that of the previous experiment, and is shown in Exhibit 4. The subjects, rats, were given training identical to that in the previous experiment, except that a fourth target stimulus, d, was introduced; this was treated in exactly the same way as stimulus c, being first conditioned

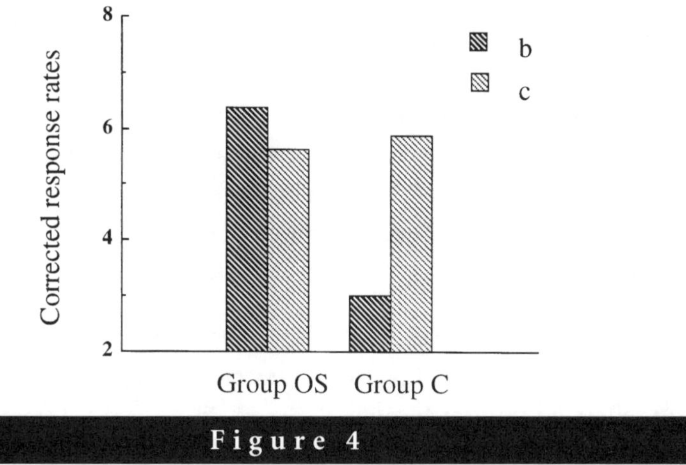

Figure 4

Group mean corrected response rates during b and c in the first two sessions of the test.

and then extinguished. Thus, at the end of training, all four target stimuli commanded a similarly low rate of responding. The animals were then divided into two groups, group OS and group C. For animals in group OS, a was paired with food reinforcement and d was nonreinforced, whereas for group C this arrangement was reversed. All animals were then given a generalization test in which the ability of b and c to provoke conditioned responding was evaluated.

The various targets were counterbalanced so that, on the basis of physical similarity alone, one would not expect differential generalization between them and hence different rates of responding to b and c at test. If the fact that a and b shared a common training history made generalization between them especially easy, however, group OS, for whom a was paired with food, would respond more to b than to c at test. In contrast, group C, for which a was nonreinforced, might be expected to show the opposite pattern of results: less responding to b than to c. The results of this experiment are shown in Figure 4, and the results were as we expected: animals in group OS responded more to b than to c, whereas animals in group C did the opposite. This is consistent with the suggestion that generalization between a and b had been enhanced as a result of their common history as the targets of occasion-setting discriminations.

In conclusion, the observation that occasion setters show selective transfer to other occasion-set cues is not as theoretically troublesome as it first appeared. There are a number of alternative explanations of this effect that do not require us to assume that occasion setters are sensitive to the training history of the transfer target. The selective transfer effect does not seem to tell us anything profound about the mechanism of occasion setting.

Incomplete Transfer to Occasion-Set Cues

The second frequent finding from transfer studies is that, although occasion setters do transfer to other occasion-set cues, that transfer tends to be incomplete. At face value this observation is also problematic for some of the theories of occasion setting that I have outlined. In particular, theories proposing that occasion setters act on the association and are therefore target-specific (e.g., Bonardi, 1991; Bouton, 1990; Holland, 1983) cannot predict any transfer without making extra assumptions. As we saw in the previous discussion, however, once it is allowed that there may be generalization between training and transfer targets and between occasion setters, some transfer might be expected.[5] The critical fact for such theories is therefore not that transfer occurs, but that it is incomplete—if the feature really acts in a target-specific manner, it should always be less effective with a transfer target than with the original training target. As this tends to be the case, furthermore, one might regard this as support for these theories.

Theories such as Rescorla's (1985), on the other hand, according to which occasion setters act on the US and are therefore not target-specific, must predict that transfer will always be complete and therefore have trouble explaining the fact that it is not. They can easily accommodate this result, however, by appealing to generalization decrement. For example, consider the most simple transfer experiment, in which animals are given training on two occasion-setting discriminations, in which X signals reinforcement of a and Y of b. Suppose that transfer is found to be incomplete,

[5] One might also expect an occasion setter to enhance responding to any transfer target through simple Pavlovian summation.

so that X, for example, has more effect on responding to a (Same trials) than to b (Different trials). On Different trials, a is signaled by the "wrong" occasion setter, Y, for the first time. This could induce generalization decrement in a, and thus produce a disruption of conditioned responding, which would look like incomplete transfer. Generalization decrement could also be produced by an associative mechanism. During training, associations might form between each feature and its own target stimulus—between X and a, and between Y and b. On Different trials when Y signals a for the first time, the Y–b association formed during training might allow Y to evoke a representation of the expected b during the presentation of a. This evoked representation could also disrupt the animal's perception of a and again produce a decrement in conditioned responding (Holland 1989b). Incomplete transfer can therefore only be taken as evidence for theories like the one proposed here if this alternative interpretation in terms of generalization decrement can be rejected. The following experiment was designed to achieve this (Bonardi, 1996, Experiment 3).

A single group of pigeons received occasion-setting training with two features, X and Y, and two occasion-set (OS) targets, a and b; X signaled reinforcement of a, and Y of b (see Exhibit 5). Responding to a and b was then examined when they were presented alone, preceded by their own features, X and Y, respectively (Same trials), and preceded by the "wrong" feature, Y and X, respectively (Different trials). It was anticipated that, as with previous findings, the birds would show transfer, but that it would be incomplete—that they would respond more on Same trials than on Different trials; the question was whether this was a result of generalization decrement of the target stimuli. To answer this question, the features X and Y were also given training with two further targets, c and d; unlike a and b, however, c and d were reinforced regardless of whether they were preceded by the features; this so-called *pseudo occasion-setting* (POS) training should not have made X and Y occasion setters for c and d (the POS targets). Finally, in order to equate the reinforcement history of a and b with that of c and d, further trials were introduced, signaled by a third feature, stimulus Z; a and b were reinforced and d and c nonreinforced

Exhibit 5

Design of Experiment 5

	Training	Test		
		Same	Different	Target
OS	X(a+) a–	X (a)	Y (a)	a
	Z(a+)			
	Y(b+) b–	Y(b)	X(b)	b
	Z (b+)			
POS	X(c+) c+	X (c)	Y (c)	c
	Z(c–)			
	Y(d+) d+	Y(d)	X(d)	d
	Z (d–)			

NOTE: X and Y were presentations of a white noise and dark (offset of the houselight); Z was the illumination of a red jewel light; these feature stimuli were of 10-sec duration and immediately preceded presentation of the target keylights, a, b, c, and d, as shown. The keylight presentations were all of 5-sec duration, as were the grain presentations on reinforced trials. For half the animals, the occasion-set targets a and b were blue and orange, and the pseudo occasion-set targets were circle and grid; for the remaining animals this arrangement was reversed. For half of each of these subgroups, blue and circle were signaled by the noise and grid and orange by dark, and for the remaining animals this arrangement was reversed. OS refers to the fact that a and b were trained in an occasion-setting discrimination and POS to the fact that c and d were trained in a pseudo occasion-setting discrimination. There were 50 sessions of training and 2 test sessions, which were conducted in extinction.

on these trials so that the total number of reinforced and nonreinforced trials with the OS and POS targets were equated. Next, c and d were tested in exactly the same way as a and b; thus, on Same trials, each was preceded by its own feature and on Different trials by the alternative feature. In this way the generalization decrement produced on Different trials with the OS targets, a and b, should have been the same as that produced with the POS targets, c and d. For example, when the animals were first presented with a preceded by Y, responding might be disrupted because this stimulus combination had never been experienced before. But exactly the same would be true of Different trials with c and d, so that generalization decrement of the OS and POS targets would be the same. It has also been argued that associations could form between features and targets during training, in this case between Y and b and also between Y and d. Thus, on Different trials when Y signaled a, Y would evoke representations of both b and d, and these evoked representations would disrupt responding to a. The same would be true, however, on Different trials in which Y was followed by c, so that again generalization decrement for the OS and POS targets would be equated. Therefore, if the greater responding to a and b on Same trials were solely a result of generalization decrement, the same pattern of responding would be observed with c and d. If the reduced responding on Different trials with a and b were in part because X and Y had become occasion setters that were specific to their training targets, however, then there would be a greater decrement of responding on Different trials with the OS targets than on those with the POS targets.

The results of this experiment are shown in Figure 5. In the top panel, responding to the occasion-set targets, a and b, is displayed. The birds responded little to these stimuli when they were presented alone but at a high rate when they were signaled by the features. The fact that responding on Different trials was higher than responding to the targets alone suggests that transfer occurred as anticipated; critical for our present purposes, however, is the fact that this transfer was incomplete—the birds responded more on Same trials than on Different trials.

In the lower panel of Figure 5, responding to the POS targets, c and d, is displayed; the birds responded at a high rate to these stimuli when they were presented alone, as they had been trained to do; they also responded at a high rate when they were signaled by the features. The critical question, however, is whether the birds would respond more on Same than on Different trials, as they did with the OS targets. It is clear, however, that this was not the case—far from obtaining less responding on Different trials with these target stimuli, the animals actually responded more.

If the imperfect transfer of occasion setting seen in this experiment had been due to generalization decrement, the same pattern of responding should have been observed in both the POS and OS targets; it was not. The implication is that the imperfect transfer must be attributed to the fact that occasion setters' effects are specific to the target CS. These results are therefore most easily accommodated by theories that, like the one

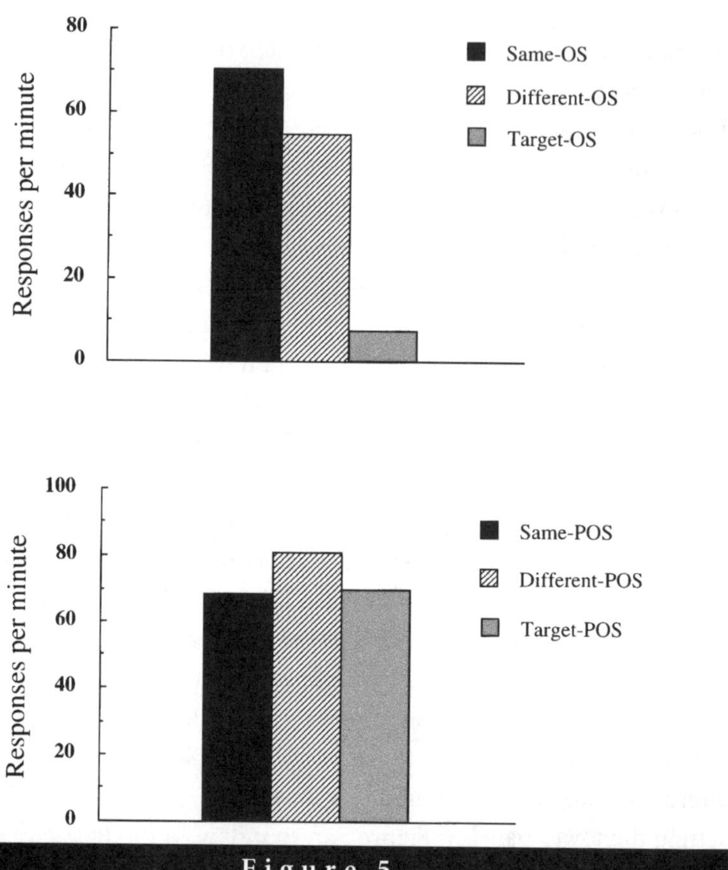

Figure 5

Mean response rates during the OS keylights a and b and the POS keylights c and d when preceded by their own features (Same trials), by the alternative feature (Different trials), and when presented alone during the test.

being proposed here, assert that the occasion setter acts at least in part on the representation of the target CS.

Conclusions

The results from experiments examining target specificity of occasion setting were at first sight daunting for any simple theory of occasion setting; but further analysis has shown that this impression was misleading. Both the selective transfer effects and the imperfect transfer to occasion-set cues are not necessarily at odds with the suggestion that occasion setters are target-specific. This accords with theories, such as the one outlined in this chapter, that assert that the occasion setter acts on the target–US association. These results are not sufficient support for such a theory, however. It might be, for example, that the occasion setter simply facilitates activation of the CS representation and has no effect on the US representation at all. Therefore, the present account also requires evidence that occasion setters are specific to the US representation. I will deal with this prediction next.

Reinforcer Specificity

All theories of occasion setting predict that occasion setters should be US-specific (Bouton, 1990; Holland, 1983; Rescorla, 1985). Surprisingly, however, this is a topic that has received almost no experimental attention. The exception is an experiment on negative occasion setting by Holland (1989a), conducted with two appetitive reinforcers. He found no evidence for US specificity, provided that the transfer US had been part of an occasion-setting discrimination. At face value this finding is inconsistent with almost all standard theories of occasion setting—but there might be alternative explanations of this result. For example, in a negative occasion-setting discrimination, the occasion setter tells the animals that a CS will not be followed by a particular US—in other words, that the CS is acting as a conditioned inhibitor in the occasion setter's presence. Conditioned inhibitors do not always convey precise information about the sensory properties of the US whose omission they signal (e.g., Pearce, Montgomery, & Dickinson, 1981), however, and if the target association encodes no specific information about the US other than its motivational characteristics, it is unclear how an occasion setter that modulates that association should be able to do so. Therefore, the fact that negative occasion setters are not always US-specific does not necessarily preclude the possibility that positive occasion setters might be. The next and final experiment indirectly examined this suggestion by addressing the prediction made by the account being proposed here, that the occasion setter's effects should be specific to the target–US association with which it was trained.

Association Specificity

In this experiment, an occasion setter was established as a signal for two associations, between CS1 and US1, and between CS2 and US2 (Bonardi, 1997). The question of interest was whether this occasion setter would be more effective with these original associations than with a new one that had been formed by recombining two of the original events—CS1 and US2, for example (cf. Jenkins, 1985). A result of this type would allow us to draw several conclusions: First, it would make it clear that the occasion setter is not only target-specific but also US-specific; if it were not, its effects would not be attenuated when the US that follows the training target was switched. Second, it would rule out the possibility that the occasion setter was acting independently on target and US representations, as this would imply that it should be insensitive to the combination in which these stimuli were presented. The only possible interpretation of such a result would therefore be that the occasion setter was acting on the target–US association—and would therefore provide powerful evidence in favor of the account I am suggesting.

A single group of pigeons was trained on four occasion-setting discriminations, with two features, X and Y, two targets, a and b, and two reinforcers (see Exhibit 6). The features were 10-sec presentations of a clicker, and of dark (produced by turning off the houselight); the targets were 5-sec presentations of a keylight (either green or a grid composed of three horizontal and three vertical lines); on compound trials, target onset coincided with feature offset. The reinforcers were 5-sec presentations of lentils of the same size and shape but of different colors (white and orange); these supported almost identical rates of responding. Animals were trained on a switching task in which each feature signaled the operation of two different associations. Thus, X signaled that a would be followed by orange lentils, b by white lentils, and Y signaled the converse arrangement; the physical nature of the features, targets, and reinforcers was fully counterbalanced.

The aim was to examine whether X and Y told the animals anything about the specific CS–US combinations that they signaled by examining

Exhibit 6

Design of Experiment 6

Stage 1		Stage 2	
		Same	Different
X (a→orange)	a–	X(aS→orange)	X(aD→white)
X (b→white)	b–	X(bS→white)	X(bD→orange)
Y (a→white)	a–	Y(aS→white)	Y(aD→orange)
Y (b→orange)	b–	Y(bS→orange)	Y(bD→white)

NOTE: X and Y were presentations of a click and offset of the houselight, respectively; these feature stimuli were of 10-sec duration and immediately preceded presentation of the target keylights, a and b, which were green and a grid composed of three vertical and three horizontal lines. S and D were purple and diamond-shaped, counterbalanced, and immediately followed a and b presentations; all keylight presentations were of 5-sec duration, as were the reinforcer presentations on reinforced trials. Orange refers to the orange lentil reinforcer and white to the white lentil reinforcer. For half the animals, orange and white reinforcers were presented as shown above, and for the remainder the identity of these reinforcers was reversed. There were 32 training sessions and 2 test sessions.

whether the birds could correctly anticipate which US would follow a particular target when it was signaled by a particular feature; this would not be manifest in discrimination performance, because both reinforcers supported the same conditioned response. Therefore, in the second phase of training, a blocking technique was employed in which the birds were given two types of trials, Same trials and Different trials. Same trials were identical to the training trials, except that a further 5-sec stimulus, S, a diamond-shaped keylight, was inserted after the offset of a or b and before the delivery of the reinforcer. Different trials were identical to Same trials except that, first, a different stimulus, D, a purple keylight, replaced S; S and D were counterbalanced. Second, the USs were switched; Thus, if during training animals had received orange lentils, on these trials they received white, and vice versa. S and D were novel but during the course of this phase would presumably become associated with reinforcement and elicit conditioned responding. Of interest was the relative speed with which this response would be acquired by the two stimuli. If the occasion setters acted on specific associations, so that, for example, X acted as a

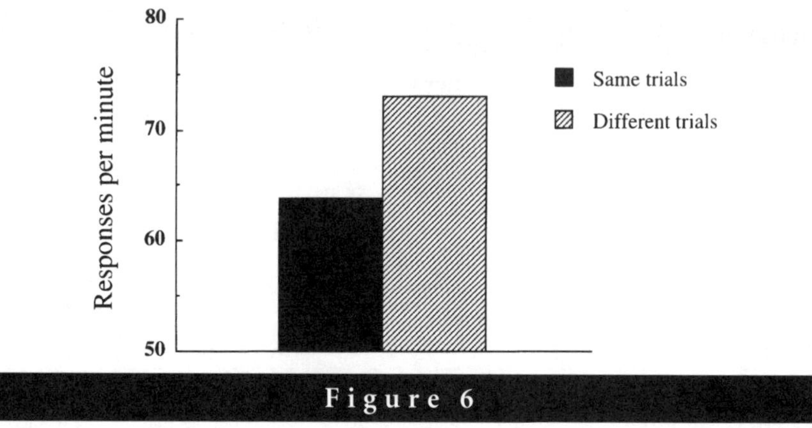

Figure 6

Mean response rates during S and D keylights during the two sessions of the test.

signal that a would be followed by orange lentils and b by white, then on Same trials the reinforcers would have been correctly signaled by a and b and thus would have been unsurprising. S would therefore be paired with a predicted reinforcer, and so it would be difficult for these events to become associated, and responding to S would therefore be poor. On Different trials, on the other hand, on being given X, the animal would expect a to be followed by orange lentils and would be surprised when white lentils were actually presented. D would therefore be paired with a surprising reinforcer, and learning about this stimulus should be good and responding to it strong. In other words, if occasion setters act on specific associations, one would predict more responding to D than to S in this phase. If instead the occasion setters act independently on CS and US representations, the occasion setters would be equally effective in allowing the targets to predict the reinforcer on Same trials as on Different trials, and one would not expect any difference in responding to S and D.

The results of this experiment are presented in Figure 6, and they are quite clear: there was more responding to D than to S, and this difference was significant, $F(1, 15) = 6.00$, $p < .03$. The results therefore support the suggestion that, at least in the case of positive occasion setting, the occasion setter can be sensitive to the specific CS–US combination that it signaled in training; this is, of course, consistent with the predictions of the account of occasion setting that I have outlined.

CONCLUSION

I have considered two sets of experiments that address the predictions of an account of occasion setting in which the occasion setter's properties derive from an association between it and a representation of the target-US pairing. The results of these experiments are broadly in agreement with this analysis. First, the conditions under which occasion setters form are those in which one would expect formation of such an association to be favored. Second, the pattern of results from transfer experiments suggests that, at least in some cases, the action of occasion setters seems to be specific to the CS–US association. These findings are inconsistent with several theories of occasion setting. For example, Rescorla's original (1985) suggestion was that occasion setters modulated activation of the US representation and encoded no information about the identity of the CS that signaled that US. Both the results described here and more recent experiments reported by Rescorla himself now suggest that some degree of CS specificity must be accommodated within any viable theory of occasion setting (Rescorla, 1991a, 1991b; see Swartzentruber, 1995). Second, the present findings are inconsistent with Holland's more recent formulation (1989a) that occasion setters act on both the CS and US, but separately so that they are not sensitive to the CS–US combination. These results are perhaps more easily accommodated by Holland's original (1983) suggestion that occasion setters act on the CS–US association. The present approach differs from his, however, in explicitly attributing occasion-setter formation to association formation. In this regard it is perhaps similar to the view that occasion setting is actually the result of a configural cue forming between the occasion setter and the target stimulus (e.g., Wilson & Pearce, 1989, 1990, 1992). It is difficult to discriminate between these two possibilities (but see, e.g., Holland, 1989c). There are, however, certain considerations that make interpretation of these results in terms of configuring less likely, and these arise from considering the relationship of occasion setting to instrumental learning.

The term *occasion setting* was not originally intended to refer to Pavlovian conditioning at all; it was coined by Skinner (1938) to refer to the relationship between a discriminative stimulus and the instrumental responding that was reinforced in its presence. Its adoption by Holland (1983) to describe the Pavlovian phenomenon was, of course, not accidental, because there is a direct operational analogy between an occasion setter in whose presence a CS–US relationship holds and a discriminative stimulus in whose presence a response-US contingency operates. Moreover, the suggestion that the properties of an occasion setter derive from an association between it and the CS–US pairing is directly analogous to Mackintosh's (1983) proposal that the power of a discriminative stimulus comes from an association between it and the response-reinforcer relationship. Not surprisingly, Mackintosh's account of discriminative stimulus formation yields a set of predictions similar to that outlined here for occasion setters. According to this view, a discriminative stimulus should form under conditions where formation of an association between it and the response-reinforcer pairing is favored, and its action should be specific to the entire response-reinforcer association. This point of view has more recently been supported by several sets of experiments by Rescorla (e.g., 1990a, 1990b). This parallel is of interest for two reasons: First, it may throw light on the contribution of configural cues to conditional control, because it is more difficult to see how configural cues could control instrumental responding; this is because the animal cannot experience the critical configural cue that predicts reinforcement until it performs the response, so it is difficult to see why it would ever do so if all that it had learned was that the configuration of discriminative stimulus and response predicted reinforcement. More fundamentally, in recent years there has been increasing support for the view that Pavlovian and instrumental conditioning arise from the same basic learning mechanism (e.g., Mackintosh & Dickinson, 1979). It would therefore be appealing, on grounds of parsimony if nothing else, if the hierarchical control of Pavlovian and instrumental associations was also the result of the same type of learning.

REFERENCES

Bonardi, C. (1988). Associative explanations of discriminative inhibition effects. *Quarterly Journal of Experimental Psychology, 40B,* 63–82.

Bonardi, C. (1991). Blocking of occasion setting in feature-positive discriminations. *Quarterly Journal of Experimental Psychology, 43B,* 431–448.

Bonardi, C. (1992). Occasion setting without feature-positive discrimination training. *Learning and Motivation, 23,* 343–367.

Bonardi, C. (1996). Transfer of occasion setting: The role of generalization decrement. *Animal Learning & Behavior, 24,* 277–289.

Bonardi, C. (1997). *Occasion setters are specific to the CS–US association.* Manuscript in preparation.

Bonardi, C., & Hall, G. (1994). Occasion-setting training renders stimuli more similar: Acquired equivalence between the targets of feature-positive discriminations. *Quarterly Journal of Experimental Psychology, 47B,* 63–81.

Bouton, M. E. (1990). Context and retrieval in extinction and in other examples of interference in simple associative learning. In L. W. Dachowski & C. F. Flaherty (Eds.), *Current topics in animal learning: Brain, emotion and cognition* (pp. 25–53). Hillsdale, NJ: Erlbaum.

Bouton, M. E. (1993). Context, time, and memory retrieval in the interference paradigm of Pavlovian learning. *Psychological Bulletin, 114,* 80–99.

Hall, G. (1996). Learning about associatively activated representations: Implications for acquired equivalence and perceptual learning. *Animal Learning & Behavior, 24,* 233–255.

Hall, G., & Honey, R. C. (1989). Contextual effects in conditioning, latent inhibition, and habituation: Associative and retrieval functions of contextual cues. *Journal of Experimental Psychology: Animal Behavior Processes, 15,* 232–241.

Hall, G., & Honey, R. C. (1990). Context-specific conditioning in the conditioned-emotional-response procedure. *Journal of Experimental Psychology: Animal Behavior Processes, 16,* 271–278.

Holland, P. C. (1983). Occasion-setting in Pavlovian feature positive discriminations. In M. L. Commons, R. J. Herrnstein, & A. R. Wagner (Eds.), *Quantitative analyses of behavior: Discrimination processes* (Vol. 4, pp. 183–206). New York: Ballinger.

Holland, P. C. (1989a). Transfer of negative occasion setting and conditioned inhibition across conditioned and unconditioned stimuli. *Journal of Experimental Psychology: Animal Behavior Processes, 15,* 311–328.

Holland, P. C. (1989b). Feature extinction enhances transfer of occasion setting. *Animal Learning & Behavior, 17,* 269–279.

Holland, P. C. (1989c). Acquisition and transfer of conditional discrimination performance. *Journal of Experimental Psychology: Animal Behavior Processes, 15,* 154–165.

Holland, P. C., & Gory, J. (1986). Extinction of inhibition after serial and simultaneous feature-negative discrimination training. *Quarterly Journal of Experimental Psychology, 38B,* 245–265.

Honey, R. C., & Hall, G. (1989). Acquired equivalence and distinctiveness of cues. *Journal of Experimental Psychology: Animal Behavior Processes, 15,* 338–346.

Jenkins, H. M. (1985). Conditioned inhibition of keypecking in the pigeon. In R. R. Miller & N. E. Spear (Eds.), *Information processing in animals: Conditioned inhibition* (pp. 327–353). Hillsdale, NJ: Erlbaum.

Kimmel, H. D., & Ray, R. L. (1978). Transswitching: Conditioning with tonic and phasic stimuli. *Journal of Experimental Psychology: General, 107,* 187–205.

Lamarre, J., & Holland, P. C. (1987). Transfer of inhibition after serial feature negative discrimination training. *Learning and Motivation, 18,* 319–342.

Mackintosh, N. J. (1983). *Conditioning and associative learning.* Oxford: Clarendon Press.

Mackintosh, N. J., & Dickinson, A. (1979). Instrumental (Type II) conditioning. In A. Dickinson & R. A. Boakes (Eds.), *Mechanisms of learning and motivation* (pp. 143–167). Hillsdale, NJ: Erlbaum.

Pearce, J. M., Montgomery, A., & Dickinson, A. (1981). Contralateral transfer of inhibitory and excitatory eyelid conditioning in the rabbit. *Quarterly Journal of Experimental Psychology, 33B,* 45–61.

Rescorla, R. A. (1985). Conditioned inhibition and facilitation. In R. R. Miller & N. E. Spear (Eds.), *Information processing in animals: Conditioned inhibition* (pp. 299–326). Hillsdale, NJ: Erlbaum.

Rescorla, R. A. (1986). Extinction of facilitation. *Journal of Experimental Psychology: Animal Behavior Processes, 12,* 16–24.

Rescorla, R. A. (1990a). Evidence for an association between the discriminative stimulus and the response-outcome association in instrumental learning. *Journal of Experimental Psychology: Animal Behavior Processes, 16,* 326–334.

Rescorla, R. A. (1990b). The role of information about the response-outcome relation in instrumental discrimination learning. *Journal of Experimental Psychology: Animal Behavior Processes, 16,* 262–270.

Rescorla, R. A. (1991a). Transfer of inhibition and facilitation mediated by the original target stimulus. *Animal Learning & Behavior, 19,* 65–70.

Rescorla, R. A. (1991b). Combinations of modulators trained with the same and different target stimuli. *Animal Learning & Behavior, 19,* 355–360.

Skinner, B. F. (1938). *The behavior of organisms.* New York: Appleton-Century-Crofts.

Swartzentruber, D. E. (1995). Modulatory mechanisms in Pavlovian conditioning. *Animal Learning and Behavior, 23,* 123–143.

Wilson, P. N., & Pearce, J. M. (1989). A role for stimulus generalisation in conditional discrimination learning. *Quarterly Journal of Experimental Psychology, 41B,* 243–273.

Wilson, P. N., & Pearce, J. M. (1990). Selective transfer of responding in conditional discriminations. *Quarterly Journal of Experimental Psychology, 42B,* 41–58.

Wilson, P. N., & Pearce, J. M. (1992). A configural analysis for feature-negative discrimination learning. *Journal of Experimental Psychology: Animal Behavior Processes, 18,* 265–277.

3

Mechanisms of Feature-Positive and Feature-Negative Discrimination Learning in an Appetitive Conditioning Paradigm

Mark E. Bouton and James B. Nelson

Most experiments on occasion setting involve some form of either a feature-positive (FP) or feature-negative (FN) discrimination. In such discriminations, the presence of one stimulus (the *feature* stimulus) marks trials on which another stimulus (the *target* stimulus) is either paired with an unconditioned stimulus (US) or not. Not surprisingly, the feature comes to influence performance to the target. Although these discriminations seem straightforward, the psychological mechanisms that control them can be multiple and complex. This chapter describes some recent research that explored the mechanisms behind the two discriminations as they are represented in a commonly used conditioning paradigm in which food is the US and the rat's investigation of the food cup provides the measure of conditioned responding (e.g., Brooks & Bouton, 1993, 1994; Bouton & Ricker, 1994; Delamater, 1995; Farwell & Ayres, 1979; Hall & Channell, 1985; Kaye & Mackintosh, 1990; Pearce & Wilson, 1991).

The FP and FN procedures are operationally symmetrical, and it is

This research was supported by Grant IBN 92-09454 from the National Science Foundation. We thank Russ Frohardt and Fay Guarraci for their comments on the manuscript.

natural to think of them as opposites (e.g., Rescorla, 1985). In both cases, the target conditioned stimulus (CS) is presented with the US on some trials and without it on others. In the FP procedure, the feature CS accompanies the target on the positive trials—that is, trials with the US. The feature therefore excites or enables performance in the presence of the target. It may do so by becoming a conditioned excitor, acquiring a direct association with the US (e.g., Rescorla & Wagner, 1972; see also Wagner & Brandon, 1989); it may enter into a unique configuration with the target that becomes associated with the US (e.g., Pearce, 1987, 1994); or it may become a positive occasion setter (e.g., Holland, 1983) or facilitator (e.g., Rescorla, 1985). In the FN procedure, the feature CS marks the negative trials—that is, the trials on which there is no US. Here the feature comes to suppress performance in the presence of the target. It may do so by becoming a conditioned inhibitor (e.g., Rescorla & Wagner, 1972), by entering into a configuration with the target that acquires an inhibitory association with the US, or by becoming a negative occasion setter (e.g., Holland, 1985). There are many paths to any behavioral outcome. The goal of much occasion-setting research is to distinguish among the various mechanisms that can account for a given example of an FP or FN discrimination.

The starting point for the research presented here was the possible connection between FP and FN learning and extinction. In extinction, a CS is presented alone repeatedly after it has been paired with a US. Although the extinction procedure decreases the responding acquired during conditioning, we know that it does not destroy what was originally learned. Instead, the CS takes on a second meaning, becomes "ambiguous," and the performance it evokes becomes determined by the current *context* (e.g., Bouton, 1991, 1993, 1994). The possible relevance of extinction to FP and FN learning is straightforward. Like an extinguished CS, the target CS in both procedures has a mixed history of reinforcement and nonreinforcement. Perhaps our knowledge of what is learned in extinction can illuminate the mechanisms of FP and FN learning.

We have explored this possibility in both *simultaneous* and *serial* versions of the FP and FN discriminations. In the simultaneous version, the feature and target are presented at the same time when they occur, and in the serial version the feature is presented before the target when compound trials occur. Simultaneous procedures tend to give the feature inhibition or excitation, whereas serial procedures tend to generate occasion setting (e.g., see Holland, 1992; Swartzentruber, 1995). Our overarching goal was to characterize what is learned in these two versions of the FP and FN procedures. In the first section of the chapter, we summarize our published work on FN learning. The results suggest an insight into the content of inhibition and negative occasion setting, and they confirm the connection with extinction. In the second part of the chapter, we present some new experiments that were designed to extend the analysis to the FP paradigm. These experiments begin to establish a connection between FP learning and extinction, but, somewhat unexpectedly, they also raise questions about the generality of positive occasion setting and the conditions that are thought to produce it.

FEATURE-NEGATIVE LEARNING

A Model of Extinction

Our research on FN and FP discriminations followed directly from previous work in our laboratory on the role of context in extinction and other "interference paradigms" in associative learning (e.g., Bouton, 1991, 1993). The results of that research strongly suggest that extinction performance is often specific to the context in which it is learned—typically the apparatus or chamber in which conditioning events are presented. For example, if we move the rat to a different context after extinction, extinction performance is lost, and conditioned responding is *renewed* when the CS is tested again (e.g., Bouton & King, 1983; Bouton & Peck, 1989; Bouton & Ricker, 1994; Brooks & Bouton, 1994; Rosas & Bouton, 1997). The experiments on the "renewal effect" also uncovered a second important finding: Although extinction performance is highly specific to its context, conditioned performance seems much less so—that is, when we switch the context after simple CS–US pairings, we observe *no corresponding loss* of conditioned

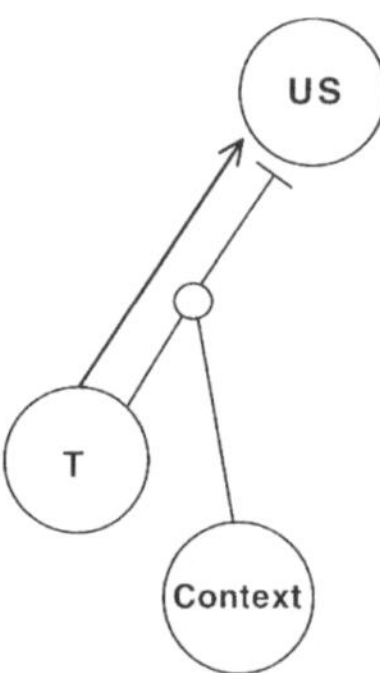

Figure 1

The extinction model. T = tone CS; US = unconditioned stimulus. Arrow indicates excitatory association; blocked line indicates inhibitory association.

performance. This conclusion is consistent with a number of experiments in other laboratories (e.g., Grahame, Hallam, Geier, & Miller, 1990; Hall & Honey, 1989; Kaye & Mackintosh, 1990; Kaye, Preston, Szabo, Druiff, & Mackintosh, 1987). Although a drop in responding has been observed under some conditions (e.g., Good & Honey, 1991; Hall & Honey, 1989; Honey, Willis, & Hall, 1990), conditioning performance is more difficult to disrupt with a change of context than is extinction.

The results of a number of experiments on the effects of context in extinction are consistent with the memory structure depicted in Figure 1, which we view as the content of what is learned in extinction (Bouton, 1994; Bouton & Nelson, 1994). During simple conditioning, the animal associates the CS and US; if a tone and food pellet are paired, an association is learned. If the tone is now presented on its own, its activation excites the representation of food and thereby generates behavior (e.g., Rescorla, 1974). During extinction, that association is spared and a new inhibitory association is learned. When the CS is now presented, both the excitatory and inhibitory links are activated, and the inhibitory association cancels the effect of the excitatory association by resuppressing the US representation. The CS thus has two associations available after extinction; its meaning is ambiguous (Bouton, 1984; Bouton & Bolles, 1985).

The context hypothetically works to disambiguate the meaning of the

CS through the mechanism shown in Figure 1. It does not work through a direct association with the US (e.g., Bouton & King, 1983; Bouton & Swartzentruber, 1986); instead, it provides an input (along with the CS) to an intermediate memory node or element that functions as an AND gate. Because of the AND gate, the crucial associative link that inhibits the US representation is only activated when the CS *and* the appropriate context are present. One can think of the AND gate as a hidden unit with a threshold like the one created by nonlinear activation functions used in connectionist backpropagation models (Rumelhart, Hinton, & Williams, 1986; see also Lamoureux, Buhusi, & Schmajuk, chapter 13, this volume; Zackheim, Myers, & Gluck, chapter 11, this volume). The main point, however, is that input from both the CS and the extinction context is necessary to activate the inhibitory link that produces extinction performance. When the CS is tested outside the extinction context, the inhibitory link is not activated, and renewed responding occurs. Similarly, if time provides part of the context, the passage of time following extinction will produce spontaneous recovery of responding (e.g., Bouton, 1988; Brooks & Bouton, 1993, 1994). Spontaneous recovery is the renewal effect that occurs when the CS is tested outside the temporal context of extinction.

The context's influence is on the CS's second, inhibitory association with the US. Not all types of knowledge are context-dependent; recall that conditioning is not as disrupted as extinction by a context switch. The model accepts this state of affairs and stipulates that the context modulates the CS's second association (e.g., Nelson, 1997; Swartzentruber & Bouton, 1992). In extinction, that is the target's inhibitory link.

This simple approach to extinction can account for a range of extinction results (e.g., Bouton, 1994). As we noted earlier, however, it may also be a part of the classic FN and FP discriminations. In those discriminations, the target CS is like an extinguished CS in that it is both reinforced and nonreinforced. The importance of the target's training history is now widely recognized in the occasion-setting literature (e.g., Holland, 1986; Lamarre & Holland, 1987; Rescorla, 1985; Swartzentruber & Rescorla, 1994). Therefore, it is worth considering the possibility that the target enters into an associative structure like the one presented in Figure 1.

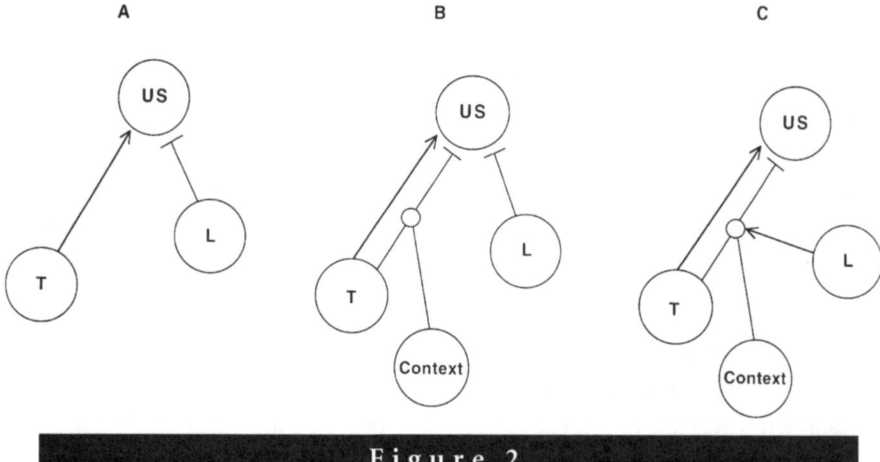

Figure 2

Three models of the content of feature-negative (FN) learning. T = tone target CS; L = light feature CS; US = unconditioned stimulus; arrow indicates excitatory association; blocked line indicates inhibitory association. (A) FN discrimination as a standard elemental model views it. (B) FN discrimination in which target enters the extinction structure (Figure 1) and the feature has a direct inhibitory association with the US. (C) FN discrimination in which target enters the extinction structure and the feature activates the target's gated inhibitory association. (C) is a model of negative occasion setting.

Among other things, this view suggests some novel effects of context on discriminative performance and occasion setting.

Three Models of the Content of FN Learning

Figure 2 illustrates three models describing how a light feature (L) might suppress responding to a tone target (T) after FN training in which the tone was reinforced when it occurred alone (T+) but not when it was combined with the light (LT–). Model A represents the content of the discrimination as a standard elemental model of conditioning (e.g., Rescorla & Wagner, 1972) might view it. Very simply, the tone acquires an excitatory association with the US, while the light acquires an inhibitory one. When the tone is presented alone, the US representation is activated, and responding occurs. When the light accompanies the tone, however, the light's inhibitory link cancels activation of the US representation.

The other models in Figure 2 accept the idea that the target might enter into the Figure 1 extinction structure. The first of these (Model B) accepts the extinction model along with the idea that the feature might suppress the US representation directly (e.g., Rescorla & Holland, 1977). Like the inhibitory association in Model A, the direct inhibitory association between the feature and the US makes it difficult to convert the feature into an excitor when it is subsequently paired with a US (the retardation test). It also allows the inhibitor to suppress responding to other excitors (besides the tone) that have been associated with the same US. The research presented next suggests that this model, rather than Model A, may be the more accurate model of what is learned in a simultaneous FN discrimination.

The third model (Model C) describes a mechanism by which negative occasion setters might operate. According to our results, this sort of learning dominates the serial FN procedure, and it plays a minor role in simultaneous FN procedures as well. In this case, the feature does not inhibit performance by directly inhibiting the US representation but, instead, activates the target's own inhibitory association. In our scheme, it provides a third input to the AND gate of the extinction model. Thus, to observe suppressed responding to the tone, this model requires input from the target, the feature, and also the context. Both the feature and the context function to activate the target's inhibitory association with the US.

Because the Model C mechanism operates on an association between the target and the US nodes, rather than on the US node directly, it is consistent with three hallmarks of negative occasion setting. First, as we just noted, a simple inhibitor (Model A or B) is slow to convert into an excitor when it is paired with a US in a retardation test. In contrast, negative occasion setters produce less retardation (e.g., Holland, 1984; Nelson & Bouton, 1997). This occurs because the feature has no direct inhibitory association with the US; its inhibition is not manifest unless the target is also present. Second, after a negative occasion setter is converted into an excitor, it can still inhibit responding to the target, while the same conversion of a simple inhibitor abolishes its ability to inhibit (Holland, 1984; Nelson & Bouton, 1997; see also Holland, 1991). For the simple inhibitor, even if the original inhibitory association remained intact after excitatory conditioning (e.g., Bouton, 1993; Nelson, 1997), converting the stimulus to a net excitor would cause net excitation, and thus excitatory summation, in the compound. In contrast, excitatory conditioning of a negative occasion setter would add an excitatory link between the feature and the US in Model C, but it would not necessarily change the links already shown. Therefore, although the new excitatory link might attenuate the feature's ability to suppress responding to the target, the feature would still activate the target's inhibitory association and thus produce some inhibition. This pattern was observed in one of our recent experiments (Nelson & Bouton, 1997, Experiment 2; see also Pearce & Wilson, 1991).

The model also begins to address a third hallmark of negative occasion setting: the peculiarities of a negative occasion setter's ability to "transfer" and suppress performance to a separately trained CS. Although a traditional inhibitor's ability to suppress responding to its target should transfer and suppress responding to a second target, an occasion setter's does not (e.g., Holland & Lamarre, 1984). Because the inhibitor has a direct inhibitory association with the US, it should suppress responding to any excitor that activates it. Because the negative occasion setter has no direct link to the US representation, however, it should not suppress responding to a separate CS unless that CS has an inhibitory association of its own. In fact, a negative occasion setter does transfer and suppress responding to targets that have been in occasion-setting relationships themselves (e.g., Holland, 1989c; Lamarre & Holland, 1987; Rescorla, 1985) or that are under the influence of extinction (e.g., Swartzentruber & Rescorla, 1994). In either case, the transfer target's training history might give it an inhibitory association that the occasion setter can modulate. Although the model is not specific about how transfer would occur (but see Bouton & Nelson, 1994), it nonetheless suggests why the transfer target's conditioning history may be important.

Effects of Context Switches on FN Performance

Model C also makes a unique prediction that we have tested in several experiments (Bouton & Nelson, 1994; Nelson & Bouton, 1997). If the

Exhibit 1

Designs of Experiments on the Effects of Context Switches on FN Performance

(from Bouton & Nelson, 1994, and Nelson & Bouton, 1997)

	Training		Testing
Context specificity of target			
	A: T+, LT−		A: T, LT
	B: N+, LN−	and/or	B: T, LT
Context specificity of feature			
	A: T+, LT−		A; T, LT
	B: T+, KT−	and/or	B: T, LT

NOTE: A and B are contexts; T, L, N, and K are tone, light-off, intermittent noise, and keylight CSs, respectively. + = reinforced, − = nonreinforced. During training, the rats received intermixed training with both session types shown. The first design tests the context specificity of inhibition of the target; the second tests context specificity of inhibition to the feature.

negative occasion setter works by activating the target's context-specific inhibitory association with the US, it should be harder to suppress responding elicited by the target when the target is tested outside the context in which it was trained. This is because activation of the crucial inhibitory link depends on input from the target, the feature, and the right context. The upper part of Exhibit 1 presents an experimental design that examines this prediction (Nelson & Bouton, 1997, Experiment 1). In the training phase, rats received two conditioning sessions a day, one in Context A and the other in Context B; the contexts were counterbalanced. (These contexts differed in many ways, including the rooms in which they were housed and in their visual, olfactory, and tactile characteristics.) In Context A, a 30-sec tone was paired with food when it occurred alone, but there was no food when the tone was combined with a 30-sec termination of the houselight (light)—that is, the animals learned a T+, LT− FN discrimination. A similar discrimination was trained in Context B, except that the light inhibited an intermittent white noise (i.e., N+, LN−). In a final test, we tested the tone and the light-tone compound in both Contexts A and B. The light had been an inhibitory feature in both contexts, but the test included the first presentation of the tone target in Context B. The experiment thus tested the effects of a context switch on responding to the *target* CS.

Rats were trained on these discriminations with either simultaneous or serial procedures. In the simultaneous discriminations, the onsets and offsets of the feature and target were simultaneous when the compound was presented, whereas in serial discriminations the target came on at the instant the feature went off. Our research has established that the serial procedure produces a feature having the three hallmarks of negative occasion setters described earlier (Nelson & Bouton, 1996, 1997). Therefore, if Model C in Figure 2 is correct, we expected an especially complete loss of inhibition in Context B for the serial group given the negative occasion-setting procedure.

The results of the test are presented in Figure 3, which shows the number of food cup entries to T (the excitor) and LT (the compound) in both contexts for both groups. The results with the simultaneous group (at left) replicated those of a previous experiment (Bouton & Nelson, 1994, Experiment 3, in which the roles of the tone and light stimuli were reversed). While the light inhibited responding to the tone in Context A, where the discrimination had been trained, it was significantly less effective at doing so in Context B. The tone's excitation transferred to the new context completely, but the context switch made responding to the tone more difficult to inhibit. The serial group (at right) demonstrated the same pattern, although here the loss of the tone's ability to be inhibited was more complete. The light inhibited responding to the tone in Context A (there was no statistical difference in responding to the serial and simultaneous compounds), but there was no evidence that responding was inhibited at all in Context B. Remember that the tone target, not the light feature, received the context switch. The results are consistent with the idea that the occasion setter established in the serial procedure worked exclusively by activating the tone target's context-specific inhibitory link.

These results are all the more interesting when one considers the results of the companion experiment described in the lower part of Exhibit 1 (Nelson & Bouton, 1997, Experiment 2; see also Bouton & Nelson, 1984, Experiment 2). This experiment tested the effect of switching the feature,

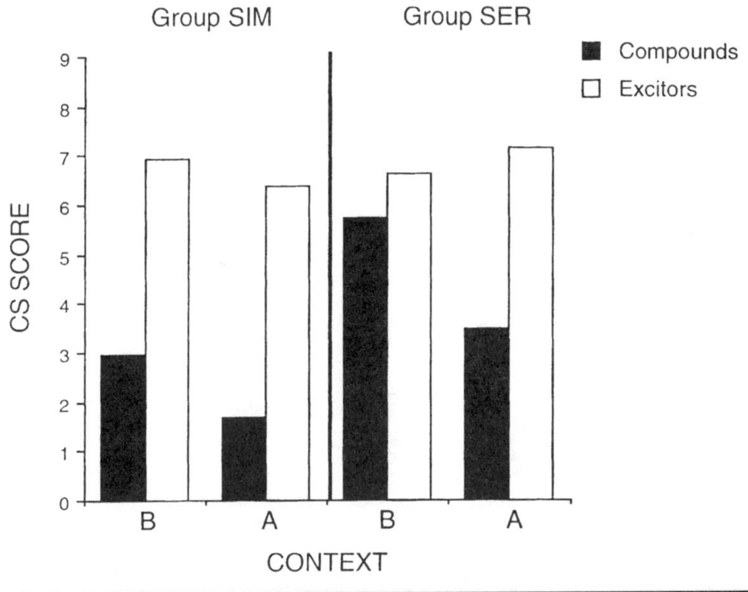

Figure 3

Effects of a context switch on inhibition conditioned to the *target* after feature-negative (FN) training. Group SIM received a simultaneous FN discrimination; Group SER received a serial one. Context A was the context in which the discrimination was trained; the target had never been presented before in Context B. From "The Effects of a Context Switch Following Serial and Simultaneous Feature Negative Discriminations," by J. B. Nelson and M. E. Bouton, 1997, *Learning and Motivation, 28,* p. 67. Copyright 1997 by Academic Press, Inc. Adapted with permission.

rather than the target, to the different context. Once again, there were intermixed sessions in Contexts A and B during training. In Context A, the animals learned the T+, LT– discrimination, and in Context B they learned T+, KT– (K was a keylight, a 2.5-cm-diameter light mounted on a side wall of the chamber). The test focused on the light feature. Each rat was tested with the tone and the light-tone compound in both contexts. This time, the tone target had been trained in both contexts before but the test contained the first test of the *feature* in Context B. If inhibition to the feature were context-specific, then we would observe more responding to the LT compound in Context B than in Context A.

The test results are presented in Figure 4. As before, the experiment

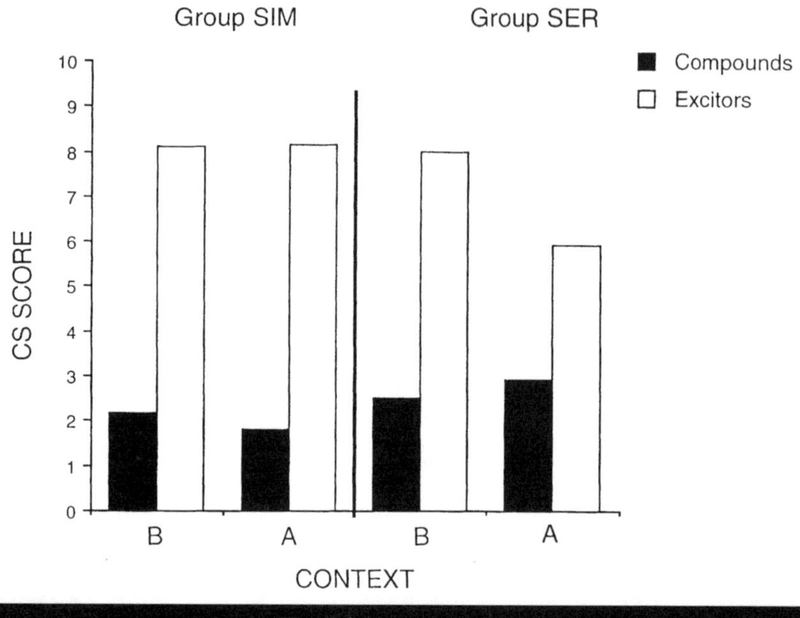

Figure 4

Effects of a context switch on inhibition conditioned to the *feature* after feature-negative (FN) training. Group SIM received a simultaneous FN discrimination; Group SER received a serial one. Context A was the context in which the discrimination was trained; the feature had never been presented before in Context B. From "The Effects of a Context Switch Following Serial and Simultaneous Feature Negative Discriminations," by J. B. Nelson and M. E. Bouton, 1997, *Learning and Motivation, 28,* p. 75. Copyright 1997 by Academic Press, Inc. Adapted with permission.

arranged a comparison between groups that received simultaneous and serial versions of the FN procedure. Not surprisingly, in the context in which the T+, LT– discrimination had been trained (Context A), there was responding to the tone alone and little responding to the compound. In both groups, however, exactly the same pattern was observed in Context B, where the feature had never been presented before. Whether we are concerned with simple inhibition or negative occasion setting, the inhibitory control exerted by the feature transfers well to a new context.

We have performed another experiment that further confirms that the context switch has a bigger impact on the target than the feature (Bouton & Nelson, 1994, Experiment 4). In that experiment, rats received

T+, N+, and LT– training in Context A intermixed with T+, N+, and KN– training in Context B. This procedure arranged matters so that one feature provided inhibition and one target was inhibited in each of the two contexts. During testing, each rat was tested with T, N, LN, and KT in both contexts. To understand the logic of the design, consider the elements of the LN compound during the tests in Contexts A and B. In Context A, the feature (L) was in the context where it had inhibited before, and the target (N) was in the context where it had never been inhibited. In Context B, the reverse was true: The feature (L) was in a new context, and the target (N) was in a context where it had been inhibited before. The elements of the KT compound had a complementary arrangement. Thus, the compounds were constructed so that they set possible context-specificity of feature and target inhibition against one another. The results were clear: there was significantly more responding to the compounds when the *target* was in the context where it had not been inhibited before, even though that was the place where the feature had inhibited. When the feature was in a new context (and the target was in the one where it had been inhibited), inhibition was more evident. The results indicate that inhibition to the target is more disrupted by context change than inhibition to the feature—in other words, a context switch has a bigger impact on the target than the feature after FN training.

The results fit Models B and C in Figure 2. Occasion setters established in our serial FN procedure appear to work—perhaps exclusively—by activating the target's own context-specific inhibitory association with the US; in our method, the simultaneous procedure appears to produce a mixture of both Models B and C. Thus, the target is modestly more difficult to inhibit after a context switch. Other experiments showed that the simultaneous feature was able to inhibit performance to a separately trained CS for which we had no grounds to expect an inhibitory link (Bouton & Nelson, 1994, Experiment 1); it was also slower than the serial feature to be converted into an excitor in a retardation test (Nelson & Bouton, 1997). Thus, a direct inhibitory link between the feature and the US is implicated. In our simultaneous procedure, both direct feature-US inhibition and the gated mechanism seem to be learned.

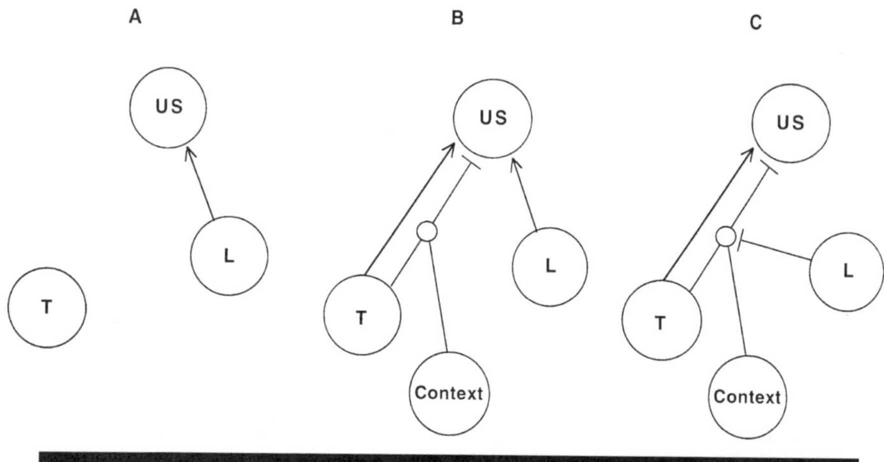

Figure 5

Three models of the content of feature-positive (FP) learning. T = tone target CS; L = light feature CS; US = unconditioned stimulus; arrow indicates excitatory association; blocked line indicates inhibitory association. (A) FP discrimination as a standard elemental model views it. (B) FP discrimination in which target enters the extinction structure (Figure 1) and the feature has a direct excitatory association with the US. C. FP discrimination in which target enters the extinction structure and the feature inhibits the target's gated inhibitory association. (C) is a model of positive occasion setting.

In summary, the extinction model applies to FN learning. In both extinction and FN learning, the target CS enters into an inhibitory association with the US that is encoded with, and influenced by, the context. In extinction, this makes extinction performance relatively specific to its context; in FN learning, it makes responding to the target more difficult to inhibit in a new context. The content of extinction, inhibition, and negative occasion setting fit together rather well (see also Bouton, 1997).

FEATURE-POSITIVE LEARNING

Three Models of the Content of FP Learning

Our understanding of FN learning can readily be extended to the FP discrimination. This idea is summarized in the models shown in Figure

5, which depict three versions of what might be learned after a tone target has been reinforced in combination with a light (LT+) but nonreinforced alone (T–). In the simplest model (Model A), we again present the discrimination as a standard elemental model of conditioning might view it (Rescorla & Wagner, 1972). According to such a model, the feature (L) can acquire so much direct excitatory conditioning that it will block (Kamin, 1969; Wagner, 1969) learning to the target . Thus, there is no association between the tone and the US representation after FP learning. The feature controls FP performance because it is the only thing associated with the US.

As before, Models B and C recognize that the target might enter into our extinction model. The target thus has both an excitatory association and a contextually gated inhibitory association with the US. In the FP paradigm, the feature accompanies the trials in which the target is paired with the US, and it might be directly associated with the US (Model B). To complete the parallel with the FN models, however, we might also expect circumstances in which the feature might work via the mechanism in Model C, a model of positive occasion setting. Instead of the feature activating the target's inhibitory association (as the negative occasion setter did), a positive occasion setter might *inhibit* it. On this view, responding to the target is ordinarily inhibited by its own inhibitory association; the effect of the feature is to cancel that inhibition.

The inhibition-of-inhibition concept is related to Rescorla's idea (e.g., 1985) that facilitators lower a raised threshold for activation of the US representation. (Our negative occasion-setting formulation is likewise related to his idea that inhibitors may raise the threshold.) The threshold-lowering idea is consistent with the results of several experiments. Swartzentruber and Rescorla (1994) found that features from both FN and FP discriminations are most effective at modulating targets that are under the influence of extinction—that is, they both may operate on the target's inhibitory link (see also Rescorla, 1985, 1987). Our models of positive and negative occasion setting are also consistent with those recently proposed by Schmajuk, Lamoureux, and Holland (1998; see also Schmajuk &

Buhusi, 1997; Lamoureux, Buhusi, & Schmajuk, chapter 13, this volume). In their scheme, occasion setters work by exciting or inhibiting a hidden unit that has an inhibitory association with the US.

In principle, a simple FP discrimination (e.g., T–, LT+) can be "solved" by any of several mechanisms. Another possibility (not represented in Figure 5 or our discussion until now) is *configural conditioning:* The animal might associate a configural cue arising from the LT compound directly with the US. In one version of this idea, a "unique cue" (X) might arise from the compound, and X would be associated with the US (e.g., Rescorla, 1973; see also Brandon & Wagner, chapter 12, this volume). In another, the aggregate of stimulation from LT might become associated with the US, with performance on positive and negative trials depending on generalization between them (Pearce, 1987, 1994). Any or all of these possibilities might contribute to a given example of FP learning. We must therefore be ready to distinguish among them.

General Method

To discover the potential role of the various mechanisms in our instance of FP discrimination learning, we used the following general procedure in a number of new experiments. The rats first received training with an FP procedure, typically one in which the tone target was nonreinforced on its own and reinforced when it was combined with the houselight-off feature (T–, LT+). Because the experiments were an extension of our FN experiments, we used the same apparatus and rats from the same population (Wistar females). We also used the same stimuli and response measure, as well as comparable session lengths and intertrial intervals. The results were also analyzed with similar analyses of variance (ANOVAs) with a rejection criterion set at $p < .05$.

After the FP discrimination was learned, we ran two kinds of tests to evaluate the mechanism(s) that might control it. First, in a *feature extinction test,* we removed the feature (L) from the compound and extinguished responding to it—that is, the feature was presented by itself repeatedly before the compound was tested again. This type of test is often used to test occasion setting (e.g., Holland, 1989a, 1989b; Rescorla, 1986; but see

Ross, 1983). If the feature controls discriminative performance through its direct association with food (e.g., Model A or B in Figure 5), feature extinction should reduce its ability to augment performance to the target. If it controls through occasion setting (e.g., Model C), however, feature extinction should have relatively little effect on responding to the compound (e.g., Holland, 1989a, 1989b; Rescorla, 1986).

A configural learning mechanism predicts the same effect of feature extinction as an occasion-setting mechanism; extinction of an element should not affect the associative strength of a configural cue emerging from the compound. To separate these possibilities, we next performed a *transfer test.* At this point, a new CS (e.g., N) was reinforced (N+) and occasionally tested in compound with the feature (e.g., LN). If the feature were a simple excitor, it would increase responding to N; but if the feature controlled performance through configural conditioning, it would not. The same would be true if the feature were an occasion setter, except in special circumstances. To investigate these, in some experiments we further examined the feature's ability to augment responding to N while N was being extinguished. If occasion setters modulated the target's inhibitory association (e.g., Model C in Figure 5), the feature would augment responding to N only during the extinction phase, when N might be acquiring an inhibitory association (e.g., Rescorla, 1985, 1987; Swartzentruber & Rescorla, 1994). Note that if the feature were a simple excitor (with a direct association with the US), it would instead augment responding to N during both conditioning and extinction.

Serial Versus Simultaneous FP Learning

Our earliest experiments compared simultaneous and serial FP discriminations. Previous research on FP learning, like that on FN learning, suggests that occasion setting is most likely to develop when there is a serial relationship between the feature and target (e.g., Holland, 1986; Ross & Holland, 1981). In one experiment, different groups ($n = 8$) received one of three serial feature–target arrangements: one in which the target came on at the instant the feature went off, one in which there was a 15-sec gap between feature offset and target onset, and one in which there was a 30-sec gap.

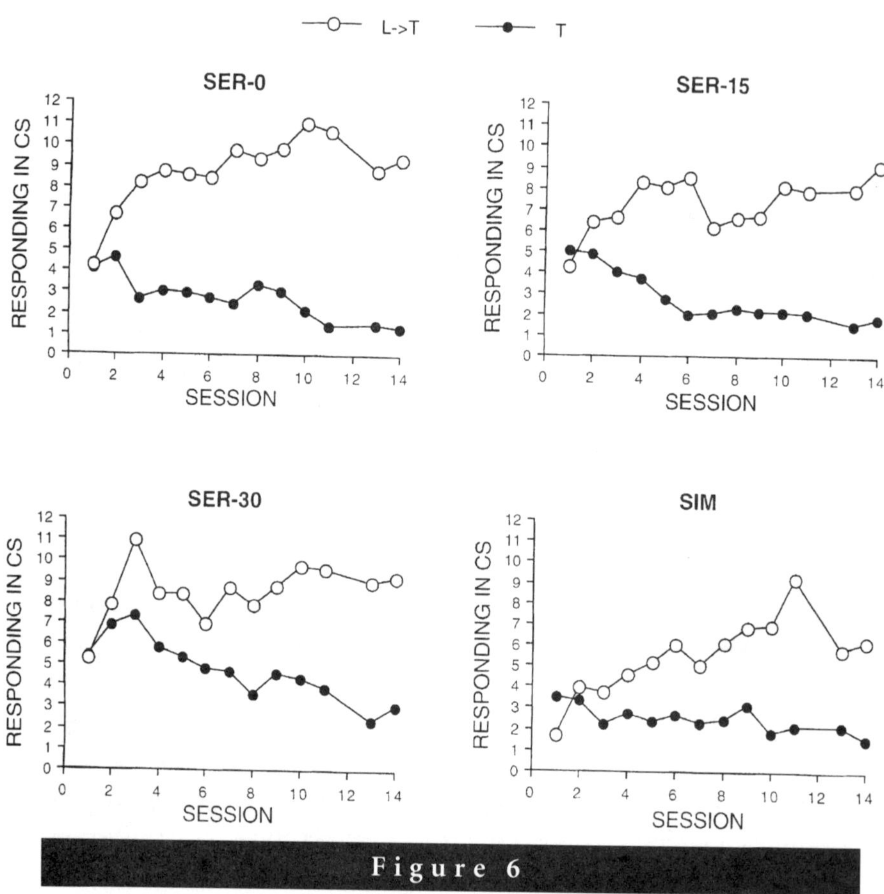

Figure 6

Results of feature-positive discrimination training in different groups. Three groups (SER-0, SER-15, and SER-30) received serial training with 0-, 15-, and 30-sec gaps between feature (L) and target (T); a fourth group (SIM) received simultaneous presentation of feature and target.

These groups were labeled SER-0, SER-15, and SER-30, respectively. A fourth group (SIM) received an FP discrimination in which the feature and target (L and T) were always simultaneous. For all groups, each session contained 4 LT+ trials and 12 T– trials, with the intertrial interval (ITI, defined as offset of trial n to onset of trial $n + 1$) varying around a mean of 3.25 min.

The results of FP discrimination training are shown in Figure 6. There

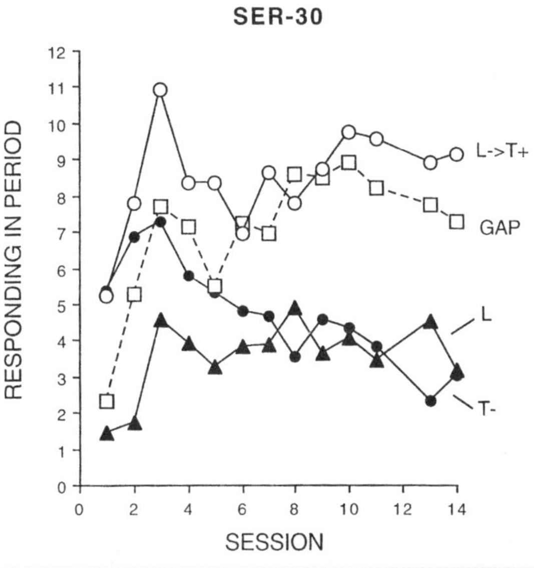

Figure 7

Responding in group SER-30 during the 30-sec feature (L), gap, and target (L→T+) periods during the sessions of feature-positive training. Responding during target during the nonreinforced trials (T–) is also shown.

were five initial sessions of T+ alone training, and then two sessions of T– training (each with 12 trials), which are not shown. (These sessions were included to give the rats a "head start" in learning the extinction structure shown in Figure 1.) As the figure indicates, the FP discrimination was readily learned in all groups, regardless of the temporal arrangement. An ANOVA incorporating group, trial type, and session confirmed that impression; most important, the group effect and the three-way interaction were not significant, *p*s > .05.

A clear pattern of behavior also developed during the compound trials. Figure 7 shows Group SER-30's performance on each session during the feature, gap, and target periods (Group SER-30 was isolated because each of these periods was an equal 30 sec in duration). Over sessions, although little responding occurred during the feature on its own (L), responding during the gap increased. Thus, by late in training, the rats waited until the feature went off and then began responding. There was a small further increase in responding once the target CS was presented after the gap, $p < .02$. Although the target contributed to responding, the rats appeared to treat the offset of the feature as a signal for the US.

This impression was further confirmed by the results of the feature extinction test, which are summarized in Figure 8. Each panel in the figure depicts performance of one group. In every panel, responding to the target during the last two compound trials of FP training is shown by the open circles at left; all rats responded to the target quite strongly on those trials. The first and last four extinction trials with L (out of a total of 34) are then shown (Xs). Extinction eliminated responding elicited by the feature in all groups. (Responding is shown at the point in time when the target would have otherwise been presented.) Finally, on the right, each panel shows all the trials on which the tone target was tested after extinction—those when it was presented alone (filled circles) and those when it was reinforced again in its usual temporal arrangement with the light (open circles). Responding during the first compound trial clearly indicates that feature extinction abolished the discrimination in every group. Discriminative performance recovered quickly after that (this was a savings test). But the feature extinction treatment had a devastating effect at first on all of the discriminations.

These observations were confirmed by an ANOVA comparing responding on the compound trials immediately before and immediately after feature extinction. There was an effect of extinction, $F(1, 27) = 19.22$, but no group effect or interaction, $Fs \leq 1.55$. Moreover, a group × trial-type ANOVA that compared the target-alone and compound trials after extinction confirmed that feature extinction abolished the discrimination, $F < 1$, with no group effects or interaction, $Fs \leq 1.22$. There was no evidence of positive occasion setting or configural conditioning here. FP performance was controlled by the rats associating the feature with food.

This conclusion was also consistent with the results of the transfer test, which followed an additional session of light extinction. At this time the light was presented in its usual temporal arrangement with a new noise that was being reinforced. In all groups, the light increased responding to

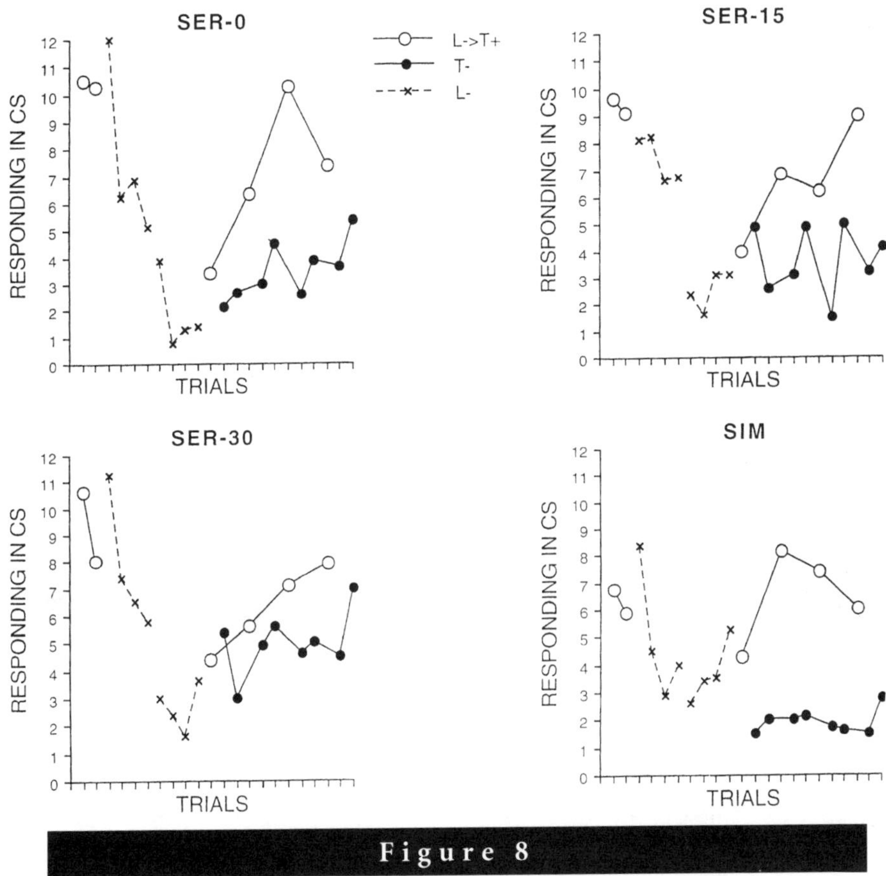

Figure 8

Responding of Groups SER-0, SER-15, SER-30, and SIM during trials connected with the feature test. In each panel, responding to the tone target on compound trials just before feature extinction is shown at left; the first and last four extinction trials with the feature (L–) are shown in the middle; responding to the tone target on the compound trials (open circles) and target alone trials (closed circles) that followed feature extinction are shown at right. Feature extinction reduced responding to the tone on the compound trials.

the noise: mean responding to the compound was 9.23, whereas to the noise alone it was 7.48. This difference was reliable, $F(1, 28) = 19.47$, and did not interact with group or any other factor, *F*s < 1.17. The fact that the light still augmented performance despite its previous extinction is consistent with the known effects of compounding an extinguished CS with an established excitor (e.g., Reberg, 1972). The main point, however,

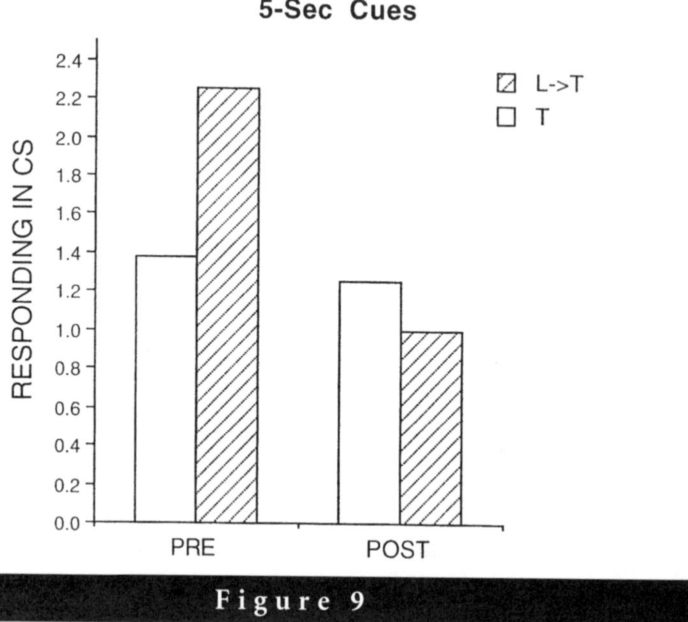

Figure 9

Responding to the tone target during the feature extinction test at the end of an experiment using short (5-sec) feature and target cues separated by a 30-sec gap. PRE = before feature extinction; POST = after feature extinction; L→T = compound trial; T = target alone trial.

is that, regardless of the temporal arrangement of feature and target during conditioning, FP performance was controlled by direct conditioning of the feature.

We have observed the same results with a number of variations in method. We obtained identical results when we extended the feature–target gap to 60 sec. We also obtained compatible results when our keylight served as the feature and our intermittent noise served as the target (with a 30-sec gap) in N–, KN+ training. Furthermore, we have seen the same pattern when we have shortened the light-off and tone stimuli to 5 sec (with a 30-sec gap), in an effort to use parameters more consistent with those of Holland's laboratory. The results from the feature extinction test phase of that experiment are presented in Figure 9. There we show responding on the first T and LT trials before (PRE) and after (POST) the light was extinguished. (The stimuli were tested in the order T, LT.) Before feature extinction, L augmented responding to T; after feature extinction, however, the augmentation was no longer evident. Responding to the compounds decreased between the tests, $F(1, 7) = 9.46$; the difference between T and LT before extinction was significant, $F(1, 13) = 4.70$, whereas after extinction it was not, $F(1, 13) < 1$. Thus, over a range of conditions, the serial FP discrimination is controlled by a simple feature–US association. These results surprised us, and we therefore set out to create conditions that might produce better positive occasion setting.

Effects of Feature–Target Overlap and Previous Inhibitory Conditioning of the Target

Experiments on positive occasion setting have often employed two types of serial arrangements between feature and target: the *gap* procedure used earlier, and an *overlap* procedure in which the feature precedes the target but remains on and terminates when the target terminates. The gap procedure is typical of Holland's laboratory, whereas the overlap procedure is more typical of Rescorla's (e.g., Davidson & Rescorla, 1986; Rescorla, 1985). In a separate experiment we compared the two procedures using the 30-sec time base established in our FN research—that is, the gap procedure involved 30-sec feature, gap, and target events, and the overlap procedure involved a 90-sec feature that terminated at the same time as an embedded 30-sec target. These 30-30-30 and 90-30 sequences contrast with the 5-5-5 and 15-5 procedures used, respectively, in Holland's and Rescorla's laboratories.

To improve the odds of generating occasion setting, we also examined the effect of another variable suggested by previous research and theory. There is evidence that positive occasion setting involves the learning of inhibition to the target and that procedures that facilitate that inhibition can also facilitate acquisition of occasion setting. Rescorla (1988) found that training the target as an inhibitor before beginning FP training increased the subsequent development of occasion setting (i.e., facilitation). Other variables that appear to promote occasion setting (e.g., temporal and salience factors) might also work because they promote target inhibi-

Exhibit 2

Treatment of Groups Before Testing in an Experiment on the Effect of Inhibitory Preconditioning of the Target Before FP training

Group	FN Training	FP Training
Inhibitor	K+, XK–	X–, L→X+
Control	K+, YK–	X–, L→X+

NOTE: K, L, X, and Y are different conditioned stimuli. K = keylight, L = houselight off, X and Y were tone and intermittent noise stimuli and were counterbalanced, + = reinforced trials, – = nonreinforced trials. → = serial presentation.

tion (see Holland, 1992, for a review). Thus, inhibitory preconditioning of the target might help generate positive occasion setting in our conditioning paradigm.

Two groups each received the gap and overlap procedures described earlier. One group from each condition ($n = 8$) also received initial inhibitory conditioning with the target, and the other group did not. The procedure for manipulating inhibitory conditioning is summarized in Exhibit 2. All rats received 14 initial sessions of FN training. At this time, a keylight (K) was reinforced on its own and nonreinforced when it was combined in simultaneous compound with either X (group Inhibitor) or Y (group Control). X and Y were counterbalanced between our tone and intermittent noise stimuli. There were 4 reinforced trials and 12 nonreinforced trials in each session. The next phase constituted FP training; our usual light-off feature marked trials on which X was now reinforced. For Group Inhibitor, the target (X) during this phase was the CS that had been the inhibitory feature from the preceding phase, and for Group Control, it was a novel stimulus. There were 16 sessions, each containing five positive and five negative trials separated by an average intertrial interval of 4.5 min. Following the conclusion of FP training, all groups underwent the usual feature extinction and transfer tests (not shown in the table). In this experiment, the transfer target was a "flasher," a wall-mounted jeweled light that flashed on for 5 of every 40 ms.

Figure 10 presents the results of the FP discrimination phase. Both

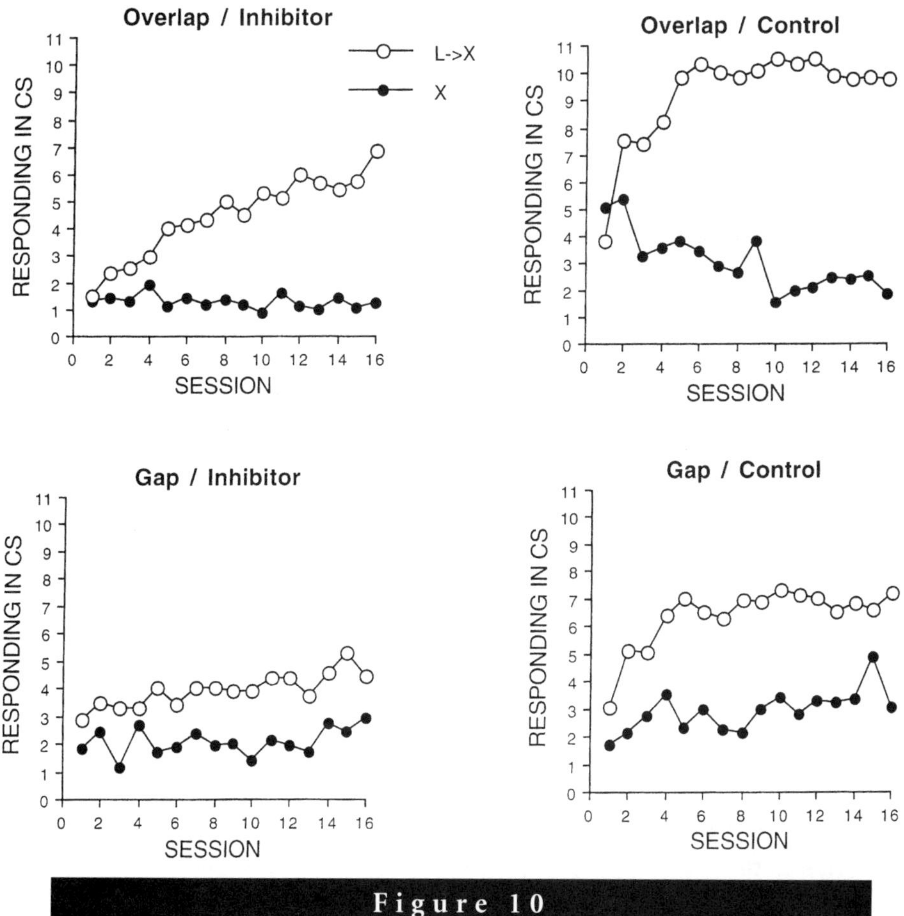

Figure 10

Responding to the target during feature-positive discrimination training in four different groups. Overlap = procedure in which 30-sec target (X) terminated with the offset of a 90-sec feature; Gap = procedure in which 30-sec target (X) followed 30-sec feature and a 30-sec gap; Inhibitor = target (X) previously conditioned as an inhibitor; Control = target X is novel at the start of this phase; L = usual houselight-off feature; X = tone or intermittent noise target.

temporal arrangement and inhibitory preconditioning had an impact on discrimination learning, as confirmed by an ANOVA that included temporal arrangement, inhibitory preconditioning, session, and trial type as factors. When the target had been an inhibitor, discrimination learning was slower; the preconditioning x trial type x session interaction was reliable,

$F(15, 405) = 2.25$. Because the inhibitory target was being converted into an excitor, this is a retardation test. In addition, discrimination learning was more rapid with the overlap procedure, as indicated by the other three-way interaction, $F(15, 405) = 6.03$. This result presumably reflects the fact that the overlap procedure requires less working memory capacity, that the feature is contiguous with the US, or both. The temporal arrangement and inhibitory conditioning factors did not interact in any way, $Fs < 1.67$.

FP training was followed by 14 feature extinction trials. The results of the feature extinction tests are presented in Figure 11. As in the previous experiments, extinction of the feature (POST) reduced the discrimination that was otherwise evident at the end of FP training (PRE). A pre-post ANOVA that included temporal arrangement, inhibitory preconditioning, and trial type as factors revealed an extinction by trial type interaction, $F(1, 27) = 7.70$, indicating that the discrimination was lost after extinction. There was also a three-way interaction, however, $F(1, 27) = 5.52$. As suggested in Figure 12, extinction of L abolished the discrimination in the overlap groups, $F < 1$, but, although it reduced responding to the compound in the gap groups, $F(1, 53) = 4.89$, a reliable discrimination still remained, $F(1, 51) = 6.24$.

The fact that extinction of L decreased but did not abolish the discrimination in the gap/control group is surprising in that this group had been run in several other experiments (e.g., Figures 8 and 15). The incomplete effect of extinction here was presumably because the experiment used a smaller number of extinction trials. The idea that even the gap discriminations were controlled by a simple feature–US association is consistent with the results of the subsequent transfer test in which the light was combined with the flasher CS. That test revealed excitatory summation in all groups: an ANOVA including temporal arrangement, pretraining, phase (conditioning or extinction of the new CS), and trial type showed an effect of trial type, $F(1, 27) = 7.93$, that did not interact with temporal arrangement or pretraining, $Fs < 1$. The results of summation testing in the gap groups are shown in Figure 12. Regardless of the overlap or gap procedure, or the inhibitory preconditioning of the target, the FP discrimination was

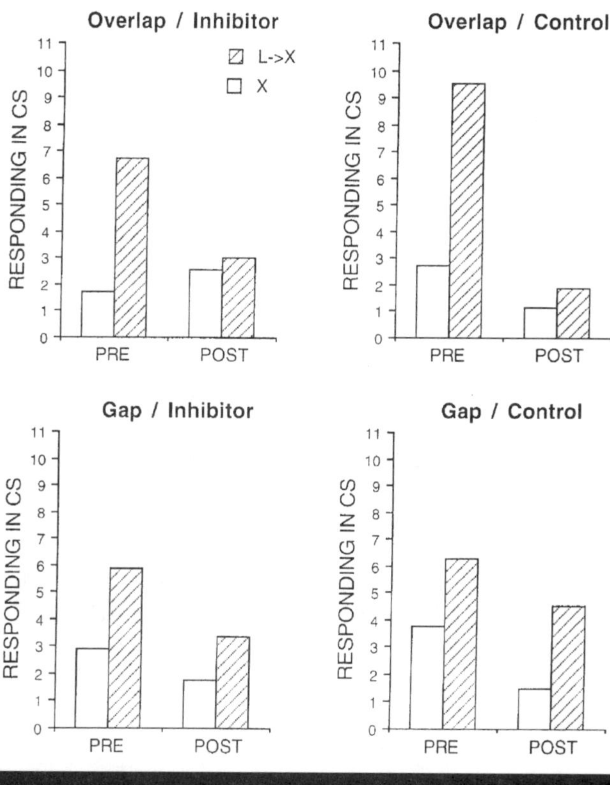

Figure 11

Responding to the target (X) during the feature extinction test. PRE = before feature extinction; POST = after feature extinction; L→X = compound trial; X = target alone trial; Overlap = procedure in which 30-sec target (X) terminated with the offset of a 90-sec feature; Gap = procedure in which 30-sec target (X) followed 30-sec feature and a 30-sec gap; Inhibitor = target (X) previously conditioned as an inhibitor; Control = target X is novel at the start of this phase.

once again solved by excitatory conditioning of the feature. Over a range of conditions, our FP discriminations are solved by a direct association between the feature and the US.

Relative Salience of the Feature and Target

In addition to manipulating temporal and associative factors, we examined the effects of manipulations that might influence the rat's perception of

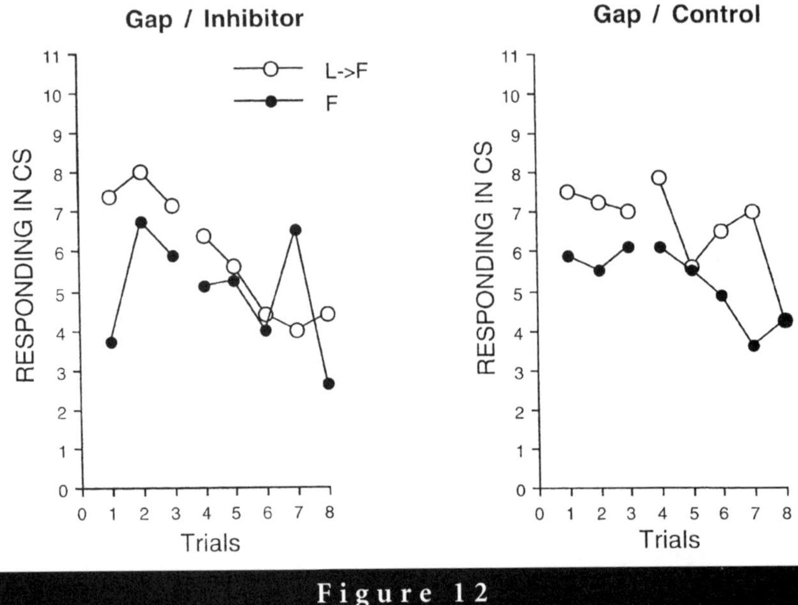

Figure 12

Responding of the gap groups during individual trials of the transfer test. F = flashing light CS; L→F = flashing light CS preceded by feature (L); Gap = procedure in which 30-sec target (X) followed 30-sec feature and a 30-sec gap; Inhibitor = target (X) previously conditioned as an inhibitor; Control = target X is novel at the start of this phase.

the compound. Holland (1989b; see also Holland & Haas, 1993) found that positive occasion setting—defined in part as resistance of the discrimination to the effects of feature extinction—can be obtained even with simultaneous compounds if the target is highly salient and the feature is relatively weak. A relatively salient target might increase the "perceptual discontinuity" between the feature and target, which has been thought to influence occasion setting (e.g., Holland, 1986). Alternatively, a relatively salient target would compete more effectively with the feature for associative strength during FP training. Therefore, it might acquire more excitation on reinforced trials and, consequently, more inhibition during nonreinforced trials (e.g., see Holland, 1992). If inhibition to the target is important in promoting occasion setting (an idea not particularly encouraged by the results of the preceding experiment), a relatively salient target might thus encourage it. By either of these perceptual or associative processes, manipulating feature and target salience could lead to better positive occasion setting.

At least one theory of configural learning (Pearce, 1987, 1994) also recommends the manipulation of relative salience. We have already noted that configural learning theories are like occasion-setting hypotheses in predicting little effect of feature extinction on responding to the compound. Thus, they are equally embarrassed by our finding that feature extinction abolishes the FP discrimination. The Pearce model does suggest, however, that the impact of feature extinction will depend on how much the animal generalizes between the extinguished feature (L) and the tested compound (LT). If there is a great deal of generalization, feature extinction can have an impact. We therefore sought to reduce generalization between L and LT. According to the model, generalization between two stimuli depends on the relative salience of their common elements, in this case L. Thus, by making T relatively salient or L relatively weak, we should decrease generalization between L and LT. On these grounds, relative salience manipulations might further decrease the impact of feature extinction.

We have run two experiments testing the effects of relative salience. In one, we weakened the salience of the feature. Two groups received the serial 30-sec gap procedure. Our usual 30-sec, 80-dB tone (above 65 dB background) was the target. The feature was once again offset of the houselight. In this experiment, however, incident light provided by the houselight was decreased from approximately 8 to 4 foot-candles (as measured at the food cup by a Sekonic Studio Delux exposure meter, model L-28c2). For the Weak Feature group, we further shortened the feature from 30 sec to 5 sec in duration. After the usual FP discrimination training (with intertrial intervals averaging 3.75 min), we ran our standard feature extinction test.

In the second experiment, we manipulated the salience of the target. The two groups both received our ordinary 30-sec houselight-off feature in the 30-30-30 gap arrangement (the intertrial interval was 4.5 min). One group received the usual 80-dB tone as the target. But the new group, Strong Target, received a louder, 95-dB tone. Following FP discrimination

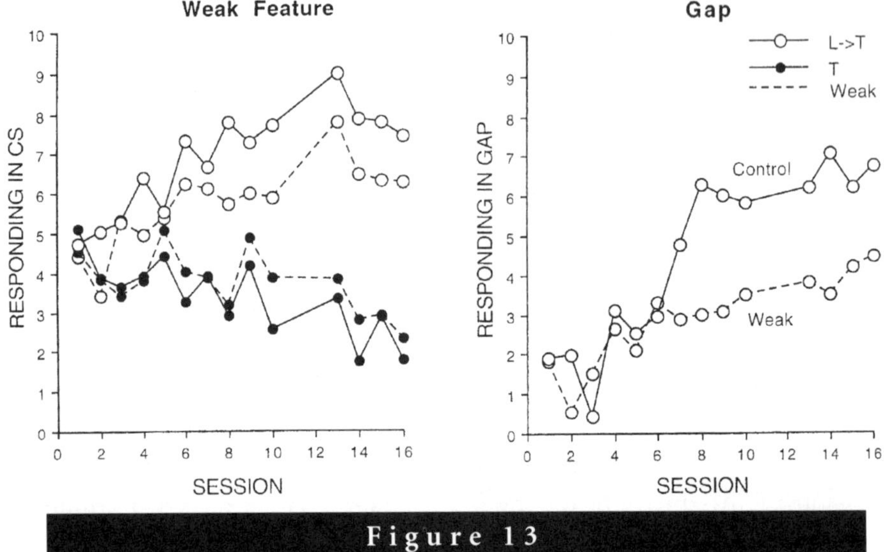

Figure 13

Responding over sessions of feature-positive training during the Weak Feature study described in the text.

training, the groups underwent our usual feature extinction and transfer tests.

The FP discrimination phases of the Weak Feature and Strong Target studies are presented in Figures 13 and 14, respectively. Both manipulations had an impact on FP learning. As shown in the left panel of Figure 13, the Weak Feature group learned the discrimination at roughly the same rate as the control. As the right-hand panel suggests, however, there was significantly less gap behavior after the weak feature, which was confirmed by a group-by-session interaction, $F(13, 182) = 2.00$. The increase of target volume in the Strong Target study likewise influenced discrimination learning (Figure 14). A comparison of the groups' responding to T on the first 10 sessions of FP training revealed a reliable effect of group, $F(1, 17) = 7.35$.

Although the salience manipulations were thus effective, they did not reduce the impact that feature extinction had on discriminative performance. The results of the feature extinction tests are summarized in the

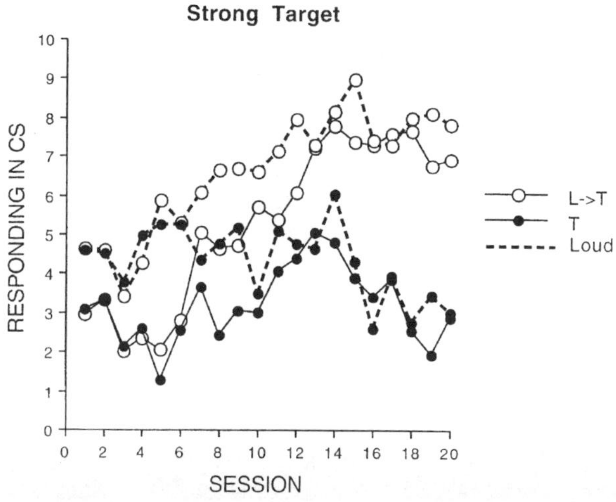

Figure 14

Responding to the target during sessions of feature-positive training during the Strong Target study described in the text.

separate panels of Figure 15. As in the other experiments, the feature extinction treatment again abolished the discriminations. Group x trial type x extinction ANOVAs on the test data revealed trial type by extinction interactions in both the Weak Feature and Strong Target experiments, $F(1, 14) = 8.08$ and 5.06, respectively. These effects did not further interact with group three-way interaction, *F*s < 1. Quite generally, with our methods, rats solve FP discriminations by learning that the feature predicts food. We have produced no evidence of either configural learning or positive occasion setting in our experiments on FP learning.

Choosing Among the Models

Our evidence that the FP discrimination is controlled by a simple feature–US association is consistent with either Model A or Model B in Figure 5; Model C may remain a viable model of positive occasion setting, but we were not able to test it because of our failure to produce the phenomenon. Although Models A and B correctly emphasize the role of the direct feature–US association operating here, how can we choose between them?

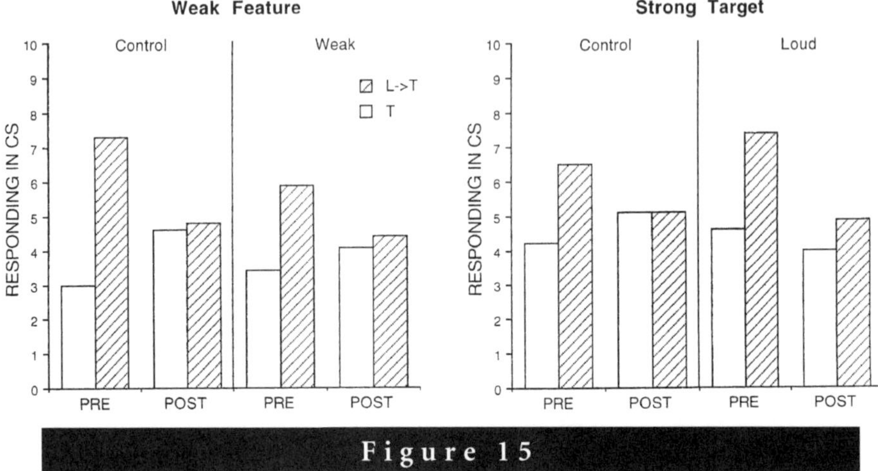

Figure 15

Responding to the target during the feature extinction tests of the Weak Feature (left) and Strong Target (right) studies described in the text. In both experiments, PRE = before feature extinction; POST = after feature extinction; L→T = compound trial; T = target alone trial; Control = group given control discrimination with 30-sec feature, gap, and target periods; Weak = weak feature; Loud = loud target.

Model A illustrates how a standard elemental model of conditioning (e.g., Rescorla & Wagner, 1972) might account for FP learning. Unlike Model B, it does not incorporate our extinction model and, instead, accepts the familiar "unlearning" approach to extinction. In other words, the Rescorla-Wagner model (and other models using the delta rule, e.g., McClelland & Rumelhart, 1985; Rumelhart et al., 1986) supposes that any association learned between the target and US early in training (either through an explicit pretraining phase or before the feature acquires enough conditioning to cause complete blocking) will ultimately be destroyed by presenting the target without the US. Our results begin to suggest, however, that this is an oversimplification for FP learning, just as it is for extinction. As is true of an extinguished CS, responding to the target after FP training can recover with manipulations of time and physical context.

Figure 16 illustrates a common finding in our FP experiments—namely that responding to the target can recover spontaneously over the 24-hr intervals that come between successive sessions. The figure shows

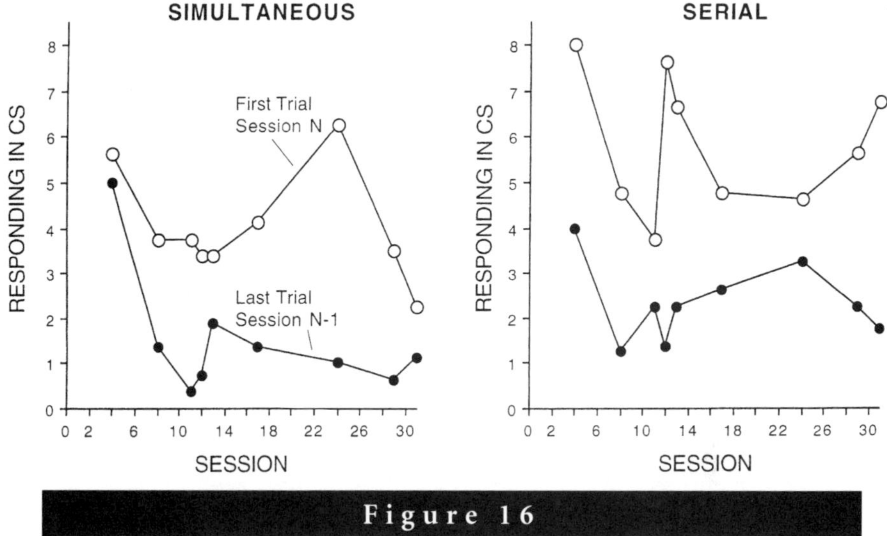

Figure 16

Spontaneous recovery of responding to the target between sessions of feature-positive (FP) training in groups given simultaneous and serial FP discriminations.

the results of an experiment in which simultaneous and serial (30-30-30) procedures (*ns* = 8) were conducted for a large number of sessions with our usual 80-dB tone target and houselight-off feature. In each session, there were five LT+ and five T–trials. There was no preconditioning of the target CS; FP training started with novel CSs. The figure focuses on sessions in which the tone target was presented first. It shows responding to the tone on its first presentation in those sessions (session N) along with responding on the preceding trial—that is, on the tone's last presentation during the preceding session (session N-1). With both the simultaneous and serial procedures, response recoveries were observed throughout training. A group × trial × session ANOVA revealed a clear spontaneous recovery effect, trial $F(1, 14) = 86.76$, that did not interact with session, $F(8, 112) < 1$. Such findings strongly suggest that the target acquires and retains an association with the US during simultaneous and serial FP learning (see also Nakajima, 1997).

Figure 17 presents the results of a complementary experiment that performed a context switch after simultaneous or serial (30-30-30) FP

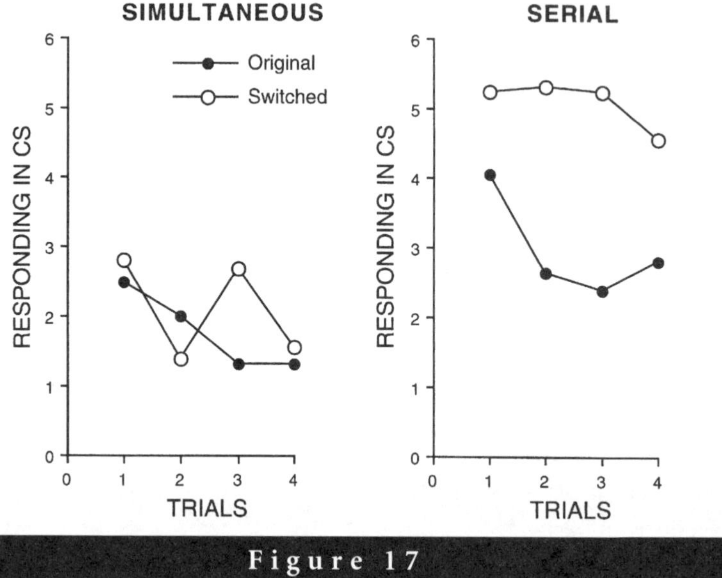

Figure 17

Effect of a context switch on responding to the target after simultaneous or serial feature-positive training. Target stimuli were tested in the context in which they were originally trained (Original) or in a different context (Switched).

training. Here the rats received 10 sessions of T–, LT+ training in Context A intermixed with 10 sessions of N–, LN+ training in Context B; T and N were also initially reinforced alone in their respective contexts. During the trials shown, T and N were both tested (nonreinforced) in both contexts. As the figure suggests, there was more responding to the targets when they were tested outside the original context in which they were trained, particularly after serial training. An ANOVA revealed both a context effect, $F(1, 14) = 16.47$, and a group x context interaction, $F(1, 14) = 8.83$. (The identity of the target had no effect, $ps > .10$, and the figure therefore collapses over them.) The context-switch effect was only reliable in the serially trained group, $Fs\ (1, 14) = 12.60$ and < 1, respectively. The failure to observe the effect in the simultaneous group may be the result of a possible floor effect.

Overall, these effects of time and context change are consistent with the idea that the target acquires both excitatory and context-dependent inhibitory associations during FP training. Thus, Model B in Figure 5 fares better than Model A as a description of our FP results. That model predicts spontaneous recovery between sessions because cues that correlate with time are assumed to be a part of the context that gates the target's inhibitory association with the US (e.g., Brooks & Bouton, 1993).

CONCLUSION

Taken together, the results of the experiments described in this chapter provide a preliminary understanding of the content of FN and FP discriminations as they are represented in one widely used conditioning paradigm. In the FN procedure, there appear to be two separable inhibition mechanisms (Figure 2). One, which is observed primarily in the simultaneous procedure, involves direct inhibition of the US representation. The other, which dominates the serial FN procedure but is also present to some extent in the simultaneous procedure, involves the feature activating the target's own context-specific inhibitory link. The FP discrimination, in contrast, is evidently solved by a single mechanism. There is evidence that the target again acquires both excitation and a context-specific inhibitory link. Over a range of procedures, however, discriminative responding is controlled by the rat associating the feature with food. The content of FP learning in either the serial or simultaneous procedures appears to be best described by Model B in Figure 5. The target acquires an excitatory association and a context-specific inhibitory one, as our extinction model would suppose, but the main effect of presenting the feature is to excite the US representation directly.

One surprising finding was our persistent failure to produce positive occasion setting. With the methods used here, positive occasion setting is more difficult to produce than simple feature conditioning, and it seems more difficult to produce than negative occasion setting. Our inability to produce positive occasion setting does *not* call previous results into question: there is good evidence from other methods that features can control FP performance by some mechanism other than simple feature excitation (e.g., see Holland, 1992; Swartzentruber, 1995, for reviews). Instead, our results reinforce the idea that there are many ways to reach a single behavioral outcome. They recommend caution in how we go about studying the occasion-setting phenomenon. Lengthy gaps between feature and target, salience asymmetries, and inhibitory preconditioning of the target do not carry any guarantees. They also suggest some limitations to our current understanding of occasion setting. Available theories suggested several leads in our effort to change the mechanism from feature excitation to positive occasion setting, but each came up short. Evidently, there is much we still do not know about the conditions that yield positive occasion setting.

The results also provide surprisingly little support for a configural conditioning account of FN and FP learning. For example, although the Pearce model (1987, 1994) has been successful with several other examples of discrimination learning (e.g., Pearce & Redhead, 1993), it failed to anticipate the present results with both FP and FN learning. It did not predict that feature extinction would have such an unambiguous effect on FP performance. Reducing the relative salience of the elements common between the L– and LT test trials did not change that outcome. In the end, the FP discrimination appears to be best explained by an *elemental* model that emphasizes conditioning of the feature. Second, as we have discussed in detail elsewhere (Bouton & Nelson, 1994; Nelson & Bouton, 1997), the Pearce model makes incorrect predictions concerning the effects of context switches on the FN discrimination. The model predicts that inhibition to the feature should be attenuated with a context switch, whereas responding to the target should not be affected. The results here were precisely the reverse: Inhibition to the feature is unaffected by a context switch, whereas responding to the target is affected. The Pearce model made several clear and interesting predictions within the domain we investigated, but, unfortunately, none of them was confirmed.

At a more general level, the results suggest a certain asymmetry between FN and FP discriminations that is reminiscent of earlier research with them (e.g., Hearst, 1984; Jenkins & Sainsbury, 1970). The main previous finding was that FP discriminations were learned faster than FN discriminations, although that result might depend on how responding is measured (e.g., Hearst, 1987). The asymmetry uncovered in the experiments presented here was that the FP discrimination is solved by a simple feature–US association, whereas the FN discrimination involves multiple mechanisms, including an indirect (occasion-setting) one. In retrospect, it may make sense that the system is organized this way: the organism does not need to learn very much to respond appropriately in an FP discrimination. If it can learn that the feature signals food, the discrimination is solved—behavior is already directed efficiently and adaptively toward the appropriate stimulus. The situation is different with the FN procedure, where the animal must learn about both the feature *and* the target to respond adaptively. Responding must occur when the target is presented alone, but not when it is combined with the feature. There is an inherent asymmetry between the FP and FN discriminations. The FN discrimination requires attention to *two* stimuli, but the FP discrimination requires attention to one.

A similar asymmetry has been evident for years in our research on contextual control (e.g., Bouton, 1991, 1993). As we noted earlier, our experiments on the renewal effect (e.g., Bouton & King, 1983; Bouton & Peck, 1989; Bouton & Ricker, 1994) uncovered an inequality in the behavioral control provided by the contexts of conditioning and extinction. In those experiments, we often reinforced a tone in Context A and then extinguished it in Context B. When we returned the tone and tested it in Context A, we observed a renewal of the extinguished response. Extinction performance is thus specific to Context B, but conditioning performance was *not* specific to Context A. When we first switched the tone to Context B and presented it there, we saw no decrement in responding to the tone. There is no apparent effect of a context switch after conditioning, although there is one after extinction. There is a difference in the degree to which the two contexts control.

It is worth noting that an FP discrimination is embedded in the conditioning phase of the renewal procedure, just as it is in any simple conditioning experiment—that is, during conditioning the animal must learn to discriminate the background alone from the background combined with the CS. To formalize it, the animal must discriminate nonreinforced exposure to Context A alone during the intertrial intervals (A–) from trials in which the context and CS are combined and reinforced (e.g., AT+). In a reversal of the way we often think about the roles of context and CS (e.g., Bouton & Swartzentruber, 1986; Hall & Mondragón, chapter 7, this volume), the context is the *target* in this discrimination, and the CS is the *feature.* In our laboratory, the feature–US association tends to dominate behavior, exactly as we found in the present FP experiments: The rat behaves as if the context is almost irrelevant. Performance is controlled primarily by the feature, the CS, which elicits responding regardless of the context. Once again, the feature–US association is all the animal really needs to learn to respond efficiently.

Whatever the usefulness of this parallel, our results support several conclusions about the nature of FN and FP learning. FN learning involves two inhibitory mechanisms, one in which the feature directly suppresses activation of the US representation, and one in which it inhibits performance less directly by activating the target's own inhibitory link; by contrast, in our method FP learning is fundamentally controlled by a simple excitatory link learned between the feature and the US. Although the pattern suggests an incomplete parallel between the contents of FN and FP learning in our paradigm, there are still important similarities between them. Configural learning of the type captured by the Pearce model (1987, 1994) appears to play little role in either case. And the target seems to enter into an associative structure resembling the one we have identified in extinction. Although our research uncovered surprisingly little evidence of positive occasion setting, there does appear to be a fundamental compatibility between the mechanisms of extinction, FN learning, and FP learning.

REFERENCES

Bouton, M. E. (1984). Differential control by context in the inflation and reinstatement paradigms. *Journal of Experimental Psychology: Animal Behavior Processes, 10,* 56–74.

Bouton, M. E. (1988). Context and ambiguity in the extinction of emotional learning:

Implications for exposure therapy. *Behaviour Research and Therapy, 26,* 137–149.

Bouton, M. E. (1991). Context and retrieval in extinction and in other examples of interference in simple associative learning. In L. W. Dachowski & C. F. Flaherty (Eds.), *Current topics in animal learning: Brain, emotion, and cognition* (pp. 25–53). Hillsdale, NJ: Erlbaum.

Bouton, M. E. (1993). Context, time, and memory retrieval in the interference paradigms of Pavlovian learning. *Psychological Bulletin, 114,* 80–99.

Bouton, M. E. (1994). Context, ambiguity, and classical conditioning. *Current Directions in Psychological Science, 3,* 49–53.

Bouton, M. E. (1997). Signals for whether versus when an event will occur. In M. E. Bouton & M. S. Fanselow (Eds.), *Learning, motivation, and cognition: The functional behaviorism of Robert C. Bolles* (pp. 385–409). Washington, DC: American Psychological Association.

Bouton, M. E., & Bolles, R. C. (1985). Contexts, event-memories, and extinction. In P. D. Balsam & A. Tomie (Eds.), *Context and learning* (pp. 133–166). Hillsdale, NJ: Erlbaum.

Bouton, M. E., & King, D. A. (1983). Contextual control of the extinction of conditioned fear: Tests for the associative value of the context. *Journal of Experimental Psychology: Animal Behavior Processes, 9,* 248–265.

Bouton, M. E., & Nelson, J. B. (1994). Context-specificity of target versus feature inhibition in a feature negative discrimination. *Journal of Experimental Psychology: Animal Behavior Processes, 20,* 51–65.

Bouton, M. E., & Peck, C. A. (1989). Context effects on conditioning, extinction, and reinstatement in an appetitive conditioning preparation. *Animal Learning & Behavior, 17,* 188–198.

Bouton, M. E., & Ricker, S. T. (1994). Renewal of extinguished responding in a second context. *Animal Learning & Behavior, 22,* 317–324.

Bouton, M. E., & Swartzentruber, D. (1986). Analysis of the associative and occasion-setting properties of contexts participating in a Pavlovian discrimination. *Journal of Experimental Psychology: Animal Behavior Processes, 12,* 333–350.

Brooks, D. C., & Bouton, M. E. (1993). A retrieval cue for extinction attenuates spontaneous recovery. *Journal of Experimental Psychology: Animal Behavior Processes, 19,* 77–89.

Brooks, D. C., & Bouton, M. E. (1994). A retrieval cue for extinction attenuates response recovery (renewal) caused by a return to the conditioning context. *Journal of Experimental Psychology: Animal Behavior Processes, 20,* 366–379.

Davidson, T. L., & Rescorla, R. A. (1986). Transfer of facilitation in the rat. *Animal Learning & Behavior, 14,* 380–386.

Delamater, A. R. (1995). Outcome-selective effects of intertrial reinforcement in a Pavlovian appetitive conditioning paradigm with rats. *Animal Learning & Behavior, 23,* 31–39.

Farwell, B. J., & Ayres, J. J. B. (1979). Stimulus-reinforcer and response-reinforcer relations in the control of conditioned appetitive headpoking (goal tracking) in rats. *Learning and Motivation, 10,* 295–312.

Good, M., & Honey, R. C. (1991). Conditioning and contextual retrieval in hippocampal rats. *Behavioral Neuroscience, 105,* 499–509.

Grahame, N. J., Hallam, S. C., Geier, L., & Miller, R. R. (1990). Context as an occasion setter following CS acquisition and extinction or CS acquisition alone. *Learning and Motivation, 21,* 237–265.

Hall, G., & Channell, S. (1985). Differential effects of contextual change on latent inhibition and on the habituation of an orienting response. *Journal of Experimental Psychology: Animal Behavior Processes, 11,* 470–481.

Hall, G., & Honey, R. C. (1989). Contextual effects in conditioning, latent inhibition, and habituation: Associative and retrieval functions of contextual cues. *Journal of Experimental Psychology: Animal Behavior Processes, 15,* 232–241.

Hearst, E. (1984). Absence of information: Some implications for learning, performance, and representational processes. In H. L. Roitblat, T. G. Bever, & H. S. Terrace (Eds.), *Animal cognition* (pp. 311–332). Hillsdale, NJ: Erlbaum.

Hearst, E. (1987). Extinction reveals stimulus control: Latent learning of feature-negative discriminations in pigeons. *Journal of Experimental Psychology: Animal Behavior Processes, 13,* 52–64.

Holland, P. C. (1983). Occasion setting in Pavlovian feature positive discriminations. In M. L. Commons, R. J. Herrnstein, & A. R. Wagner (Eds.), *Quantitative analyses of behavior: Discrimination processes* (Vol. 4, pp. 183–206). New York: Ballinger.

Holland, P. C. (1984). Differential effects of reinforcement of an inhibitory feature after serial and simultaneous feature negative discrimination training. *Journal of Experimental Psychology: Animal Behavior Processes, 10,* 461–475.

Holland, P. C. (1985). The nature of conditioned inhibition in serial and simultaneous feature negative discriminations. In R. R. Miller & N. E. Spear (Eds.), *Information processing in animals: Conditioned inhibition* (pp. 267–297). Hillsdale, NJ: Erlbaum.

Holland, P. C. (1986). Temporal determinants of occasion setting in feature-positive discriminations. *Animal Learning & Behavior, 17,* 269–279.

Holland, P. C. (1989a). Feature extinction enhances transfer of occasion setting. *Animal Learning & Behavior, 17,* 269–279.

Holland, P. C. (1989b). Occasion setting with simultaneous compounds in rats. *Journal of Experimental Psychology: Animal Behavior Processes, 15,* 183–193.

Holland, P. C. (1989c). Transfer of negative occasion setting and conditioned inhibition across conditioned and unconditioned stimuli. *Journal of Experimental Psychology: Animal Behavior Processes, 15,* 183–193.

Holland, P. C. (1991). Acquisition and transfer of occasion setting in operant feature positive and feature negative discriminations. *Learning and Motivation, 22,* 366–387.

Holland, P. C. (1992). Occasion setting in Pavlovian conditioning. In G. Bower (Ed.), *The psychology of learning and motivation* (Vol. 28, pp. 69–125). Orlando, FL: Academic Press.

Holland, P. C., & Hass, M. L. (1993). The effects of target salience in operant feature positive discriminations. *Learning and Motivation, 24,* 119–140.

Holland, P. C., & Lamarre, J. (1984). Transfer of inhibition after serial and simultaneous feature negative discrimination training. *Learning and Motivation, 15,* 219–243.

Honey, R. C., Willis, A., & Hall, G. (1990). Context specificity in pigeon autoshaping. *Learning and Motivation, 21,* 125–136.

Jenkins, H. M., & Sainsbury, R. S. (1970). Discrimination learning with the distinctive feature on positive or negative trials. In D. Mostofsky (Ed.), *Attention: Contemporary theory and analysis* (pp. 239–273). New York: Appleton-Century-Crofts.

Kamin, L. J. (1969). Predictability, surprise, attention, and conditioning. In B. A. Campbell & R. B. Church (Eds.), *Punishment and aversive behavior* (pp. 279–296). New York: Appleton-Century-Crofts.

Kaye, H., & Mackintosh, N. J. (1990). A change of context can enhance performance of an aversive but not of an appetitive conditioned response. *Quarterly Journal of Experimental Psychology, 42B,* 113–134.

Kaye, H., Preston, G., Szabo, L., Druiff, H., & Mackintosh, N. J. (1987). Context specificity of conditioning and latent inhibition: Evidence for a dissociation of latent inhibition and associative interference. *Quarterly Journal of Experimental Psychology, 39B,* 127–145.

Lamarre, J., & Holland, P. C. (1987). Transfer of inhibition after serial feature negative discrimination training. *Learning and Motivation, 18,* 319–342.

McClelland, J. L., & Rumelhart, D. E. (1985). Distributed memory and the representation of general and specific information. *Journal of Experimental Psychology: General, 114,* 159–188.

Nakajima, S. (1997). Long-term retention of Pavlovian serial feature-positive and feature-negative discriminations. *Behavioural Processes, 39,* 223–229.

Nelson, J. B. (1997). *The context specificity of second learned information.* Unpublished doctoral dissertation, University of Vermont, Burlington.

Nelson, J. B., & Bouton, M. E. (1996). [Transfer of feature inhibition after simultaneous and serial feature-negative training]. Unpublished raw data.

Nelson, J. B., & Bouton, M. E. (1997). The effects of a context switch following serial and simultaneous feature-negative discriminations. *Learning and Motivation, 28,* 56–84.

Pearce, J. M. (1987). A model for stimulus generalization in Pavlovian conditioning. *Psychological Review, 94,* 61–73.

Pearce, J. M. (1994). Similarity and discrimination: A selective review and a connectionist model. *Psychological Review, 101,* 587–607.

Pearce, J. M., & Redhead, E. S. (1993). The influence of an irrelevant stimulus on two discriminations. *Journal of Experimental Psychology: Animal Behavior Processes, 19,* 180–190.

Pearce, J. M., & Wilson, P. N. (1991). Failure of excitatory conditioning to extinguish the influence of a conditioned inhibitor. *Journal of Experimental Psychology: Animal Behavior Processes, 17,* 519–529.

Reberg, D. (1972). Compound tests for excitation in early acquisition and after prolonged extinction of conditioned suppression. *Learning and Motivation, 3,* 246–258.

Rescorla, R. A. (1973). Evidence for "unique stimulus" account of configural conditioning. *Journal of Comparative and Physiological Psychology, 85,* 331–338.

Rescorla, R. A. (1974). Effect of inflation of the unconditioned stimulus value following conditioning. *Journal of Comparative and Physiological Psychology, 86,* 101–106.

Rescorla, R. A. (1985). Conditioned inhibition and facilitation. In R. R. Miller & N. E. Spear (Eds.), *Information processing in animals: Conditioned inhibition* (pp. 199–326). Hillsdale, NJ: Erlbaum.

Rescorla, R. A. (1986). Extinction of facilitation. *Journal of Experimental Psychology: Animal Behavior Processes, 12,* 16–24.

Rescorla, R. A. (1987). Facilitation and inhibition. *Journal of Experimental Psychology: Animal Behavior Processes, 13,* 250–259.

Rescorla, R. A. (1988). Facilitation based on inhibition. *Animal Learning & Behavior, 16,* 169–176.

Rescorla, R. A., & Holland, P. C. (1977). Associations in Pavlovian conditioned inhibition. *Learning and Motivation, 8,* 429–447.

Rescorla, R. A., & Wagner, A. R. (1972). A theory of Pavlovian conditioning: Variations in the effectiveness of reinforcement and nonreinforcement. In A. H. Black & W. F. Prokasy (Eds.), *Classical conditioning II: Current research and theory* (pp. 64–99). New York: Appleton-Century-Crofts.

Rosas, J. M., & Bouton, M. E. (1997). Renewal of a conditioned taste aversion upon return to the conditioning context after extinction in another one. *Learning and Motivation, 28,* 216–229.

Ross, R. T. (1983). Relationships between the determinants of performance in serial feature positive discriminations. *Journal of Experimental Psychology: Animal Behavior Processes, 9,* 349–373.

Ross, R. T., & Holland, P. C. (1981). Conditioning of simultaneous and serial feature-positive discriminations. *Animal Learning & Behavior, 9,* 293–303.

Rumelhart, D. E., Hinton, G. E., & Williams, R. J. (1986). Learning internal representations by error propagation. In D. E. Rumelhart & J. L. McClelland (Eds.), *Parallel distributed processing: Explorations in the microstructure of cognition. Vol 1: Foundations* (pp. 318–362). Cambridge, MA: Bradford.

Schmajuk, N. A., & Buhusi, C. V. (1997). Stimulus configuration, occasion setting, and the hippocampus. *Behavioral Neuroscience, 111,* 235–258.

Schmajuk, N. A., Lamoureux, J. A., & Holland, P. C. (1998). Occasion setting: A neural network approach. *Psychological Review, 105,* 3–32.

Swartzentruber, D. (1995). Modulatory mechanisms in Pavlovian conditioning. *Animal Learning & Behavior, 23,* 123–143.

Swartzentruber, D., & Bouton, M. E. (1992). Context sensitivity of conditioned suppression following preexposure to the conditioned stimulus. *Animal Learning & Behavior, 20,* 97–103.

Swartzentruber, D., & Rescorla, R. A. (1994). Modulation of trained and extinguished stimuli by facilitators and inhibitors. *Animal Learning & Behavior, 22,* 309–316.

Wagner, A. R. (1969). Stimulus selection and a "modified continuity theory." In G. H. Bower & J. T. Spence (Eds.), *The psychology of learning and motivation* (Vol. 3, pp. 1–41). New York: Academic Press.

Wagner, A. R., & Brandon, S. E. (1989). Evolution of a structured connectionist model of Pavlovian conditioning: AESOP. In S. B. Klein & R. R. Mowrer (Eds.), *Contemporary learning theories: Pavlovian conditioning and the status of traditional learning theory* (pp. 149–190). Hillsdale, NJ: Erlbaum.

4

What Can Nontraditional Features Tell Us About Conditioning and Occasion Setting?

Darlene M. Skinner, Murray J. Goddard, and Peter C. Holland

Simple conditioned stimuli (CSs) are assumed to elicit conditioned responses (CRs) because they signal the occurrence of an unconditioned stimulus (US). In contrast, an occasion setter (Holland, 1983, 1992; Swartzentruber, 1995) is thought to modulate responding generated by another CS by indicating the relation between that CS and the US. In the serial feature-positive and feature-negative discrimination procedures frequently used to study occasion setting, subjects must learn that reinforcement of a target CS depends on the previous presentation of a feature cue. In positive occasion setting, subjects normally receive F→ST+, T− trials and must learn that a target cue (T) is only reinforced when it is preceded by a particular feature cue (F) (but see Bonardi, chapter 2, this volume). In negative occasion setting, subjects receive F→ST−, T+ trials and must learn that a target cue is only reinforced when it is not preceded by a particular feature cue.

The research described in this chapter was funded by grants from the Human Frontier Science Program to D. M. Skinner, from the National Science Foundation to P. C. Holland, from the Natural Sciences and Engineering Research Council of Canada to M. J. Goddard, and from the Medical Research Council of Canada to D. van der Kooy.

Studies of occasion setting have predominately used relatively neutral feature cues. For example, in positive occasion setting, a tone target cue may be reinforced only when it is preceded by a light feature cue. The chapters presented in this book complement this observation—most authors reported using relatively neutral feature cues (but see Davidson, chapter 8, this volume). Perhaps it is not surprising, therefore, that theories of occasion setting, such as layered network models (for example, see Lamoureux, Buhusi, & Schmajuk, chapter 13, this volume; Zackheim, Myers, & Gluck, chapter 11, this volume), have been carefully structured to account for a database that has been obtained using neutral feature cues such as lights and tones.

Recently, however, we have been studying occasion setting with less traditional feature cues. For example, Skinner and Martin (1992) used morphine as a feature cue that signaled when saccharine would be followed by illness. Rats rapidly learned this positive occasion-setting relation by consuming significantly less saccharine when saccharine was preceded by morphine than when saccharine was preceded by saline. Similarly, Goddard and Holland (1996) used flavored Kool-Aid as the feature cue that signaled when responding during a tone target would be reinforced by more of the same Kool-Aid. Rats learned this positive occasion-setting relation by responding significantly more when the tone was preceded by flavored Kool-Aid than when the tone was presented alone.

This chapter describes some of our recent investigations of occasion setting using foods, external contexts, and drug states as occasion setters. First, we describe a series of studies of operant occasion setting in which flavored liquids served as both features and reinforcers. Second, we present studies in which internal or external contextual cues modulated flavor–illness learning. Finally, we suggest how these kinds of features may provide useful analytic tools for exploring a variety of general issues in conditioning and behavior that are less easily addressed with use of simple lights and tones.

Although most of the results of these studies were comparable to the data previously collected with more traditional features, we found several differences as well. An appreciation for the influence of different kinds of feature events on the nature of learning may provide a more complete understanding of occasion setting and challenge and extend current theories of occasion setting. Similarly, the study of occasion setting with a variety of feature cue types may provide better models of real-world behavior systems in which, for example, biologically potent external and internal events may modulate an organism's response to other events in its environment.

OCCASION SETTING WITH FLAVORED LIQUID AS BOTH FEATURE AND REINFORCER

Although most investigations of occasion setting in feature-positive (FP) and feature-negative (FN) discriminations have used visual or auditory cues as features, some of the earlier studies used events that might otherwise be classed as reinforcers or USs. For example, Holland and Forbes (1982), using a preparatory-releaser procedure (Konorski & Lawicka, 1959; Terry and Wagner, 1975) with rats, paired a tone with food pellets on some trials and presented the tone without food on other trials. In FP training, the tone was paired with food only when it was preceded by a liquid sucrose feature; in FN training, the tone was paired with food only when it was not preceded by a sucrose feature. In both cases, the rats rapidly learned to respond appropriately to the tone.

Although most of the results from these early experiments with reinforcers as features were similar to those from comparable experiments in which more neutral events were used as features, some outcomes differed. For example, although most investigations of FP and FN training find superior FP performance (Hearst, 1978, 1984; Hearst & Wolff, 1989; Jenkins & Sainsbury, 1969), both Holland and Forbes (1982) and Reberg and Memmot (1979) found superior FN performance when reinforcers were used as feature cues (cf. Bottjer & Hearst, 1979). It is possible that highly salient, biologically meaningful events possess attributes or generate consequences that may alter their cuing properties compared to those of less significant events. Indeed, some theorists have suggested that learning of relations among USs may differ qualitatively from CS-US learning (e.g., Garcia, 1986; Solomon, 1977).

Recently, Goddard and Holland (1996, 1997) examined rats' solution of operant serial FP and FN discriminations when the feature cues were flavored liquids like those used as the reinforcers and when they were more typical auditory or visual cues. Although this research was primarily empirically motivated, we were not without expectations. For example, there are several reasons why using features that can also serve as reinforcers might encourage solutions based on simple feature–US associations rather than occasion setting. First, it is likely that reinforcer features are more salient than typical visual or auditory features. Both previous data (e.g., Holland, 1989b; Holland & Haas, 1993) and several theories of occasion setting (e.g., Lamoureux, Buhusi, & Schmajuk, chapter 13, this volume; Schmajuk, Lamoureux, & Holland, in press) suggest that use of occasion-setting strategies is favored when the feature is less salient relative to the target, and simple conditioning is favored when the feature is more salient. Second, a number of investigators have reported that associations are more readily formed between similar cues than between dissimilar cues (Holland & Ross, 1981; Rescorla & Furrow, 1977). The use of features similar (or identical) to the reinforcer might especially encourage formation of simple feature–reinforcer associations, at the expense of occasion setting. Third, Goddard (1995) has reported that US presentation is a particularly effective cue for the subsequent absence of that event. Thus, use of reinforcers as features might especially encourage solution of FN discriminations by forming inhibitory feature–reinforcer associations rather than occasion setting.

Feature-Positive Discrimination Learning

Holland (1983, 1992) noted three classes of evidence that suggested differences between solutions of FP discriminations that involved simple conditioning and those that involved occasion setting. First, in conditioning preparations in which the form of the CR depends on the nature of the CS, the form of the CR displayed during the target CS can indicate whether performance is controlled by associations between the feature and the reinforcer (simple conditioning) or by associations between the target and the reinforcer (occasion setting). Second, although posttraining presentations of the feature alone abolish discrimination performance that is based on simple feature–US associations, they have little effect on that feature's occasion-setting ability. Third, although feature cues elicit their CRs when presented with their original targets, with other target cues, or even by themselves, their occasion-setting ability is more limited to particular kinds of target cues. Transfer experiments with traditional auditory or visual feature cues typically show reliable transfer to targets trained in other occasion-setting discriminations, but little transfer to cues that have simply been preexposed or have received only simple conditioning (e.g., see Holland, 1989a; Rescorla, 1985). Mixed results have been found when transfer tests are conducted with test targets that have received both excitatory and inhibitory training but not explicit training as targets of occasion setters; although some studies show transfer (Jarrard and Davidson, 1991), others do not (Holland, 1986). Regardless of this, transfer of occasion setting is more limited than transfer of simple conditioning.

Goddard and Holland (1996) used these criteria to compare the solution of operant serial FP discriminations when the feature stimuli were themselves reinforcers and when they were more typical visual or auditory stimuli. Food-deprived rats were given concurrent training on two serial FP discriminations. On feature-target trials, on which the feature cue was presented 30 sec before the target cue, performance of the correct operant during the 10-sec auditory target cues was reinforced with the delivery of a flavored liquid sucrose; but on target-alone trials, reinforcement was unavailable. Each discrimination involved a different feature, target, and response, but the same reinforcer. The nature of the feature cues for these discriminations varied across three groups. For the rats in group CS–CS, the features were a light and a clicker; for the rats in group US–US, the features were two Kool-Aid flavors; and for the rats in group US–CS, one feature was a light or clicker and the other was one flavor of Kool-Aid. The targets were a noise or a tone, the responses were lever pressing or chain pulling, and the reinforcers were grape or orange Kool-Aid, all counterbalanced. The Kool-Aid reinforcer was identical to the Kool-Aid feature in group US–CS and for one discrimination in group US–US. The measures of conditioning used were the percentage of trials on which correct responses occurred, the latency of the first correct response, and the rate of correct responding.

The identity of the feature cue had little or no impact in training: The rats acquired accurate discrimination performance at about the same rate in all conditions. Furthermore, extensive posttraining presentations of the features alone had no discernible effect on responding to the original feature–target compound. Thus, the effects of feature extinction suggested that the discriminative responding was based on occasion setting rather than simple feature conditioning in all conditions.

Additional similarities between the action of Kool-Aid and auditory or visual features were revealed by transfer tests administered after training (both before and after feature extinction), but one substantial difference was observed as well. In agreement with Holland (1989a) and Rescorla (1985), Goddard and Holland (1996) found that auditory or visual features readily modulated responding to a cue that had been trained as a target in another serial FP discrimination with an auditory or visual feature (Figure 1, left bars). Similarly, the occasion-setting power of Kool-Aid features readily transferred to the target of another Kool-Aid feature (Figure 1, right bars). Furthermore, responding to the transfer compounds was almost exclusively of the form appropriate to the target presented rather than the feature. Thus, the transfer observed was of the features' occasion-setting powers rather than of simple conditioning. Furthermore, the performance of control groups (not shown), which received training with one serial FP discrimination and one pseudodiscrimination (F→SA+, A+), showed that this transfer was not easily attributable to simple generalization between the features or targets and that transfer did not occur to a target that had not been trained within a serial FP discrimination.

Goddard and Holland (1996), however, found little transfer of occasion setting when a Kool-Aid feature was tested with a target that had been trained with a light or tone feature, or when a light or tone feature was tested with a target that had been trained with a Kool-Aid feature

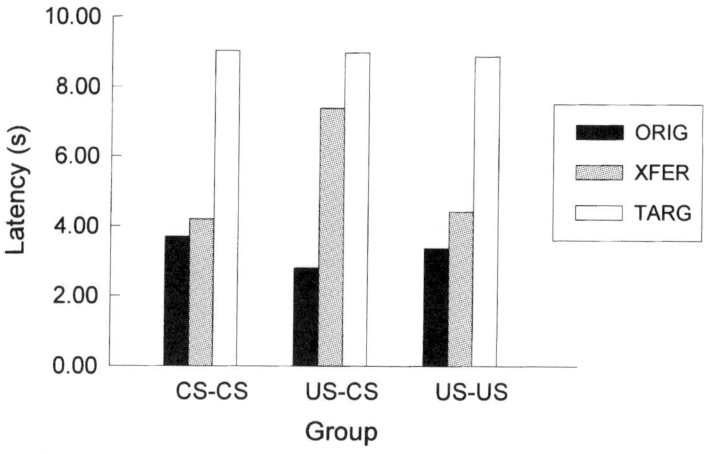

Figure 1

Latency to the first correct response during transfer testing of rats in Goddard and Holland's (1996) Experiment 2. All rats received training on two serial feature-positive discriminations. The features were auditory or visual stimuli for both discriminations in group CS–CS, Kool-Aid for both in group US–US, and one auditory or visual cue and one Kool-Aid in group US–CS. The bars labeled ORIG show responding to original training feature-target compounds, those labeled XFER show responding on transfer compounds comprising the feature from one discrimination and the target from the other, and those labeled TARG show responding on target-alone trials.

(Figure 1, middle bars). The absence of occasion-setting transfer between Kool-Aid and auditory or visual features was shown regardless of whether the features also evoked significant levels of feature-specific responding (Goddard and Holland, 1996, Experiment 1) or not (Goddard and Holland, 1996, Experiment 2). Furthermore, the observation of substantial transfer *within* both classes of features showed that the lack of transfer *between* feature classes was not due to a general inability of one or the other feature to show transfer.

These results seriously constrain theories of occasion setting that predict transfer to targets trained in other occasion-setting discriminations (as most theories do) and suggested that occasion-setting transfer is affected not only by the training contingencies, but also by the intrinsic properties of the events involved in those contingencies. For example, one explanation for the greater transfer of a feature's occasion setting to the targets of other occasion setters than to separately trained cues is that similar training procedures enhances the normal stimulus generalization between the features (e.g., Bonardi, chapter 2, this volume; Honey & Hall, 1989). Such enhancement of generalization might demand some initial similarity among the features and, thus, would not be observed when one feature is a light or tone and the other is Kool-Aid. On the other hand, within this view it is not clear why we typically observe excellent transfer when one feature is a visual cue and the other is an auditory cue (e.g., Figure 1, left bars).

We have begun to consider what properties of Kool-Aid features make them and their trained targets distinct from auditory or visual features and their targets. For example, it is possible that it is not the nature of the features themselves that matters but the confounded differences in the event contingencies. For example, the delivery of a Kool-Aid feature can be viewed as a response-independent reinforcer, and the delivery of the Kool-Aid reinforcer contingent on the first response after target presentation can be viewed as the presentation of a feature simultaneously with target presentation. Neither of these relations between feature and reinforcer occurs in occasion setting with auditory or visual features. Furthermore, the use of Kool-Aid features demands greater feature-reinforcer similarity than the use of auditory or visual features, Alternatively, it may be that properties that are intrinsic to the feature cues themselves are indeed critical—for example, flavor, sweet, or reinforcing stimuli may be processed in a different way than auditory or visual cues.

A recent, unpublished experiment provides some hints that these factors are important. In this study (Skinner & Holland, 1997), food- and water-deprived rats were trained with the same procedures that were used to train the rats in group US–CS in Goddard and Holland's (1996) study, except that the response-contingent reinforcer was always plain sucrose solution and the feature cues were a visual cue and a flavored but unsweetened Kool-Aid solution. Figure 2 shows the results of a transfer test identical to that administered by Goddard and Holland (1996). As in that study, transfer responding was entirely appropriate to the target cue and hence

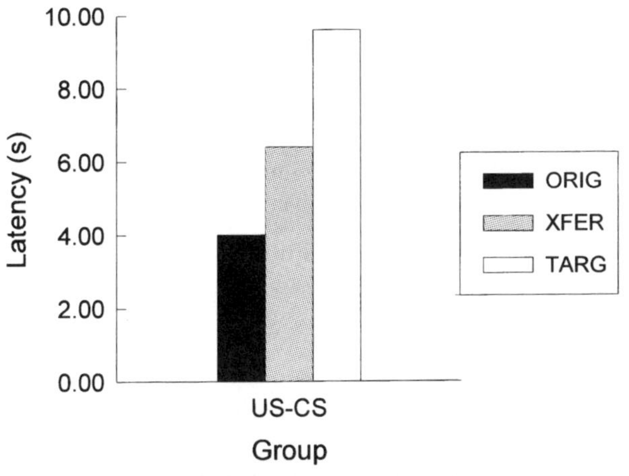

Figure 2

Latency to the first correct response in an unpublished experiment (Skinner & Holland, 1997), in which one feature was unsweetened Kool-Aid and the other was a visual cue. The bars labeled ORIG show responding to original training feature–target compounds, those labeled XFER show responding on transfer compounds comprising the feature from one discrimination and the target from the other, and those labeled TARG show responding on target-alone trials.

was likely the result of occasion setting rather than simple feature-US conditioning. Unlike the Goddard and Holland study, there was substantial transfer of both the visual and unsweetened Kool-Aid features' occasion-setting powers to targets trained with the other feature (compare to Figure 1, middle bars). Thus, elimination of the feature's sweetness and the use of different events as feature and reinforcer resulted in a pattern of data more like that found with more typical auditory or visual features. Subsequent studies will consider the separate contributions of feature-reinforcer similarity and the removal of sweetness from the feature.

Feature-Negative Discrimination Learning

Using experimental procedures similar to those they used earlier (1996), Goddard and Holland (1997) compared operant serial FN discrimination learning of food-deprived rats when the features were the same as the reinforcers and when they were auditory or visual stimuli. Dramatic differences were found in both the rate and nature of learning as a function of feature type.

Discrimination learning was much more rapid with Kool-Aid features than with auditory or visual features. For example, in group US–CS, subjects were exposed to two operant serial FN discriminations, one with a Kool-Aid feature and one with an auditory or visual feature. With the Kool-Aid feature, robust, nearly asymptotic discrimination performance was shown after 5 training sessions; with the auditory or visual feature, however, discrimination performance was still relatively poor (although reliable) after 50 training sessions. Similarly, rats in group US–US, which were exposed to one FN discrimination with one Kool-Aid flavor and another FN discrimination with a different Kool-Aid flavor, showed acquisition of reliable discrimination performance *within the first training session.* In contrast, rats in group CS–CS, which were exposed to two FN discriminations with auditory or visual features, showed relatively poor discrimination performance after 50 training sessions.

In contrast to these results, using very similar procedures, Goddard and Holland (1996, described earlier) found FP learning to proceed at about the same rate regardless of the nature of the feature cue. Indeed, comparisons across these studies revealed a typical FP advantage with auditory or visual features but a substantial FN advantage with Kool-Aid features. In a recent unpublished experiment (Skinner & Holland, 1997), we directly compared the acquisition of operant FP and FN discriminations in food- and water-deprived rats when the feature cues were either visual cues or unsweetened Kool-Aid and the reinforcer was a plain sucrose solution (Figure 3). Although in this study the Kool-Aid feature was superior to the auditory or visual feature for both FP and FN learning, the FP and FN effects were comparable to those found in Goddard and Holland's (1996, 1997) studies. Interestingly, both the observation of FP superiority with auditory or visual features and FN superiority with Kool-Aid features are consistent with previous findings in the literature, which are described at the beginning of this chapter.

The results of transfer tests after serial FN training (Goddard & Holland, 1997) were very different from those obtained after FP training

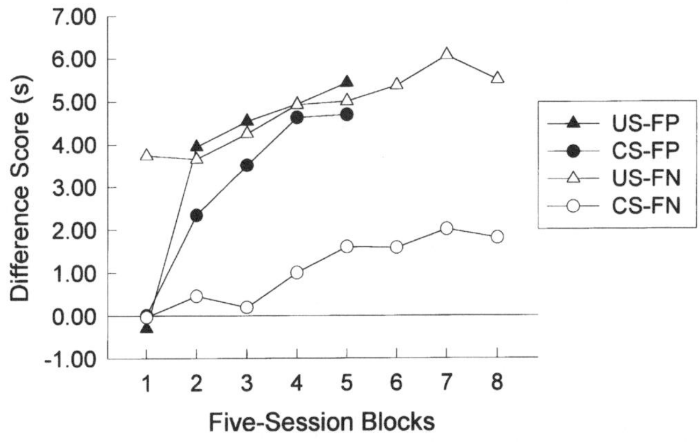

Figure 3

Acquisition of discrimination performance in an unpublished experiment (Skinner & Holland, 1997). One group of rats received training with two feature positive (FP) discriminations, and another group received training with two feature negative (FN) discriminations. In each group, one feature was unsweetened Kool-Aid (US) and one was a visual cue (CS). The index of discrimination performance is a difference score: latency of the first correct response to the target on nonreinforced trials minus that latency on reinforced trials.

(Goddard & Holland, 1996). Consistent with previous findings, auditory or visual features' negative occasion-setting powers transferred to targets of another auditory or visual occasion setter but not to a separately trained excitatory CS or a target of a Kool-Aid occasion setter (Figure 4, left and middle bars). A Kool-Aid feature almost completely suppressed responding to all kinds of targets, however, including targets of another Kool-Aid occasion setter, targets of an auditory or visual occasion setter, and separately trained exciters (Figure 4, middle and right bars).

Goddard and Holland's (1997) data clearly show that the acquisition and transfer of inhibitory control in serial FN discriminations with Kool-Aid reinforcer features is very different from that with auditory or visual cues. We suspect that these differences are related to the observation that the delivery of temporally separated biologically potent cues (such as flavored sucrose or USs in general) leads to powerful inhibitory learning, apart from specific contingencies that engender occasion setting (see

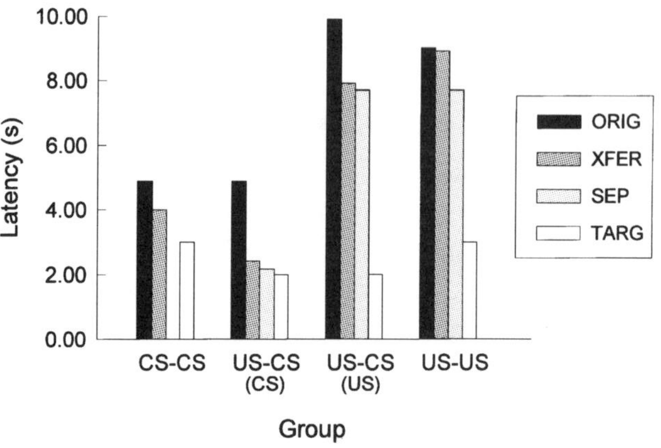

Figure 4

Latency to the first correct response during transfer testing of rats in Goddard and Holland's (1997) Experiment 1. All rats received training on two serial feature-negative discriminations. The features were auditory or visual stimuli for both discriminations in group CS–CS, Kool-Aid for both in group US–US, and one auditory or visual cue and one Kool-Aid in group US–CS. The bars labeled ORIG show responding on the original training feature–target compounds, those labeled XFER show responding on transfer compounds comprising the feature from one discrimination and the target from the other, those labeled SEP show responding to compounds that included a separately trained target cue, and those labeled TARG show responding on target-alone trials.

Moore & Choi, chapter 10, this volume). For example, Burdick and James (1973) found in fear conditioning that preceding a well-trained CS with a US presentation produced a reduction of the conditioned suppression previously produced by that CS. More recently, Goddard (1995) reported that when rats received temporally separated food deliveries, they showed a significant loss in the number of magazine entries shortly after a food pellet.

Goddard and Holland (1997) also observed a significant loss in magazine entries shortly after delivery of the Kool-Aid features, suggesting that the Kool-Aid features in their study had acquired simple inhibitory properties. This postfeature inhibition might serve both to facilitate FN discrimination performance significantly and to contribute to the robust transfer shown to targets with a variety of training histories. Thus, unlike Goddard and Holland's (1996) findings with FP training, in FN training these Kool-Aid features may more closely resemble simple inhibitors rather than true modulators.

The results of another experiment (Goddard and Holland, 1997, Experiment 2) suggest that acquisition of inhibitory powers by the Kool-Aid features did not depend on the arrangement of explicit FN discrimination contingencies. In that experiment, a Kool-Aid feature presented explicitly unpaired with an excitatory target CS developed equivalent inhibitory powers (as revealed in subsequent transfer tests), suggesting that the mere temporally spaced presentation of Kool-Aid was sufficient to endow that cue with inhibitory powers. Thus, it seems that the inhibitory potential of spaced reinforcer presentations is so great that it overpowers any additional effects of explicit FN contingencies. Interestingly, a Kool-Aid feature trained within a pseudodiscrimination (F→ST+, T+), in which the Kool-Aid feature was not a consistent predictor of a Kool-Aid-free interval, did not possess these inhibitory powers, at least not by the time transfer tests were administered. Other tests of stimulus control after similar pseudodiscrimination training (Goddard & Holland, 1996) showed that this procedure generated little excitation or occasion-setting power to the pseudofeature, either.

Summary

The action of Kool-Aid features differed from that of auditory or visual features. First, unless delivery of a Kool-Aid feature was explicitly paired with delivery of Kool-Aid reinforcers (as in FP or pseudodiscrimination procedures), it acquired broad-ranging suppressive powers more akin to simple conditioned inhibition than negative occasion setting. Furthermore, the acquisition of this inhibitory control was considerably more rapid than the acquisition of either inhibitory control by auditory or visual features or positive occasion setting by Kool-Aid features. Second, although the acquisition and transfer of positive occasion setting was similar with Kool-Aid and auditory or visual features, positive occasion setting established with one set of cues did not transfer to targets trained with the other.

Data like these, although unexpected, are not necessarily incompatible with theories of occasion setting. The readiness of reinforcer-like features to serve as predictors of their own absence can be superimposed on any theory of occasion setting. Within most such theories, occasion-setting strategies are engaged when simple excitatory or inhibitory conditioning strategies are unable to solve the discrimination. To the extent that FN tasks are solved very rapidly by the conditioning of inhibition to reinforcer features, that solution would be anticipated to dominate over negative occasion setting. Likewise, most theories are readily modified to deal with the failure to find transfer of positive occasion setting across feature types. For example, as described earlier, Honey and Hall's (1989) account for transfer target training effects can be extended to these findings simply by assuming that the enhancement of generalization by comparable training procedures demands some intrinsic similarity of the cues. Similarly, within Schmajuk, Lamoureux, and Holland's (1998) network model (see Lamoureux, Buhusi, & Schmajuk, chapter 13, this volume), one could make the plausible assumption that features like auditory and visual stimuli gain access to different configural units than do Kool-Aid features.

INTERNAL (DRUG STATES) AND EXTERNAL CONTEXTS AS OCCASION SETTERS IN FLAVOR AVERSION LEARNING

An occasion-setting analysis has been applied to the modulation of conditioned flavor aversions by contextual cues in drug discrimination procedures (Martin, Gans, & van der Kooy, 1990; Skinner, Martin, Pridgar, & van der Kooy, 1994). In initial experiments, an internal context produced by a drug-induced state was used to modulate a conditioned flavor aversion (Martin et al., 1990). On some trials a morphine-induced drug state (the feature) preceded exposure to a flavored solution (the target), which in turn was followed by injection of the toxin lithium chloride (LiCl). On other trials, the target was presented alone and was not followed by the toxin. Over several trials, the rats decreased their fluid consumption on drug trials relative to nondrug trials, as if the drug state set the occasion for the flavor-illness relation.

It might be argued that the morphine state acted as a simple Pavlovian CS for illness and suppressed fluid consumption more directly, for example, by eliciting a conditioned illness response (but see Lett, 1983) that would compete with ingestive behavior, or by generating a conditioned motivational state that interferes with states thought to underlie ingestion (as in traditional two-process theory, e.g., Rescorla & Solomon, 1967). Several kinds of data led Martin et al. (1990) to claim, however, that in these experiments the morphine state suppressed fluid consumption by acting as an occasion setter rather than as a simple Pavlovian CS. First, explicit pairings of morphine with LiCl without a flavor did not endow the morphine state with the ability to suppress water consumption when the rats were later presented with water while in the morphine state. Thus, the simple CR produced by morphine-illness associations apparently does not include suppression of water consumption. Second, after FP drug discrimination training like that just described, the morphine feature failed to block simple conditioning of an aversion to a novel flavor when morphine was interposed between that flavor and LiCl administration (see also Lett, 1983). In contrast, after simple morphine-LiCl pairings, interposed morphine did block acquisition of an aversion to the new flavor. Thus, the drug discrimination procedure generated more control over fluid consumption than simple morphine-LiCl pairings but less ability to block fluid consumption, implying that the suppression of fluid consumption in the former procedure was due more to morphine's role as an occasion setter than to its simple association with illness.

Nevertheless, the results of transfer tests in experiments like these initially suggested that occasion setting in drug discrimination tasks might be very different from that found in other conditioning preparations. Although much evidence from studies with auditory or visual features and food or shock USs suggested that the transfer of occasion setting is limited to targets with specific kinds of training histories, transfer seemed to be much broader within the discriminated flavor aversion preparation. Indeed, Martin et al. (1990) showed that rats trained on a drug discrimination procedure in which morphine modulated a saccharine–illness association also suppressed their consumption of plain tap water while they were in the drug-induced state. Thus, transfer occurred even to a previously untrained target stimulus. Note, too, that in that same experiment, simple pairings of morphine with illness did not endow the morphine state with the ability to suppress consumption of tap water (described earlier), so it is unlikely that the transfer of morphine's suppressive powers after FP drug discrimination training was the consequence of simple morphine–illness associations.

Recent data from conditioning preparations like these suggest that the extensive transfer observed by Martin et al. (1990) at least in part reflects the features' modulation of the consummatory response or the response–illness relation rather than the flavor–illness relation. An initial, unpublished experiment (Skinner & van der Kooy, 1994) demonstrated substantial transfer to a novel flavor after FP drug discrimination training. In a discrimination group, on reinforced trials, morphine was injected before the availability of a saccharine solution, which was then followed by LiCl injection. On nonreinforced trials, saccharine was preceded by an injection of the (inactive) morphine vehicle and followed by a (nontoxic) saline injection. A Pavlovian control group received direct pairings of morphine and LiCl and separate unpaired presentations of saccharine.

After six discrimination cycles, rats in the discrimination group consumed reliably less after morphine injection (2 ml) than after vehicle injection (18 ml). Of most interest are the results of a transfer test, in which a novel flavor, vinegar, was administered after injection of either morphine or the vehicle alone in each group (Figure 5). The discrimination group showed transfer to the novel target, consuming significantly less vinegar in the drug state than in the nondrug state. The Pavlovian control group, given fluid in the drug state for the first time, did not show differential consumption but instead consumed equal amounts of vinegar in the presence and absence of the morphine drug state.

In a second experiment (Skinner et al., 1994, Experiment 1), the performance of rats trained on a drug discrimination was compared to that of rats trained on a discrimination that used external contextual cues. The drug discrimination task was similar to the one just described, with a morphine feature and a saccharine target. In the context discrimination

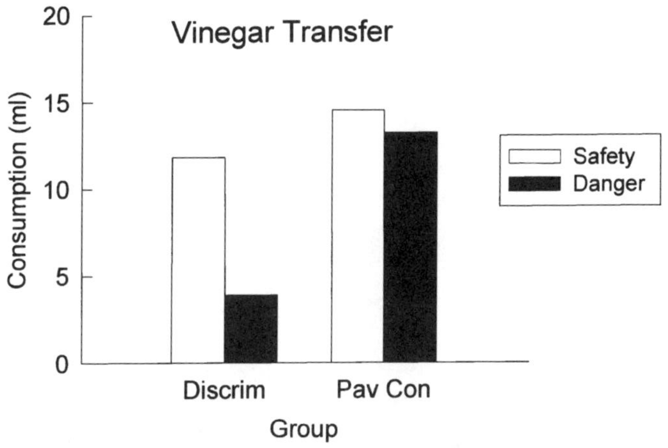

Figure 5

Consumption of a novel vinegar solution in an unpublished experiment (Skinner & van der Kooy, 1994). The rats in Group Discrim (discrimination) first received feature-positive training with a morphine feature, a saccharine target, and a lithium chloride reinforcer on reinforced trials, and a vehicle injection and saccharine alone on nonreinforced trials. Rats in Group Pav Con (Pavlovian Control) received direct pairings of morphine with lithium chloride, in the absence of saccharine. The bars labeled Safety show consumption of the vinegar after a vehicle injection, and those labeled Danger show vinegar consumption after morphine injection.

task, placement in distinctive boxes (which differed in odor, brightness, and floor construction) replaced morphine and vehicle injections as the danger and safety signals in both the discrimination and Pavlovian control groups.

Both the drug and context discrimination groups learned to suppress saccharine consumption on toxin trials relative to no-toxin saline trials. Of most interest are the data from a variety of transfer tests. Figure 6, Panel A, shows the results of a transfer test with a novel vinegar solution. The rats in both discrimination groups suppressed consumption of a novel vinegar solution in the presence of the appropriate danger signal relative to their consumption during the safety signal. In contrast, rats in the Pavlovian context control group showed high levels of consumption in both contexts, suggesting that contextual modulation of drinking in the context discrimination group was not because of direct context–illness

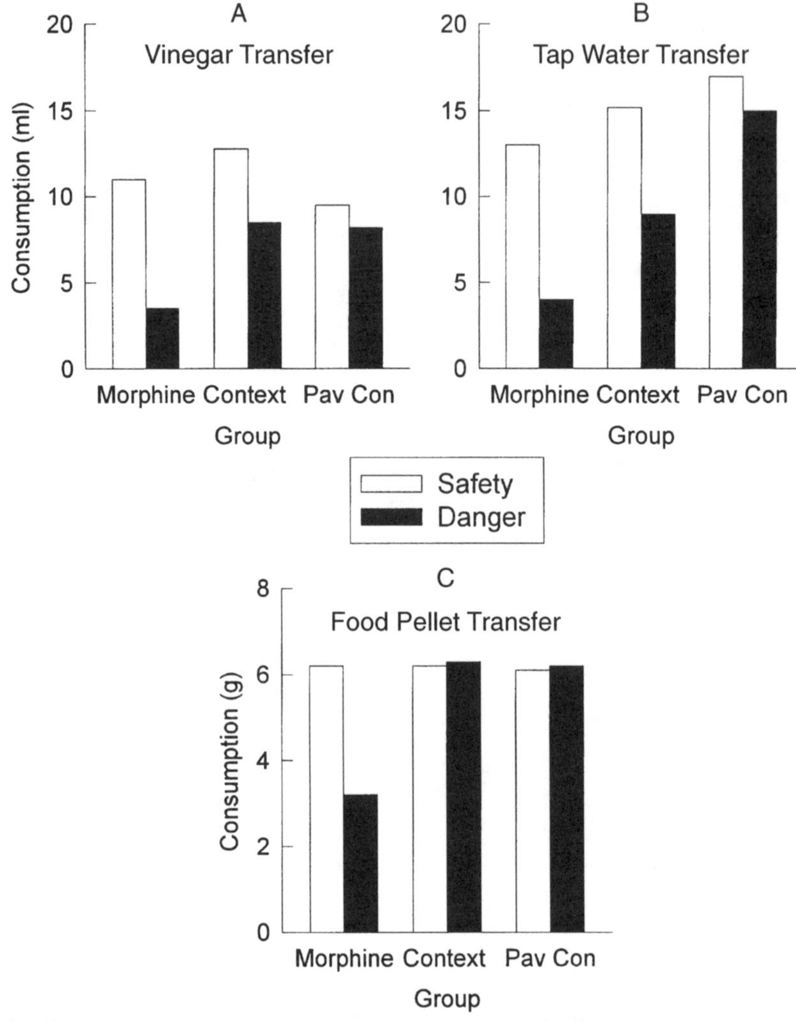

Figure 6

Results of transfer tests of rats in Experiment 1 of Skinner et al. (1994). The rats in Morphine and Context received saccharine–lithium chloride pairings after either morphine injection or being placed in a particular context (Danger) and saccharine-alone presentations after either a vehicle injection or placement in a second context (Safety). The rats in group Pav Con received direct context–lithium chloride pairings in the absence of saccharine. Panel A shows the results of a transfer test with vinegar, Panel B the transfer to tap water, and Panel C the transfer to food pellets.

associations. Furthermore, the results of a subsequent context preference test showed that those direct associations were at least as strong in the control rats as in the discrimination rats. In that test, the rats in the context discrimination group spent 71% of their time in the safety context, and the rats in the Pavlovian context control group spent 85% of their time in the safety context.

Figure 6, Panel B, shows the results of a transfer test with a familiar fluid (tap water). As in the novel fluid (vinegar) test, both the drug and context discrimination groups showed substantial suppression of fluid consumption during their danger signal relative to their safety signal, and the Pavlovian context control group showed no such differential consumption. Finally, Figure 6, Panel C, shows the results of a transfer test with a familiar solid food (standard lab chow). In contrast to the results of the fluid transfer tests, in this test only the drug discrimination group showed any evidence of differential consumption. Thus, although the occasion-setting powers of morphine transferred broadly to both novel and familiar fluids as well as to a familiar solid food, the occasion-setting powers of context transferred only to other fluids and did not extend to the modulation of consumption of a solid food.

One reason for this specificity in the case of external contexts is that the contextual cues acquired the ability to modulate *drinking* or the drinking–illness relation rather than a flavor–illness association. In contrast, Skinner et al. (1994) suggested that morphine's broader transfer across a variety of consummatory responses may reflect a special relation between opiates and ingestive behavior: Considerable evidence assigns a role for endogenous opiates in the control of ingestive behavior (e.g., Gosnell & Majchzak, 1989; Sanger & McCarthy, 1981).

Recent unpublished experiments in our laboratory shed light on some of these issues of transfer. The first of these studies (Skinner, 1997) simply replaced morphine with a non-opiate drug, pentobarbital. If the broader transfer observed with morphine features reflects a special role for opiates in the control of ingestion, then other endogenous drug states should show more limited transfer, as observed with external contextual features

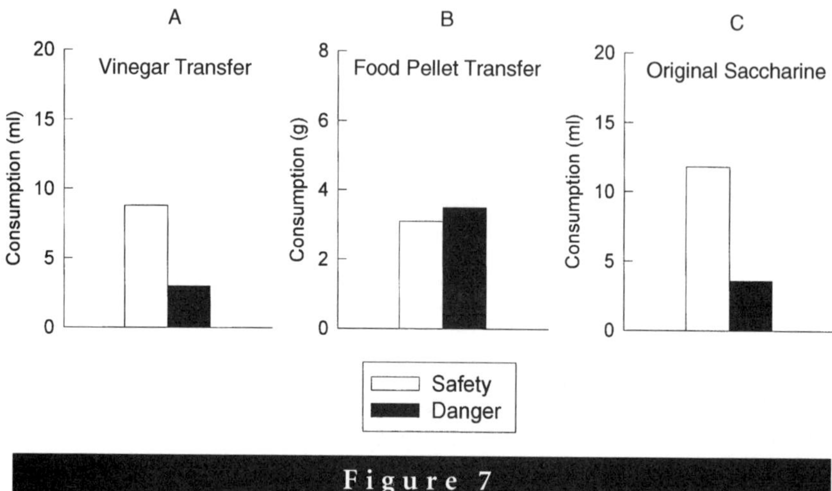

Figure 7

Results of transfer tests of rats in an unpublished experiment (Skinner, 1997). The rats had received feature-positive discrimination training in which, after pentobarbital injection, saccharine was paired with lithium chloride, but after saline injection, saccharine was presented alone. Panel A shows the results of a transfer test with vinegar, Panel B the transfer to food pellets, and Panel C the consumption with the original saccharine target. The bars labeled Safety show consumption on trials preceded by saline injection, and the bars labeled Danger show consumption on trials preceded by pentobarbital.

in the Skinner et al. (1994) study. Thus, with pentobarbital features, transfer should occur only to targets that share a consummatory response with the original target.

A pentobarbital-induced drug state was used to modulate a flavor aversion based on saccharine–LiCl pairings, as described earlier for morphine discriminations. With the drug injection serving as the danger signal and saline injection as the safety signal, rats showed differential consumption of the saccharine target. Furthermore, in subsequent transfer tests, the rats showed transfer to another, novel fluid (vinegar, Figure 7, Panel A), but not to solid food (45 mg standard food pellets, Figure 7, Panel B). For comparison, Figure 7, Panel C shows the results of a final test of performance on the initial saccharine discrimination that was administered after the transfer tests.

Thus, as with external context cues, arrangement of serial FP discrimination contingencies might be described as endowing pentobarbital features with the ability to modulate the drinking response or, more specifically, to set the occasion for not drinking. Of course, at this point it is not possible to distinguish modulation of consummatory responding from modulation of some stimulus property common to a variety of fluids. Nevertheless, these results suggest that the exceptionally broad transfer of morphine's ability to modulate consummatory responding in the Skinner et al. (1994) study reflects a special role for opiates in the control of ingestion rather than a general characteristic of endogenous drug cues.

Response specificity, rather than stimulus specificity, of occasion setting in flavor-aversion learning might not be surprising if one considers that, in this task, the rats must generate a response to gain access to the target cue. Thus, both stimulus and response are important attributes of the target event; either or both could serve as targets of the feature's modulation. Indeed, there is ample precedent for modulation of responses by features in operant occasion-setting experiments. For example, Holland (1995) trained rats with two operant serial FP discriminations, each demanding a unique response (R1 or R2) to obtain food, F1→T1R1+, T1–; F2→T2R2+, T2–. Thus, as suggested for flavor aversion modulation tasks, both stimulus and response properties of the target events were salient. A third target cue was first trained and then extinguished by itself. For some rats, the response required during that stimulus was identical to the response required in one of the discriminations (T3R2+), and for other rats it was a unique response (T3R3+). In transfer tests, the features showed transfer to targets that included either stimulus or response aspects that had been trained as targets of occasion setters in the two FP discriminations. Most relevant here is that feature F1's occasion setting transferred to T3 only if that cue had been trained with R2, a response that had previously been trained within an occasion-setting task. Other comparisons showed that transfer was best if both the stimulus and response had been trained within occasion-setting tasks. Comparable transfer data after operant serial FN discrimination training were described by Holland and Coldwell (1993). Note, too, that assigning importance to response properties of target cues is consistent with the large body of data collected by

Colwill and Rescorla (e.g., Colwill, 1993; Colwill & Rescorla, 1986; Rescorla, 1992), which shows the critical importance of response–reinforcer associations in operant conditioning and the modulation of those associations by discriminative stimuli.

The modulatory action of internal and external contextual cues on consummatory responding might also provide a simple account for an otherwise anomalous finding of Skinner et al. (1994). In that experiment, rats were trained with external contextual (box) cues that modulated an aversion to a saccharine solution. As in previous experiments in that series, contextual occasion-setting transferred to another, novel fluid, but not to a solid food. After this training, Skinner et al. attempted to eliminate direct context–illness associations by extinguishing the contexts: The rats were alternately placed in the danger or safety contexts with a bottle of tap water until water consumption was equivalent in both contexts. Skinner et al. found that this extinction procedure abolished the contexts' ability to modulate consumption of saccharine (Figure 8, top panel). Interestingly, simple context–illness associations were apparently little affected by this extinction procedure: in a context preference test, the rats still spent more time in the previous safety context than the danger context (Figure 8, bottom panel). Thus, the results of this feature–extinction procedure were precisely the opposite of what has been found in most occasion-setting experiments: the feature's occasion-setting powers were eliminated but not its simple associations.

On the other hand, if contextual cues modulated *drinking* rather than, for example, the palatability of saccharine, these results are less bothersome. From this perspective, the Skinner et al. (1994) extinction procedure involved not feature-alone presentations but extinction of the feature in the presence of an appropriate target event (the drinking response). Rescorla (1986) has shown in pigeon autoshaping that, although a feature's occasion-setting powers are not disrupted by feature-alone presentations, they are severely impaired if the feature is extinguished in the presence of an appropriate target. Thus, the expression of tap water drinking during the context extinction procedure would be expected to permit the extinction of the context's ability to modulate drinking.

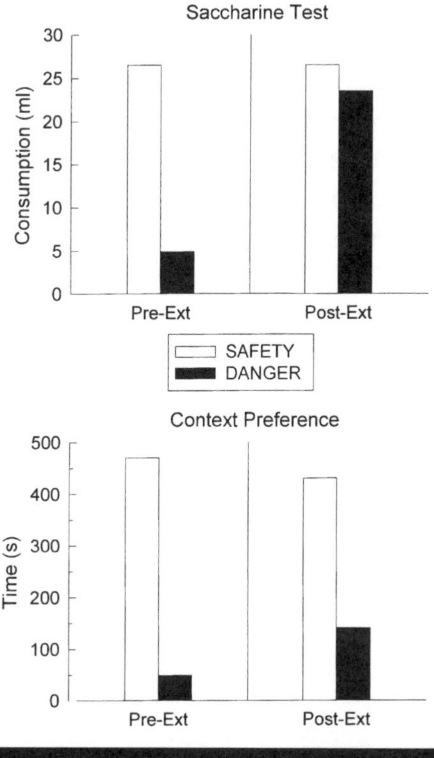

Figure 8

Results of consumption (top panel) and context preference (bottom panel) tests in an experiment by Skinner et al. (1994). The rats first received feature-positive discrimination training with a context feature, saccharine target, and then lithium chloride reinforcer on Danger trials and a second context and saccharine alone on Safety trials. The left bars show responding at the end of training, and the right bars show responding after extended training in which rats drank tap water in both contexts in the absence of lithium chloride.

Summary

Contexts and drug states displayed some properties of more traditional occasion setters, but not others. For example, as in more traditional preparations, the consequences of simple feature–illness associations and occasion-setting relations were distinguishable in terms of response form: Although simple context–illness associations resulted in an aversion to that context, only the occasion-setting relations established control over consummatory responding. In contrast, at least on the surface, both transfer and extinction effects were very different with context and drug features than is typical of other occasion-setting preparations. First, transfer was very broad; even consumption of novel foodstuffs was modulated by these features; second, simple extinction procedures eliminated a context's modulatory power but not a direct aversion to that context, the opposite pattern of data found in more traditional preparations. On the other hand, at least with context and pentobarbital features, these data can be subsumed under existing views of occasion setting if it is assumed that these features come to modulate the consummatory response–illness relation. More investigation is needed to determine whether morphine's across-the-board modulation of consumption reflects broader occasion setting or a direct effect of the drug on consumption. Similarly, it is not known whether the atypical transfer and extinction data obtained in these studies are more determined by the nature of the features themselves or by the system (flavor aversion/consumption) being modulated by those features.

THE USE OF NONTRADITIONAL FEATURES AS A RESEARCH TOOL

A novel conditioning paradigm may be important not only because it extends knowledge in a particular domain, but also because it provides a useful tool for studying other important issues in conditioning and behavior. For example, studies in second-order conditioning showed that an association may be learned not only between a CS and a US, but also between two CSs. Although this knowledge is certainly significant in its own right, Rescorla (1980) noted that an equally important and possibly more lasting legacy was that second-order conditioning would be useful for investigating other important issues in conditioning and behavior. For example, second-order conditioning enabled systematic study of how similarity influenced associative formation (Rescorla and Furrow, 1977), an issue that could not easily be addressed using CSs and USs that are usually quite dissimilar.

Occasion-setting with nontraditional feature cues may also be useful for investigating important issues in conditioning and behavior. Konorski and Lawicka (1959) and Terry and Wagner (1975) described the use of reinforcers as features in occasion setting–like tasks as providing a particularly effective test of various short-term memory phenomena. For example, Holland and Forbes (1982) used sucrose as a feature cue signaling that a tone would (in positive occasion setting) or would not (in negative occasion setting) be followed by food. Subjects learned both discriminations, but of most interest was Holland and Forbes's demonstration that a visual cue previously paired with sucrose could substitute for sucrose as a conditional cue; thus, occasion setting with a reinforcer feature allowed them to conveniently show that retrieval-generated event representations could substitute for the events themselves (see also Holland, 1990). In subsequent test sessions, Holland and Forbes (1982) also showed that when a flavored feature cue was surprising (because it was preceded by a CS that previously signaled the absence of that flavor), subjects showed significantly better discriminative performance than when the feature was expected, because it was preceded by a previously trained signal for that flavor. Here again, occasion setting with a reinforcer feature showed that expected events may be less well processed than surprising events (see also Brandon & Wagner, chapter 12, this volume; Terry & Wagner, 1975; Wagner, 1981).

Similarly, occasion-setting procedures may provide particularly sensitive measures for characteristics of various nontraditional cues that can be used as features. Skinner and Martin (1992) gave rats positive occasion-setting training in which, on danger days, an injection of 4.0 mg/kg morphine served as a feature cue signaling that a saccharine solution would be followed by illness; on safety days, an injection of saline signaled that saccharine would be followed by more saline. The rats showed rapid discrimination learning: they significantly reduced saccharine consumption on danger days relative to safety days. Of most interest, however, Skinner and Martin showed reliable discriminative performance when the dosage of morphine was systematically reduced to dosages as low as 0.5 mg/kg. Similar results were shown when 1.0 mg/kg morphine was used as the original feature cue, although initial discrimination learning was more protracted. Thus, the occasion-setting paradigm used by Skinner and Martin was useful for measuring an organism's sensitivity to a drug discriminative cue. Notably, this procedure resulted in more rapid acquisition of discriminative performance than other drug cuing paradigms (e.g., see Overton & Batta, 1979), making it especially attractive for investigating drug effects. A similar design has also been used to test for the action of drug antagonists (e.g., see Martin, Bechara, & van der Kooy, 1991; Martin, Gans, & van der Kooy, 1990). In addition, the interval between the feature and target cue, over which discriminative performance can be maintained, may be useful for measuring the decay of drug effects.

The use of various nontraditional events as features in investigations of occasion setting also may suggest the importance of variables that may be important in occasion setting in general. For example, in a previous section, on the basis of data from contextual modulation of saccharine consumption, we suggested that the role of simultaneously present responses might influence the content of learning. It is also worth noting, however, that practical concerns in the design of experiments with many kinds of nontraditional features lead to use of procedures that might uncover important effects of contingencies that otherwise would be ignored.

For example, most studies of positive occasion setting simply intermix reinforced feature–target trials with nonreinforced target-alone trials. When drugs are used as features, however, it is important to precede both reinforced and nonreinforced trials with some sort of injection to show that discriminative performance does not result simply from the injection procedure rather than the drug state. This procedural variation on FP and FN discriminations (F1→T1+, F2→T1−) naturally raises a question regarding how much of the discrimination performance results from the presence of an explicit safety cue on nonreinforced trials; this question has led to extensive investigation (e.g., Skinner et al., 1995). Only recently has the study of such "ambiguous target" discriminations begun with more traditional procedures (e.g., Bueno & Moreira, in press; Bueno & Holland, 1997). Interestingly, some evidence (Alvarado & Rudy, 1995) suggests that signaling both reinforced and nonreinforced target trials may change the character of what is learned, as compared to simple FP or FN procedures.

Similarly, the use of potent drugs as features largely demands that only one trial be presented in each daily session, whereas more typical occasion-setting studies involve intermixing all trial types within each session. Recent studies by Alvarado and Rudy (1995, Experiment 2) suggest that the apportionment of trial types to sessions can have a substantial influence on the way in which some discrimination tasks are learned. In their studies, rats received training on negative patterning discriminations (A+, B+, AB–). The results of transfer tests depended on whether all three trial types were presented in the same sessions or some sessions included only A+ and AB– trials and others only B+ and AB– trials. We have started similar investigations in our laboratory.

Finally, it is worth noting that features like drug states, foods, and contexts are long lasting, overlap the target cues and reinforcers, and often produce their own perseverating behavioral consequences. Most investigations of occasion setting have largely ignored the extent to which behavioral aspects of the elements involved may be important parts of the content of learning.

CONCLUSION

The use of a variety of conditioning preparations and a range of stimuli within those preparations may encourage broader perspectives on conditioning, including occasion setting and other modulatory processes. The defining characteristics of occasion setting proposed by Holland (1983, 1992), although useful for guiding early research, may be more task-specific than originally thought. The notion of modulation is widely applicable, as the variety of topics in this book attests. It is probably unrealistic, however, to expect many of these applications to be consistent with the details found in one or two popular conditioning preparations. For example, motivational states have commonly been described as exerting modulatory influence on learned associations (e.g., Davidson, 1993, chapter 8, this volume; Holland, 1983, 1991). But the duration and intensity of these states, as well as their typical targets (consummatory responding), are probably more akin to some of the nontraditional features described in this chapter than to the discrete auditory or visual events that are more typically investigated. It is important to recognize a range of phenomena that is potentially a part of the occasion-setting realm, as well as any relation to simple conditioning those phenomena might have.

REFERENCES

Alvarado, M. C., & Rudy, J. W. (1995). A comparison of "configural" discrimination problems: Implications for understanding the role of the hippocampal formation in learning and memory. *Psychobiology, 23,* 178–184.

Bottjer, S. W., & Hearst, E. (1979). Food delivery as a conditional stimulus: Feature-learning and memory in pigeons. *Journal of the Experimental Analysis of Behavior, 31,* 189–207.

Bueno, J. L. O., & Holland, P. C. (1997). *Occasion setting in ambiguous target tasks.* Manuscript submitted for publication.

Bueno, J. L. O., & Moreira, R. C. M. (in press). Conditional discrimination: The role of CS-alone trials. *Behaviourial Processes.*

Burdick, C. K., & James, J. P. (1973). Effects of a backward conditioning procedure following acquisition on extinction of conditioned suppression. *Animal Learning & Behavior, 1,* 137–139.

Colwill, R. M. (1993). An associative analysis of instrumental learning. *Current Directions in Psychological Science, 2,* 111–116.

Colwill, R. M., & Rescorla, R. A. (1986). Associative structures in instrumental learning. In G. H. Bower (Ed.), *The psychology of learning and motivation* (Vol. 20, pp. 55–104). San Diego, CA: Academic Press.

Davidson, T. L. (1993). The nature and function of interoceptive signals for food: Toward an integration of physiological and learning perspectives. *Psychological Review, 100,* 640–657.

Garcia, J. (1986). *Food for Tolman: Cognition and cathexis in context.* Paper presented at the celebration of the centennial of Edward C. Tolman's birth, University of California, Berkeley.

Goddard, M. J. (1995). Acquisition of US–no US associations in Pavlovian conditioning. *Learning and Motivation, 26,* 264–277.

Goddard, M. J., & Holland, P. C. (1996). Type of feature affects transfer in operant serial feature-positive discriminations. *Animal Learning & Behavior, 24,* 266–276.

Goddard, M. J., & Holland, P. C. (1997). The effects of feature identity in operant serial feature-negative discriminations. *Learning and Motivation, 28,* 577–608.

Gosnell, B. A., & Majchzak, M. J. (1989). Centrally administered opioid peptides stimulate saccharine intake in nondeprived rats. *Pharmacology, Biochemistry, and Behavior, 33,* 805–810.

Hearst, E. (1978). Stimulus relationships and feature selection in learning and behavior. In S. Hulse, H. Fowler, & W.K. Honig (Eds.), *Cognitive processes in animal behavior* (pp. 51–88). Hillsdale, NJ : Erlbaum.

Hearst, E. (1984). Absence as information: Some implications for learning, performance, and representational processes. In H. L. Roitblat, T. G. Bever, & H. S. Terrace (Eds.), *Animal cognition* (pp. 311–332). Hillsdale, NJ : Erlbaum.

Hearst, E., & Wolff, W. T. (1989). Addition versus deletion as a signal. *Animal Learning & Behavior, 17,* 120–133.

Holland, P. C. (1983). Occasion-setting in Pavlovian feature positive discriminations. In M. L. Commons, R. J. Herrnstein, & A. R. Wagner (Eds.), *Quantitative analyses of behavior: Discrimination processes* (Vol. 4, pp. 183–206). New York: Ballinger.

Holland, P. C. (1986). Transfer after serial feature positive discrimination training. *Learning and Motivation, 17,* 243–268.

Holland, P. C. (1989a). Transfer of negative occasion-setting and conditioned inhibition across conditioned and unconditioned stimuli. *Journal of Experimental Psychology: Animal Behavior Processes, 15,* 311–328.

Holland, P. C. (1989b). Occasion setting with simultaneous compounds in rats. *Journal of Experimental Psychology: Animal Behavior Processes, 15,* 183–193.

Holland, P. C. (1990). Event representation in Pavlovian conditioning: Image and action. *Cognition, 37,* 105–131.

Holland, P. C. (1991). Learning, thirst, and drinking. In D. J. Ramsey and D. Booth (Eds.), *Thirst: Physiological and psychological aspects* (pp. 279–295). New York: Springer-Verlag.

Holland, P. C. (1992). Occasion setting in Pavlovian conditioning. In D. Medin (Ed.), *The psychology of learning and motivation* (Vol. 28, pp. 69–125). San Diego: Academic Press.

Holland, P. C. (1995). Transfer of occasion setting across stimulus and response in operant feature positive discriminations. *Learning and Motivation, 26,* 239–263.

Holland, P. C., & Coldwell, S. E. (1993). Transfer of inhibitory stimulus control in operant feature negative discriminations. *Learning and Motivation, 24,* 345–375.

Holland, P. C., & Forbes, D. T. (1982). Control of conditional discrimination performance by CS-evoked event representations. *Animal Learning & Behavior, 10,* 249–256.

Holland, P. C., & Haas, M. L. (1993). The effects of target salience in operant feature positive discriminations. *Learning and Motivation, 24,* 119–140.

Holland, P. C., & Ross, R. T. (1981). Within-compound associations in serial compound conditioning. *Journal of Experimental Psychology: Animal Behavior Processes, 7,* 228–241.

Honey, R. C., & Hall, G. (1989). The acquired equivalence and distinctiveness of cues. *Journal of Experimental Psychology: Animal Behavior Processes, 15,* 338–346.

Jarrard, L. E., & Davidson, T. L. (1991). On the hippocampus and learned conditioned responding: Effects of aspiration versus ibotenate lesions. *Hippocampus, 1,* 107–117.

Jenkins, H. M., & Sainsbury, R. S. (1969). The development of stimulus control through differential reinforcement. In N. J. Mackintosh & W. K. Honig (Eds.), *Fundamental issues in associative learning* (pp. 123–161). Halifax, Nova Scotia: Dalhousie University Press.

Konorski, J., & Lawicka, W. (1959). Physiological mechanism of delayed reactions. I. The analysis and classification of delayed reactions. *Acta Biologiae Experimentalis, 19,* 175–197.

Lett, B. T. (1983). Pavlovian drug-sickness pairings result in the conditioning of an antisickness response. *Behavioral Neuroscience, 97,* 779–784.

Martin, G. M., Bechara, A., & van der Kooy, D. (1991). The perception of emotion: Parallel neural processing of the affective and discriminative properties of opiates. *Psychobiology, 19,* 147–152.

Martin, G. M., Gans, M., & van der Kooy, D. (1990). Discriminative properties of morphine that modulate associations between tastes and lithium chloride. *Journal of Experimental Psychology: Animal Behavior Processes, 16,* 56–68.

Overton, D. A., & Batta, S. K. (1979). Investigation of narcotics and antitussives using drug discrimination techniques. *Journal of Pharmacology and Experimental Therapeutics, 211,* 401–408.

Reberg, D., & Memmott, J. (1979). Shock as a signal for shock or no-shock: A feature-negative effect in conditioned suppression. *Journal of the Experimental Analysis of Behavior, 32,* 387–397.

Rescorla, R. A. (1980). *Pavlovian second-order conditioning: Studies in associative learning.* Hillsdale, NJ: Erlbaum.

Rescorla, R. A. (1985). Conditioned inhibition and facilitation. In R. R. Miller & N. E. Spear (Eds.), *Information processing in animals: Conditioned inhibition* (pp. 299–326). Hillsdale, NJ : Erlbaum.

Rescorla, R. A. (1986). Extinction of facilitation. *Journal of Experimental Psychology: Animal Behavior Processes, 12,* 16–24.

Rescorla, R. A. (1992). Hierarchical associative relations in Pavlovian conditioning and instrumental training. *Current Directions in Psychological Science, 1,* 66–70.

Rescorla, R. A., & Furrow, D. R. (1977). Stimulus similarity as a determinant of Pavlovian conditioning. *Journal of Experimental Psychology: Animal Behavior Processes, 3,* 203–215.

Rescorla, R. A., & Solomon, R. L. (1967). Two process learning theory: Relationships between classical conditioning and instrumental learning. *Psychological Review, 74,* 151–182.

Sanger, D. J., & McCarthy, P. S. (1981) Increased food and water intake produced in rats by opiate receptor antagonists. *Psychopharmacology, 74,* 217–220.

Schmajuk, N. A., Lamoureux, J. A., & Holland, P. C. (1998). Occasion setting: A neural network approach. *Psychological Review, 105,* 3–32.

Skinner, D. M. (1997). [Modulation of taste aversions by pentobarbital]. Unpublished raw data.

Skinner, D. M., & Holland, P. C. (1997). [Acquisition and transfer of feature-positive and feature-negative discriminations with Kool-Aid features]. Unpublished raw data.

Skinner, D. M., & Martin, G. M. (1992). Conditioned taste aversions support drug discrimination learning at low dosages of morphine. *Behavioral and Neural Biology, 58,* 236–241.

Skinner, D. M., Martin, G. M., Howe, R. D., Pridgar, A., & van der Kooy, D. (1995). Drug discrimination learning using a taste aversion paradigm: An assessment of the role of safety cues. *Learning and Motivation, 26,* 343–369.

Skinner, D. M., Martin, G. M., Pridgar, A., & van der Kooy, D. (1994). Conditional control of fluid consumption in an occasion setting paradigm is independent of Pavlovian associations. *Learning and Motivation, 25,* 368–400.

Skinner, D. M., & van der Kooy, D. (1994). [Modulation of taste aversions by morphine]. Unpublished raw data.

Solomon, R. L. (1977). An opponent-process theory of motivation: V. Affective dynamics of eating. In L. M. Barker, M. R. Best, & M. Domjan (Eds.), *Learning mechanisms in food selection* (pp. 255–269). Waco, TX: Baylor University Press.

Swartzentruber, D. (1995). Modulatory mechanisms in Pavlovian conditioning. *Animal Learning & Behavior, 23,* 123–143.

Terry, W. S., & Wagner, A. R. (1975). Short-term memory for "surprising" vs. "expected" unconditioned stimuli in Pavlovian conditioning. *Journal of Experimental Psychology: Animal Behavior Processes, 1,* 122–133.

Wagner, A. R. (1981). SOP: A model of automatic memory processing in animal behavior. In N. E. Spear & R. R. Miller (Eds.), *Information processing in animals: Memory mechanisms* (pp. 5–47). Hillsdale, NJ: Erlbaum.

PART II

Conditional Discriminations

5

Pavlovian Feature-Ambiguous Discrimination

Sadahiko Nakajima

Pavlovian hierarchical event learning has been frequently studied with serial feature-positive (FP) and feature-negative (FN) discrimination tasks (see Holland, 1992; Swartzentruber, 1995, for reviews). In the serial FP task (X→A+, A–), an unconditioned stimulus (US) follows a target stimulus (A) only when A is preceded by a feature stimulus (X). On the other hand, in the serial FN task (X→A–, A+), the US follows A only when A is presented alone. In these tasks, one stimulus (X) modulates or sets the occasion for responding to another stimulus (A), and thus X facilitates responding to A in the FP task and inhibits such responding in the FN task.

Holland (1983, 1985) proposed that learning under these event contingencies is indeed hierarchical: Animals learn hierarchical event relationships to solve the FP and FN tasks. According to Holland, conditioned responses (CRs) to a conditioned stimulus (CS) can be controlled by another stimulus, called an *occasion setter,* which acts on specific CS–US

Preparation of the manuscript was supported by the Japanese Society for Promotion of Science: Postdoctoral Fellowship for Research Abroad. I thank Robert A. Rescorla for his support for my recent study conducted in his laboratory, and Matthew Lattal for improving the manuscript's English.

associations. Thus, X sets a positive occasion for an A–US association in the FP task and a negative occasion for it in the FN task. Rescorla (1979, 1985), however, claimed that X lowers the activation threshold of the US representation for A to elicit strong CRs in the FP task, and that it raises the threshold for A to elicit weak CRs in the FN task. The learning is hierarchical in the sense that a stimulus modulates responding that comes from learning an association of another stimulus and a US. Thus, both of these early hypotheses claimed hierarchical event learning in Pavlovian conditioning, but they differed in their underlying mechanisms.

FEATURE-AMBIGUOUS DISCRIMINATION TASK

Pavlovian serial FP and FN tasks can be combined into a single task with one feature stimulus (X) and two target stimuli (A and B). The combined task (X→A+, A–, X→B–, B+), a serial feature-ambiguous (FA) discrimination,[1] is theoretically intriguing. Mastery of this task troubles the US-threshold-changing hypothesis proposed by Rescorla (1979, 1985), because X cannot both lower and raise the threshold of US representation at the same time. The specific occasion-setting hypothesis of Holland (1983, 1985), however, allows for mastery of this task by assuming that X acts positively on the A–US association and negatively on the B–US association.

Temporal Factors in Feature-Ambiguous Discriminations

My first experiment (Nakajima, 1992) on FA discrimination had two purposes: the first was to examine whether animals can learn this task. As described earlier, Rescorla's hypothesis does not allow for mastery of the FA task. The second purpose was to investigate the temporal relationship

[1] Although I have used the term *bidirectional occasion-setting task* for this task (Nakajima, 1994a), this name makes assumptions about the underlying mechanism. In order to avoid such assumptions, the more theoretically neutral name *feature-ambiguous (FA) discrimination* is used hereinafter. This task has also been called *ambiguous discrimination* (Holland, 1991; Holland & Reeve, 1991) or *ambiguous cue training* (Rescorla, 1993), but these names are confusing with an "ambiguous-cue task" (A–/B+, B–/C+) where animals have to choose or avoid the same stimulus (B) when it is presented with different stimuli (A and C; e.g., Hall, 1980).

of feature and target stimuli in compound trials. My original intention of this manipulation was simply empirical: Under what temporal conditions do animals learn FA discrimination? Theoretical implications of manipulations of the feature–target interval will be discussed later.

Six homing pigeons were used as subjects, and the feature stimulus (X) was an intermittent tone. Target stimuli (A and B) were red and green lights projected on a key. Pecks to the key were recorded as CRs. The duration of both feature and target stimuli was 5 sec. A food US was followed for 5 sec after XA compound or B-alone trials, but not after A-alone or XB compound trials. Three temporal relationships between feature and target stimuli were arranged on compound trials. Feature and target stimuli were presented simultaneously (SIM), the feature was immediately followed by the target (SER), or the feature was followed by a 5-sec temporal gap and then by the target (GAP). Each condition continued for 60 days. The order of these three temporal conditions was different among birds. The discrimination performance was indexed by dividing pecks to target keylights on reinforced trials by total pecks to the targets for each FP (X-A compound versus A-alone) and FN (X-B compound versus B-alone) subtask. Random responding would yield a value of 1.0, and complete discrimination would yield a value of 1.0. The final individual performances averaged over the last three days of each condition are shown in Figure 1. All birds learned the FA task under the SER condition. Some birds also showed mastery of the task under the SIM and GAP conditions, but it was worse than that under the SER condition in almost all cases. This experiment revealed two points: First, animals can learn an FA discrimination. This is inconsistent with the US-threshold–changing hypothesis that predicted poor performance in this task. Rescorla (1993) also demonstrated acquisition of an FA discrimination in autoshaping with pigeons (see also Bottjer & Hearst, 1979, Experiment 3), and Holland (1991) and Holland and Reeve (1991) published mastery of the task in instrumental conditional lever-press learning with rats. All of these results indicate that a mechanism other than a change in the US threshold is operating here. Second, performance was better when the feature was immediately followed by the target on compound trials than when they

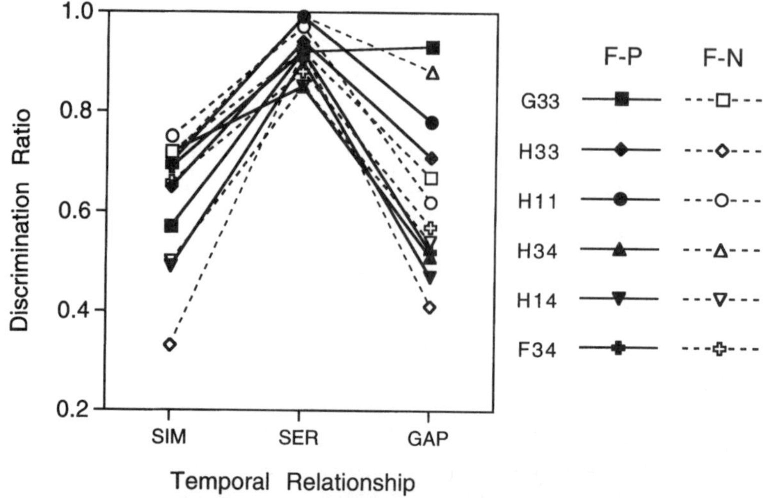

Figure 1

Discrimination performance of each pigeon averaged over the last three sessions of each temporal condition. FP = feature-positive discrimination subtask; FN = feature-negative discrimination subtask. SIM = simultaneous presentation of feature and target stimuli on compound trials; SER = serial presentation of these stimuli with no gap; GAP = serial presentation with a 5-sec gap between the stimuli. The figure was drawn from the data of Nakajima (1992).

were presented simultaneously or when a 5-sec temporal gap was inserted between them. A theoretical implication of these results will be discussed later.

Configural Account

A configural learning account treats each stimulus compound as a unitary stimulus (cf. Kehoe & Gormezano, 1980; Pearce, 1987). Thus, in the FA task of the experiment described earlier, stimuli XA and B signal reinforcement, and stimuli A and XB signal nonreinforcement. Instead of a hierarchical structure, this solution relies on simple CS–US and CS–no US associations. The finding that serial presentation of feature and target stimuli results in better discrimination performance than simultaneous presentation, however, is unfavorable to the configural account, because configuration seems more likely to occur in simultaneous stimulus compounds than in the serial ones (Hull, 1943). If there is a limitation in ability to process simultaneously presented stimuli (cf. Riley & Roitblat, 1978), however, animals might not fully process feature and target stimuli in the SIM condition. The serial presentation of these stimuli could reduce the processing load and make it easier for the birds to integrate the stimuli into a unitary configural stimulus. Furthermore, the AESOP theory of Pavlovian conditioning (Wagner & Brandon, 1989), revised to include a configuration factor, predicts that configuration is more likely in serial stimulus compounding than in simultaneous compounding (Brandon & Wagner, chapter 12, this volume).

Transfer Effects of Features and Targets

The underlying mechanisms of conditioned modulation have been assessed by using novel feature–target combinations. As described earlier, mastery of the FA task is possible either by occasion setting of specific CS–US linkages (Holland, 1983, 1985) or by learning specific feature–target configurations. Thus, these mechanisms do not allow a feature of an FA task to have a transfer effect on targets that have not been trained with that feature stimulus.

Contrary to this prediction of no transfer, studies of serial FA discriminations showed transfer of modulatory control by a feature over some kinds of targets. In an autoshaping preparation with pigeons, Rescorla (1993, Experiment 4) demonstrated that a feature of a serial FA task controlled CRs to targets of separately trained serial FP and FN tasks: an FA feature increased CRs to an FP target and decreased CRs to an FN target. In addition, he found that features of the FP and FN tasks controlled CRs to targets of the FA task: a feature of the FP task increased CRs to a target trained in an FP subtask of the FA task, and a feature of the FN task decreased CRs to a target trained in an FN subtask of the FA task.

The mutual transfer effects between a serial FA task and serial FP and FN tasks were also reported by Holland (1991) in an instrumental lever-press preparation with rats. He also demonstrated transfer between two concurrently trained serial FA tasks. Furthermore, Holland and Reeve

(1991) revealed that a feature of a serial FA task increased CRs to a separately reinforced and then extinguished stimulus. Transfer of modulation seems to have some specificity, however. A feature of a serial FA task did not affect CRs to a continuously reinforced stimulus (Holland & Reeve, 1991) or CRs to a partially reinforced stimulus (Holland, 1991). Holland also revealed that reversal training of targets of a serial FA task did not invert the effect of original features on those targets: Reinforcement of A and extinction of B after X→A+, A–, X→B–, B+ training did not make X decrease CRs to A or X increase CRs to B. Indeed, X still increased CRs to A and decreased CRs to B, despite the fact that A alone evoked more CRs than B alone.

These transfer results help to clarify the mechanism underlying this kind of conditioned modulation. As noted earlier, neither specific CS–US occasion setting nor specific feature–target configuration allows such transfers. Because a feature stimulus of an FA task controls CRs to targets trained in another FA task, to targets of FP and FN tasks, and to a reinforced and then extinguished target, one may assume that it works as an inverter for current patterns of responding to ambiguous targets: namely, increasing CRs to a CS with weak associative strength, but decreasing CRs to a CS with strong associative strength. The failure to invert patterns of responding to its own targets after reversal training does not conform to this hypothesis, however.

The multiple memory system proposed by Holland (1989) posits that targets trained in a conditional discrimination are stored in a separate memory system from that of simple conditioned stimuli. This can account for transfer between two FA tasks and mutual transfer between FA and FP or FN tasks, because targets of these tasks are in the same conditional memory system. This hypothesis may also explain the finding that target reversal training did not invert the direction of conditional control by the feature on the original targets, because their status in the conditional memory system did not change. This hypothesis cannot explain transfer with a reinforced and then extinguished target, however, because the target must have been stored in the simple memory system. Thus, these studies of modulatory transfer of serial FA discrimination challenged the theories of hierarchical event learning. In spite of the theoretical implications, few studies have examined modulatory transfer with an FA task. I briefly report here some of my transfer experiments on FA discrimination in autoshaping.

The first study used complex contingencies (Nakajima, 1994a). Five pigeons were trained with eight different kinds of trials in a given session (D:X→A+, D:A–, D:X→B–, D:B+, L:X→A–, L:A+, L:X→B+, and L:B–). In the darkened chamber (D), a keylight, A, was followed by food only when a tone preceded it, and another keylight, B, was followed by food only when it was presented alone. When the chamber was lit (L), the contingencies were reversed. Thus, this was a higher order occasion-setting task (cf. Arnold, Grahame, & Miller, 1991; Nakajima, 1994b). The tone feature, the keylight targets, and the food were each presented for 5 sec with no overlap and no between-stimuli gap. After mastery of the task, the targets' contingencies were reversed in the dark condition (D:A+, D:B–). This training, however, had little effect on CRs on the other kinds of trials in the postreversal test (Figure 2). Hence, as in Holland (1991), the feature did not invert patterns of responding to these targets.

Modulatory transfer has been explored with simpler contingencies (Nakajima, 1997). In the first experiment, 16 pigeons were trained with a serial FA task with pseudomodulator treatment (X→A+, A–, X→B–, B+; P→E±, E±), where X and P were a diffuse flashing light and a noise, each counterbalanced, and A, B, and E were different figures projected on the key. The diffuse features, X and Y, were 15 sec long, and the keylight targets were illuminated during the last 5 sec of the compound trials. After mastery of this task, the contingencies of the targets of the true modulator (X) were reversed (A+, B–), and modulatory effects of X and the pseudomodulator (P) were examined. As shown in Figure 3 (left panel), none of the features affected CRs to A or B. Thus, as in Holland (1991), the modulator of this Pavlovian FA task did not work as an inverter. Figure 3 (center panel) indicates the second test after A and B received re-reversal training (A–, B+). Only X had effects on CRs to these stimuli, suggesting that the failure of transfers in the first test is not attributable to forgetting modulation during target reversal training that preceded the test.

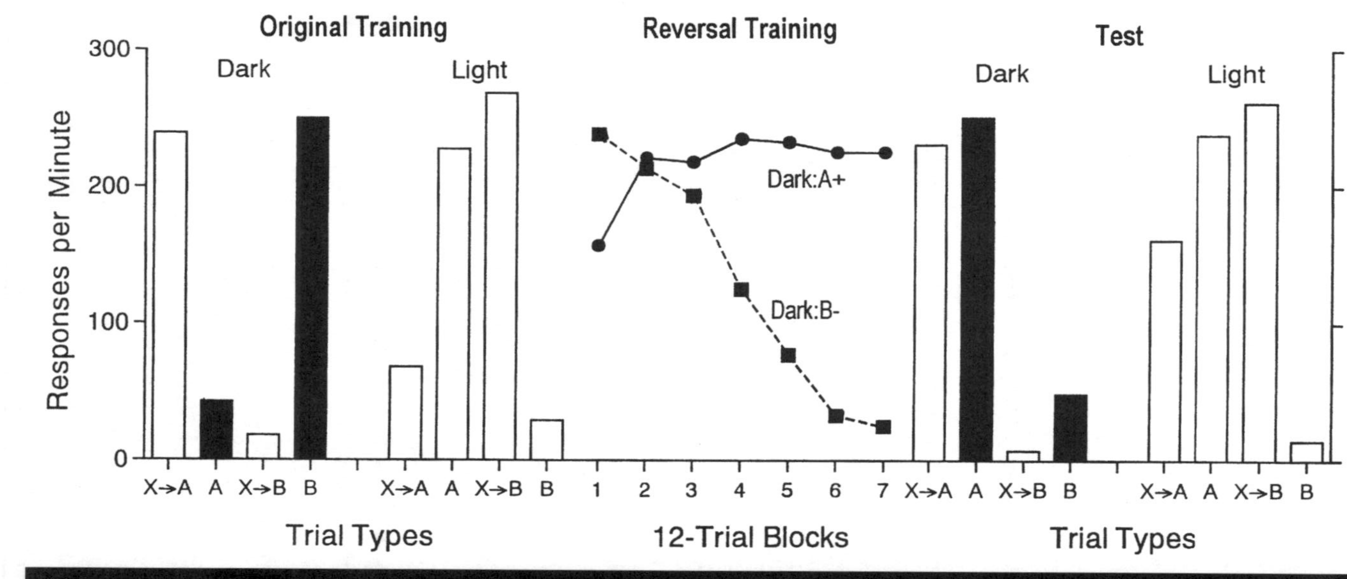

Figure 2

Mean rates of pecks to the targets averaged over the last three sessions of higher order feature-ambiguous discrimination training *(left)*, those during the targets' reversal *(center)*, and those of testing *(right)*. The figure was drawn by averaging the data for five individual pigeons (Nakajima, 1994a).

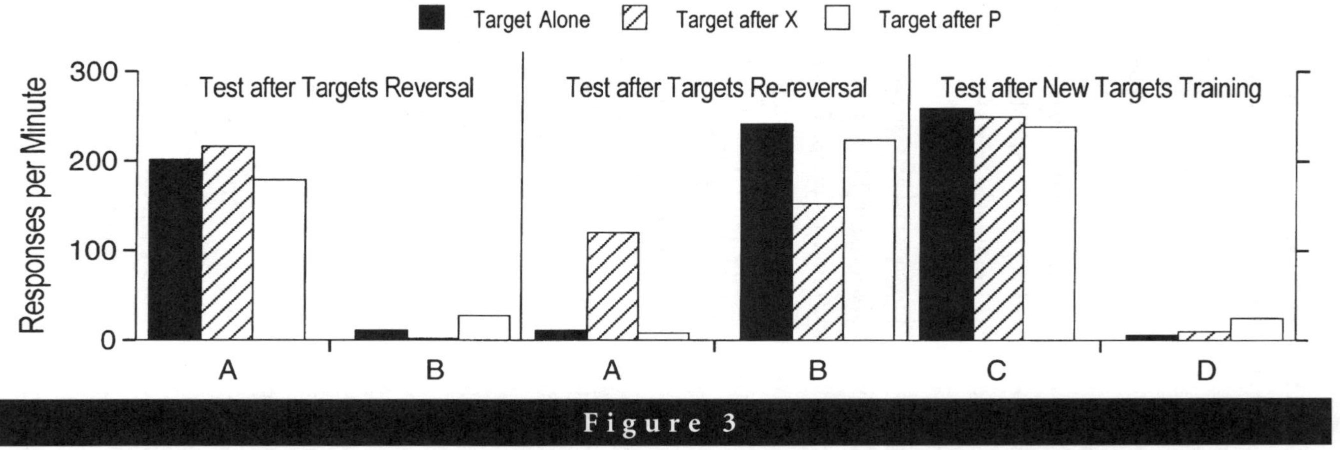

Figure 3

Mean rates of pecks to the targets after feature-ambiguous discrimination training and target reversal training *(left)*, after target re-reversal training *(center)*, and after new target training *(right)*.

After retraining with the original FA task, two different keylight figures of 5-sec duration (C and D) were trained as targets for the third test. First, both stimuli were reinforced (C+, D+), then one of them was extinguished while the other continued to be reinforced (C–, D+), and, finally, the contingency was reversed (C+, D–). Thus, these targets had histories of reinforcement and extinction, and one of them (C) was now evoking CRs but the other (D) was not. As mentioned earlier, Holland and Reeve (1991) demonstrated a transfer effect of a modulator on a reinforced and extinguished target—that is, the modulator increased CRs to it. Figure 3 (right panel) shows that the true modulator (X), as well as the pseudomodulator (P), had no effect on CRs to these targets, suggesting a more specific modulatory control than that observed in Holland and Reeve (1991).

The next experiment (Nakajima, in press, Experiment 2) explored modulatory transfer across two concurrently trained FA tasks. Fifteen birds received two serial FA tasks with pseudomodulator treatment (X→A+, A–, X→B–, B+; Y→C+, C–, Y→D–, D+; P→E+, E±), where X was a diffuse flashing light. For some birds Y was the noise used in the preceding experiment, and P was a tone. The identities of Y and P were reversed for the remaining birds. The targets (A, B, C, D, and E) were different keylight figures. Figure 4 (left panel) depicts CRs to A and B in a test. The auditory feature (Y), which had been used in another FA task, had no more modulatory control over these targets than did the pseudomodulator (P)—that is, there were no transfer effects across the two serial FA tasks. The second test was conducted after reversal training of A and B (A+, B–), and test results were similar to Test 1 of the preceding experiment: No feature stimuli had detectable control over the targets, as shown in Figure 4 (center panel). The results after re-reversal training of A and B (A–, B+), shown in Figure 4 (right panel), revealed that the original feature stimulus (X) maintained its control over these stimuli but that there was no transfer control by another modulator (Y). Therefore, as in the previous experiment, modulatory control by a feature of a serial FA task was very specific—the underlying mechanism could not involve inverting patterns of responding. Similar results were obtained in an experiment of the same design but without a pseudomodulation treatment

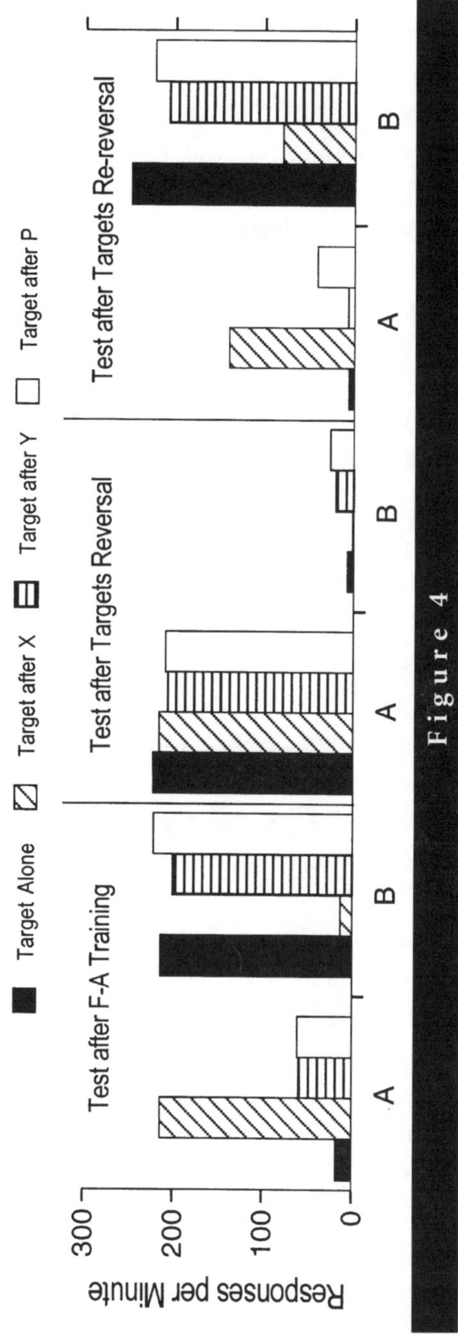

Figure 4

Mean rates of pecks to the targets after feature-ambiguous discrimination training *(left)*, after target reversal training *(center)*, and after target re-reversal training *(right)*.

(Nakajima, in press, Experiment 3). This experiment controlled for nonmodulatory factors by using a false feature that had merely been exposed to the birds before the discrimination training began.

Thus, experiments examining modulatory transfer in autoshaping clearly indicate specificity of control by a feature stimulus from a serial FA discrimination. On the other hand, Rescorla (1993, Experiment 4) demonstrated modulatory transfers between an FA task and an FP or FN task after concurrent training of these tasks (X→A+, A–, X→B–, B+; Y→C+, C–; Z→D–, D+). Rescorla's experiment did not control for nonmodulatory factors, however: there were no tests of feature stimuli that did not have modulatory training. Thus, his results may not have reflected true modulatory transfers between the tasks. This is quite likely because he used three white-and-black circular keylight stimuli as training features, X, Y, and Z. Thus, the modulatory transfer he reported may have been caused by simple stimulus generalization among similar features. An experiment on serial FA discrimination that used the same features and temporal parameters as Rescorla (Nakajima, in press, Experiment 4) showed that this is plausible. "Transfer" across two FA tasks was observed, but the same amount of conditional control was obtained with a nonmodulatory feature. Thus, the transfer was ascribed to simple stimulus generalization in this experiment. The same factor may have caused transfer in Rescorla's experiment. This series of experiments on modulatory transfer (Nakajima, in press) revealed that conditioned modulation is specific to original feature–target combinations and that transfer to new combinations is caused by simple stimulus generalization.

The specificity of conditioned modulation in serial FA discriminations demonstrated in this study indicates that the underlying mechanism of modulatory control in these tasks is either specific CS–US occasion setting (Holland, 1983, 1985) or specific configuration learning. Holland (1991) and Holland & Reeve (1991) showed with an adequate control for nonmodulatory factors that modulatory control of a feature from an FA discrimination is less specific: It affected CRs to targets of concurrently trained FP, FN, and FA tasks and to a conditioned and extinguished stimulus. These two studies used rats as subjects in an instrumental conditional discrimination. Thus, the exact nature of the process underlying FA discrimination learning may differ in species, in experimental preparations, or in both (see Nakajima, in press).[2]

FEATURE-AMBIGUOUS DISCRIMINATION AND RELATED TASKS

The FA task is not the only offspring of the FP and FN tasks. A sibling of the FA task is the paradigm used by Udell and Rescorla (1979), X→A+, P→A+, X→B–, P→B±, where one feature keylight (X) gave information about whether food followed target keylights (A and B), but the other feature keylight (P) did not. Thus, X played a role of a conditioned modulator, and P was a pseudomodulator. This task is interesting because, as in the FA task, the US-threshold–changing hypothesis has trouble handling mastery of this task: stimulus X signals reinforcement and nonreinforcement at the same time for the different targets. Unfortunately, the analysis of the learning underlying this task was limited in that study, in part because the research was conducted before the rise of interest in conditioned modulation. Another factor that makes the analysis difficult comes from the fact that partial reinforcement results in just as many or more CRs than does continuous reinforcement (e.g., Gibbon, Farrell, Locurto, Duncan, & Terrace, 1980; Perkins et al., 1975). In Udell and Rescorla's study, the rates of CRs to both targets after the pseudomodulator (P) were equal to the rate of CRs to A after the modulator (X). Thus, it is difficult to know what kind of information X and P gave the birds in these three trials (X→A+, P→A±, P→B±).

Another sibling of the FA task is more famous and brings up many implications. If a second feature is put in target-alone trials of the feature-ambiguous task, the contingency (X→A+, Y→A–, X→B–, Y→B+) becomes the task used by Looney, Cohen, Brady, and Cohen (1977). Rescorla, Grau, and Durlach (1985, Experiment 4) tested CRs to keylight

[2] It is worth mentioning that there are some inconsistencies in modulatory transfer, even among serial FP and FN studies that use different species or preparations (see Swartzentruber, 1995, for a review).

targets (A and B) after their pigeons' mastery of the Looney task, and the rate on these trials was lower than that of the reinforced compounds (X→A and Y→B) but higher than that of nonreinforced compounds (Y→A and X→B). This result indicates that both X and Y can work as FA features in the Looney task.

The Looney task is interesting because it is essentially identical to that of a classic switching study conducted by Shitov (cited in Asratian, 1965, pp. 129–130). He trained dogs in differential conditioning with loud and soft tones. The loud tone was a signal of food in the morning sessions, and the soft tone played the same role in the afternoon sessions. The loud tone in the afternoon sessions and the soft tone in the morning sessions were not followed by food. Some but not all animals learned this task and showed much alimentary responding to the loud tone in the morning sessions and to the soft tone in the afternoon sessions. Nonreinforced combinations, the loud tone in the afternoon sessions and the soft tone in the morning sessions, elicited little responding. If we consider environmental cues of the morning and afternoon as X and Y, respectively, and consider the loud and soft tones as A and B, respectively, the paradigm used by Shitov is essentially the same as that used by Looney et al. Studies of switching have a long history, and many kinds of tasks have been called *switching* simply because the same CSs evoked a different amount of CRs in different circumstances (Wyrwicka, 1993). The variety of the switching tasks has made sensible analyses difficult. Careful examination of the specific contingencies set by experimenters in these tasks as well as finding similarities among the tasks are probably instructive.

The task used by Looney et al. (1977) is the same as that devised by Konorski (1959; cf. Chorazyna, 1959) and brought to the forefront of current research on animal cognition as a *successive matching-to-sample paradigm* (Wasserman, 1976). This is a Go/No-Go version of delayed matching-to-sample (DMTS) procedures,[3] and it has been widely used to investigate the basic characteristics of pigeons' short-term memory.

[3] Because the term *successive DMTS* also has been used as a more generic name for the DMTS procedures that include a "Yes/No"–type variant (cf. Mackay, 1991), I use the term *Go/No-Go DMTS* here to specify the paradigm of current interest.

Contingencies of the Go/No-Go DMTS are almost the same as the Looney task. Two stimuli are presented in succession and the outcome depends on their conditional relations: X→A is reinforced, Y→A is nonreinforced, X→B is nonreinforced, and Y→B is reinforced. Different terms for the stimuli are used in Go/No-Go DMTS tasks. X and Y are called *samples* rather than *features,* and A and B are called *test stimuli* or *comparison stimuli* rather than *targets.* Short-term memory is assessed with the Go/No-Go DMTS paradigm by inserting a delay or retention interval between the sample and test stimuli—one may call it a *temporal gap,* as in the serial FA task. There is only one difference between the Looney task and the typical Go/No-Go DMTS task: Animals have to respond to the second stimuli to get reinforcement on positive trials. This is an instrumental task, but this contingency is a trivial difference because the usual pigeon studies use short-duration keylights as the second stimuli, and the intertrial intervals are long enough to establish and maintain required responses (i.e., keypecks) via a Pavlovian process (i.e., autoshaping; cf. Perkins et al., 1975; Terrace, Gibbon, Farrell, & Baldock, 1975). Thus, the Go/No-Go DMTS task with pigeons is probably controlled by a Pavlovian process.

Conclusion

Experimental analysis of FA discrimination contributes to the understanding of properties and mechanisms of occasion setting. In addition, its similarity to related tasks including a Go/No-Go DMTS task suggests the same or similar underlying mechanisms in these tasks.

The corpus of data on Go/No-Go DMTS might help our examination of Pavlovian conditioned modulation phenomena. Many topics investigated in Go/No-Go DMTS tasks could also be studied in conditioned modulation paradigms such as serial FP, FN, and FA discriminations. For example, an interesting theoretical question in working memory research is whether animals use retrospective or prospective memory codes during the retention interval. Whereas some Go/No-Go DMTS studies suggest that pigeons use retrospective memory codes (e.g., Guttenberger & Wasserman, 1985; Wasserman, Bhatt, Chatlosh, & Kiedinger, 1987), other reports that use different Go/No-Go DMTS procedures support prospective coding (e.g., Grant & Spetch, 1991; Jackson-Smith, Zentall, & Steirn, 1993; Spetch & Grant, 1993). Nakajima (1994a) interpreted differences in acquisition performance among serial FP, FN, and FA tasks from the retrospective versus prospective coding approach. Swartzentruber (chapter 6, this volume) used discriminal distance analysis (Roitblat, 1980; Wilkie & Willson, 1990) to test the nature of the memory codes used by pigeons in Pavlovian conditioned modulation. These approaches provide fresh perspectives for future studies on conditioned modulation.

On the other hand, our knowledge of conditioned modulation may further our understanding of Go/No-Go DMTS performance. Little is known about the basic learning mechanisms in these tasks: Are they hierarchical or configural? Does the specific occasion-setting hypothesis work here, or is the US-threshold mechanism a more plausible assumption? Are the variables found to be effective in conditioned modulation also effective in Go/No-Go DMTS? Synthesis of these two important areas of research could considerably extend our understanding of animal learning and cognition.

REFERENCES

Arnold, H. M., Grahame, N. J., & Miller, R. R. (1991). Higher order occasion setting. *Animal Learning & Behavior, 19,* 58–64.

Asratian, E. A. (1965). *Compensatory adaptations, reflex activity, and the brain* (S. A. Corson, Trans.). Oxford: Pergamon Press.

Bottjer, S. W., & Hearst, E. (1979). Food delivery as a conditional stimulus: Feature-learning and memory in pigeons. *Journal of the Experimental Analysis of Behavior, 31,* 189–207.

Chorazyna, H. (1959). Investigation of recent memory of acoustic stimuli in normal dogs. *Bulletin de l'Académie Polonaise des Sciences: Série des Sciences Biologiques, 7,* 119–121.

Gibbon, J., Farrell, L., Locurto, C. M., Duncan, H. J., & Terrace, H. S. (1980). Partial reinforcement in autoshaping with pigeons. *Animal Learning & Behavior, 8,* 45–59.

Grant, G. S., & Spetch, M. L. (1991). Pigeons' memory for event duration: Differences between choice and successive matching tasks. *Learning and Motivation, 22,* 180–199.

Guttenberger, V. T., & Wasserman, E. A. (1985). Effects of sample duration, retention interval, and passage of time in the test on pigeons' matching-to-sample performance. *Animal Learning & Behavior, 13,* 121–128.

Hall, G. (1980). An investigation of ambiguous-cue learning in pigeons. *Animal Learning & Behavior, 8,* 282–286.

Holland, P. C. (1983). Occasion setting in Pavlovian feature positive discriminations. In M. L. Commons, R. J. Herrnstein, & A. R. Wagner (Eds.), *Quantitative analyses of behavior, Vol. 4: Discrimination processes* (pp. 183–206). New York: Ballinger.

Holland, P. C. (1985). The nature of conditioned inhibition in serial and simultaneous feature negative discriminations. In R. R. Miller & N. E. Spear (Eds.), *Information processing in animals: Conditioned inhibition* (pp. 267–297). Hillsdale, NJ: Erlbaum.

Holland, P. C. (1989). Transfer of negative occasion setting and conditioned inhibition across conditioned and unconditioned stimuli. *Journal of Experimental Psychology: Animal Behavior Processes, 15,* 311–328.

Holland, P. C. (1991). Transfer of control in ambiguous discriminations. *Journal of Experimental Psychology: Animal Behavior Processes, 17,* 231–248.

Holland, P. C. (1992). Occasion setting in Pavlovian conditioning. In D. L. Medin (Ed.), *The psychology of learning and motivation* (Vol. 28, pp. 69–125). San Diego, CA: Academic Press.

Holland, P. C., & Reeve, C. E. (1991). Acquisition and transfer of control by an ambiguous cue. *Animal Learning & Behavior, 19,* 113–124.

Hull, C. L. (1943). *Principles of behavior: An introduction to behavior theory.* New York: Appleton-Century-Crofts.

Jackson-Smith, P., Zentall, T. R., & Steirn, J. N. (1993). Prospective and retrospective memory processes in pigeons' performance on a successive delayed matching-to-sample task. *Learning and Motivation, 24,* 1–22.

Kehoe, E. J., & Gormezano, I. (1980). Configuration and combination laws in conditioning with compound stimuli. *Psychological Bulletin, 87,* 351–378.

Konorski, J. (1959). A new method of physiological investigation of recent memory in animals. *Bulletin de l'Académie Polonaise des Sciences: Série des Sciences Biologiques, 7,* 115–117.

Looney, T. A., Cohen, L. R., Brady, J. H., & Cohen, P. S. (1977). Conditional discrimination performance by pigeons on a response-independent procedure. *Journal of the Experimental Analysis of Behavior, 27,* 363–370.

Mackay, H. A. (1991). Conditional stimulus control. In I. H. Iversen & K. A. Lattal (Eds.), *Experimental analysis of behavior: Part I* (pp. 301–350). Amsterdam: Elsevier.

Nakajima, S. (1992). The effect of temporal relationship of stimulus compound on ambiguous discrimination in the pigeon's autoshaping. *Behavioural Processes, 27,* 65–74.

Nakajima, S. (1994a). Contextual control of Pavlovian bidirectional occasion setting. *Behavioural Processes, 32,* 53–66.

Nakajima, S. (1994b). Contextual control of Pavlovian feature-positive and feature-negative discriminations. *Animal Learning & Behavior, 22,* 34–46.

Nakajima, S. (1997). Transfer testing after serial feature-ambiguous discrimination in Pavlovian keypeck conditioning. *Animal Learning & Behavior, 25,* 413–426.

Pearce, J. M. (1987). A model for stimulus generalization in Pavlovian conditioning. *Psychological Review, 94,* 61–73.

Perkins, C. C., Jr., Beavers, W. O., Hancock, R. A., Jr., Hemmendinger, P. C., Hemmendinger, D., & Ricci, J. A. (1975). Some variables affecting rate of key pecking during response-independent procedures (autoshaping). *Journal of the Experimental Analysis of Behavior, 24,* 59–72.

Rescorla, R. A. (1979). Conditioned inhibition and extinction. In A. Dickinson & R. A. Boakes (Eds.), *Mechanisms of learning and motivation: A memorial volume to Jerzy Konorski* (pp. 83–110). Hillsdale, NJ: Erlbaum.

Rescorla, R. A. (1985). Conditioned inhibition and facilitation. In R. R. Miller & N. E. Spear (Eds.), *Information processing in animals: Conditioned inhibition* (pp. 299–326). Hillsdale, NJ: Erlbaum.

Rescorla, R. A. (1993). Interference among modulators. *Animal Learning & Behavior, 21,* 179–186.

Rescorla, R. A., Grau, J. W., & Durlach, P. J. (1985). Analysis of the unique cue in configural discriminations. *Journal of Experimental Psychology: Animal Behavior Processes, 11,* 356–366.

Riley, D. A., & Roitblat, H. L. (1978). Selective attention and related cognitive processes in pigeons. In S. H. Hulse, H. Fowler, & W. K. Honig (Eds.), *Cognitive processes in animal behavior* (pp. 249–276). Hillsdale, NJ: Erlbaum.

Roitblat, H. L. (1980). Codes and coding processes in pigeon short-term memory. *Animal Learning & Behavior, 8,* 341–351.

Spetch, M. L., & Grant, D. S. (1993). Pigeons' memory for event duration in choice and successive matching-to-sample tasks. *Learning and Motivation, 24,* 156–174.

Swartzentruber, D. (1995). Modulatory mechanism in Pavlovian conditioning. *Animal Learning & Behavior, 23,* 123–143.

Terrace, H. S., Gibbon, J., Farrell, L., & Baldock, M. D. (1975). Temporal factors influencing the acquisition and maintenance of an autoshaped keypeck. *Animal Learning & Behavior, 3,* 53–62.

Udell, H., & Rescorla, R. A. (1979). Conditioning of simultaneous and successive common elements in a discrimination and pseudodiscrimination. *Bulletin of the Psychonomic Society, 14,* 453–456.

Wagner, A. R., & Brandon, S. E. (1989). Evolution of a structured connectionist model of Pavlovian conditioning (AESOP). In S. B. Klein & R. R. Mowrer (Eds.), *Contemporary learning theories: Pavlovian conditioning and the status of traditional learning theory* (pp. 149–189). Hillsdale, NJ: Erlbaum.

Wasserman, E. A. (1976). Successive matching-to-sample in the pigeon: Variations on a theme by Konorski. *Behavior Research Methods and Instrumentation, 8,* 278–282.

Wasserman, E. A., Bhatt, R. S., Chatlosh, D. L., & Kiedinger, R. E. (1987). Discrimination of and memory for dimension and value information by pigeons. *Learning and Motivation, 18,* 34–56.

Wilkie, D. M., & Willson, R. J. (1990). Discriminal distance analysis supports the hypothesis that pigeons retrospectively encode event duration. *Animal Learning & Behavior, 18,* 124–132.

Wyrwicka, W. (1993). The problem of switching in conditional behavior. *Integrative Physiological and Behavioral Science, 28,* 239–257.

6

Perspectives on Modulation: Modulator- and Target-Focused Views

Dale Swartzentruber

Pavlovian occasion setting has traditionally been examined with a procedure in which a feature stimulus signals whether a target conditioned stimulus (CS) will be followed by an unconditioned stimulus (US). In the feature-positive (FP) discrimination, the feature is present when the target CS is paired with the US. In the feature-negative (FN) discrimination, the feature is present when the target is not paired with the US. Traditional associative models of learning, such as the Rescorla–Wagner (1972) model, predict that successful performance on these discriminations results from acquisition of feature–US associations. In the FP discrimination, greater responding to the feature–target compound than to the target alone occurs because the feature acquires an excitatory association with the US, whereas the target eventually attains a neutral associative status. In the FN discrimination, weaker responding to the compound than to the target occurs because an inhibitory feature–US association subtracts from the target's excitation. Much of our interest in occasion

Preparation of this manuscript was partially supported by National Institute of Mental Health Grant MH54490.

setting comes from the now extensive body of research showing that, under certain circumstances, the differential responding to the compound and target alone cannot be readily explained in terms of these simple binary associations between stimuli.

Ross and Holland's (1981) early work on occasion setting with rat subjects exploited Holland's (1977) finding that visual and auditory stimuli paired with food USs elicit topographically different conditioned responses (CRs). They showed that, when a visual cue preceded occasions on which an auditory cue was followed by the US, the visual cue became excitatory and elicited CRs indicative of visual cue–US associations, as predicted by the Rescorla–Wagner model. The auditory cue also remained excitatory, however, and elicited auditory cue–US responses. Over repeated trials, these auditory CRs were confined primarily to those times when the auditory target was preceded by the visual feature. Because our popular associative theories failed to account for this pattern of responding, their results required researchers to consider mechanisms that went beyond the traditional binary associative mechanism.

Ross and Holland (1981) used the term *positive occasion setting* to describe the modulatory role that the feature played in these discriminations. The feature appeared to modulate responding to the target independently of its own direct associations with the US. Within several years, researchers were examining the analogous *negative occasion setting*, where the animals use the feature to signal when the target is not reinforced (e.g., Holland, 1985; Rescorla, 1985). Much of the ensuing research compared the direct US associations of the feature to its ability to *set the occasion* for the target–US pairings. As is now well known, positive occasion setters can modulate responding to a target without exhibiting evidence of direct excitation, and negative occasion setters can modulate responding in spite of their own excitatory associations with the US. This book demonstrates the wealth of existing data on this function. There is general agreement that the modulatory and simple associative roles appear independent; there is less agreement about the mechanism through which this Pavlovian modulation occurs.

In this chapter, I suggest that our emphasis on comparing the associative and modulatory properties of the feature has limited the range of modulatory mechanisms that we have explored so far.

PERSPECTIVES

Most current theories posit that modulation depends on acquisition of a type of associative or active relationship between the modulator and some component of the CS–US relationship. These theories differ on the locus of the modulator's action (see Rescorla & Holland, 1977, for an analysis of inhibition that uses this framework).

One of Holland's (1983) early characterizations, for example, was that the modulator acts on an element that controls the target–US association. For example, in the FP discrimination, the feature facilitates the response to the target by activating or enabling the target–US control element. In an FN discrimination, the feature acts in the opposite manner by inhibiting the control element, thus suppressing the response. Correct discrimination performance thus depends on the extent to which the control element is activated.

Rescorla (e.g., 1985) has advocated a mechanism that is not specific to the target CS. He suggested that the modulator changes the threshold for activation of the US representation—a positive modulator lowers the threshold, thus facilitating the CR, and a negative modulator raises the threshold, thus inhibiting the response.

Bouton (e.g., 1991; Bouton & Swartzentruber, 1986) has compared the modulatory function of discrete stimuli to that of contexts. His extensive research on the role of contexts in Pavlovian interference paradigms has shown that contexts play the strongest role in situations where a CS has been treated differently in different phases of a study. For example, in the most basic interference paradigm, extinction, responding to a CS that has been paired with a US in one context, but extinguished in a different context, is renewed when the stimulus is then presented in the conditioning context (e.g., Bouton & King, 1983). Bouton (1991) has suggested that contexts and modulators might work by retrieving memories of the events that have occurred in their presence. From this perspective, occasion setting depends on the ability of the modulator to retrieve an appropriate memory of the target CS's reinforcement contingencies.

More recently, Schmajuk, Lamoureux, and Holland (1998; Lamoureux, Buhusi, & Schmajuk, chapter 13, this volume) have examined the ability of a modification of Schmajuk and DiCarlo's (1992) neural network model to predict performance on modulatory discriminations accurately. They found that an appropriately designed model of stimulus units, hidden units, and output units was remarkably successful in producing results that are consistent with the discrimination performance reported in much of the occasion-setting literature. In essence, the modulator activates a hidden unit that shares connections with units representing the target CS and the output response.

Note that in each of these potential mechanisms, presentation of the modulator actively changes the animal in some way. In Holland's target-specific account, the modulator enables or inhibits a control element specific to the target–US association; Rescorla's account gives the modulator the role of changing the threshold for activation of the US representation; Bouton's account provides the modulator with the ability to retrieve memories of events; and Schmajuk's modulators activate hidden units. Although these are not all necessarily associative in the traditional sense of the modulator having an excitatory or inhibitory bond with another event, in each case the modulator acquires a property from its having been presented as an informationally valid signal of target reinforcement or nonreinforcement. The theories differ regarding the nature of that property.

An alternative to the common focus on the ability of the modulator to actively change the animal in some way is to focus on the role that the modulator plays in providing the animal with information about the target. In modulatory discriminations, the animal is presented with two discrepant experiences with the target CS. In effect, the CS is partially reinforced; it has an associatively ambiguous status (e.g., Bouton & Bolles, 1985). Under these circumstances, an adaptive strategy would be to attend to otherwise extraneous cues in an attempt to categorize CS reinforcement and nonreinforcement. If the animal can effectively place the reinforced and nonreinforced experiences with that CS into different stimulus contexts, the stimulus contexts begin to modulate appropriate performance to the CS.

This target-focused perspective is not dependent on an active modulatory role. Presentation of the modulator might simply produce a passive memory trace. The animal encodes the stimulus as it would any neutral stimulus and retains its representation in working memory. Because responding to the target has become dependent on the modulator's representation in working memory, the modulator plays a role only at presentation of the ambiguous target CS.

My thinking about an alternative to the active associative role for modulators was motivated by a concern about the adaptive value of modulation in the animal's environment. Because the occasion-setting process appears to depend on the development of ambiguity to a stimulus (see Bonardi, 1992, for an alternative view), it seems likely that the animal is focusing on resolving the ambiguity and is thus focusing on the extent to which the target's reinforcement contingencies are dependent on other cues. The occasion-setting mechanism allows the animal to categorize events effectively that have multiple incongruent associates and, thus, provides an efficient hierarchical structure for storage of the animal's experiences.

SEMANTICS

Although, in my view, researchers have tended to emphasize the associative structure of occasion setting and therefore the active properties of the modulator, much of the occasion-setting research can be examined from either the modulator- or target-focused views. An example can be seen in an experiment designed to examine transfer of contextual control across target CSs with different training histories (Swartzentruber, 1993, Experiment 2).

The experiment used 16 pigeons in an autoshaping procedure where stimuli were presented on small, computer-controlled television screens mounted on the sides of the operant chambers. The televisions were mounted behind a transparent key that, when pecked, closed a switch that registered a response. The target CSs consisted of small white stimuli that were presented for 5 sec with a mean intertrial interval (ITI) of 60 sec. The CSs were a horizontal line, a vertical line, a square, and a triangle. The contexts consisted of colored backgrounds that remained on throughout the ITIs and during presentation of the target CSs. On reinforced trials, a target CS was followed by 5-sec access to grain.

The experiment differed from traditional occasion-setting experiments in that there was only a single reversal of each target's reinforcement contingencies. One target CS, x, was reinforced in Context A, then extinguished in Context B, and a second CS, y, was nonreinforced in Context A and reinforced in Context B.[1] Thus, Phase 1 consisted of Ax+,Ay– training, and Phase 2 consisted of Bx–,By+ training. In order to examine the extent to which the training history of the contexts and targets affects the extent of modulatory control transfer, two more stimuli, z and w, were treated identically to x and y, in two different contexts, C and D. Thus, the Ax+,Ay– discrimination was conducted concurrently with a Cz+,Cw– discrimination. The Bx–,By+ discrimination that followed was conducted concurrently with a Dz–,Dw+ discrimination.

Phase 1 training consisted of five two-session cycles. In each session, subjects received 16 reinforced trials and 16 nonreinforced trials in either Context A or Context C. Phase 2 consisted of two two-session cycles, during which the reinforcement contingencies of all four stimuli were reversed in Contexts B and D. There were 36 reinforced and 36 nonreinforced trials in each session.

Contextual control and transfer were then examined by presenting each of the four target CSs in each context. Note that there were two pairs of contexts, as well as two pairs of targets, that were treated identically. To present the results, I will use a single context or target designation to refer to data collapsed over two conditions. For example, responding to the conditioned-then-extinguished targets, x and z, in their original Phase 1 contexts, A and C, respectively, is simply referred to as Ax but includes

[1] Throughout this chapter, the uppercase letters A–D represent modulatory contextual or punctate stimuli. Lowercase letters w–z represent target conditioned stimuli.

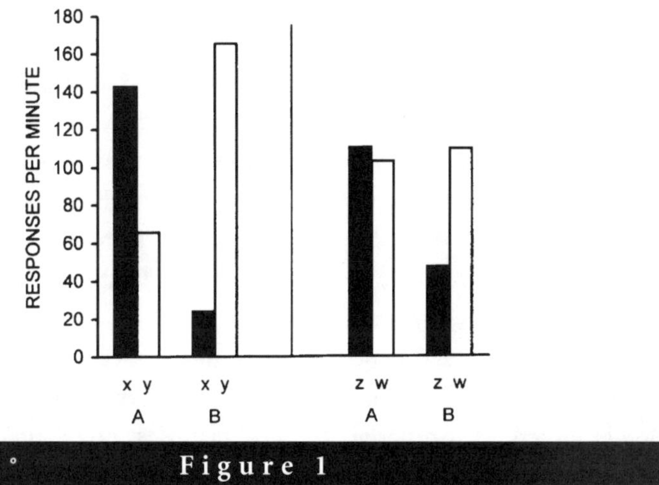

Figure 1

Responding to original and transfer context–target combinations. The left panel shows responding to the context–CS combinations that were experienced during training. The right panel shows responding when the CSs that were trained in one pair of contexts were tested in the alternate pair of contexts. Data are from Swartzentruber (1993).

the combined data from the Ax and Cz tests. The results of the test are shown in Figure 1. The left side of the figure shows the ability of Contexts A and B to control responding to the target CSs that had been trained in them. The first pair of bars reveals responding to the targets in Context A, the Phase 1 context. Responding to x was high when it was presented back in A after being extinguished in B. Responding to y, which had been most recently reinforced in B, was relatively low. The second pair of bars shows the effect of the Phase 2 context, Context B, on responding to x and y. It is not surprising to see that responding to x was low and responding to y was high; the birds had most recently received extinction of x and reinforcement of y in Context B.

The right side of the Figure 1 shows the extent to which Contexts A and B controlled responding to the transfer targets, z and w, that were treated identically to x and y, but in different contexts. Note that Context A evoked little differential control of responding to z and w, whereas in Context B responding to w was reliably higher than responding to z.

The results shown in Figure 1 are presented from the traditional modulator-focused perspective. They examine the abilities of Contexts A and B to transfer control of responding across original and transfer targets. One interpretation from this perspective is that, although the contexts controlled responding to the original CSs in a manner consistent with the original training, only the Phase 2 Context B was able to modulate responding to the transfer targets. The extinction of x and conditioning of y that occurred in Context B apparently gave the context the ability to transfer control across targets z and w.

These data can also be viewed from the target-focused perspective. To do so, instead of examining the abilities of Contexts A and B to transfer across targets with different training histories, one should examine the extent to which responding to the targets transferred across contexts with different training histories. Note that, because the treatments of z and w in Contexts C and D were identical to the treatments of x and y in Contexts A and B, the right side of Figure 1 also shows the extent to which the targets z and w transferred to Contexts A and B. From this perspective, the results show that only z, which was first conditioned in C then extinguished in D, was sensitive to the differential properties of A and B. When conditioning and extinction of a target occur in different contexts, differential responding to the target apparently transfers across multiple contexts.

To summarize, this experiment can be viewed as an examination of the ability of contexts to transfer control across original and transfer targets with different properties, but it can also be viewed as an examination of how responding to targets transfers across original and transfer contexts with different properties. The use of the same data for both perspectives might suggest that the distinction is merely semantic; I would argue, however, that the conclusions drawn could be importantly affected by one's perspective.

ACTIVE AND PASSIVE ROLES FOR THE MODULATOR

Although much of the occasion-setting literature can be evaluated by focusing on either the active properties of the modulator or the potentially passive role where the animal uses the modulator to resolve the target's ambiguous reinforcement contingencies, there is evidence that is more easily explained from one or the other perspective.

For example, Rescorla published two series of experiments that suggest that the modulator elicits some form of expectation about a specific target CS. In one set of experiments (Rescorla, 1991a), he trained four stimuli as either negative (Experiment 1) or positive (Experiment 2) modulators. Two of the stimuli were trained as modulators of one target CS; the other two were trained as modulators of another target CS. Finally, he examined the ability of the modulators to control responding to a new target CS when they were combined with either the modulator that shared a training target or the modulator that was trained with a different target. In both experiments, Rescorla found that combinations of two modulators that had been trained with the same target CS were more effective in transferring to a new target than were combinations of modulators that had been trained with different target CSs.

In the other set of experiments, Rescorla (1991c) trained two stimuli as modulators for different targets. Then he changed the associative status of one of the two targets. When the modulators had signaled reinforcement of the targets (Experiment 1), one of the targets was extinguished in the presence of another positive modulator. When the modulators had signaled nonreinforcement (Experiment 2), one of the targets was reinforced in the presence of another negative modulator. Finally, he tested the modulatory strength of the two modulators on a transfer target CS. In both experiments, Rescorla found that changing the associative status of a target reliably decreased the modulatory effectiveness of that target's original modulator.

Both of these experiments suggest that a modulator's effectiveness on a transfer target is at least partly mediated by a representation of that modulator's training target CS. These results are readily explained from a modulator-focused view, because the modulator's effectiveness depended on its ability to elicit a representation of the target CS actively.

Although most of the evidence is indirect, the target-focused view is more intuitively appealing when we examine data that suggest a nonassociative, or passive, role for the modulator. Perhaps the best evidence is that nonreinforced exposure to both positive and negative modulators typically has little impact on the ability of the modulator to control responding to a target—in other words, modulatory strength is not prone to extinction (e.g., Holland, 1989b, 1995; Rescorla, 1986). Although there are other explanations, if the modulator acts associatively, then it seems likely that exposure to the modulator without the necessary conditions for acquiring its associative capacity would degrade its modulatory ability. If the modulator plays no role until presentation of the target, however, then presenting the modulator without the target should have little impact.

In a similar vein, the target-focused view provides a ready framework for the findings that a modulator can be both a positive signal for one target and a negative signal for another. For example, Holland and Reeve (1991) examined the ability of rats to learn that a stimulus signals that responding will be reinforced during one target but nonreinforced during another. They found that the rate of learning about this *ambiguous cue* was no different from the rate of learning that a stimulus was exclusively a signal that responses would be either reinforced or nonreinforced. Again, although the data do not demand a specific view, an active role for the modulator would require simultaneous action on more than one upcoming target–US relationship. A passive role, as provided in the target-focused view, would predict that the modulator would not play a role until presentation of a specific target stimulus—in other words, from a target-focused view, an animal could use a single modulator to resolve the ambiguity of multiple targets.

RETROSPECTIVE AND PROSPECTIVE STRATEGIES

Once we shift the focus to the animal's goal of solving the target discrimination, we must consider the different types of information that the modulator can provide. In a target-focused approach, as target reinforcement becomes ambiguous, responding to the target becomes increasingly sensitive to the contents of the subject's working memory store. At presentation of the target, the subject examines the working memory contents, or code, and responds in a manner that is appropriate to the subject's previous experiences with the target and reinforcement in the presence of that code.

This has been one approach taken by researchers in the analysis of response choice in the instrumental matching-to-sample (MTS) paradigm with pigeons. In the typical MTS paradigm, one of two sample stimuli is presented to subjects, and it is followed by the simultaneous presentation of two comparison stimuli. Responses to one of the comparison stimuli are reinforced following one sample, and responses to the other comparison stimulus are reinforced following the other sample.

There are several strategies for solving this type of discrimination, but researchers typically focus on two types of information that could be used at the time of choice responding (e.g., Honig & Thompson, 1982; Wasserman, 1986). One possibility is that the animal is retaining a representation of the sample stimulus at the time of choice. Under this strategy, the animal has learned that reinforcement of responding to a specific comparison stimulus depends on the specific representation available in working memory. This *retrospective coding strategy* in MTS is analogous to the passive role for the modulator that I have been advocating. Another possibility is that presentation of the sample elicits an associatively generated expectation. In the MTS paradigm, working memory might then contain a representation of a specific comparison stimulus. This *prospective coding strategy* is analogous to the active role for the modulator; the modulator affects some component of the target–US association.

Many researchers have compared these strategies, and the results are somewhat mixed. For example, Zentall, Jagielo, Jackson-Smith, and Urcuioli (1987) changed either the number of possible sample stimuli that corresponded to comparison stimuli or the number of comparisons that were correct choices following each sample stimulus. Their logic was that, because responding depends on the contents of working memory, increasing the demands on working memory should interfere with choice accuracy. They showed that increasing the number of comparison stimuli had a greater effect on discrimination performance than did increasing the number of sample stimuli. This suggests that the pigeons use a prospective coding strategy, because the memory requirement for prospective coding is to retain the comparisons. If there are more comparisons, the memory requirement is greater.

On the other hand, Urcuioli and Zentall (1986) found that increasing the discriminability of the samples improved discrimination performance more than increasing the discriminability of the comparison stimuli. Assuming that the animals are using the contents of working memory in their solution of the discrimination, greater discriminability of working memory representations would improve choice accuracy. Their results suggest that the pigeons are retaining representations of the sample in working memory and, thus, are using a retrospective code. Zentall, Urcuioli, Jackson-Smith, and Steirn (1991) summarized a number of findings and suggested that the pigeons might have both types of coding strategies in their repertoire and use the one that is most efficient for the given task.

In order to examine the code used by pigeons to solve Pavlovian modulatory discriminations, I used a strategy analogous to one used by Roitblat (1980; see also Wilkie & Willson, 1990). Using an apparatus similar to that described earlier in my investigation of transfer of Pavlovian contextual control, I trained eight pigeons on a rather complicated conditional discrimination. Three stimuli served as modulators, A, B, and C, and three stimuli as targets, x, y, and z. On every trial one of the modulators was presented for 5 sec and followed by one of the 5-sec targets. Each modulator was followed an equal number of times by each target. Modulator A signaled that 4 sec of grain reinforcement would follow the x target, B signaled reinforcement of y, and C signaled reinforcement of z. No reinforcement was made available on the remaining 6 types of trials; there were 12 of each type of trial in each session.

The goal of the experiment was to examine the nature of the working memory code that the pigeons use in their decisions to respond to the targets. The retrospective code would consist of a representation of the physical characteristics of the modulators; a prospective code would consist of an associatively generated expectation of an upcoming event, presumably the physical characteristics of the target that was followed by reinforcement. Following Roitblat's logic, a decision about the type of code that controls responding can be made by systematically modifying

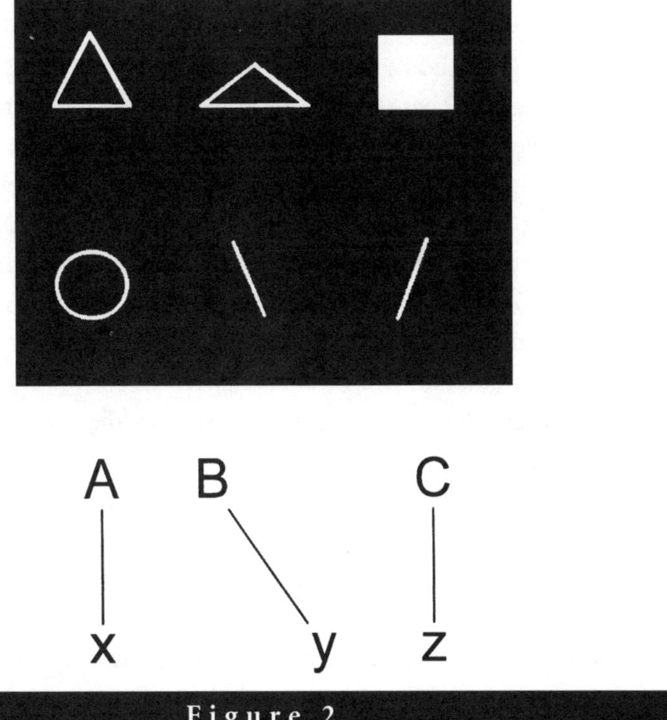

Figure 2

The top panel shows the stimuli that were used to train the conditional discrimination. Note that the triangles and lines were white, the square was green, and the circle was red. All stimuli were presented on a dark background. For half the subjects, the top stimuli were modulators and the bottom stimuli were the targets; for the other half, these roles were reversed. The bottom panel shows a theoretical characterization of the discrimination. A, B, and C modulated responding to the x, y, and z target CSs. The lines designate reinforced compounds. The physical proximity of the modulators and targets indicates their physical similarities.

the discriminability of the modulators and the targets. The pattern of errors, in this case responding on nonreinforced trials, would indicate the nature of the code. To accomplish this, the A and B modulators were similar to each other, but different from C, and the y and z targets were similar to each other, but different from x.

The stimuli used in the discrimination are shown at the top of Figure 2. For four of the birds, the stimuli playing the role of A, B, and C, respectively, were a white equilateral triangle with 14 mm sides, a white isosceles triangle with 11.5 mm sides and a 20 mm base, and a green square with 12 mm sides. These three stimuli were always presented on the left side of the display. The stimuli playing the roles of x, y, and z, respectively, were a red empty circle with a 14 mm diameter, a white 23 mm line slanted −12.5°, and a white 23 mm line slanted +12.5°. For the other four birds the identities of A, B, and C were switched with the identities of z, y, and x. Note that, for all birds, confusion should occur between A and B and between y and z.

The discrimination can be characterized as shown at the bottom of Figure 2, where the A and B modulators, and the y and z targets, are shown physically closer because of their physical similarities. According to the logic, if the pigeons are using a working memory of the physical characteristics of the modulators to control responding to the targets, then we would expect to see the greatest confusion between the A and B modulators. On the other hand, if correct responding to the targets is controlled by an anticipation of the targets, then we would expect to see the greatest confusion between the y and z targets. Note that the counterbalancing between the modulators and the targets precluded an explanation in terms of greater physical similarity between the similar modulators or the similar targets.

The top three panels of Figure 3 show the rate of discrimination learning separately for the x, y, and z targets. In an effort to increase the difficulty and thus the potential confusion, for the first 32 sessions a 5-sec empty trace interval was inserted between the modulators and the targets. Because there was no evidence of learning with that procedure, for the next 68 sessions of training the gap was removed. Note that, as learning progressed, a general pattern of errors emerged so that subjects responded similarly to compounds involving the A and B modulators.

The focus of the investigation was to compare the degree of confusion between the similar modulators and the similar targets. Confusion between the A and B modulators would produce a high degree of incorrect responding to the y target when y followed A and to the x target when x followed B. Alternatively, confusion between y and z would be indicated

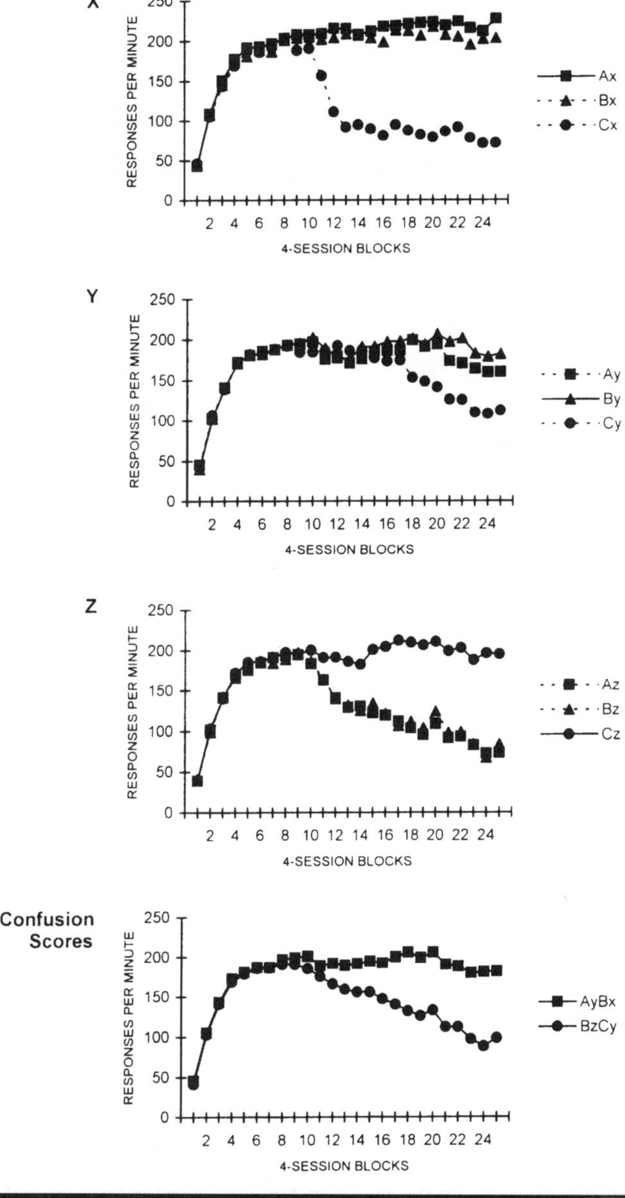

Figure 3

The top three panels show discrimination learning with the x, y, and z targets, respectively. Solid lines show responding to reinforced compounds; dotted lines show responding to nonreinforced compounds. The bottom panel shows "confusion scores" during training. Responding to the Ay and Bx nonreinforced compounds indicates confusion between the A and B modulators; responding to the Bz and Cy compounds suggests confusion between the y and z targets.

by incorrect responding to y following C, and to z following B. To make this comparison, each bird's data were converted to *confusion scores,* which consisted of the mean rate of incorrect responding to the Ay and Bx compounds and the mean rate of incorrect responding to the Bz and Cy compounds. These means are shown in the bottom panel of Figure 3. By the end of training, all eight subjects were responding more to Ay and Bx than to Bz and Cy, suggesting a greater degree of confusion between the A and B modulators than between the y and z targets.

The final training session was followed by eight additional sessions, in which a temporal gap was reinserted between the termination of the modulators and the onset of the targets. Each session began with four of each of the nine trial types with no gap, followed by four of each of the trial types with a gap. The length of the gap in seconds differed across sessions in the order 1, 2, 3, 5, 5, 3, 2, and 1. Although discrimination performance generally became poorer as the length of the gap increased, as shown by greater responding to all nonreinforced compounds, confusion between A and B remained higher than that between y and z.

If confusion can indeed be used to examine the contents of working memory, as assumed by the logic of this design, these results suggest that the birds are using a retrospective working memory representation of the modulators to control responding to the targets. For example, when target x is presented, the subjects presumably respond if they have a representation of A, or something similar to A, in working memory. The alternative prospective account, where the birds are anticipating a specific target, is not supported by these data. Thus, if we view occasion setting from a perspective where the primary emphasis is on learning about the target and the conditions that signal its reinforcement, it appears that the present discrimination paradigm encourages the subject to use a working memory representation of the modulator, as opposed to an expectation of a specific target.

Although this experiment suggests that Pavlovian modulation involves a retrospective coding strategy, the conditional discrimination that was used might have encouraged that type of strategy. An occasion-setting mechanism is probably present in a number of Pavlovian paradigms, and certain types of training procedures might affect the nature of the coding strategy (see Zentall et al., 1991).

For example, in a situation in which the modulator provides discrepant information about multiple targets, such as in the ambiguous cue training administered by Holland and Reeve (1991; Holland, 1991; Wilson & Pearce, 1989), a retrospective code would be more efficient because the animal would not have to retain the representations of multiple CSs.

Situations that discourage use of an expectation of the target might also encourage use of a retrospective code. For example, positive and negative patterning discriminations, in which the modulator is frequently presented without the target, might reduce the extent to which the modulator controls respond through an associative mechanism. Similarly, retrospective processing might be likely during contextual control of responding to targets. Because contexts are present before, during, and after the target, it seems implausible that the context elicits an active expectation of a target–US relationship, whereas the subject's response to the target could easily depend on an active working memory representation of the contextual stimuli.

On the other hand, when the traditional FP and FN discrimination procedures are used to generate modulatory control, a prospective strategy is both efficient and effective. The modulator could act directly on a representation of the target, the US, or the response.

Although all of these ideas are somewhat speculative, our animal subjects probably have large repertoires of cognitive strategies. The strategy may depend at least in part on its efficiency and perhaps the animal's previous experiences, and it may even change during the course of training or even during a trial (see Cook, Brown, & Reilly, 1985; Zentall, Steirn, & Jackson-Smith, 1990).

PERSPECTIVES AND EXPERIMENTAL DESIGN

The difference between a focus on the modulator's active role and a focus on the target and the conditions of its reinforcement becomes apparent and theoretically important when we examine the experimental strategies used in our investigations of occasion setting.

Conditional Discrimination Learning

Most of our research on Pavlovian modulation involves either the FP or FN discrimination paradigm. The often-stated conclusion is that, under certain circumstances, the feature can enhance (positive) or depress (negative) responding to the target independent of the feature's own direct Pavlovian associations with the US. The use of these discrimination paradigms, where a single feature stimulus provides information about the target reinforcement, has perhaps encouraged us to focus on the single feature's properties. In the target-focused perspective, however, we examine the animal's ability to discriminate episodes of target reinforcement from episodes of target nonreinforcement. I adapted this perspective in the design of a series of experiments that examined the role of feature excitation in modulatory control.

Rescorla (1991b) has shown that modulatory strength can be enhanced by increasing the simple excitatory strength of positive and negative modulators. There are at least two possible mechanisms through which excitatory training of a stimulus can enhance its modulatory role—one is that enhancement results from increased attention directed at the modulators, and another is that the excitatory conditioning endows the modulator with additional stimulus properties and that these excitatory properties, in addition to the physical properties, acquire modulatory control. The designs of Rescorla's experiments ruled out the latter possibility as a complete account of the enhanced effectiveness, but I thought it worth exploring the extent to which this factor could play a role (Swartzentruber, 1997).

The experiments used pigeons in a within-subject autoshaping preparation where 5-sec visual target CSs were presented on the television monitors and were followed by grain on reinforced trials. Modulation training was conducted by signaling the target CSs with 5-sec visual modulatory stimuli on both reinforced and nonreinforced trials. On these compound trials the modulators were presented and followed by a 5-sec empty interval before presentation of the targets. In the first two experiments, I was interested in comparing discrimination performance when both the positive and negative modulators were explicitly made excitatory to performance when only the positive modulator (Experiment 1) or the negative modulator (Experiment 2) was made excitatory. In Experiment 1, the pigeons were trained on two discriminations. Target x was reinforced when it followed Modulator A but not when it followed B, and Target y was reinforced following C but not following D. For half the subjects, A and B were red and green circles, respectively, and C and D were yellow and blue circles; for the remaining subjects these identities were reversed. Within each of these treatments, x and y were counterbalanced between a horizontal white line and a white star. To examine the effect of excitation, A, C, and D were each made excitatory by following them with grain on additional trials. If excitation did enhance modulatory effectiveness by increasing attention directed at the modulators, then the Cy+/Dy– discrimination would be learned faster than the Ax+/Bx– discrimination, because both of y's modulators were excitatory. If excitation played a modulatory role, however, then we would expect faster learning of the Ax+/Bx– discrimination, because the subjects could use the differential excitatory strength of the modulators as additional cues for x's reinforcement contingencies.

During each session, there were six of each of the four compound trials and six presentations each of the four modulators. When the modulators were presented separately, A, C, and D, but not B, were each followed by 5-sec access to grain. Discrimination learning over the 16 sessions of training is shown in Figure 4. The subjects learned the discrimination involving x significantly faster than the discrimination involving y. These results demonstrate that excitatory training of just the positive modulator is more effective in enhancing discrimination performance than excitatory training of both the positive and negative modulators. Although this suggests that the subjects were using the differential excitation of the modulators to discriminate reinforcement and nonreinforcement of x, it is possi-

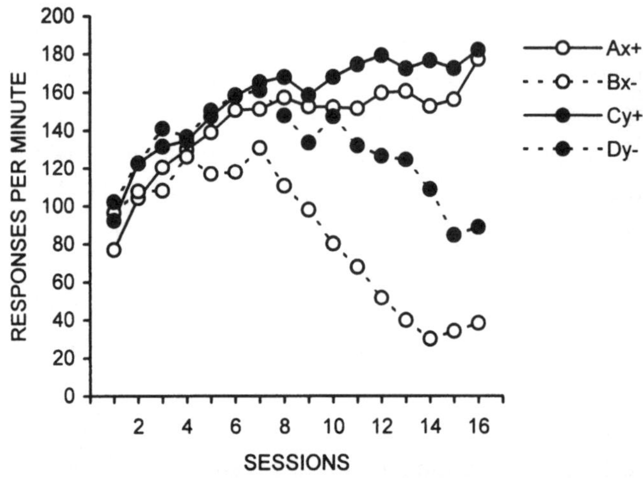

Figure 4

Responding to the x and y target stimuli during discrimination training. A and B signaled reinforcement and nonreinforcement of x, respectively, whereas C and D signaled reinforcement and nonreinforcement of y. On additional trials, A, but not B, was paired with the US, and C and D were both paired with the US. Data are from Swartzentruber (1997). Copyright 1997 by the American Psychological Association.

ble that the excitation of A, C, and D was merely summating with the targets, thus enhancing responding on Ax, Cy, and Dy trials; this possibility could also produce the observed results.

Experiment 2 was designed to rule out the summation explanation by comparing excitatory conditioning of both modulators to excitatory conditioning of just the negative modulator. Training was identical to the training used in Experiment 1, with the exception that B was made excitatory instead of A. Results of the 36 sessions of training are shown in Figure 5. Again, excitatory training of just one modulator produced a faster rate of discrimination learning than did excitatory training of both modulators.

When combined, these experiments suggest that the pigeons were using the excitatory properties of the modulators as signals for the reinforcement contingencies of the x target. The differential excitation of A and B provided a means for discriminating that went beyond physical

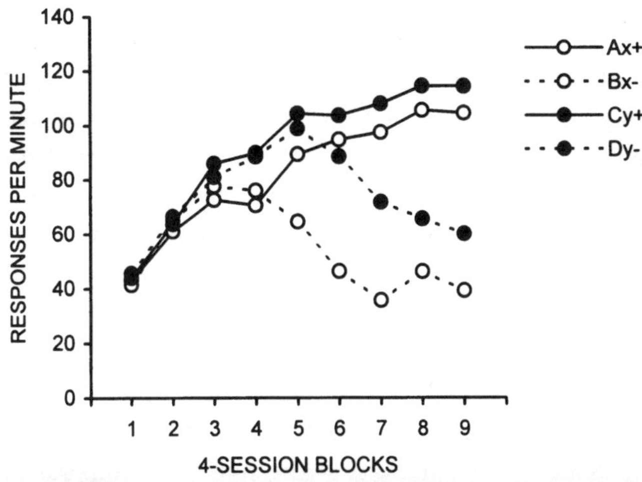

Figure 5

Responding to the x and y target stimuli during discrimination training. A and B signaled reinforcement and nonreinforcement of x, respectively, whereas C and D signaled reinforcement and nonreinforcement of y. On additional trials, B, but not A, was paired with the US, and both C and D were paired with the US. Data are from Swartzentruber (1997). Copyright 1997 by the American Psychological Association.

differences. When both the positive and negative modulators were excitatory, the excitatory properties presumably decreased their discriminability, thus slowing discrimination learning.

Note how these experiments were designed from a target-focused perspective. The designs emphasize the role of learning about the target and the cues for differentiating the target's reinforcement contingencies. Excitation plays an important role, not by directly enhancing the modulatory strength of the stimulus but by enhancing the discriminability of the reinforced and nonreinforced conditions.

Transfer Tests

As researchers have become convinced that occasion setting represents a learning mechanism that is distinct from simple excitation and inhibition, one issue that has received some attention is the set of factors that might affect the strength of modulation. For example, as mentioned earlier, Rescorla (1991b) has argued that increasing the direct excitatory strength of a modulator can enhance its modulatory effectiveness, and Holland (e.g., 1986) has considered the role and length of the temporal interval in modulatory strength. How does one go about testing modulatory strength? An initial indication of strength can be seen during training where the extent to which the modulator enhances or depresses the response to the target CS is simply compared to the response to the target when presented alone. We know that an excitatory modulator is more effective than a more associatively neutral modulator (Rescorla, 1991b) partly because training with an excitatory modulator produces greater differential responding to the target. Similarly, we know that insertion of a temporal interval is important because the differential responding to the target is greater than when training is conducted with no empty interval.

Modulatory strength is not so easily assessed, however. There is now a fair amount of research suggesting that the properties of the target can affect the extent to which a target is sensitive to modulatory control (e.g., Holland, 1989a; Lamarre & Holland, 1987; Rescorla, 1985). As a result, if the modulation training procedure produces a target that is sensitive to modulatory control, the likely conclusion is that the modulator is very effective. Similarly, a training target that is less sensitive to control might lead one to underestimate the effectiveness of the modulator. In other words, when using the differential responding observed during training as an indication of the modulator's strength, the conclusion is confounded by the target's sensitivity.

Some researchers have argued that a more accurate test is one in which modulatory control is expressed on a target that has not previously been presented in compound with the modulator (Detke, 1991; Rescorla, 1991b; Swartzentruber, 1995). There are at least two reasons, however, for questioning the validity of this assertion. First, the fact that both modulators are being tested on a target other than the target that was involved in their training requires the assumption that a modulator's power is independent of the identity of the specific CS. Although this assumption has some support, it is clear from research, such as that described earlier (Rescorla,

1991a, 1991c), that a CS-independent account cannot accommodate all the data. Using a single transfer target to compare the strengths of two modulators will only provide evidence for the extent to which they differ in the strength of their CS-independent modulatory properties.

The second reason for questioning the validity of single-target tests follows from the target-focused perspective presented here. Although the focus on learning about the target and the conditions that signal target reinforcement is naturally a CS-specific modulatory account, it is clear that modulators can transfer control of responding across multiple targets. This transfer has been taken as evidence that the modulator acts on some aspect of the association other than the specific CS, such as the US representation. One way to reconcile transfer with the present CS-specific account is to consider the role of stimulus generalization. For example, there is general agreement that the most sensitive transfer target is one that has participated as a target of another modulatory discrimination (see Swartzentruber, 1995). This sensitivity may be due to several factors. First, there is the possibility that the subject generalizes across the two targets—the target used in the training of the test modulator and the transfer target that will be used in the test. Second, the subject might generalize across the two modulators—the modulator whose strength is being assessed and the modulator used to train the transfer target. Either of these possibilities would provide evidence of transfer, even if modulation is a CS-specific process.

To return to the problem of testing modulatory strength on a common transfer target, one must consider the second possibility. Because of the modulatory training that it receives, responding to the transfer target may become sensitive to a property of its original modulator that may or may not be shared by the modulator whose strength is being assessed. If the shared properties were the underlying reason for transfer, then control of responding to the transfer target during the test would indicate the test modulator's strength only to the extent that the test modulator had the critical properties.

Evidence for this concern is shown in the third of the series of experiments that examined the modulatory properties of excitation (Swartzentruber, 1997). The experiment was designed to assess more directly the possibility that the excitatory properties of a modulator could themselves acquire modulatory control. Eight pigeons were trained on a conditional discrimination of the form Ax+,Bx–/Ay–,By+. Thus, x was reinforced following A, but not B, whereas y received the opposite treatment, being reinforced following B, but not A. On additional trials, A and B were each presented separately, but only B was followed by reinforcement. This differential excitatory treatment of A and B allowed the pigeons to use excitation to discriminate reinforcement and nonreinforcement of x and y. The A and B stimuli were composed of horizontal and vertical white lines and were counterbalanced. The x and y targets were counterbalanced between a cyan "bulls-eye" stimulus made of concentric circles 2 mm in width and a "pinwheel" stimulus made by dividing a circle into 16 black-and-white alternating pie-shaped wedges. In each of the 60 training sessions, there were 12 presentations of each compound trial. There were six additional presentations of the A and the B modulators, during which B, but not A, was followed by grain. By the end of training, the pigeons were showing more responding to x when it was preceded by A than by B, and more responding to y when it was preceded by B than by A.

The goal of the experiment was to examine the extent to which the pigeons used the differential excitatory properties of A and B in their solution of the discrimination. Thus, two new stimuli, C and D, were introduced and given differential excitatory training. They consisted of +45° and –45° white lines, which were counterbalanced across the identities of A and B. For 10 sessions, the birds received 16 presentations each of A, B, C, and D; A and C were nonreinforced, and B and D were reinforced. To test the extent of control by the excitatory properties, the x and y targets were presented in compound with C and D. The results of this transfer test are shown in Figure 6, which shows responding to x and y when they were preceded by C and D. Recall that C and D had received differential excitatory training analogous to that received by A and B, that x had been reinforced following A, and that y had been reinforced following B. As expected, the pattern of responding on the transfer test suggested that the birds had learned that reinforcement of x and y had

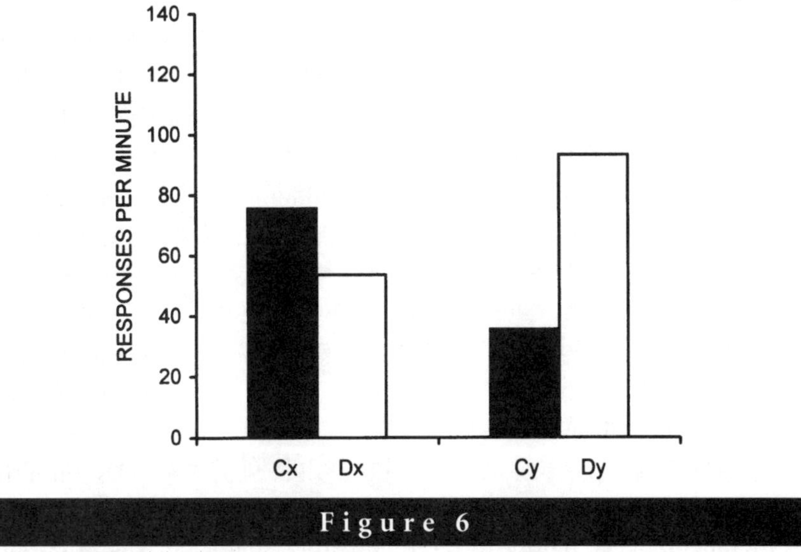

Figure 6

Responding to the x and y target stimuli following two stimuli, C and D, that had received differential excitatory training analogous to that administered to the training modulators, A and B. Data are from Swartzentruber (1997). Copyright 1997 by the American Psychological Association.

been at least partly signaled by the differential excitatory properties of A and B. All but one bird showed more responding to x following C than D, and more responding to y following D than C.

Because the traditional emphasis has been on the properties of modulators, most transfer tests have examined the ability of modulators to transfer control across targets with different training histories. Most of our evidence on the extent to which targets can be controlled by different modulators comes from the use of a control condition, where the effects of a known modulator on responding to a target are compared to the effects of a neutral stimulus, or *pseudomodulator* (e.g., Davidson, Aparicio, & Rescorla, 1988; Wilson & Pearce, 1989). The pseudomodulator is used to rule out the nonassociative, or unlearned, effects of preceding the target with a stimulus and typically show little evidence of pseudomodulatory control.

The present test, however, revealed that stimuli that had received no explicit modulatory training were capable of controlling responding to targets of modulatory discriminations. The C and D stimuli acquired *modulatory control* by virtue of the simple differential excitatory training that they received. Although it might not be readily predicted from a focus on the properties of modulators, this finding follows naturally from the target-focused perspective. The experiment was designed to examine the nature of the cues that the birds were using to solve the discrimination, and it provides compelling evidence that the birds focused on the differential properties of the modulators in their solution of the discrimination (see Peterson, 1984; and Urcuioli & DeMarse, 1996, for analogous transfer across samples with MTS procedures).

Of most importance, however, the results of this experiment urge caution when using a common transfer target to compare the effectiveness of modulators. The nature of the modulatory abilities of C and D (and the original modulators, A and B) was entirely dependent on what the animals had learned about x and y. Although the nature of the target CS's training history can have an important effect on the target's sensitivity to modulation, this experiment suggests that a target's sensitivity depends on the interaction between the training histories of the target and modulator. When responding to a target is sensitive to the particular properties of a modulator, a modulator with those properties will have a stronger influence over responding to that target than will a modulator without those properties. A target with a different training history, however, might be sensitive to different properties or even to the absence of a specific property. Thus, a perspective that focuses on learning about the target suggests the presence of an important modulator history–target history interaction.

CONCLUSION

In this chapter, I attempted to demonstrate that there are fundamental differences in the perspectives that one can take on modulation. If the focus is on the active role of the modulator, there is a tendency to assume that presentation of a modulator changes the organism in some way that differs from the effect of the presentation of a neutral stimulus. Although there may be little evidence of such a change before presentation of the target, the assumption is that the modulator actively evokes a change. Experiments that are designed from this perspective focus on the modulator's ability to enable or inhibit a specific CS–US association, shift the threshold for activation of the US representation, or retrieve memories of events that have occurred in the presence of the modulator.

The alternative discussed here is to focus on the learning that occurs regarding the target and the extent to which its reinforcement is specific to other stimuli. A focus on the target emphasizes the nature of the memory code that the animal uses in solving the discrimination; the solution requires that the animal determine the conditions that are present when the CS is or is not followed by the US.

Within this perspective, it is possible that the modulatory role is nonassociative, or essentially passive, and that presentation of the modulator produces a working memory trace of its physical properties. The animal would thus use a retrospective coding strategy to solve the discrimination. The target-focused perspective does not restrict the modulator to a nonassociative role, however. Over the course of training, the modulator can and frequently does acquire associations with certain aspects of the training situation, such as the target CS, the US, or the CS–US association. The animal might be using expectations, or prospective codes, in solving the discrimination.

As with a number of paradigms in learning, it is likely that animals have a repertoire of several different strategies for solving complex discriminations. A number of variables might interact to determine the strategies that animals use.

In any event, the occasion-setting mechanism, however it is viewed, is adaptive in the sense that it allows the animal to categorize and retain multiple incongruent experiences with stimuli. The hierarchical structure of the memory system provides the animal with a rich representation of the events that it has experienced and helps to ensure that expectations and responses are appropriate to the animal's environment.

REFERENCES

Bonardi, C. (1992). Occasion setting without feature-positive discrimination training. *Learning and Motivation, 23,* 343–367.

Bouton, M. E. (1991). Context and retrieval in extinction and in other examples of interference in simple associative learning. In L. W. Dachowski & C. F. Flaherty (Eds.), *Current topics in animal learning: Brain, emotion, and cognition* (pp. 25–53). Hillsdale, NJ: Erlbaum.

Bouton, M. E., & Bolles, R. C. (1985). Contexts, event-memories, and extinction. In P. D. Balsam & A. Tomie (Eds.), *Context and learning* (pp. 133–166). Hillsdale, NJ: Erlbaum.

Bouton, M. E., & King, D. A. (1983). Contextual control of the extinction of conditioned fear: Tests for the associative value of the context. *Journal of Experimental Psychology: Animal Behavior Processes, 9,* 248–265.

Bouton, M. E., & Swartzentruber, D. (1986). Analysis of the associative and occasion-setting properties of contexts participating in a Pavlovian discrimination. *Journal of Experimental Psychology: Animal Behavior Processes, 12,* 333–350.

Cook, R. G., Brown, M. F., & Riley, D. A. (1985). Flexible memory processing by rats: Use of prospective and retrospective information in the radial maze. *Journal of Experimental Psychology: Animal Behavior Processes, 11,* 453–469.

Davidson, T. L., Aparicio, J., & Rescorla, R. A. (1988). Transfer between Pavlovian facilitators and instrumental discriminative stimuli. *Animal Learning & Behavior, 16,* 285–291.

Detke, M. J. (1991). Extinction of sequential conditioned inhibition. *Animal Learning & Behavior, 19,* 345–354.

Holland, P. C. (1977). Conditioned stimulus as a determinant of the form of the Pavlovian conditioned response. *Journal of Experimental Psychology: Animal Behavior Processes, 3,* 77–104.

Holland, P. C. (1983). Occasion setting in Pavlovian feature positive discriminations. In M. L. Commons, R. J. Herrnstein, & A. R. Wagner (Eds.), *Quantitative analyses of behavior: Discrimination processes* (Vol. 4, pp. 183–206). New York: Ballinger.

Holland, P. C. (1985). The nature of conditioned inhibition in serial and simultaneous feature negative discriminations. In R. R. Miller & N. E. Spear (Eds.),

Information processing in animals: Conditioned inhibition (pp. 267–297). Hillsdale, NJ: Erlbaum.

Holland, P. C. (1986). Temporal determinants of occasion setting in feature-positive discriminations. *Animal Learning & Behavior, 14,* 111–120.

Holland, P. C. (1989a). Acquisition and transfer of conditional discrimination performance. *Journal of Experimental Psychology: Animal Behavior Processes, 15,* 154–165.

Holland, P. C. (1989b). Feature extinction enhances transfer of occasion setting. *Animal Learning & Behavior, 17,* 269–279.

Holland, P. C. (1991). Transfer of control in ambiguous discriminations. *Journal of Experimental Psychology: Animal Behavior Processes, 17,* 231–248.

Holland, P. C. (1995). Transfer of occasion setting across stimulus and response in operant feature positive discriminations. *Learning and Motivation, 26,* 239–263.

Holland, P. C., & Reeve, C. E. (1991). Acquisition and transfer of control by an ambiguous cue. *Animal Learning & Behavior, 19,* 113–124.

Honig, W. K., & Thompson, R. K. R. (1982). Retrospective and prospective processing in animal working memory. In G. H. Bower (Ed.), *The psychology of learning and motivation* (Vol. 16, pp. 239–283). New York: Academic Press.

Lamarre, J., & Holland, P. C. (1987). Transfer of inhibition after serial feature negative discrimination training. *Learning and Motivation, 18,* 319–342.

Peterson, G. B. (1984). How expectancies guide behavior. In H. L. Roitblat, T. G. Bever, & H. S. Terrace (Eds.), *Animal cognition* (pp. 135–148). Hillsdale, NJ: Erlbaum.

Rescorla, R. A. (1985). Conditioned inhibition and facilitation. In R. R. Miller & N. E. Spear (Eds.), *Information processing in animals: Conditioned inhibition* (pp. 299–326). Hillsdale, NJ: Erlbaum.

Rescorla, R. A. (1986). Extinction of facilitation. *Journal of Experimental Psychology: Animal Behavior Processes, 12,* 16–24.

Rescorla, R. A. (1991a). Combinations of modulators trained with the same and different target stimuli. *Animal Learning & Behavior, 19,* 355–360.

Rescorla, R. A. (1991b). Separate reinforcement can enhance the effectiveness of modulators. *Journal of Experimental Psychology: Animal Behavior Processes, 17,* 259–269.

Rescorla, R. A. (1991c). Transfer of inhibition and facilitation mediated by the original target stimulus. *Animal Learning & Behavior, 19,* 65–70.

Rescorla, R. A., & Holland, P. C. (1977). Associations in Pavlovian conditioned inhibition. *Learning and Motivation, 8,* 429–447.

Rescorla, R. A., & Wagner, A. R. (1972). A theory of Pavlovian conditioning: Variations in the effectiveness of reinforcement and nonreinforcement. In A. H. Black & W. F. Prokasy (Eds.), *Classical conditioning II: Current research and theory* (pp. 64–99). New York: Appleton-Century-Crofts.

Roitblat, H. L. (1980). Codes and coding processes in pigeon short-term memory. *Animal Learning & Behavior, 8,* 341–351.

Ross, R. T., & Holland, P. C. (1981). Conditioning of simultaneous and serial feature-positive discriminations. *Animal Learning & Behavior, 9,* 293–303.

Schmajuk, N. A., & DiCarlo, J. J. (1992). Stimulus configuration, classical conditioning, and the hippocampus. *Psychological Review, 99,* 268–305.

Schmajuk, N. A., Lamoureux, J. A., & Holland, P. C. (1998). Occasion setting: A neural network approach. *Psychological Review, 105,* 3–32.

Swartzentruber, D. (1993). Transfer of contextual control across similarly trained conditioned stimuli. *Animal Learning & Behavior, 21,* 14–22.

Swartzentruber, D. (1995). Modulatory mechanisms in Pavlovian conditioning. *Animal Learning & Behavior, 23,* 123–143.

Swartzentruber, D. (1997). Modulation by the stimulus properties of excitation. *Journal of Experimental Psychology: Animal Behavior Processes, 23,* 434–440.

Urcuioli, P. J., & DeMarse, T. (1996). Associative processes in differential outcome discriminations. *Journal of Experimental Psychology: Animal Behavior Processes, 22,* 192–204.

Urcuioli, P. J., & Zentall, T. R. (1986). Retrospective coding in pigeons' delayed matching-to-sample. *Journal of Experimental Psychology: Animal Behavior Processes, 12,* 69–77.

Wasserman, E. A. (1986). Prospection and retrospection as processes of animal short-term memory. In D. F. Kendrick, M. E. Rilling, & M. R. Denny (Eds.), *Theories of animal memory* (pp. 53–75). Hillsdale, NJ: Erlbaum.

Wilkie, D. M., & Willson, R. J. (1990). Discriminal distance analysis supports the hypothesis that pigeons retrospectively encode event duration. *Animal Learning & Behavior, 18,* 124–132.

Wilson, P. N., & Pearce, J. M. (1989). A role for stimulus generalization in conditional discrimination learning. *Quarterly Journal of Experimental Psychology, 41B,* 243–273.

Zentall, T. R., Jagielo, J. A., Jackson-Smith, P., & Urcuioli, P. J. (1987). Memory codes in pigeon short-term memory: Effects of varying the number of sample and comparison stimuli. *Learning and Motivation, 18,* 21–33.

Zentall, T. R., Steirn, J. N., & Jackson-Smith, P. (1990). Memory strategies in pigeons' performance of a radial-arm-maze analog task. *Journal of Experimental Psychology: Animal Behavior Processes, 16,* 358–371.

Zentall, T. R., Urcuioli, P. J., Jackson-Smith, P., & Steirn, J. N. (1991). Memory strategies in pigeons. In L. Dachowski & C. F. Flaherty (Eds.), *Current topics in animal learning: Brain, emotion, and cognition* (pp. 119–139). Hillsdale, NJ: Erlbaum.

7

Contextual Control as Occasion Setting

Geoffrey Hall and Esther Mondragón

The work described in this chapter grew out of a desire to understand how contextual cues can come to exercise control over the expression of associative information acquired in their presence. The attempt to identify this control as being a form of occasion setting equivalent to that established by feature-positive training has led to a series of experiments that investigate the conditions in which discrete cues trained as occasion setters acquire the powers they do; a description of these experiments makes up most of this chapter. Before turning to these, however, we must outline the main findings of some previously published experiments that have studied contextual control directly, because they provide the rationale for the new experiments.

CONTEXTUAL CONDITIONAL CONTROL

Appropriate training can make the effects of a conditioning procedure context-dependent. Thus, for example, Bouton and Swartzentruber (1986)

The experimental work reported here was supported in part by a grant from the United Kingdom Medical Research Council. Esther Mondragón's participation was made possible by a grant from the Spanish Ministerio de Educación y Ciencia. We thank Charlotte Bonardi and Jasper Ward-Robinson for much helpful discussion.

gave rats pairings of a tone and a shock reinforcer in one distinctive context (X), along with presentations of the tone alone in a different context (Y). The animals formed a discrimination, and showed the conditioned response (CR) to the tone only in Context X.

In a series of further tests, Bouton and Swartzentruber were able to demonstrate that this effect was independent of any excitatory or inhibitory associations that might have been acquired by the contexts themselves. The explanation preferred by Bouton and Swartzentruber was that Context X had come to act as a positive occasion setter—as a cue that could foster retrieval and use of associative information acquired in its presence (see Bouton, 1993). As they point out, their training procedure is formally very similar to the orthodox feature-positive (FP) training technique that is used to establish occasion setting. In this procedure a target conditioned stimulus (CS), A, is reinforced only when it has been accompanied or preceded by some other discrete cue (X) and not when X is absent (X:A+/A–). Support for this interpretation comes from a study by Swartzentruber (1991) that investigated the interaction between contexts and discrete cues trained as occasion setters. Animals were trained initially on the FP task, X:A+/A–, before receiving training in which contextual cues were made relevant, with X:A+ trials occurring in one context and A– trials in another. It was found that this pretraining blocked acquisition of control by the context over the ability of A to evoke its CR. A further experiment demonstrated the converse—that initial training with just the contextual cues blocked acquisition of occasion-setting power by X when that cue was subsequently introduced. This mutual blocking between context and occasion setters argues for a functional equivalence between them.

In the procedure used by Bouton and Swartzentruber (1986), contextual control was established by explicit discrimination training—context X signaled that the CS would be reinforced, and context Y that it would not. In some cases, however, context dependence has been demonstrated without such training being given. The most solidly established instance comes from the study of latent inhibition. Nonreinforced preexposure to a stimulus will retard conditioning when that stimulus is subsequently used as a CS, but only if the preexposure and conditioning treatments are given in the same context. If preexposure is given in one context and conditioning in another, the latent inhibition effect is attenuated or even abolished (e.g., Channell & Hall, 1983; Hall & Honey, 1989; Lovibond, Preston, & Mackintosh, 1984). There is no explicit discrimination training in these experiments; the animals are simply given preexposure in one context and conditioning in another. Nonetheless, the context appears to gain control over what is learned during preexposure in that the effects of preexposure are fully evident only in the context in which it was given.

Although satisfactory demonstrations are less common, there are also some examples of the failure of conditioned responding to transfer from one context to another, even when the conditioning phase involves no explicit discrimination between different contexts. Figure 1 shows the design and results of an experiment by Hall and Honey (1989). Rats received an initial phase of appetitive conditioning in which the A CS was reinforced in one context (X), and the B CS was reinforced in another (Y). The use of two contexts in this phase was meant simply to equate the animals' experience of reinforcement in the two. It should be noted that there was no explicit discrimination training—that is, there were no nonreinforced presentations of A in Y or of B in X. For the test phase, half the animals (Group Different) received presentations of the stimuli in the "wrong" context, A occurring for the first time in Y, and B in X. The lower portion of Figure 1 shows the conditioned responding evoked in the two groups over the nonreinforced trials of the test. Animals in Group Different showed less vigorous conditioned responding (indexed by approaches to the food tray in the presence of the CSs) than did the subjects (Group Same) for whom the context-stimulus pairings remained the same as in initial training.

In a discussion of these and related findings, Hall (1991) offered an explanation that was essentially the same as that proposed by Bouton and

Context-dependence of conditioning: Design and results

Training	Test
Context X: A+	Group Same
	X: A
	Y: B
and	
Context Y: B+	Group Different
	X: B
	Y: A

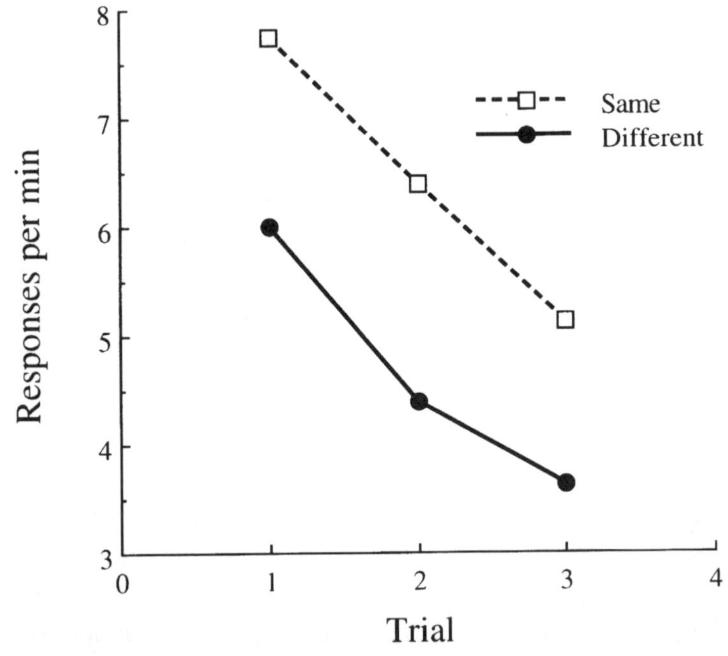

Figure 1

(Top panel) Experimental design. A and B represent different stimuli, food reinforced (+) in training. X and Y represent distinctively different experimental chambers. *(Lower panel)* Test phase magazine responding in the presence of A and B in the Same or Different context, pooled over two test sessions (one in each context). Data from Hall and Honey (1989).

Swartzentruber (1986) for their experiment in which contextual control was established after explicit discrimination training. Hall suggested that the contextual cues present during conditioning (or preexposure in the case of latent inhibition) acquire a conditional function by which they come to control retrieval of information acquired in their presence; he equated this control with that acquired by discrete stimuli trained as occasion setters.

To adopt this theoretical position, accepted opinion about the conditions necessary for occasion-setter formation must be rejected. As Swartzentruber (1995) has pointed out, it has been generally assumed that for occasion setting to occur, the occasion setter must supply information. In FP training, for instance, the feature (X) supplies information in that it resolves the ambiguity (see Bouton, 1993) regarding whether the target stimulus (A) will be reinforced. In the examples just cited there is no such ambiguity—in latent inhibition the stimulus is always nonreinforced during preexposure. In the experiment by Hall and Honey (1989), the CS was always reinforced during training. Swartzentruber also acknowledges, however, that little evidence compels us to accept the consensus view and that the exact conditions necessary for occasion-setter formation remain to specified. It is still open to us, therefore, to suppose that the contextual dependence shown by latent inhibition, and by conditioned responding in the Hall and Honey (1989) experiment, depends on acquisition of occasion-setting properties by the contextual cues.

The direct implication of this proposal is that the effects that have been demonstrated using contexts as the conditional cues should also be obtainable by using discrete events of the sort typically employed in standard studies of occasion setting. This proposal is examined in the experiments described in this chapter. The first of these, which concerns latent inhibition, asks whether conditional control over the effect can be observed when what changes between the two phases of the experiment is not the context in which the target stimulus occurs, but a discrete cue that accompanies presentation of the target stimulus. Subsequent experiments deal with conditional control over conditioned responding; they examine the implication that, if explicit discrimination training is not needed to establish a context as an occasion setter, this training should not be needed with more orthodox procedures in which a discrete cue is used.

SIGNALING THE STIMULUS IN LATENT INHIBITION

In their demonstration of the context specificity of latent inhibition, Hall and Honey (1989) gave rats a series of nonreinforced presentations of two stimuli, A being presented in one conditioning chamber (context X) and B in a different chamber (context Y). The animals were then divided into two groups for the conditioning phase, in which A and B signaled a shock reinforcer. For Group Same, the trials with A continued to occur in X, and those with B in Y. For Group Different, however, the arrangement was reversed, with A trials occurring in Y and B trials in X. Conditioning (assessed by development of conditioned suppression of instrumental food-rewarded responding) occurred more rapidly in Group Different than in Group Same, and it was concluded that the effects of preexposure had failed to transfer fully across contexts in Group Different.

The experiment summarized in the top panel of Figure 2 attempted to replicate all essential features of the Hall and Honey (1989) experiment, but with one major change of procedure: Instead of presenting A and B in different chambers, we used a different discrete stimulus to signal the occurrence of each. Sixteen rats were trained initially to perform an instrumental response, and this was maintained by food reward throughout training. In the first (preexposure) phase, all subjects received eight 40-min sessions, each containing four nonreinforced presentations of A and four of B. A and B (a tone and white noise, respectively) were each 30 sec in duration. Each A trial was preceded by stimulus X, and each B trial by stimulus Y. X and Y (illumination of a jewel light and offset of the houselight, respectively, both counterbalanced) were also 30 sec long and terminated immediately before the target stimulus (A or B) was presented. Each of the four conditioning phase sessions contained two shock-reinforced trials, the shock occurring immediately after the target stimulus was offset. For Group Same, these trials consisted of one presentation of X→A and

Signaling of latent inhibition: Design and results

Preexposure	Conditioning
	Group Same
X -> A -> 0	X -> A+ and Y -> B+
and	
	Group Different
Y -> B -> 0	
	X -> B+ and Y -> A+

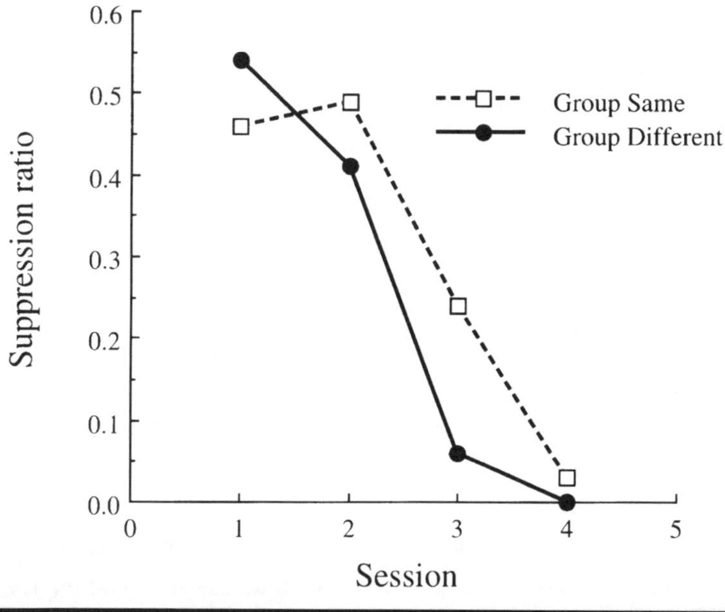

Figure 2

(Top panel) Experimental design. A and B represent two auditory stimuli, and X and Y two visual stimuli; + represents shock reinforcement. *(Lower panel)* Conditioned suppression controlled by A and B. Each daily score pools the results for two trials, one of each type.

one of Y→B, which was the arrangement used in preexposure. Group Different received X→B and Y→A trials.

The results for the four days of the conditioning phase are presented in the lower panel of Figure 2, which shows, for each group, a suppression ratio, computed as $a/a + b$, where a represents the responding shown on both target trials on that day and b the responding recorded in the 30-sec stimulus-free periods that preceded the onset of X and Y. It is apparent that suppression was more rapid in Group Different than in Group Same, and an analysis of variance with group and session as the factors showed that this difference was statistically reliable—for the group x session interaction, $F(3, 42) = 2.84$, $p < .05$. This result is susceptible to more than one explanation (as discussed in the last section of this chapter). For the time being, however, it is enough to note that, first, the pattern of results exactly matches that obtained in the experiment by Hall and Honey (1989) on the context-dependence of latent inhibition; and, second, that this effect is not surprising if successful retrieval of the information that was acquired during preexposure were dependent on the presence of the cue that had signaled the target stimulus during preexposure.

NONEXPLICIT TRAINING AND OCCASION SETTING

As we have already noted, the standard occasion-setting training procedure involves an explicit discrimination, X:A+/A–. According to the hypothesis now being considered, for X to become an occasion setter, the A– trials should not be needed; the fact that X accompanies the reinforcement of A should be enough. Evidence that seems at first sight to support this view comes from a study by Bonardi (1992; see also Bonardi, chapter 2, this volume). She gave rats food-reinforced presentations of two target stimuli, A and B (noise and a light, counterbalanced, each 5 sec long); these occurred only in the presence of longer duration feature stimuli, X and Y (a clicker and dark, respectively, each 3 min long), with A occurring in X, and B in Y. This procedure is similar to that used in studies of occasion setting by Kimmel and Ray (1978) and Wilson and Pearce (1989, 1990), but differs in that there were no nonreinforced presentations of A and B.[1] In spite of this difference, a final test revealed that the features had acquired power over the ability of "their" target CS to evoke the CR—animals given A in Y and B in X showed less vigorous responding than those tested with the usual combinations. Bonardi (1992) noted that these results were not to be explained in terms of any direct associative strength controlled by the features because the training regime that she employed ensured that the features were equated in this respect. She also presented arguments against the possibility that the loss of responding observed in the subjects that were given the novel stimulus combinations might be a result of generalization decrement.

The design of Bonardi's (1992) experiment is formally identical to that summarized in Figure 1, and it generates the same basic result—the CR is more vigorous when the CS is tested in the presence of the context, or of the feature stimulus, that was present during conditioning. If we assume that Bonardi's feature stimuli are functioning as occasion setters, we might want to conclude that the contexts in the experiment by Hall and Honey (1989) had acquired similar properties. On the other hand, it might be argued that Bonardi's experiment, with its procedure of embedding target trials in a longer stimulus, is no more than a further demonstration of the context dependency of conditioning and that neither experiment demonstrates "true" occasion setting. After all, in the usual procedure for establishing occasion setting, the reinforced target stimulus follows presentation of the feature rather than being embedded in it. It is important to ask, therefore, whether nonexplicit training with a procedure of this sort (i.e., simple, serial X→A+ conditioning) will also be capable of turning X into an occasion setter.

[1] Given the absence of these nonreinforced trials, it may be thought inappropriate to describe stimuli X and Y as *features*, but using this terminology maintains contact with studies of explicit discrimination training on which this experiment is based. It should not be assumed that the feature stimuli of this study necessarily function like true features in the explicit discrimination training procedure—that is an empirical question and one that the experiment is attempting to answer.

Our initial attempt to investigate this question employed the experimental design shown at the top of Figure 3. The eight rats that constituted Group Serial received 12 40-min sessions of training, each session containing two food-reinforced presentations of the target stimuli A and B (a white noise or a tone, 30 sec in duration). Each reinforced target was preceded by its own feature stimulus, A by X and B by Y. X and Y were visual cues—illumination of a jewel light or of the light inside the food magazine; they were 30 sec long and terminated immediately before the target stimulus was presented. This training was sufficient to establish reliable conditioned responding in the presence of A and B (indexed by scoring approaches to the food magazine in the presence of these stimuli). We also included, for purposes of comparison, a group of eight subjects (Group Discrimination) that was given standard FP training. This group was treated just like Group Serial, except for addition of nonreinforced target trials during training (two A– and two B– trials per session). By the end of training, the subjects in this group were showing a reliable discrimination, responding more to A and B when they were presented following their features than when they were presented alone.

In each of the two test sessions that immediately followed the end of training, all subjects received two Same trials in which the stimulus combinations were those used in training (i.e., X→A and Y→B) and two Different trials (X→B and Y→A). If X and Y had acquired occasion-setting properties as a result of the first stage of training, we might expect responding to the targets to be more vigorous on Same trials than on Different trials. The lower panel of Figure 3 shows the mean rate of response (magazine entry) during target stimulus presentations for the two groups, pooled over all trials of a given type in the test phase. Although the difference was not statistically reliable—an analysis of variance with group and trial type as the factors yielded $F(1, 14) = 1.66$ for the interaction between these factors—it is clear from the figure that only in Group Discrimination was there any sign of the expected effect. For Group Serial, the results were quite the opposite of those anticipated, with responding being more vigorous on Different trials than on Same trials.

Effects of intermixed nonreinforced target trials: Design and results

Training	Test
Group Serial	
X -> A+	Same trials
&	
Y -> B+	X -> A+ & Y -> B+
Group Discrimination	Different trials
X -> A+ / A-	X -> B+ & Y -> A+
&	
Y -> B+ / B-	

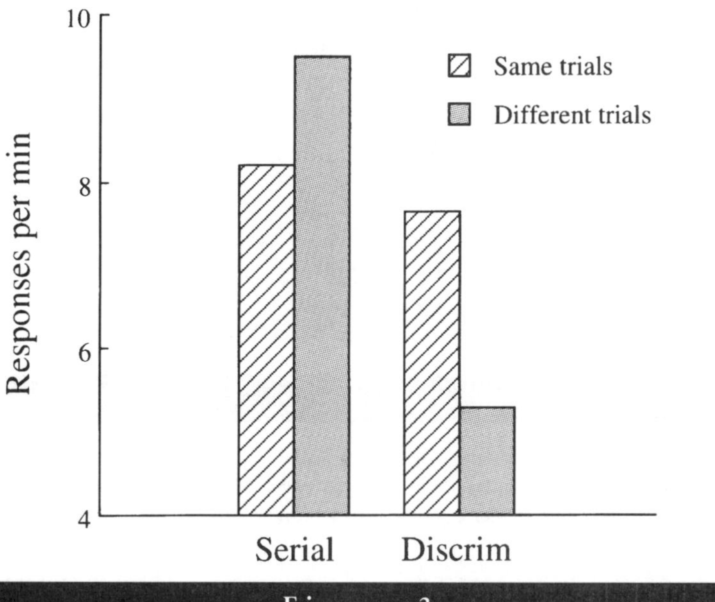

Figure 3

(Top panel) Experimental design. X and Y are visual stimuli, and A and B are auditory stimuli; + represents food reinforcement. *(Lower panel)* Magazine responding controlled by A and B during the test phase, pooled over all Different trials and all Same trials.

Nonexplicit training: Design and results

Training	Test
	Group Same
X -> A+	X -> A+ and Y -> B+
and	
	Group Different
Y -> B+	X -> B+ and Y -> A+

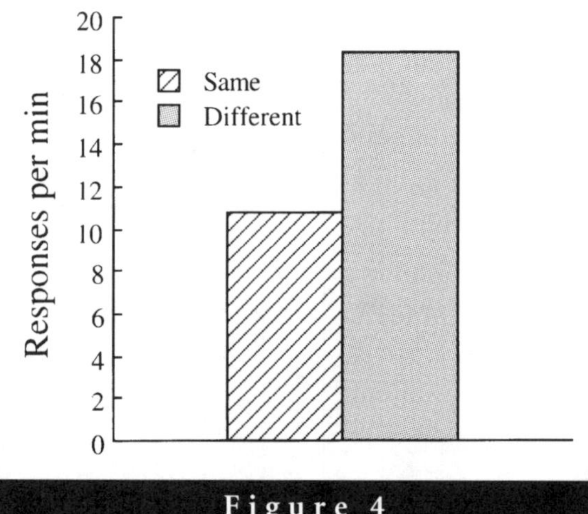

Figure 4

(Top panel) Experimental design. X and Y are visual stimuli, and A and B are auditory stimuli; + represents food reinforcement. *(Lower panel)* Magazine responding controlled by A and B during the test phase, pooled over both trial types for each group.

Intrigued by the apparent reversal of occasion setting shown by Group Different, we decided to attempt to confirm the reliability of the result in a further experiment, whose design is shown in Figure 4. All 16 rats received eight sessions of initial training, identical to that given to Group Serial in the previous experiment. In the hope of increasing the sensitivity of the test phase, we used a between-groups comparison and extended testing over three sessions. For subjects in Group Same, training continued just as before; but for those in Group Different, feature X was now used to signal B+ trials and feature Y to signal A+ trials. The lower panel of Figure 4 shows the mean rate of response (magazine entry) for the two groups, pooled over all target presentations of the test phase. Again, it was the Different condition that showed the higher rate of response, and in this experiment the difference was statistically reliable, $F(1, 14) = 9.57$, $p < .01$. As with demonstrations of contextual dependency of conditioned responding , the fact that the target CS is presented embedded within a long-duration feature stimulus evidently is critical to the occasion-setting effect produced by Bonardi's (1992) nonexplicit training procedure. In order to understand why this would occur, it helps to consider why the procedure used in this experiment not only failed to generate the occasion-setting result (more responding in Group Same) but actually produced a significant reversal (more responding in Group Different).

THE ROLE OF PRIMING

To understand the unexpected effect demonstrated in Figure 4, we conducted a further set of experiments that successfully confirmed the reliability of the effect under a range of conditions; these experiments also ruled out some uninteresting possible explanations (Honey, Hall, & Bonardi, 1993). The explanation that we finally endorsed was based on the idea that an unexpected CS is better able to evoke its CR than one that is expected. During the training stage of our experiment, it was reasonable to suppose that associations would be formed not only between the target stimulus, A, and the reinforcer, but also between the feature, X, and the target. For Group Same on the test, therefore, A would be predicted by the X presentation that precedes it. For Group Different, on the other hand, A would be preceded for the first time by Y, and to that extent its occurrence would be unexpected.

The notion that an unexpected event is likely to be more effective than one that is predicted is not arbitrary; it follows directly from Wagner's (e.g., 1976, 1981) general model of conditioning. According to this account, the existence of an associative link, such as that presumed to exist between X and A in our example, will allow the occurrence of X to *prime* the central representation of A into a secondary state of activation. The evocation of this secondary state is assumed to restrict the ability of A to generate a normal primary state of activation when stimulus A is itself presented and thus to limit the ability of A to generate a vigorous CR. Without necessarily accepting Wagner's model in its entirety (as applied to habituation, for example, the model encounters certain difficulties; see Hall, 1991), we (Honey et al., 1993) concluded that the notion of priming provided a satisfactory explanation for the type of results shown in Figure 4.

This explanation attributes the priming effect to formation of an orthodox excitatory association between the feature stimulus and the target. The fact that a stimulus can acquire associative properties as the result of a given form of training, however, does not preclude the possibility that this type of training might endow it with other properties as well. For the standard FP procedure (X:A+/A–), it is accepted that X will form direct associations with the events that follow it (in particular with the reinforcer) at the same time as it comes to act as an occasion setter—witness the various experimental procedures used to show that X's power over the ability of A to evoke the CR is not solely a consequence of the direct X–US association. What is true for the standard procedure may also be true for the nonexplicit training procedure under investigation here—that is, although, as the priming effect demonstrates, X:A+ trials establish X as a CS for A, they may also establish X as an occasion setter simultaneously. If so, then the test results of Figure 3 indicate only that the priming effect is powerful enough to overwhelm the occasion-setting effect, not that no occasion setting has occurred. The implication of this interpretation is that occasion setting is only likely to be observed when the training conditions attenuate the contribution from the priming effect.

Accepting this account also clarifies why including the A– trials of the explicit training procedure is needed to obtain occasion setting (Figure 3). Stimulus A is assumed to serve as the unconditioned stimulus (US) in the X–A association formed on the X:A+ trials. The addition of the A trials in the explicit procedure thus amounts to the addition of a set of US presentations that are not signaled by the CS (stimulus X). It is well established for standard classical conditioning paradigms that degrading the CS–US correlation in this way results in poor association formation (e.g., Rescorla, 1968). The explicit training procedure can thus be expected to allow only a weak X–A association to form; priming would not, therefore, be a powerful effect, and occasion setting might then become apparent (the result that was obtained). According to this analysis, the A– trials have their effect not because they ensure that X is informative about whether A will be reinforced, but simply because they restrict development of the direct X–A association.

The argument just presented does no more than establish that our hypothesis can *accommodate* the effects produced by adding A– trials to X:A+ training; to compel acceptance of the hypothesis would require more than this, however. What is needed is evidence that priming can be turned into occasion setting by procedures that weaken the X–A association even when these are not procedures that render X informative about whether A will be reinforced. The experiments described next attempt to achieve this.

THE EFFECTS OF FEATURE PREEXPOSURE ON PRIMING

Miller and Oberling (chapter 1, this volume) studied how preexposure to the feature stimulus affects the ability of this stimulus to acquire occasion-setting properties—that is, they gave extensive nonreinforced exposure to stimulus X before training rats on an FP, X:A+/A– discrimination. This procedure turned out to have no effect when testing the ability of X to modulate the CR evoked by A. Why such preexposure should be ineffective is of interest in itself, but that will not be discussed here. Instead, we simply want to use this finding to investigate the interrelation between occasion setting and the priming effect.

We know that simple serial (X→A+) conditioning results in a priming effect, and we have attributed this to the formation of an X–A association.

Although preexposure to X does not influence X's acquisition of occasion-setting properties, we may assume that it would detract from X's ability to enter into simple associations (the latent inhibition effect). Preexposure to X, therefore, should retard acquisition of the X–A association and attenuate or eliminate priming. According to this hypothesis, elimination of priming should allow occasion setting to show through. This suggestion was tested in the next experiment.

In this experiment (the design is summarized in the top panel of Figure 5), two groups of subjects (eight rats per group) received 12 sessions of conditioning that consisted of intermixed X→A+ and Y→B+ trials. The stimuli and training procedures were identical to those described for our previous experiments on priming. The test phase was extended to five sessions, but in other respects the procedure was the same as described for the experiment presented in Figure 3—that is, on each session all subjects experienced both Same trials (A preceded by X and B by Y) and Different trials (with the other feature–target combinations). The two groups differed only in the training they had experienced before the conditioning phase started. For Group Pre, this consisted of 12 sessions, each containing four nonreinforced presentations of X and four of Y. Group Control experienced the experimental context during these sessions, but no stimuli. Our previous results suggested that Group Control would show the priming effect by responding to the target stimuli more vigorously on Different trials than on Same trials. The central question was whether the latent inhibition training given to Group Pre would, by eliminating the priming effect, allow us to see an occasion-setting effect demonstrated by more vigorous response to the target cues on Same trials than on Different trials.

The results of the test phase (group means pooled over the responding recorded on all trials of each type on both test sessions) are shown in the lower panel of Figure 5. They exactly matched our expectations. Group Control showed the priming effect, responding more on Different than on Same trials; Group Pre showed the occasion-setting result, responding more on Same than on Different trials. An analysis of variance conducted on the Figure 5 data confirmed the reliability of the interaction between

Effects of prior exposure to the feature stimuli: Design and results

Preexposure	Training	Test
Group Pre X -> 0 & Y -> 0	X -> A+ & Y -> B+	Same trials X -> A+ & Y -> B+ Different trials X -> B+ & Y -> A+
Group Control ---------		

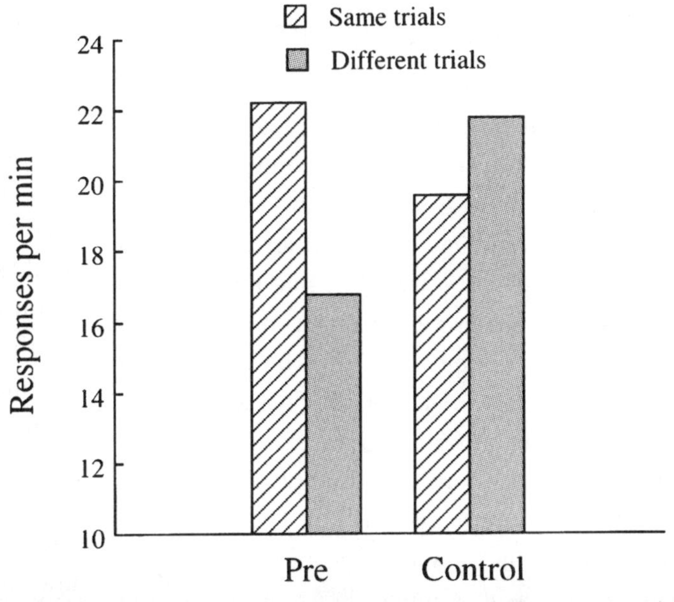

Figure 5

(Top panel) Experimental design. X and Y are visual stimuli, and A and B are auditory stimuli; + represents food reinforcement. No reinforcement occurred in the Preexposure phase. *(Lower panel)* Magazine responding controlled by A and B during the test phase, pooled, for each group, over all Different and all Same trials.

group and trial type, $F(1, 14) = 4.82$, $p < .05$. Our interpretation is that serial conditioning (X→A+) like that given to all subjects in the training phase of this experiment will normally establish A as a CS for A and also give X conditional control over the ability of A to evoke its CR. The result observed in the test phase in which X no longer precedes A will depend on the balance between the opposed effects generated by these two learning processes. Latent inhibition of X, by limiting the growth or effectiveness of the X–A association, tips the balance in favor of the occasion-setting effect. It should be noted that this latent inhibition procedure is not one that makes X informative about the outcome of A in the conditioning phase.

THE EFFECTS OF NONREINFORCED FEATURE TRIALS

The rationale for this final experiment is, in principle, identical to that for the experiment just described—that is, we again look at the effects of a procedure that might be expected to limit the growth of the X–A association during X→A+ training but does not make X informative. The procedure we used was intermixing of nonreinforced feature trials (X– trials) with the reinforced (X→A+) trials. Adding these trials makes X a poor predictor of A—and thus no very strong X–A association can be expected and hence no sizable priming effect. It has been shown a number of times (e.g., Holland, 1989; Rescorla, 1986; but see Ross, 1983), however, that occasion setting survives nonreinforced presentations of the feature—at least when this type of training is given as a separate phase, following acquisition of the relevant discrimination. There is reason to think, therefore, that X would still be able to acquire conditional control in our experiment and that, with priming eliminated, an occasion-setting result might emerge on the test.

The design of the experiment is shown in the top panel of Figure 6. The eight rats in Group Serial received 10 sessions of serial conditioning with stimuli and procedures identical to those described for the training stage of the previous experiment. Group Discrimination (a further eight

Effects of intermixed nonreinforced feature trials: Design and results

	Training	Test
Group Serial		
	X -> A+ & Y -> B+	Same trials X -> A+ & Y -> B+
Group Discrimination		Different trials
	X -> A+ / X- & Y -> B+ / Y-	X -> B+ & Y -> A+

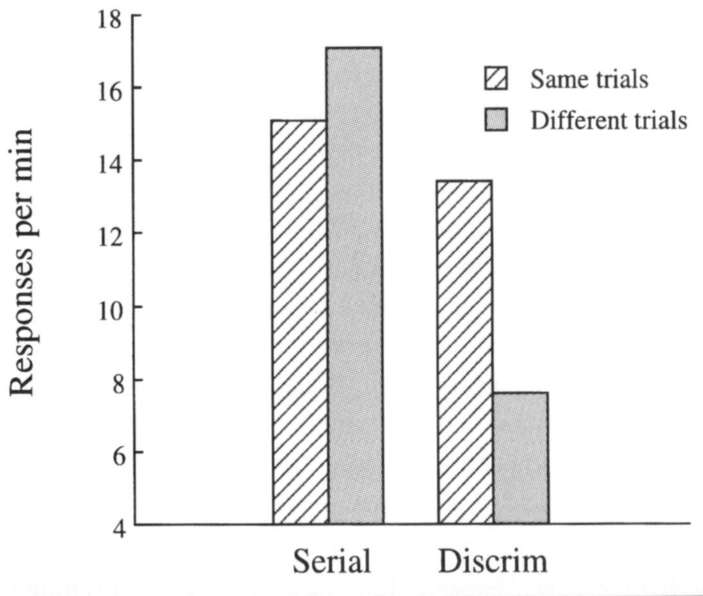

Figure 6

(Top panel) Experimental design. X and Y are visual stimuli, and A and B are auditory stimuli; + represents food reinforcement. *(Lower panel)* Magazine responding controlled by A and B during the test phase, pooled, for each group, over all Different and all Same trials.

subjects) was treated identically, except that, in addition to the four reinforced trials, they experienced two presentations of X alone and two of Y alone in each training session. The test procedure was identical to that used in the previous experiment—that is, there were five sessions with each containing two Same and two Different trials. The lower panel of Figure 6 shows the mean rate of response controlled by each target stimulus on the two trial types. The results conformed to our expectations. Group Serial showed the priming effect, responding somewhat more on Different than on Same trials; but for Group Discrimination, the pattern was reversed—that is, addition of the nonreinforced feature trials during training turned priming into occasion setting. An analysis of variance conducted on the data summarized in Figure 6 confirmed that the interaction between group and trial type was statistically reliable, $F(1, 14) = 6.54$, $p < .05$.

This result is more than just a further demonstration of how a procedure that weakens the direct feature–target association can turn priming produced by our standard nonexplicit training procedure into occasion setting—it also provides some insight into why other forms of nonexplicit training might produce occasion setting. Recall that this was the effect found in the experiment by Bonardi (1992) and in the experiment on the context specificity of the CR by Honey and Hall (1989). In both of these experiments, animals experienced reinforced presentations of the target stimulus embedded in a much longer presentation of the feature—four 5-sec targets in each 3-min feature in Bonardi's experiment, and three 30-sec targets in a "feature" (the contextual cues) that lasted for the whole 40-min session in the experiment by Hall and Honey. As a consequence, in both of these experiments the animals received extensive experience of the feature without the target, a procedure that, like the separate presentations of the feature stimuli used in our experiment, might be expected to work against development of a strong feature–target association. In both of these experiments, therefore, the priming effect can be expected to be weak, allowing us to see the occasion-setting effect that was obtained.

CONCLUSION

When target–US pairings occur in the presence of, or immediately after presentation of, some other (feature) cue, the latter cue will acquire two separable properties. First, it will enter into direct associations with the events that follow it and in particular will come to signal the occurrence of the target; it will also, presumably, form an association with the US, a fact that can be neglected in our experiments, which were designed to ensure that feature–US associations were equated in all conditions. Second, it will acquire conditional control over the target–US association acquired in its presence and will do so even when there is no ambiguity regarding whether the target will be followed by the US. The latter suggestion is contrary to what is usually supposed about the conditions needed for establishing conditional control, but there is little by way of hard evidence to support the usual view, and there are some arguments in favor of the alternative (see Bonardi, chapter 2, this volume).

These two forms of learning will have opposed effects on the ability of the target to evoke its CR. The associative link, we have argued, means that a signaled target will be less effective than one that is unexpected (the priming effect). The signal, however, to the extent that it has gained conditional control, will also act, in some way yet to be specified, to foster retrieval or use of the target–US association (the occasion-setting effect). Which of these two effects predominates will depend on the exact conditions of training. In simple serial conditioning (X→A+) it is the priming effect, and animals tend to respond to the target less when it is preceded by X than when it is not. The experiments reported in this chapter have shown, however, that training procedures that are likely to restrict development of the direct feature–target association are effective in converting priming into occasion setting, so that the animal responds more to A when it is preceded by X than when it is not.

Armed with these propositions, we can now return to the issue with which this chapter began—that of contextual control. First, we should not be surprised that a CR acquired in one context may fail to transfer fully when the CS is presented in another. We can assume that contexts, like other cues, can acquire conditional control without explicit discrimination training, and the fact that the contextual cues are often experienced without the target CS is likely to restrict any priming effect. It should be admitted, however, that we have little information about the factors that control the strength of the context–target association, and some training procedures may be more favorable regarding development of this association than others.

The latter possibility may hold the key to finding an explanation for the fact that demonstrations of the context-specificity of CRs after nonexplicit training can be hard to come by. Bouton, for example, has often found transfer across contexts to be perfect after such training (see, e.g., Bouton, 1993). Could it be that there is something about the details of his training procedure that favor formation of the direct association and thus encourage a priming effect that obscures context specificity? Certainly in one of the few experiments in which they obtained context specificity, Swartzentruber and Bouton (1992) adopted a procedure (previous exposure to the context) that would probably restrict development of the context–target association, a result that accords with the present hypothesis. We should point out, however, that these authors were also able to obtain context specificity in an experiment where the subjects were given previous exposure to the target stimulus in the context—a procedure that seems unlikely to prevent priming. The matter thus remains unresolved for the time being.

Finally, context dependence of latent inhibition must be addressed. This phenomenon, unlike the context dependence of the CR, is undoubtedly robust and readily reproducible—the theoretical position advanced here can explain why. We assume that, during preexposure, the contextual cues will form a direct association with the target stimulus and also acquire conditional control over the learning that underlies the latent inhibition effect. When it comes to the conditioning phase, both of these processes will limit the magnitude of the CR. The conditional control exerted by the contextual cues will foster retrieval of information that detracts from formation of the CS–US association, and the associative function of the contextual cues will, by way of the priming effect, mean that the CS–US association, when it does form, will not be fully effective in evoking a CR. In this case, in other words, the associative and retrieval functions of the contextual cues will be working in the same direction. If this argument is accepted, the fact that latent inhibition may show context dependence when conditioned responding does not may be taken as further evidence in support of the theoretical analysis developed in this chapter.

REFERENCES

Bonardi, C. (1992). Occasion setting without feature-positive discrimination training. *Learning and Motivation, 23,* 343–367.

Bouton, M. E. (1993). Context, time, and memory retrieval in the interference paradigms of Pavlovian learning. *Psychological Bulletin, 114,* 80–99.

Bouton, M. E., & Swartzentruber, D. (1986). Analysis of the associative and occasion-setting properties of contexts participating in a Pavlovian discrimination. *Journal of Experimental Psychology: Animal Behavior Processes, 12,* 333–350.

Channell, S., & Hall, G. (1983). Contextual effects in latent inhibition with an appetitive conditioning procedure. *Animal Learning & Behavior, 11,* 67–74.

Hall, G. (1991). *Perceptual and associative learning.* Oxford: Clarendon Press.

Hall, G., & Honey, R. C. (1989). Contextual effects in conditioning, latent inhibition, and habituation: Associative and retrieval functions of contextual cues. *Journal of Experimental Psychology: Animal Behavior Processes, 15,* 232–241.

Holland, P. C. (1989). Feature extinction enhances transfer of occasion setting. *Animal Learning & Behavior, 17,* 269–279.

Honey, R. C., Hall, G., & Bonardi, C. (1993). Negative priming in associative learning: Evidence from a serial-conditioning procedure. *Journal of Experimental Psychology: Animal Behavior Processes, 19,* 90–97.

Kimmel, H. D., & Ray, R. L. (1978). Transswitching: Conditioning with tonic and phasic stimuli. *Journal of Experimental Psychology: General, 107,* 187–205.

Lovibond, P. F., Preston, C. G., & Mackintosh, N. J. (1984). Context specificity of conditioning, extinction, and latent inhibition. *Journal of Experimental Psychology: Animal Behavior Processes, 10,* 360–375.

Rescorla, R. A. (1968). Probability of shock in the presence and absence of CS in fear conditioning. *Journal of Comparative and Physiological Psychology, 66,* 1–5.

Rescorla, R. A. (1986). Extinction of facilitation. *Journal of Experimental Psychology: Animal Behavior Processes, 12,* 16–24.

Ross, R. T. (1983). Relationships between the determinants of performance in serial feature positive discriminations. *Journal of Experimental Psychology: Animal Behavior Processes, 9,* 349–373.

Swartzentruber, D. (1991). Blocking between occasion setters and contextual stimuli. *Journal of Experimental Psychology: Animal Behavior Processes, 17,* 163–173.

Swartzentruber, D. (1995). Modulatory mechanisms in Pavlovian conditioning. *Animal Learning & Behavior, 23,* 123–143.

Swartzentruber, D., & Bouton, M. E. (1992). Context sensitivity of conditioned suppression following preexposure to the conditioned stimulus. *Animal Learning & Behavior, 20,* 97–103.

Wagner, A. R. (1976). Priming in STM: An information-processing mechanism for self-generated or retrieval-generated depression in performance. In T. J. Tighe & R. N. Leaton (Eds.), *Habituation: Perspectives from child development, animal behavior, and neurophysiology* (pp. 95–128). Hillsdale, NJ: Erlbaum.

Wagner, A. R. (1981). SOP: A model of automatic memory processing in animal behavior. In N. E. Spear & R. R. Miller (Eds.), *Information processing in animals: Memory mechanisms* (pp. 5–47). Hillsdale, NJ: Erlbaum.

Wilson, P. N., & Pearce, J. M. (1989). A role for stimulus generalization in conditional discrimination learning. *Quarterly Journal of Experimental Psychology, 41B,* 243–273.

Wilson, P. N., & Pearce, J. M. (1990). Selective transfer of responding in conditional discriminations. *Quarterly Journal of Experimental Psychology, 42B,* 41–583.

8

Hunger Cues as Modulatory Stimuli

T. L. Davidson

A starting point for many theories of energy regulation is that animals eat and engage in food-seeking behavior to maintain their supplies of metabolic fuels at homeostatic levels (see Kissileff & Van Itallie, 1982). A long-standing challenge for researchers of feeding behavior is to formulate principles that can explain how departures from homeostasis produce behavioral changes that serve to restore energy balance. It is clear that feeding behavior depends, in part, on the ability of animals to learn responses that enable them to obtain food and to learn relations between certain environmental events and food availability (see Capaldi, 1992). It is also clear that performance of these learned responses can be potentiated by fasting and other manipulations that are presumed to deplete energy stores (see Bolles, 1975). The purpose of this chapter is to consider the possibility that this type of potentiation might also be based on learning—that it is an example of Pavlovian occasion setting and related conditioned modulatory processes (e.g., Holland, 1983; Rescorla, 1985).

Support for this research was provided by grant HD28792 from the National Institutes of Health.

Hunger has traditionally been the concept most often invoked to explain increases in feeding behavior in response to food deprivation or other metabolic challenges. Hunger is typically viewed as a central state that occurs because of departure from energy homeostasis. Hunger has most often been assumed to influence feeding behavior by its effects on motivational mechanisms. For example, Hull (1943) proposed that the physiological need for food energized food intake and the responses that are instrumental to obtaining food by contributing to drive, which was viewed as the source of energy that motivated all behavior. The current prevailing view is that hunger enhances feeding behavior by increasing the palatability, attractiveness, or value of food or cues associated with food (e.g., Toates, 1994). Thus, the motivational power of incentive objects is thought to depend on the animal's level of hunger.

Hunger is also characterized as a stimulus or sensory event. For example, Cannon (1939, p. 70) identified hunger with a "very disagreeable ache or pang or sense of gnawing or pressure which is referred to the epigastrium." Although more recent discussions have not identified the sensory aspects of hunger with any specific physiological locus (e.g., Davidson, 1993; Freidman, 1990), the idea that energy need gives rise to discriminable interoceptive stimuli remains popular.

Several early theories proposed that the function of hunger in feeding behavior could be described solely in terms of learning about its cue properties (e.g., Estes, 1958; Smith & Guthrie, 1921). According to these formulations, hunger cues acquired the power to evoke directly feeding responses on the basis of their participation in simple stimulus–response (S–R) associations; it turned out to be quite difficult to establish hunger cues as direct elicitors of conditioned responses, however. This difficulty led some investigators to conclude that hunger stimuli were not important participants in the learned control of behavior (see Bolles, 1975, for review).

Contemporary views recognize that animal learning involves more than formation of simple S–R associations (e.g., Holland, 1990). It is now commonly held that animals form mental representations of the events that they experience and that they learn about the relations among those events. For example, as a result of Pavlovian conditioning, animals will form a memorial representation of an unconditioned stimulus (US). The capacity of a conditioned stimulus (CS) to excite that US memory determines the strength of the conditioned response (CR).

Of particular relevance to this analysis are situations in which the capacity of a CS to activate a US representation is augmented by presentation of another cue. For example, positive patterning is a Pavlovian discrimination problem that takes the general form X→A+, X–, A–. In these problems, stimulus X (e.g., a light) precedes and signals when stimulus A (e.g., a tone) is followed by food (+), whereas both X and A each signal nonreinforcement (–) when presented alone. The typical outcome of this type of training is that conditioned responding is promoted when X precedes A (i.e., on X→A+ trials) compared to when X and A are presented separately (e.g., Davidson & Rescorla, 1986). Thus, in positive patterning, an ordinary stimulus (e.g., a light) comes to potentiate conditioned responding evoked by a conventional CS (e.g., a tone).

This form of potentiation is not dependent on direct excitatory conditioning of the light, which evokes little or no conditioned responding when it is presented without the tone. Thus, the capacity of the light to promote performance in positive patterning and related (e.g., X→A+, A–) problems does not to appear to depend solely on its own association with the US. Nor has it been deemed necessary, or even useful, to suggest that the combination of X and A (e.g., a light cue with a tone CS) promotes behavior by increasing the value of the US or by producing some other type of motivational effect. Instead, some analyses propose that X comes to *modulate* or *set the occasion for* activation of the US representation by A (see Swartzentruber, 1995, for a review).

A MEMORY MODULATION MODEL OF HUNGER

Davidson (1993) suggested that the problem of when and when not to feed has the same general form (i.e., X→A+, X, A–,) as does the positive patterning problem. In this case, hunger cues signal that food cues will be followed by a particular postingestive US (X→A+), whereas neither hun-

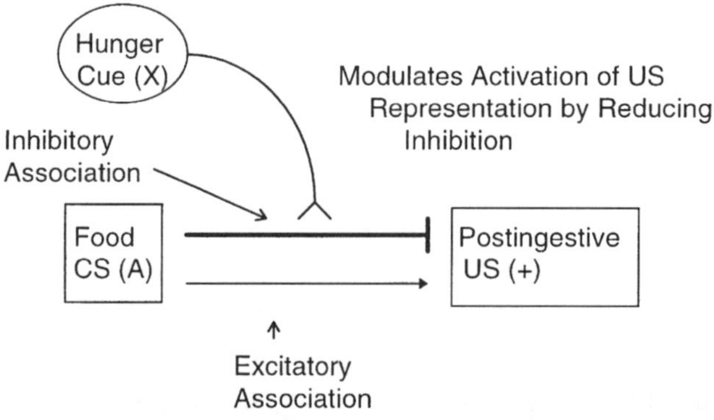

Figure 1

Hypothetical mechanism by which interoceptive hunger cues augment the capacity of a food CS to excite the memorial representation of an appetitive postingestive US. The strength of conditioned feeding behavior is assumed to be a positive function of activation of this US representation.

ger cues without food cues (X) nor food cues without hunger cues (A–) is followed by that US.

Borrowing much from accounts of occasion setting offered by Rescorla (1985) and Bouton (1994), Figure 1 describes how hunger cues might potentiate feeding behavior. According to the figure, the presence of hunger cues lowers the threshold for activation of the US representation. This enhances the capacity of conditioned food cues to evoke that memory and to elicit conditioned responses (Rescorla, 1985). Thus, stimulus control by hunger cues does not depend on the hunger cues being involved in a direct association with a US or a response. Instead, hunger cues are seen as modulating or setting the occasion for feeding behaviors to be evoked by conditioned food cues.

Two aspects of this diagram deserve special attention. First, the figure indicates that hunger potentiates feeding by influencing the memory of the *postingestive consequences* of food intake. The conditioned modulation view acknowledges that food intake produces potent orosensory and postingestive stimuli, and that both types of cues are likely to be memorially represented by animals. We suggest, however, that only activation of the postingestive US representation will be influenced by hunger cues. This may occur because hunger cues are not informative about when a given stimulus will be followed by a particular orosensory event (e.g., sweet or sour taste) but do signal that a given stimulus will be followed by a particular type of postingestive stimulation. The functional significance of this distinction is that CRs controlled only by orosensory USs (e.g., sweet tastes) will not normally be potentiated by hunger, whereas performance of learned behaviors evoked by activation of postingestive US memories will depend on the presence of hunger cues.

Second, consistent with previous interpretations that are based on learning with conventional types of Pavlovian stimuli (e.g., Bouton 1994; Rescorla, 1985; Swartzentruber & Rescorla, 1994), the diagram indicates that hunger cues lower the threshold for activation of the US representation by removing or reducing the strength of inhibitory associations between food cues and the memory of a postingestive US. Those inhibitory associations are presumably formed when animals eat food without hunger cues being present (A– trials) and do not experience the appetitive postingestive US. From a functional standpoint, this means that hunger will be unable to potentiate feeding behavior unless food cues are involved with both excitatory and inhibitory associations with the US representation. In other words, within this framework, a food CS (e.g., an orosensory cue) is followed by an appetitive postingestive US when animals are hungry, which enables an excitatory association between the CS and that US representation to be formed. The appetitive postingestive US does not follow the food CS if eating occurs when the animal is sated; this leads to an inhibitory association between the food CS and the representation of the appetitive postingestive US that coexists with the excitatory association that was mentioned earlier. Hunger cues potentiate feeding behavior by removing or reducing the effectiveness of this inhibitory association.

Empirical Support for the Model

As described earlier, the memory modulation model of hunger is based on four assumptions: (a) food cues (i.e., the immediate sensory properties of food and stimuli related to food) become associated with appetitive postingestive USs; (b) that different degrees of hunger give rise to discriminable interoceptive stimuli; (c) that hunger cues modulate the capacity of Pavlovian CSs to activate US representations; and (d) that modulation by hunger cues depends on whether there are inhibitory CS–US associations. Evidence of this is considered next.

Do Rats Associate Food Cues With Postingestive USs?

Conditioned taste aversion provides the classic demonstration that animals can learn to associate the sensory properties of food with aversive postingestive consequences produced by illness. As a consequence of this association, the capacity of a food cue to evoke appetitive behavior is greatly reduced (see Domjan, 1980, for a review). In addition, studies of *flavor-nutrient* learning show that rats can also learn about the postingestive aftereffects of consuming highly caloric or nutritious foods (see Capaldi, 1992). For example, Sclafani and his coworkers (see Sclafani, 1990, for a review) trained rats with an intragastric infusion preparation that allowed the preabsorptive stimuli arising from intake of different flavors to be dissociated from their nutritive postingestive consequences. With this procedure, rats learned a preference for a flavor associated with a nutritive US even when delivery of the US solution completely bypassed the oral cavity. The rats apparently formed an association between the neutral flavors and the appetitive postingestive consequences of intake. These data support two basic assumptions of the memory modulation model of hunger: that (a) animals encode information about postingestive USs, and (b) the memorial representation of the appetitive postingestive US can be activated by food cue CSs.

Do Different Degrees of Food Deprivation Give Rise to Discriminable Interoceptive Stimuli?

There is no basis for hunger cues to function like Pavlovian occasion setters if rats are unable to discriminate between the interoceptive sensory consequences of different levels of energy need. A number of reports provide evidence that rats can learn discrimination problems on the basis of cues arising from different levels of food deprivation. Acquisition of *deprivation intensity discrimination* is usually slow and laborious when food deprivation cues are used to reinforce different instrumental responses. For example, hundreds of trials are required before rats are able to learn that response A (e.g., turn left in a maze or press left manipulandum) leads to food only when the animal is highly food deprived and response B (e.g., turn right in a maze or press right manipulandum) leads to food only when the animal is under a lower level of food deprivation (Corwin, Woolverton, & Schuster, 1990; Jenkins & Hanratty, 1949; Schuh et al., 1994). These types of learning problems are likely to require rats to form direct S–R associations between different deprivation cues and responses.

According to the memory modulation model, the function of hunger cues in the control of food intake does not depend on their participation in S–R associations. Instead, these stimuli signal when food-related cues are likely to be followed by a US. Discrimination problems that require rats to use their deprivation intensity signals to predict the availability of food are learned much faster than those requiring rats to learn different CRs (e.g., Capaldi, Vivieros, & Davidson, 1981).

For example, in an experiment recently conducted in our laboratory (Davidson, Altizer, & Barbato, 1998), rats were trained to use cues arising from 0-hr (i.e., the rats were fed ad libitum for about 24 hr before the training session) and 24-hr (no food was available for 24 hr preceding training) food deprivation as discriminative signals for delivery of sucrose pellets. For half the rats, sucrose pellets were delivered at the end of a 4-min training session when the rats were 0-hr food deprived. Pellets were

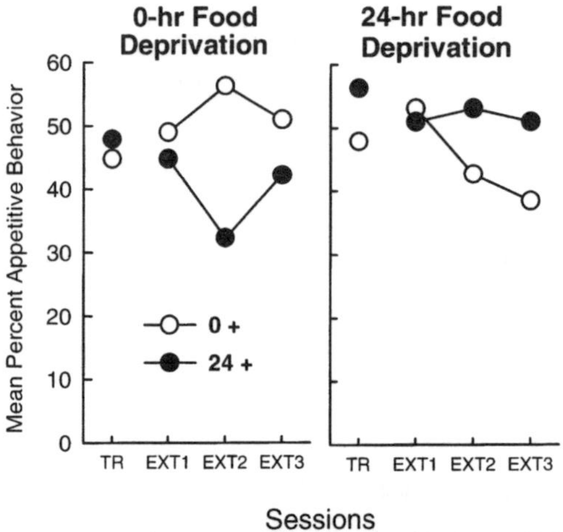

Figure 2

Mean percentage appetitive behavior (i.e., percent of time that an infrared photobeam near the food cup was interrupted) under 0- *(left panel)* and 24-hr *(right panel)* food deprivation, for rats trained to anticipate sucrose pellets under 0-hr but not 24-hr food deprivation (group 0+), and rats trained with the opposite deprivation pellet contingency (group 24+). Data are presented for the last session of training (TR) and for each extinction session (EXT1–EXT3).

not delivered when rats had been deprived for 24 hr. The remaining rats had the opposite deprivation-pellet contingency. The groups were given only four training trials under each deprivation condition. The experiment used a latent discrimination design (e.g., Davidson, Flynn, & Jarrard, 1992) in which learning emerged during a subsequent test phase rather than during initial training. Appetitive behavior (indexed by the percentage of time per trial that a photobeam closest to the food cup was broken) at the end training was high and did not differ as a function of group or deprivation level. All rats were then tested in extinction for several sessions during which their deprivation level alternated daily between 0 and 24 hr. Figure 2 shows that, for both groups, appetitive behavior extinguished significantly more slowly under the rats' previously reinforced compared to their previously nonreinforced level of food deprivation.

The results of another test confirmed that the rats were discriminating

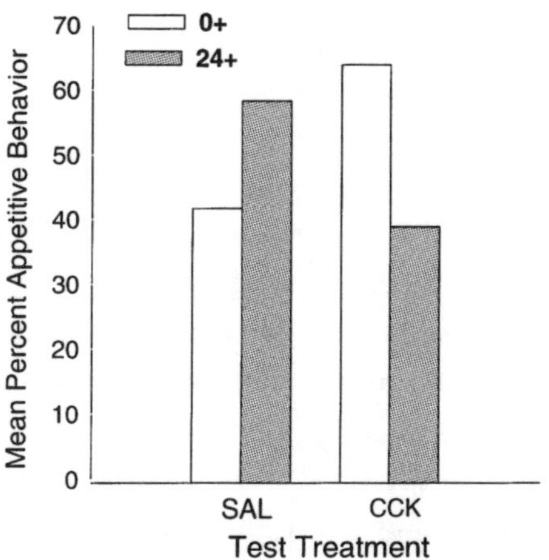

Figure 3

Mean percentage appetitive behavior for rats in groups 0+ and 24+ following intraperitoneal injection with 8 μg/kg cholecystokinin (CCK) or isotonic saline (SAL). Testing occurred when rats were food-deprived for 24 hr.

on the basis of the interoceptive stimulus consequences of their deprivation conditions rather than on exteroceptive cues that varied with the food deprivation regimen (e.g., presence or absence of food in the home cage). When under 24-hr food deprivation, half the rats in each group were injected with 8 μg/kg cholecystokinin (CCK), a peptide that is widely held to cause satiety signals in rats and other species (Gibbs & Smith, 1992). The remaining rats received control injections of isotonic saline. As shown in Figure 3, relative to saline, CCK increased appetitive behavior for rats that were previously trained to anticipate sucrose delivery at 0-hr food deprivation and decreased appetitive behavior for rats that received the sucrose pellet US only when deprived of food for 24 hr. This could not be a nonspecific effect of CCK, because both decreases and increases in conditioned responding were observed following CCK administration. Furthermore, exteroceptive stimuli were constant for both groups. Therefore, the results indicate that appetitive behavior was under the learned control of interoceptive cues produced by different levels of food deprivation. This learned control developed as a result of only four training trials under each level of food deprivation.

Previous experiments from our laboratory also provide clear evidence that rats can use their interoceptive hunger cues as discriminative signals for delivery of shock. In these studies, rats rapidly show more conditioned freezing under their shocked compared to their nonshocked level of food deprivation (see Davidson, 1993, for a review). These data reduce the plausibility of the argument that deprivation intensity discrimination could be based on incentive motivational factors associated with the food or ingestion. Moreover, we have shown that discriminative control of conditioned freezing by food deprivation intensity stimuli also generalizes to cues produced by physiological manipulations, such as administration of insulin, glucose antimetabolites, nutritive stomach loads, or CCK, all of which are known to either promote or reduce food intake (Benoit & Davidson, 1996; Davidson, 1987; Davidson & Carretta, 1993). These data provide strong evidence that hunger gives rise to discriminable internal signals and that these signals can acquire strong learned control over behavior.

Are Hunger Cues Modulatory Stimuli?

The memory modulation model proposes that the capacity of hunger stimuli to promote feeding is based on the solution of an X→A+, X, A– positive patterning problem. According to this formulation, hunger cues reduce the threshold for activation of appetitive postingestive US representations, thereby making it easier for food CSs to evoke conditioned feeding responses. An important feature of this account is that the capacity of hunger cues to modulate memory activation is *not specific to the CS with which it was originally trained*—that is, hunger cues will augment the response-promoting power of any cue associated with the same US that was subject to modulation by the hunger cue. Assuming that most food cues are followed by a similar postingestive US, hunger cues should therefore be able to promote feeding responses to a wide array of foods and food-related stimuli.

The lack of CS specificity is an aspect of the modulation model that distinguishes it from some nonmodulatory explanations of positive patterning. For example, Gibson and Booth (1989) described the influence of hunger on feeding in terms of configural learning. According to the configural learning hypothesis, a unique cue with perceptual features different from either hunger cues or food cues emerges from the combination of these stimuli. Based on the strength of its direct association with the US, this configural cue comes to activate the US representation to a degree that exceeds the threshold for response elicitation. Gibson and Booth proposed that interoceptive cues (e.g., gastric distention cues) and dietary cues (e.g., tastes) combined to form a configural stimulus that directly activates feeding behavior. As a result, changing either hunger or dietary cues should disrupt behavior control, because the configural CS that emerged from the combination of those stimuli would no longer be present.

Adapting strategies used previously to investigate learning with conventional cues (e.g., Davidson & Rescorla, 1986; Rescorla, 1985), Davidson and Benoit (1996, Experiment 1) trained rats to use food deprivation cues as discriminative signals for a mild shock, and then used transfer tests to assess whether learning was based on modulatory or configural processes. Our discrimination problem took the general form X→A+, X, A– that was described earlier. In this case, cues arising from different levels of food deprivation (X) and experimental context cues (A–) were not followed by shock when they occurred separately (i.e., deprivation cues were not shocked in the home cage, and context cues were not shocked without the appropriate food deprivation cue). Shock was only delivered when food deprivation and context cues occurred together in serial compound (X→A+).

We first trained rats in a distinctive context (A) under conditions in which their level of food deprivation at the time of training alternated between 0 and 24 hr. One group (24+) was shocked following 24-hr but not 0-hr food deprivation. Another group (24–) received the opposite deprivation level–shock contingency. A control group (+/–) received shock in a manner uncorrelated with level of food deprivation. A second control group (–/–) received no shocks during initial training. Incidence of conditioned freezing during the first 2 min of each 4-min session served as the index of learning.

By the end of training, the performance of each group under each deprivation level was appropriate to its deprivation level–shock contingency—that is, Groups 24+ and 24– froze more under their shocked than under their nonshocked level of food deprivation, Group +/– showed high, nondifferential freezing under both levels of food deprivation, and Group –/– showed essentially no freezing under either deprivation level.

Of particular interest was how behavioral control under 24-hr food deprivation was influenced by these different training histories. Figure 4 compares the freezing behavior of each group on the last block of training under 24-hr food deprivation and during subsequent transfer testing. The far left panel of Figure 4 shows that, during the last block of training, 24-hr food deprivation produced less freezing for group 24– than for group 24+. Level of freezing under 24-hr food deprivation was the same for groups +/– and 24+, whereas group –/– froze much less than the other groups.

Next, control of conditioned freezing by 24-hr food deprivation stimuli was assessed in a novel transfer context (B) that had not previously been associated with shock. Contexts varied in terms of auditory cues, olfactory cues chamber illumination, and floor surface. Despite the relatively high levels of freezing for all but group –/– at the end of training, Figure 4 (left-center panel) shows that almost no freezing was observed for any group in novel context B. This indicated that hunger cues did not control freezing in Context A on the sole basis of their direct association with the shock US. Indeed, food deprivation cues controlled no more conditioned freezing from groups that had been shocked than for group –/–, which had not been shocked during training.

The rats were then trained in another novel context (C), where they were 19-hr water- but not food-deprived. The purpose of training under water deprivation was to associate Context C with the shock US in the presence of interoceptive states signals that were different from those used in the 0- and 24-hr food deprivation conditions of the original training. All rats received three shocked trials followed by one trial without shock.

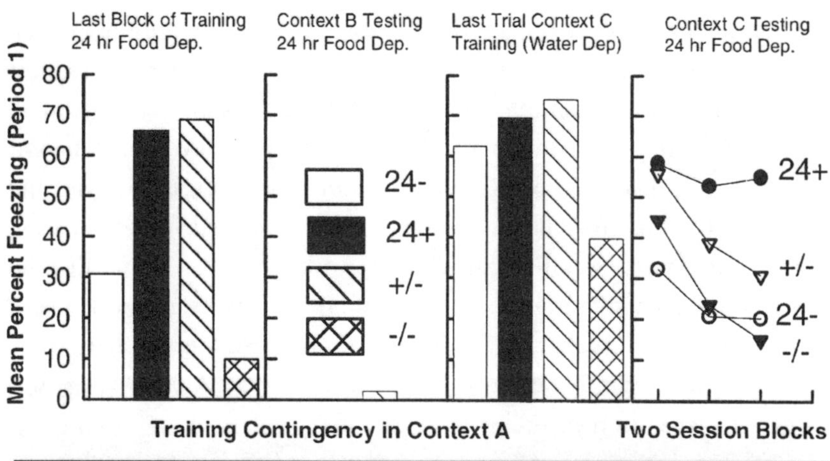

Figure 4

Mean percentage freezing under 24-hr food deprivation in Contexts A, B, and C. Open bars and circles show freeing data for Group 24–, which received foot shock after 0- but not 24-hr food deprivation in Context A. Filled bars and symbols show data from Group 24+, which received the reverse contingency between shock and food deprivation in Context A. Striped bars and triangles show data for Group +/–, which received uncorrelated pairings of deprivation and shock in Context A. The far left panel shows data for all groups during the last session of training in Context A. The left-center panel shows data for all groups during Context B testing. The right-center panel shows data for all groups at the end of Context C, which was shock training under 19-hr water deprivation. The far right panel shows two-session blocks of transfer testing under 24-hr food deprivation for all groups. From Davidson & Benoit (1996). Reprinted by permission of Purdue University.

The center-right panel of Figure 4 shows that Groups 24–, 24+ and +/– all exhibited comparable and high levels of conditioned freezing as a result of Context C training. Rats in group –/–, which had not been shocked before training in Context C, showed less freezing than rats in the other groups.

Finally, all rats were returned to the food deprivation schedule used during the training of Context A. The capacity of cues arising from 24-hr food deprivation to control conditioned freezing in Context C was then assessed for all groups. According to the memory modulation model, hunger cues trained to modulate conditioned freezing in Context A would exert similar control of freezing in Context C. This is indeed the case, because the capacity for hunger cues to lower the threshold for activating the US memory extends to other cues that are associated with that US. If hunger cues became conditioned modulators of the capacity of Context A to activate the US representation, they would also have that function for Context C, because both Contexts A and C were associated with the same US. On the other hand, if hunger cues controlled freezing during initial training as a result of participating with Context A stimuli in the production of a configural cue, there would be little basis for hunger cues to control freezing behavior in Context C, because the configural cue arising from the combination of hunger and Context A cues would not be present when hunger occurred in Context C.

The far right panel of Figure 4 shows that freezing during this test varied with the deprivation cue–shock contingencies that had been established during original training in Context A. Food deprivation promoted freezing for Group 24+ relative to the uncorrelated control (Group +/–) and inhibited freezing for Group 24– relative to that control. This outcome indicated that freezing behavior was not based on formation of a direct association involving the shock US and a "configural" CS that could have emerged from the compound of deprivation and exteroceptive contextual stimuli. Because food deprivation cues never occurred in Context C when shock was delivered, the rats had no opportunity to learn such a configural association. Instead, the finding that 24-hr food deprivation cues controlled freezing in Context C supports the idea that these signals modulated activation of the memorial representation of the shock US that was established during training in Context A. These findings are important because they show that hunger stimuli can function, in principle, as conditioned modulatory or occasion-setting cues.

There is also more direct evidence that potentiation of feeding behavior is based on appetitive postingestive US representations being modulated by hunger signals. We (Davidson, Altizer, Benoit, Walls, & Powley, 1997) trained rats with one CS (e.g., a tone) that signaled delivery of peanut oil (100% fat) and another CS (e.g., a light) that signaled delivery of sucrose pellets (100% carbohydrate). The identities of the CSs were counterbalanced for each US. After asymptotic conditioned responding (approach to the food cup), rats were food sated and given treatments designed to selectively induce lipoprivation or glucoprivation. Next, the capacities of the cue for oil and the cue for sucrose to evoke conditioned responding were compared. Testing was carried out in extinction to rule out the possibility that differences in responding were based on the orosensory or postingestive consequences of fat or carbohydrate intake. In one experiment, treating rats with Na-2-mercaptoacetate (MA), an agent that produces lipoprivation by blocking fatty acid oxidation, produced significantly more responding to the CS for oil than to the CS for sucrose pellets. Responding for rats treated with saline did not differ dependent on the CS. A second experiment showed that surgical disruption of subdiaphragmatic vagal afferent fibers abolished the capacity of MA to augment responding evoked by a CS for oil. Vagal afferent fibers are thought to provide an important neural pathway for transmission of lipoprivic signals to the brain (Ritter, Calingasan, Hutton, & Dinh, 1992). Another study in this series (Davidson et al., 1997, Experiment 4) found that central glucoprivation produced by intracerebroventricular infusion of glucose antimetabolites promoted significantly more test responding to a CS associated with sucrose than to a CS associated with oil.

These data are important for two reasons: First, they provide evidence that rats represent information about the postingestive metabolic consequences of fat and carbohydrate USs. If the US representations of the rats only contained information about the preingestive or orosensory features of peanut oil and sucrose pellets, there would seem to be little basis for different metabolic manipulations to selectively promote response evocation by the conditioned cues for these USs. Second, which postingestive US representation was activated the most depended on the type of metabolic depletion. This indicates that lipoprivic and glucoprivic treatments selectively enhanced the capacity of different CSs to activate the memories of the fat and carbohydrate USs with which they were associated. This finding is consistent with the idea that the threshold for activation of fat and carbohydrate US representations were selectively modulated by lipoprivic and glucoprivic signals, respectively.

Does Modulation by Hunger Cues Depend on Inhibitory CS–US Associations?

The memory modulation model of hunger proposes that hunger cues potentiate feeding behavior by removing or reducing inhibitory associations between food cue CSs and appetitive postingestive USs. By reducing the influence of inhibitory associations, the ability of concurrent excitatory associations between food cues and postingestive USs to evoke feeding behavior is enhanced. Thus, hunger cues potentiate feeding behavior by reducing or removing inhibition.

One implication of this model is that hunger cues will be much less effective potentiators of feeding behavior when inhibitory CS–US associations are weak or absent. Davidson and Benoit (1996, Experiment 2) provided evidence consistent with this hypothesis. Following procedures like those described earlier (Davidson & Benoit, 1996, Experiment 1), rats were trained in one context to use their hunger stimuli as discriminative signals for delivery of shock. Next, the rats were water-deprived before being given additional shock training in a different transfer context. Half of the rats received an extinction session at the end of shocked training; the remainder did not receive a session without shock. The effects of reinstating hunger cues in the transfer context was then assessed for all rats. Hunger cues promoted significantly more conditioned freezing for rats that received both training and extinction in the transfer context than for rats that received only simple excitatory training.

These results are consistent with the idea that hunger cues promoted conditioned responding by reducing the strength of the inhibitory association between context cues and the representation of the shock US. The rats that received extinction training in the transfer context would have had the opportunity to form an inhibitory association between context cues and the shock US. According to the memory modulation model, reinstating hunger cues would then reduce the strength of this inhibitory association, thereby making it easier for excitatory transfer context cues to activate the memory of the shock US. For the rats that received only simple excitatory training in the transfer context, there was little or no inhibition to be removed by the modulatory hunger cues and therefore little basis for enhanced activation of the US representation.

The results of the previous experiment were obtained under conditions in which extinction was the basis for forming an inhibitory context–shock association. According to the memory modulation model, an inhibitory association between food cues and the representation of an appetitive US would also form as a result of food satiation—that is, when an animal eats food when satiated, the appetitive postingestive US that occurred under hunger is no longer present. Therefore, food cues that are present during satiation would now become part of an inhibitory association that suppresses activation of the memory of the appetitive postingestive US. Davidson, Benoit, and Morell (1998) obtained a pattern of results consistent with this analysis. We measured the tendency of hungry rats to break an infrared photobeam that was located in front of a food cup where novel sucrose pellets were delivered. A pellet was delivered about once every 2 min. The rats received 15 pellets per session for 8 sessions (120 pellets). Within the present theoretical framework, this initial training would establish an excitatory association between the representation of sucrose pellets and the representation of the postingestive consequences of pellet consumption. Next, two groups of rats were food-sated and placed in a new context (a large white tub with wood shavings in the bottom). One group (SE) was given 60 additional sucrose pellets (which they ate), and the another group (SN) received no additional pellets. Two additional groups, one exposed to sucrose pellets in the novel context (DE) and one not exposed to pellets (DN), were also tested; the rats in these groups, however, remained food-deprived throughout the experiment. From the perspective of the conditioned modulation view, receiving pellets when food-sated would amount to an extinction trial—that is, under satiation, the sucrose pellets would not be followed by the appetitive postingestive US that occurred when the rats ate the pellets when food-deprived. Thus, viewed within the present theoretical framework, giving Group SE pellets under both

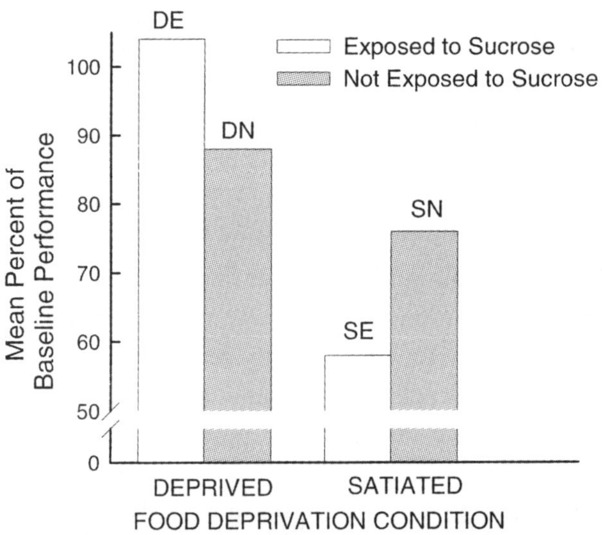

Figure 5

Mean percentage of baseline appetitive behavior during testing. Rats that were exposed to sucrose pellets when food-sated before testing are designated SE; rats that were food-sated but not exposed to pellets before testing are designated SN; rats that were exposed to pellets but were not food-sated before testing are designated DE; and rats that were not food-sated or exposed to pellets before testing are designated DN. Baseline refers to the percentage of time that a photobeam nearest the food cup was interrupted at the end of initial training.

food deprivation and satiation amounted to giving them both excitatory training and extinction with the sucrose pellet CS. On the other hand, giving groups SN, DE, and DN pellets only under food deprivation amounted to giving them only simple excitatory training with the sucrose pellet CS. After the pellet exposure phase, all groups were returned to the training apparatus for a test session that compared the effects of satiation (for groups SE and SN) with food deprivation (for groups DE and DN) on the tendency to break a photobeam near the food cup.

The test phase results of this experiment (expressed as a percentage of performance at the end of initial training) are shown in Figure 5. The effects of satiation on test performance depended on whether the rats had been exposed previously to sucrose pellets when satiated—that is, satiation had a stronger suppressive effect on food cup behavior for group SE, which had previously consumed pellets when satiated, than for group SN, which did not receive pellets when satiated. Moreover, food cup behavior for group SN was not significantly different from that of groups DN or DE, both of which were tested when food-deprived. Group SE showed significantly less food cup behavior than either of these food-deprived groups. Thus, satiation had a significant suppressive effect on food cup approach behavior only for rats that ate food pellets when sated. These findings seem to be entirely consistent with analysis in terms of satiation, setting the conditions for development of an inhibitory association between a food CS and its appetitive postingestive US. Removing hunger cues apparently reduces response evocation by food cues only for rats that have formed this inhibitory association. These findings are also interpretable within an incentive learning framework (see Dickinson & Balleine, 1994). This interpretation will be considered later.

A similar insensitivity to satiation resulting from removal of the hippocampus has been reported by Davidson & Jarrard (1993). They found that food-sated rats with selective neurotoxic lesions of the hippocampus made significantly (about 65%) more contacts with food than did controls. Curiously, although these rats made more contact with food (as measured by changes in electrical resistance of a mesh grid that covered the food hopper in the home cage), they did not consume significantly more food than controls.

There are at least three ways to interpret these findings. First, increased contact with food without increased intake might be a nonspecific consequence of greater general activity. Rats with hippocampal damage also moved about the cage more than controls. Increased contact with the food hopper may be a nonspecific consequence of a general increase in locomotor movement.

Second, rats without a hippocampus may have difficulty detecting their interoceptive satiety cues. These rats would therefore be less able to anticipate that food cues are no longer followed by the appetitive postingestive US. Under these conditions, hippocampal rats would engage in more anticipatory food approach and sampling behavior than controls, but they would not necessarily eat more food, because the postingestive consequences of intake (i.e., no postingestive US) would be the same as for controls.

A third possibility is that hippocampal rats may be impaired, not in detecting satiety cues, but in using them. According to the conditioned modulation analysis proposed here, the effects of satiation on feeding behavior depend on an inhibitory association being established between food cues and the representation of the appetitive postingestive US. If rats without a hippocampus have difficulty learning this inhibitory association, they would be less able to suppress anticipatory responses evoked by conditioned food cues when they are food-sated. It should be noted that, rather than increasing food contacts as a nonspecific consequence of increased general activity, the latter interpretation suggests that increased general activity is a specific consequence of an increased tendency of food cues to evoke approach responses to the food cup.

Recent findings in our laboratory favor the view that removal of the hippocampus impairs acquisition of inhibitory CS–US associations in many simple appetitive learning situations. Benoit, Davidson, Trigilio, Chan, and Jarrard (1997) found that rats have difficulty learning to inhibit responding to both diffuse contextual cues and punctate CSs that were associated with food USs. This impairment, however, was revealed only when those conditioned cues had also been subjected to extinction training. Removing the hippocampus did not increase responding to cues that received only simple excitatory training, nor did rats without a hippocampus show greater activity than controls in contexts that had received little or no excitatory training.

For example, rats without a hippocampus showed significantly greater (about 130%) behavioral activity in a context that had been subjected to both excitatory and extinction training. In contrast, hippocampal rats showed about 18% less activity than controls in a context that received little or no excitatory training. The latter result indicates that increased activity is not a strong, nonspecific effect of hippocampal damage.

In addition, conditioned food cup approach behavior was significantly greater for rats with hippocampal damage (about 62% greater than controls) following extinction of an excitatory punctate CS. That CS did not evoke more conditioned responding by rats without a hippocampus at the beginning of extinction training (hippocampal rats responded about 2% less than controls). The results support the hypothesis that hippocampal rats show more excitatory conditioned responses than controls because they are less able to learn the opposing inhibitory association.

This section began with the hypothesis that, when sated, intact rats learn an inhibitory association between food cues and the representation of the postingestive US. It appears that removing the hippocampus interferes with the ability of rats to learn inhibitory associations between context cues and representation of a food US and also between discrete CSs and memorial representation of food. That rats without a hippocampus also show enhanced anticipatory responding to food cues when food-sated provides converging evidence for the notion that the suppressive effects of satiation on responding to food cues depends on learning an inhibitory association between those cues and the representation of the appetitive postingestive US.

How Do Hunger Cues Reduce Inhibition?

Some of the findings mentioned so far might also be interpreted within an incentive value framework. For example, Dickinson and Balleine (1994) suggested that rats need experience with food under satiation to learn that the incentive value of the food has decreased from the relatively high value it had when the animal was hungry. It is important to note, however, that analysis in terms of conditioned modulation provides a unitary account of how hunger cues potentiate conditioned responding whether learning is based on aversive (shock) or on appetitive (food) USs. It is difficult to see how an incentive value account would explain the capacity of hunger cues to potentiate conditioned aversive responses. It would seem quite awkward to suggest that hunger somehow increases the aversive value of shock.

In addition, interpretations that are based on incentive value are typically vague about the mechanisms that enable changes in hunger to increase or decrease the value of food and cues related to food. The modula-

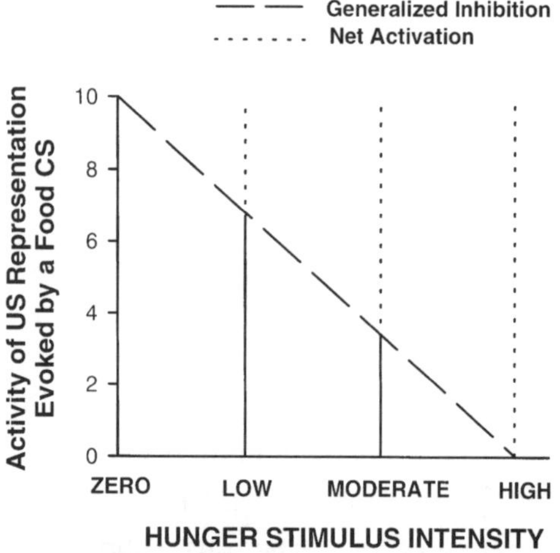

Figure 6

Hypothetical relationship between intensity of hunger stimulation and the capacity of a food CS to activate the memorial representation of an appetitive postingestive US.

tion model proposes that hunger potentiates feeding behavior by reducing the strength of inhibitory associations between food cues and the memories of the appetitive postingestive US. The way these inhibitory associations might be formed has been discussed earlier. However, the manner in which hunger cues reduce the influence of these inhibitory associations is, at present, specified no more clearly than the manner in which hunger might alter incentive value or other sources of motivation.

Figure 6 shows how a food CS might excite the memory of its appetitive postingestive US at three different intensities of hunger stimulation. The memory modulation model proposes that hunger cues signal when food cues will be followed by an appetitive postingestive US. When hunger cues are absent, that US does not occur. Under these conditions, interoceptive cues that are concomitant with satiation could be expected to become a source of inhibition. In Figure 6, these inhibitory stimuli are located at the zero point (origin) of a hypothetical hunger cue intensity continuum.

This inhibition reduces the capacity of food cues to excite the memory of the appetitive postingestive US. On the basis of principles derived from Spence (1936), it is assumed that inhibition generalizes along the intensity continuum (indicated by the dashed line in Figure 6), becoming progressively weaker as hunger stimulus intensity increases. Thus, more inhibition is present at lower relative to higher intensities of hunger stimulation.

Net activation of the US memory is determined by subtracting inhibition from the excitatory potential of the conditioned food cue. In Figure 6, the amount to which the dotted, vertical lines extend above the inhibitory gradient at each deprivation level represents net activation of the US memory at each level. Thus, net activation of the US representation by food cues is shown to be greater under higher compared to lower intensities of hunger stimulation. Because performance of feeding responses is assumed to be an increasing function of the net activation of the appetitive US representation, Figure 6 indicates that feeding behavior will be potentiated more by hunger cues of higher compared to lower intensity. This is one way that hunger cues could reduce inhibition and thereby potentiate feeding behavior.

CONCLUSION

This chapter makes the case that feeding behavior in response to departures from energy homeostasis may depend on establishment of interoceptive hunger cues as Pavlovian occasion setters. From this perspective, interoceptive cues produced by food deprivation and other types of metabolic depletion promote feeding behavior by making it easier for food CSs to excite the memorial representations of postingestive USs. Hunger cues modulate the effectiveness of excitatory food cue–postingestive US associations by reducing the strength of concurrent inhibitory associations between food CSs and the memory of the postingestive US. This approach accounts for the effects of energy need on feeding behavior without appealing to incentive value or other motivational concepts. Instead, the principles used to explain regulatory feeding are the same as the principles used to describe how animals solve conventional Pavlovian discrimination problems.

REFERENCES

Benoit, S. C., & Davidson, T. L. (1996). Interoceptive sensory signals produced by 24-hr food deprivation, pharmacological glucoprivation and lipoprivation. *Behavioral Neuroscience, 101,* 1–13.

Benoit, S. C., Davidson, T. L., Trigilio, T., Chan, K., & Jarrard, L. E. (1997). *Pavlovian conditioning and extinction of context cues and punctate CS in rats with ibotenate lesions of the hippocampus.* Manuscript submitted for publication.

Bolles, R. C. (1975). *Theory of motivation* (2nd ed.). New York: Harper and Row.

Bouton, M. E. (1994). Context, ambiguity and classical conditioning. *Current Directions in Psychological Science, 3,* 49–53.

Cannon, W. B. (1939). *The wisdom of the body.* New York: W. W. Norton.

Capaldi, E. D. (1992). Conditioned food preferences. In D. Medin (Ed.), *The psychology of learning and motivation* (Vol. 28, pp. 1–33). New York: Academic Press.

Capaldi, E. D., Viveiros, D. M., & Davidson, T. L. (1981). Deprivation stimulus intensity and incentive factors in the control of instrumental responding. *Journal of Experimental Psychology: Animal Behavior Processes, 7,* 140–149.

Corwin, R. L., Woolverton, W. L., & Schuster, C. R. (1990). Effects of cholecystokinin, d-amphetamine and fenfluramine in rats trained to discriminate 3 from 22 hr of food deprivation. *Journal of Pharmacology and Experimental Therapeutics, 253,* 720–728.

Davidson, T. L. (1987). Learning about deprivation intensity stimuli. *Behavioral Neuroscience, 101,* 198–208.

Davidson, T. L. (1993). The nature and function of interoceptive signals to feed: Toward integration of physiological and learning perspectives. *Psychological Review, 100,* 640–657.

Davidson, T. L., Altizer, A. M., & Barbato, J. (1998). *Deprivation intensity discrimination based on a sucrose pellet US generalizes to cues produced by injection of cholecystokinin.* Manuscript in preparation.

Davidson, T. L., Altizer, A. M., Benoit, S. C., Walls, E. K., & Powley, T. L. (1997). Encoding and selective activation of "metabolic memories" in the rat. *Behavioral Neuroscience, 111,* 1014–1030.

Davidson, T. L., & Benoit, S. C. (1996). The learned function of food deprivation cues: A role for conditioned modulation. *Animal Learning & Behavior, 24,* 46–56.

Davidson, T. L., Benoit, S. C., & Morell, J. A. (1998). *Formation of Pavlovian associations as a consequence of eating food when satiated.* Unpublished manuscript, Purdue University, West Lafayette, IN.

Davidson, T. L., & Carretta, J. C. (1993). Cholecystokinin, but not bombesin, has interoceptive sensory consequences like 1-hr food deprivation. *Physiology and Behavior, 53,* 737–735.

Davidson, T. L., Flynn, F. W., & Jarrard, L. E. (1992). Potency of food deprivation intensity cues as discriminative stimuli. *Journal of Experimental Psychology: Animal Behavior Processes, 18,* 174–181.

Davidson, T. L., & Jarrard, L. E. (1997). A role for hippocampus in the utilization of hunger signals. *Behavioral and Neural Biology, 59,* 167–171.

Davidson, T. L., & Rescorla, R. A. (1986). Transfer of facilitation in the rat. *Animal Learning & Behavior, 4,* 380–386.

Dickinson, A., & Balleine, B. W. (1994). Motivational control of goal-directed action. *Animal Learning & Behavior, 22,* 1–18.

Domjan, M. (1980). Ingestional aversive learning: Unique and general processes. In J. S. Rosenblatt, R. A. Hinde, C. Beer, & M. C. Busnel (Eds.), *Advance in the study of behavior* (Vol. 11, pp. 275–336). New York: Academic Press.

Estes, W. K. (1958). Stimulus-response theory of drive. In M. R. Jones (Ed.), *Nebraska symposium on motivation.* Lincoln: University of Nebraska Press.

Friedman, M. I. (1990). Making sense out of calories. In E. M. Stricker (Ed.), *Handbook of Behavioral Neurobiology* (Vol. 10, pp. 513–529). New York: Plenum Press.

Gibbs, J., & Smith, G. P. (1992). Peripheral signals for satiety in animals and humans. In G. H. Harvey & S. H. Kennedy (Eds.), *The biology of feast and famine: Relevance to eating disorders* (pp. 61–72). San Diego, CA: Academic Press.

Gibson, E. L., & Booth, D. A. (1989). Dependence of carbohydrate-conditioned flavor preference on internal state in rats. *Learning and Motivation, 20,* 36–47.

Holland, P. C. (1983). Occasion-setting in Pavlovian feature positive discrimination. In M. L. Commons, R. J. Herrnstein, & A. R. Wagner (Eds.), *Quantitative analyses of behavior: Discrimination processes* (Vol. 4, pp. 183–206). New York: Ballinger.

Holland, P. C. (1990). Event representation in Pavlovian conditioning: Image and action. *Cognition, 37,* 105–131.

Hull, C. L. (1943). *Principles of behavior.* New York: Appleton.

Jenkins, J. J., & Hanratty, J. A. (1949). Drive intensity discrimination in the white rat. *Journal of Comparative and Physiological Psychology, 42,* 228–232.

Kissileff, H. R., & Van Itallie, T. B. (1982). Physiology of the control of food intake. *American Review of Nutrition, 2,* 371–418.

Rescorla, R. A. (1985). Facilitation and inhibition. In R. R. Miller & N. E. Spear (Eds.), *Information processing in animals: Conditioned inhibition* (pp. 299–326). Hillsdale, NJ: Erlbaum.

Ritter, S., Calingasan, N. Y., Hutton, B., & Dinh, T. T. (1992). Cooperation of vagal and central neural systems in monitoring metabolic events controlling feeding behavior. In S. Ritter, R. C. Ritter, & C. D. Barnes (Eds.), *Neuroanatomy and physiology of abdominal vagal afferents* (pp. 249–277). Boca Raton, FL: CRC Press.

Schuh, K. J., Schaal, D. W., Thompson, T., Cleary, J. P., Billington, C. J., & Levine, A. S. (1994). Insulin, 2-deoxy-d-glucose, and food deprivation as discriminative stimuli in rats. *Pharmacology, Biochemistry, and Behavior, 47,* 317–324.

Sclafani, A. (1990). Nutritionally based learned flavor preferences in rats. In E. D. Capaldi & T. L. Powley (Eds.), *Taste, experience, and feeding* (pp. 139–178), Washington, DC: American Psychological Association.

Smith, S., & Guthrie, E. R. (1921). *General psychology in terms of behavior.* New York: Appleton.

Spence, K. W. (1936). The nature of discrimination learning in animals. *Psychological Review, 43,* 427–449.

Swartzentruber, D. (1995). Modulatory mechanisms in Pavlovian conditioning. *Animal Learning & Behavior, 23,* 123–143.

Swartzentruber, D., & Rescorla, R. A. (1994). Modulation of trained and extinguished stimuli by facilitators and inhibitors. *Animal Learning & Behavior, 22,* 309–316.

Toates, F. M. (1994). Comparing motivational systems—An incentive motivation perspective. In C. R. Leg & D. Booth (Eds.), *Appetite: Neural and behavioral bases* (pp. 305–327). Oxford: Oxford University Press.

9

The Role of Attention in the Solution of Conditional Discriminations

John M. Pearce, David N. George, and Edward S. Redhead

A number of changes may take place when an animal solves an occasion-setting discrimination. The most obvious changes will be in the way that the animal responds to the experimental stimuli. Much of the theoretical discussion that relates to occasion setting has been concerned with identifying the associations that are responsible for these changes in behavior. Another change that may take place involves the extent to which the animal attends to the stimuli that are used for the occasion-setting task. With the exception of a few studies (e.g., Rescorla, 1991), relatively little interest has been directed at this possible influence of occasion setting. The experiments described in this chapter go some way toward redressing this imbalance by specifically looking for changes in attention to the stimuli used for an occasion setting, or, as we refer to it, a *conditional discrimination.* There were two reasons for conducting this research. First, there is some uncertainty about the changes in attention that take place during even a simple discrimination. By using condi-

This research was supported by grants from the Biotechnology and Biological Sciences Research Council of Great Britain.

tional discriminations, we hoped to derive a clearer understanding of the way in which attentional processes operate not only in occasion setting, but also in discriminations in general. The second reason is more directly related to the analysis of occasion setting. If it can be shown that there are changes in attention to the stimuli used in an occasion-setting discrimination, any satisfactory theory of occasion setting must consider these changes.

The first experimental study of the involvement of attentional processes in discrimination learning was reported by Lawrence (1949). Rats were trained to approach one stimulus, and avoid another from the same dimension, in order to obtain reward. At the same time, they were presented with stimuli from a different dimension that were irrelevant to solving the problem. The rats were then divided into two groups for a second stage of the experiment. One group was required to solve a new discrimination for which the previously relevant stimuli remained relevant, and those that were irrelevant continued to be irrelevant. For the second group these relationships were reversed so that the previously irrelevant stimuli were now relevant. The first group learned the new discrimination more rapidly than the second, which suggests that the first stage of training resulted in more attention being paid to the stimuli that belonged to the relevant than the irrelevant dimension.

The experiment by Lawrence has had a considerable influence on subsequent experimental research and theory. In particular, a number of formal theories have been developed that are based on the assumption that more attention is paid to relevant than irrelevant stimuli. As well as offering an explanation for the changes in attention that take place as a discrimination is solved (e.g., Sutherland & Mackintosh, 1971), these theories have also clarified many of the findings that have been revealed with Pavlovian conditioning (e.g., Mackintosh, 1975).

The idea that animals will pay more attention to a stimulus if it is relevant rather than irrelevant to the solution of a discrimination is intuitively attractive. This idea has not gone unchallenged, however. In the original experiment by Lawrence (1949), animals necessarily responded in different ways to the signals for reward and nonreward as they solved the first discrimination. Because these stimuli were presented to both groups for the second discrimination, the responses they elicited may have aided the discrimination for one group or interfered with its development for the other. Lawrence took steps to minimize the likelihood of this explanation being correct, but it now appears that these steps were inadequate (Pullen & Turney, 1977; Siegel, 1967, 1969). The Lawrence study is not the only one that has been said to show that animals attend more to stimuli that are relevant than irrelevant to a discrimination. In a thorough review of these studies, however, Hall (1991) concluded that there is very little evidence that unequivocally lends support to this theoretical principle.

A second reason for questioning whether changes in attention take place in the manner envisaged by Lawrence is based on results like those described by Hall and Pearce (1979). In a study of conditioned suppression with rats, we found that conditioning with a strong unconditioned stimulus (US) progressed rather slowly if the conditioned stimulus (CS) had previously been paired with a moderately intense US. According to a theory such as that proposed by Mackintosh (1975), the pretraining would allow animals to discover that the CS is the best available predictor of the moderate US, and it would receive the animal's full attention. The theory thus predicts that conditioning with the strong US in the study by Hall and Pearce should have progressed more rapidly than was the case (see also Swan & Pearce, 1988; Wilson, Boumphrey, & Pearce, 1992).

On the basis of these findings, we proposed that the attention of animals is guided by a rather different set of rules from those described by Lawrence (1949). Specifically, we suggested that substantial attention would be paid to a stimulus only for so long as an animal is learning about its relationship with a reinforcer (Pearce & Hall, 1980). Considerable attention will thus be directed to a stimulus during the initial trials of conditioning, but once conditioning has reached a stable asymptote, attention to it can cease, as far as learning is concerned. The animal must obviously continue to detect the stimulus in order to perform the appropriate responses in its presence. Pearce and Hall (1980) regard this as a rather different attentional process from the one that determines the conditionability, or associability, of a stimulus.

There is, therefore, rather little experimental support for the principle that more attention is paid to stimuli that are relevant than irrelevant to the solution of a discrimination. There is also some evidence that contradicts this principle by showing that animals may ultimately pay relatively little attention to stimuli that reliably signal an important outcome. Despite this pattern of experimental evidence and despite the affection that one of us holds for the Pearce and Hall (1980) theory, we could not shake off the nagging belief that, in certain circumstances, animals will pay more attention to stimuli that are relevant rather than irrelevant to the outcome of a discrimination. Indeed, this belief was so strong that we were led to conduct the experiments that are described in the next section. In essence, these experiments were conducted in order to determine if stimuli that are relevant to the solution of a conditional discrimination acquire distinctiveness.

ACQUIRED DISTINCTIVENESS IN A CONDITIONAL DISCRIMINATION

Experiment 1

The patterns in the two left-hand columns of Figure 1 portray the stimuli that were used for the 50 sessions of discrimination training in the first stage of Experiment 1; pigeons were the subjects of the experiment. Food was presented after patterns shown in column +, but not after patterns shown in column –. The method of training was autoshaping. Each pattern was composed of stimuli belonging to three dimensions: brightness (black or white) in the lower quadrant, color (red or green) in the upper quadrant, and orientation (+45° and –45°). The patterns were presented on a television screen behind a clear Perspex response key.

For the first stage, the dimensions of color and orientation were relevant to solution of the discrimination, and brightness was irrelevant. Furthermore, the outcome of a trial was indicated by combinations of stimuli rather than individual stimuli. By way of example, food was always delivered on any trial when red and lines of –45° were displayed, but food was not presented after patterns containing red and lines oriented at +45°.

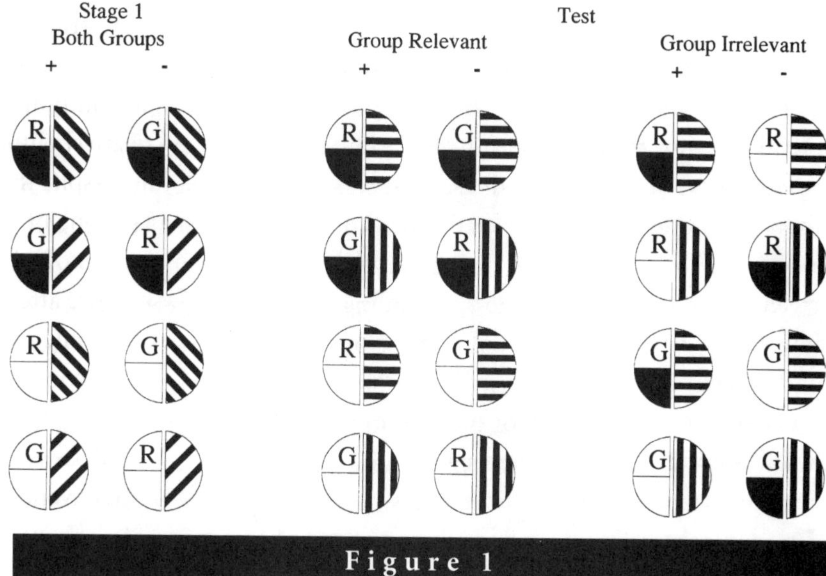

Figure 1

Diagrams of the stimuli used in Experiment 1. The patterns in the two left-hand columns depict training stimuli. The test stimuli used for Group Relevant and Group Irrelevant are shown, respectively, in the central and right-hand columns (+ = patterns that signaled food, – = patterns that signaled the absence of food, R = red, G = green). When measured on the television screen, the diameter of a pattern was 2.5 cm.

None of the combinations involving white or black was followed consistently by the same outcome. If animals paid more attention to stimuli that were relevant rather than irrelevant to the solution of a discrimination, this training would result in more attention being paid to the dimensions of color and orientation than to brightness. To test this prediction, the birds were divided into two groups and given a new discrimination. Group Relevant was trained with the patterns shown in the two central columns in Figure 1. The new problem was very similar to the original problem, except that the orientation of the stripes was changed to horizontal and vertical. Once again combinations of colors and orientations signaled the outcome of the trials, and brightness was irrelevant. Group Irrelevant was trained with the same patterns as Group Relevant, but the significance of the patterns was changed so that brightness was relevant and color irrelevant to the solution of the conditional discrimination (see the two right-hand columns in Figure 1). For example, food was signaled by the combination of black and horizontal stripes, with variations of color being irrelevant to the outcome of a trial. If the training in Stage 1 resulted in more attention being paid to relevant than irrelevant stimuli, the two groups would behave differently in the second stage. Group Relevant would be disposed to attend to the correct dimensions from the outset of Stage 2 and would thus acquire the discrimination rapidly; by contrast, Group Irrelevant would start this stage by attending more to the irrelevant dimension of color than the relevant dimension of brightness, which would hinder development of the discrimination.[1]

Despite the complexity of the discrimination used for the first stage, the birds eventually responded significantly faster on the reinforced than the nonreinforced trials. In the final session of this stage, the mean number of responses per min for all pigeons was 151 during the patterns that signaled food, and 52 during the patterns that were followed by nothing.

In order to present the test stage results as simply as possible, discrimination ratios were computed for every bird by dividing the mean number of responses made on the reinforced trials of a session by the sum of the responses made on both types of trials. A ratio 0.5 indicates a failure to discriminate, and a ratio of 1.0 indicates that responding occurred exclusively on the reinforced trials. Figure 2 portrays the mean discrimination ratios for the two groups for each of the ten sessions in Stage 2. The discrimination was acquired more rapidly by Group Relevant than Group Irrelevant, which is in keeping with the expectation that, at the end of Stage 1, more attention was devoted to the stimuli belonging to the relevant than the irrelevant dimensions. A two-way ANOVA of individual discrimination ratios for each of the test sessions revealed a significant group x session interaction, $F(9, 270) = 2.4$. Subsequent tests of simple main effects

[1] In order to ensure that the stimuli were properly counterbalanced, only half the birds received the training that has been described. For the remaining birds, the dimensions of brightness and orientation were relevant and color was irrelevant in the first stage. Furthermore, to prevent the birds from solving the discrimination by focusing on a particular region of the television screen, the quadrants showing the stimuli from the color and brightness dimensions were switched randomly from trial to trial.

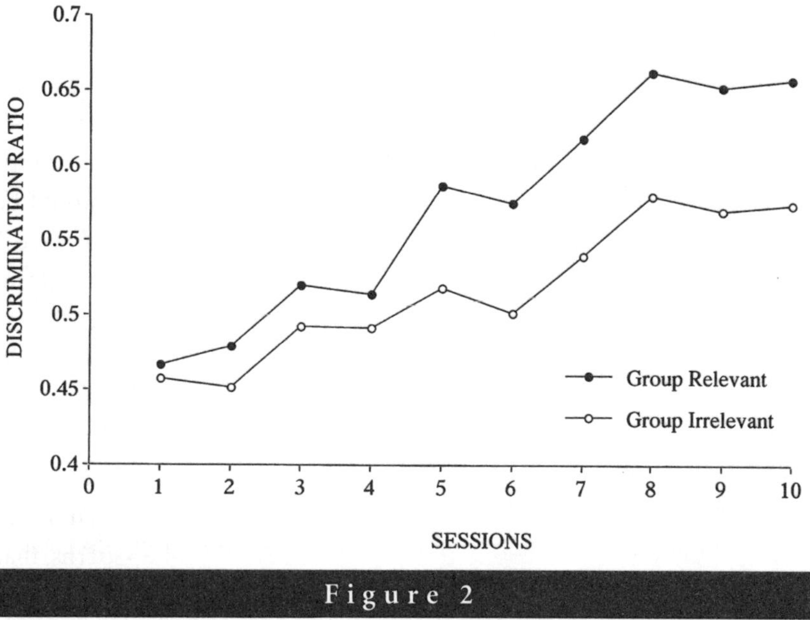

Figure 2

The group mean discrimination ratios for the two groups during the ten test sessions of Experiment 1.

indicated a significant difference between the groups from session 6 onward, $Fs(1, 300) > 3.9$.

Before leaving this experiment, we should emphasize that it is very difficult to explain our results by appealing to the sort of explanation that proved troublesome for the Lawrence (1949) study. The design of the experiment ensured in Stage 1 that each element of each dimension was followed by food on half of the trials. As a result, the associative properties of these elements must have been equal when they were combined for the compounds used in Stage 2. Therefore, there is no good reason for thinking that Group Relevant entered Stage 2 with a stronger tendency to respond on the reinforced than the nonreinforced trials than Group Irrelevant. Instead, the rapid mastery of the second discrimination by Group Relevant must have occurred because, from the outset, more attention was paid to stimuli that belonged to the relevant than to the irrelevant dimension.

A number of our additional experiments (George, 1998) have confirmed the reliability of the previous findings. For example, pigeons were trained in one experiment with patterns similar to those in Figure 1, except that the left half of the pattern was entirely red or green. On some trials the whole pattern was on the left-hand side of the television screen, and on other trials it was on the right-hand side. The training and testing was very much the same as that described earlier, except that for some birds the conditional discrimination involved the dimensions of color and orientation, with the position of the pattern on the screen being irrelevant. Alternatively, birds were trained with position and orientation being relevant and color being irrelevant. The discrimination in the test phase was acquired significantly more rapidly by the group for which the same dimensions remained relevant for both stages of the experiment.

An assumption found in a number of theories of discrimination learning (e.g., Sutherland & Mackintosh, 1971) is that when there is a shift of attention, it is to all of the values on a particular dimension. One implication of this type of theory for the experiment described earlier is that the original training resulted in more attention being paid to some dimensions (such as brightness) than others (such as color). An alternative assumption is that changes in attention are more specific to the stimuli that are used (e.g., Mackintosh, 1975; Pearce & Hall, 1980). Such an assumption would imply that our pigeons paid more attention, for example, to the red-and-green than the black-and-white quadrants of the circle. If certain assumptions are made about how attention may generalize from one stimulus to another, it may be difficult ultimately to choose between these alternatives. Even so, the results from one further experiment point to the conclusion that the shifts in attention that we observed were specific to entire dimensions, rather than to individual stimuli. The experiment was identical in all respects to Experiment 1, except that, instead of using black and white to occupy one quadrant of the pattern, we used blue and yellow. Thus, for some birds in Stage 1, red and green were relevant to the solution of the discrimination, but blue and yellow were not. The training in the initial stage progressed entirely as expected on the basis of our other experiments; there was not even a suggestion in the second stage, however, of the relevant group acquiring the discrimination more rapidly than the irrelevant group. There is obviously a need for caution when interpreting this failure to find a difference between the groups, but the results can be readily explained if we assume that a change in attention to some of the colors resulted in a similar change to the other colors that were used. By contrast, we can be more forceful about the principal conclusion that we draw from these experiments; given the appropriate choice of stimuli, it is possible to demonstrate that pigeons will pay more attention to stimuli that are relevant rather than irrelevant to the solution of an occasion-setting discrimination.

ATTENTION AND IRRELEVANT STIMULI

During the course of a discrimination, there are stimuli present that are incidental to its solution. An obvious source of incidental stimuli are those provided by the internal state of the animal and the apparatus. Other incidental stimuli may also be introduced by the experimenter to accompany every trial of the discrimination. The following experiments are based on the supposition that the more attention animals pay to these incidental stimuli, the less attention they will be able to devote to those used for the discrimination. As a consequence, animals are likely to be able to solve a discrimination more readily when it is accompanied by incidental stimuli that can be ignored rather than those that must receive substantial attention.

The experiments, which once again used autoshaping with pigeons, were based on a negative patterning discrimination. Food was presented after each of two stimuli when they were presented separately, but not when they were presented together, A+ B+ ABo. In each experiment there was a group that received this training but with an incidental stimulus, C, present on every trial, AC+ BC+ ABCo. Pearce and Redhead (1993) have shown that the presence of C makes the discrimination more difficult to solve. The experiments that follow examine if this disruptive influence of C can be modified by altering the attention that it receives. In each experiment, A, B, and C were numerous rectangles of different colors that were dispersed at random on the television screen (for further details, see Pearce & Redhead, 1993). The duration of each trial was 10 sec.

Experiment 2

There were three groups for the second experiment. Group Simple received a standard negative patterning discrimination, A+ B+ ABo; and Group Common received the same training, except that a common element, C, was present on every trial, AC+ BC+ ABCo. Finally, Group Continuous received the training given to Group Common, but the common element, C, remained on during the intertrial interval so that this stimulus was present throughout each experimental session. The previous findings of Pearce and Redhead (1993) indicated that the discrimination for Group Simple would be easier to master than for Group Common. We assumed that, by leaving C on permanently, attention to this stimulus would decline and that Group Continuous would then be able to pay more attention to A and B than Group Common. If this line of reasoning was correct, Group Continuous would master the negative patterning discrimination more readily than Group Common.

The results from each session of discrimination training are shown as discrimination ratios in Figure 3. Group Simple acquired the discrimination more rapidly than Group Common; these results replicate those reported by Pearce and Redhead (1993). The novel finding from the experiment is that leaving the irrelevant stimulus on continuously resulted in the discrimination being easier to acquire for Group Continuous than for Group Common. A two-way ANOVA revealed a significant group x session interaction, $F(12, 180) = 2.6$. Subsequent comparisons then revealed that the discrimination ratios for Group Simple were greater than for Group Continuous on sessions 2 and 3, and the ratios for Group Continuous were significantly greater than for Group Common for sessions 3, 4, 6, and 7. Thus, by leaving an irrelevant stimulus permanently on, its disruptive influence on a discrimination can be reduced. The purpose of the next experiment was to determine if the disruptive influence of an irrelevant stimulus can be altered in other ways.

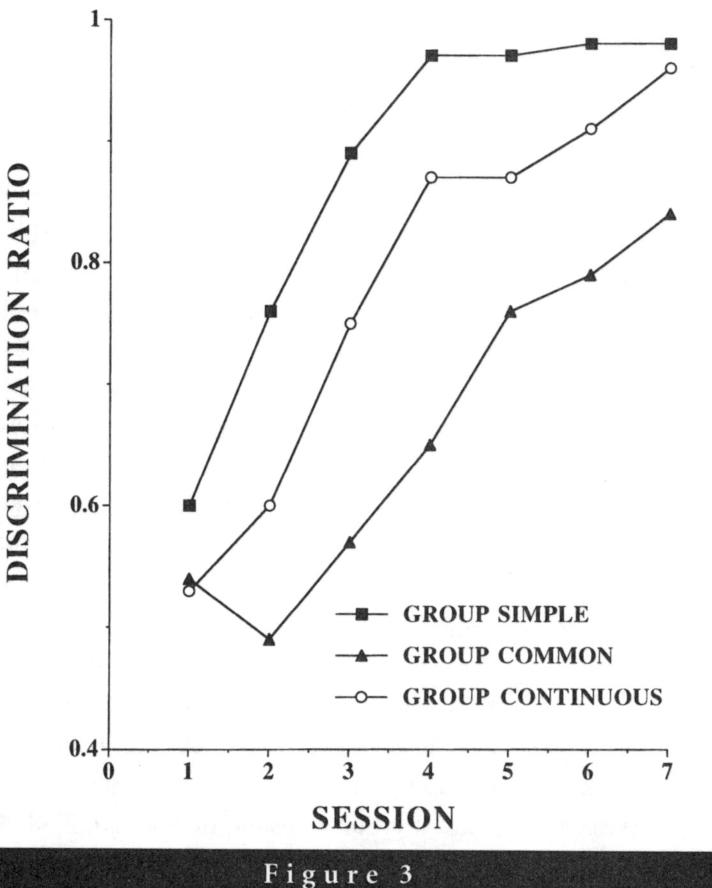

Figure 3

The group mean discrimination for the three groups during the seven test sessions of Experiment 2.

Experiment 3

In essence, the third experiment was designed to assess the effect of presenting C by itself for brief periods during the course of an AC+ BC+ ABCo discrimination. Group Common received training similar to that it received in the previous experiment. This training was given to the remaining two groups, except that in each session there was a relatively large number of trials in which C was presented alone for 10 sec. Each independent presentation of C was followed by nothing for Group Co and by food for Group C+.

The repeated exposure to C in the absence of food was expected to encourage Group Co to ignore this stimulus and thus reduce its disruptive impact on the discrimination. This outcome would not be particularly surprising, given the results from the previous experiment, but the results from Group C+ may be of more theoretical interest. We argued earlier that pigeons attend more to stimuli that are relevant, rather than irrelevant, to the delivery of a reinforcer. If this is always true, then C would receive more attention from Group C+, for whom the independent trials with C are followed by food, than from Group Co, for whom the trials with C signal nothing. As a result, the presence of C on the trials of the discrimination would attract attention away from A and B to a greater extent for Group C+ than for Group Co, and make the discrimination harder for Group C+.

The discrimination ratios for the 20 test sessions are shown in Figure 4.[2] The independent presentations of C had the expected effect of making the AC+ BC+ ABCo discrimination easier for Group Co than for Group Common. These trials also had the unexpected effect of making the discrimination easier for Group C+ than for Group Common. A two-way ANOVA revealed a significant group x session interaction, $F(38, 570) = 1.8$. Subsequent comparisons revealed that the discrimination ratios for Group Common were significantly lower than for Group Co on sessions, 15, 16, 18, and 19, and for Group C+ on sessions 13, 15, and 16. The difference between Groups Co and C+ was not significant on any session.

The results from Group C+ clearly show that pairing C by itself with food reduced the disruptive influence of this stimulus on acquisition of the discrimination. This conclusion does not mean that it is no longer appropriate to explain the results from Experiments 2 and 3 by referring to changes in the attention that is paid to C—instead, if the results are

[2] In this experiment, the intertrial interval was considerably greater than in the previous experiment in order to accommodate the additional trials with C in Groups Co and C+. Because of this, there were fewer trials of the discrimination in each session of Experiment 3 than in Experiment 2, which accounts for the greater number of sessions of discrimination training that were required.

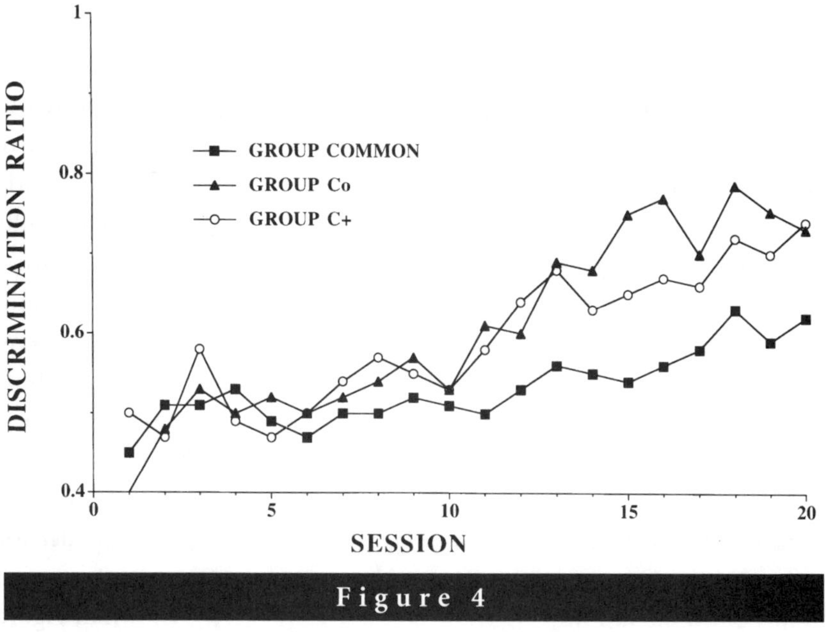

Figure 4

The group mean discrimination for the three groups during the 20 test sessions of Experiment 3.

explained by appealing to attentional processes, they must have operated in a rather different manner from that described by Lawrence (1949; see also Mackintosh, 1975). One possible way that the results from Experiment 3 might be explained is provided by the Pearce and Hall (1980) theory.

We noted earlier that the Pearce and Hall theory predicts that attention to a stimulus will decline once the events that follow it can be accurately predicted. Every test session contained 24 trials with C alone, followed either by nothing for Group Co or by food for Group C+. This training may have been sufficient to allow both groups to appreciate that C by itself was an accurate predictor of its consequences, and thus for both groups attention to C might have declined to a lower level than for group Common. If this is correct, then C would have more of a disruptive influence on acquisition of the discrimination for Group Common than for the other two groups.

Experiment 4

A straightforward prediction from the Pearce and Hall (1980) theory is that attention to a stimulus will be sustained if it is followed by unpredictable events. For instance, a stimulus that is followed by food according to a random partial reinforcement schedule is predicted to receive the full attention of an animal no matter how many times it is presented. Experiments with rats have supported this idea by showing that the orienting response to a stimulus is stronger when it is followed by food on randomly selected trials than on every trial. Similarly, the conditionability of a CS has been shown to be greater when it is intermittently rather than consistently followed by a reinforcer (Kaye & Pearce, 1984; Swan & Pearce, 1988; Wilson et al., 1992). Thus, if C had been paired with food according to a partial reinforcement schedule in the previous experiment, it might have continued to receive considerable attention and exerted a more disruptive influence on the discrimination.

The three groups in the next experiment were designed to test the foregoing prediction. Group Common and Group Co were treated in the same way as in the previous study. Group C+/o received the same training as Group Co, except that food was presented after the trials with C alone on the basis of a 50% random reinforcement schedule. If the analysis of the results from Experiment 3 in terms of the Pearce and Hall theory were correct, Group C+/o would acquire the discrimination more slowly than Co, and Group C+/o would not find the discrimination any easier than Group Common would. The results from the experiment, which are shown in Figure 5, confirmed these predictions. A two-way ANOVA revealed a significant group x session interaction, $F(38, 551) = 1.5$. Subsequent comparisons revealed that the discrimination ratios were significantly lower for Group Co than for Group C+/o on sessions 12, 14, 18, and 19, and for Group Common on sessions 9, 12, 14, and 18–20. The difference between Groups C+/o and Common was not significant in any session.

There is one prediction from the Pearce and Hall (1980) theory concerning these experiments that has not been directly tested—the theory predicts that pairing C repeatedly with food would result in an eventual

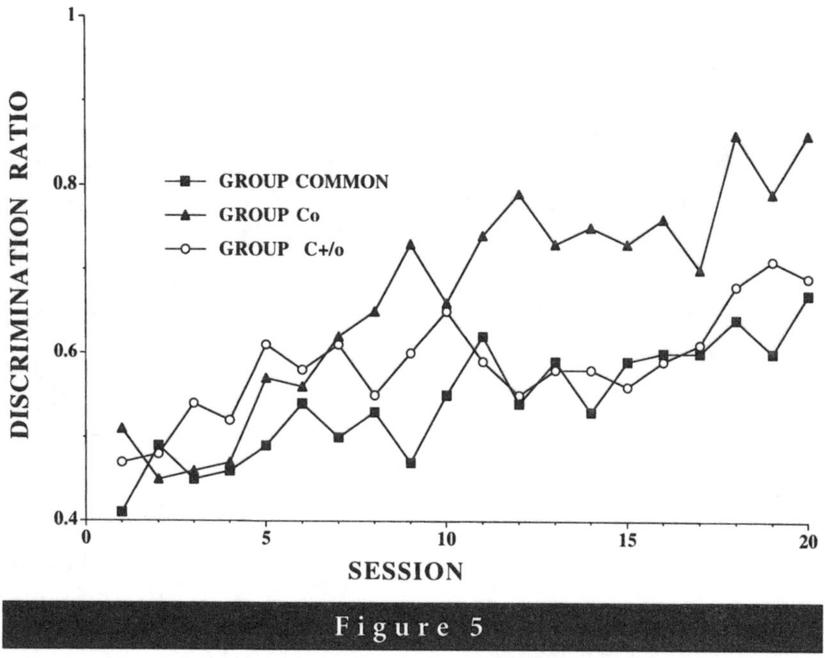

Figure 5

The group mean discrimination for the three groups during the 20 test sessions of Experiment 4.

loss of attention to C, and attention to C would be maintained by pairing it with food using a partial reinforcement schedule. A comparison of the results shown for the relevant groups in Figures 4 and 5 reveals indirect support for this prediction, but we have looked for more direct support in an additional experiment using two groups. One group received discrimination training similar to that for group C+ in Experiment 4, and a second group received the training given to Group C+/o in Experiment 5. We found that pairing C consistently with food resulted in a significantly more rapid acquisition of the discrimination than when C was paired with food intermittently.

Exposure to C by itself in each of the experiments described in this section made it possible to alter the associative strength of this stimulus. As a result, we need to consider whether changes in the associative properties of C were by themselves directly responsible for our experimental findings; in fact, that is unlikely. We found that manipulations designed to leave C either with little or with high associative strength (for example, Groups Co and C+ of Experiment 3), had the same effect of facilitating the acquisition of the AC+ BC+ ABCo discrimination. On the other hand, a manipulation that might leave C with intermediate associative strength (Group C+/o of Experiment 4) had no effect on discrimination learning. It is very difficult to understand how these different associative strengths could directly influence the solution of the discriminations in the ways that were observed. Instead, a more plausible explanation is that the attention paid to C was altered by the trials with this stimulus alone, and that this then affected the ease with which the discrimination could be solved. If this is correct, then all of the changes in attention that we have proposed in this section would be consistent with predictions from the Pearce and Hall (1980) theory.

THEORETICAL DISCUSSION

The experiments that we have described indicate that attentional processes can influence the ease with which a conditional discrimination is solved. They further indicate that these processes operate in different ways in different tasks. The purpose of this section is to attempt to integrate these conclusions within the framework of an associative learning theory. There are a variety of ways in which the ability of animals to solve conditional discriminations can be explained (Holland, 1985; Rescorla, 1985; Rescorla & Wagner, 1972; Wagner & Brandon, 1989; Wilson & Pearce, 1989). Rather than explore the implications of our findings for each of these theories, we will concentrate on one theory in some detail—the configural theory proposed by Pearce (1987, 1994). One justification for choosing this theory is its ability to account for the influence of similarity on discrimination more effectively than some of the other theories (see Pearce, 1994). Thus, the theory of Pearce (1994) correctly predicts that an A+ B+ ABo discrimination will be more difficult to solve than one in which the signals for reward and nonreward are made more similar by adding a common element, AC+ BC+ ABCo. The Rescorla and Wagner (1972)

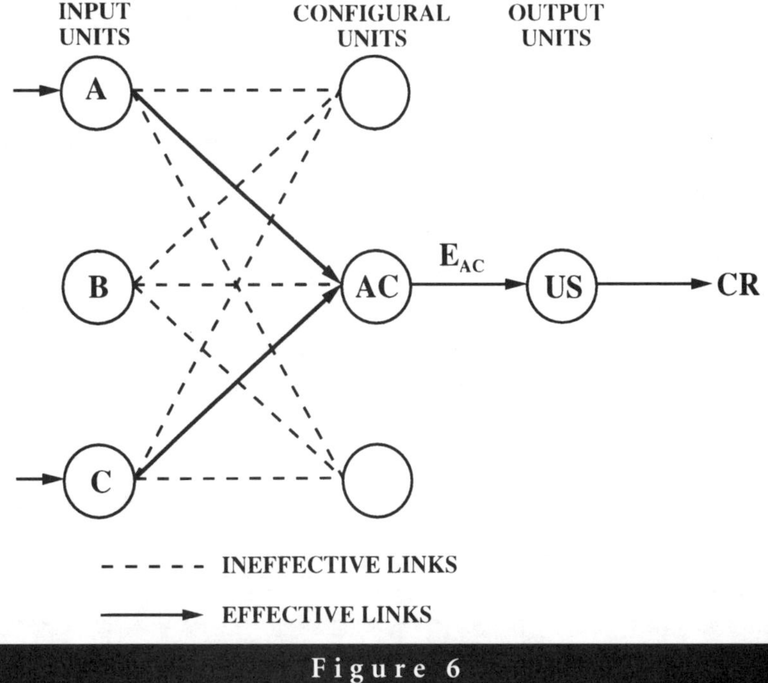

Figure 6

The connections that will be formed in a configural connectionist network after a conditioning trial in which the compound AC has been paired with food.

model incorrectly predicts that the presence of C will make the discrimination easier to solve (Pearce & Redhead, 1993).

Pearce (1994) proposed a connectionist network, similar to that shown in Figure 6, to account for associative learning. There is a layer of input units, which are activated by individual stimuli, and a layer of configural units. Each input unit has the potential to be connected to each configural unit. The figure shows the connections that will develop in the network if excitatory conditioning takes place with AC. When AC is first presented, connections will rapidly form between the input units for A and C and a randomly selected configural unit. Once these connections have been formed, the configural unit will be fully activated whenever AC is presented. The occurrence of a US after AC will permit a connection to grow between the AC configural unit and a US center. The strength of this

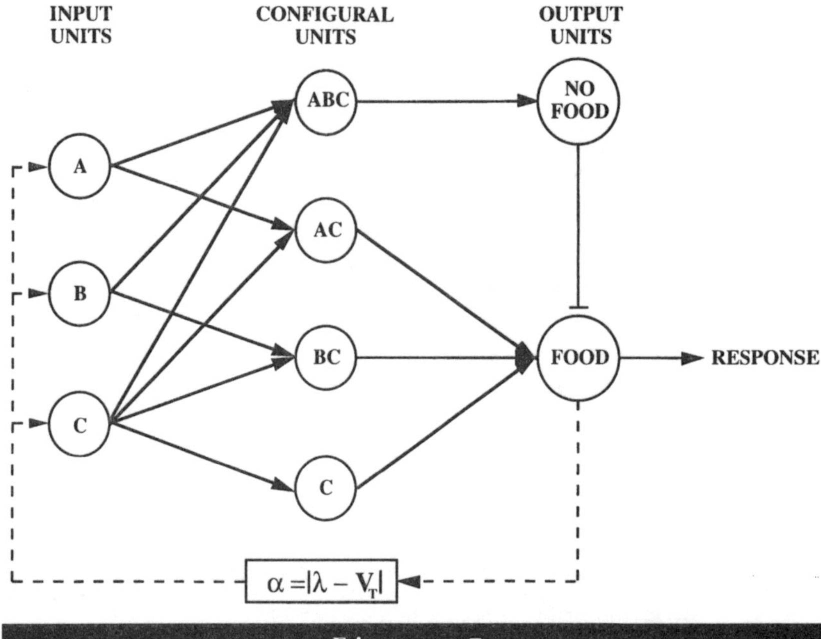

Figure 7

The connections that will be formed in a configural connectionist network after training with an AC+ BC+ ABCo C+ discrimination. The dashed line at the bottom allows an error signal to be fed from the output unit to all of the input units.

connection, E_{AC}, is assumed to grow over successive trials. Subsequent presentations of AC will activate the AC configural unit, which will then activate the US center and lead to a conditioned response (CR). The strength of the CR is determined by the extent to which the configural unit is activated, multiplied by E_{AC}. Hence, if A is presented by itself, it will activate the AC configural unit to a fraction of its maximum value, and a relatively weak CR will be performed. At the same time, the input unit for A will become connected to a new configural unit, which will be maximally excited whenever A is presented by itself. On those occasions when the configural unit for A is fully activated, it will itself be capable of entering into either excitatory or inhibitory associations.

Figure 7 shows the connections that will be formed during an AC+ BC+ ABCo discrimination with additional C+ trials; the feedback loop at the bottom should be ignored for now. Configural units for AC, BC, and C are all connected with the food center. As a result of the nonreinforced trials, the configural unit ABC will become connected to the food center through an inhibitory link. Activation of the ABC configural unit will then dampen activity in the food output unit. According to Pearce (1994), the strength of the CR on any trial is given by the sum of the effects on the US center by each of the configural units that are activated (V_T). When learning has reached a stable asymptote, V_T will equal λ. On trials when the US is omitted, the value of λ is 0; otherwise its value is determined by the magnitude of the US.

The loop at the bottom of Figure 7 allows an error signal, α, to be fed back from the US center to the input layer. The value of α is given by the absolute magnitude of the discrepancy λ-V_T (see Pearce & Hall, 1980). For any input unit that has been activated on the current trial, the value of α will influence the extent to which that input unit will be activated when the stimulus is next presented.[3] If the value of α is high, the input unit will be strongly activated on a subsequent trial, but if α is low, the input will be weakly activated. When the network accurately predicts the outcome of a trial, the value of α will be close to zero, and stimuli belonging to the current pattern of stimulation will weakly activate their input units on a subsequent trial. When the outcome of a trial is not accurately predicted, such as when a discrimination is developing or when a CS is intermittently followed by a US, α will be high. In these circumstances, the input units for the stimuli that have just been presented will be strongly activated on subsequent trials. In summary, the feedback loop will ensure that input units will be excited more strongly by stimuli that are followed by consequences that have been inaccurately rather than accurately predicted by the network.

How will these changes affect the development of a discrimination?

Consider the AC+ BC+ ABCo discrimination with added C+ trials. In our experiments, there were more C+ trials than any other type. Thus,

[3] To prevent unduly rapid changes in the sensitivity of input units, we assume that these changes are determined by a weighted moving average of α based on all trials for which the stimulus was presented (see Pearce, Kaye, & Hall, 1982).

the network will soon accurately predict the outcome of the trials with C, and the extent to which C is able to activate its input unit will be reduced. Note that, provided that C is activated to some extent, it will continue to activate its configural unit maximally and thus elicit a CR of normal magnitude. Because the occurrence of C will only weakly activate its input unit, however, its effective salience relative to that of A and B will be reduced. As a consequence, according to the rules specified by Pearce (1987, 1994), the similarity of AC and BC to ABC will be reduced, and the network will find the discrimination easier to solve. A similar prediction follows if the independent trials with C are all followed by the absence of food. When C by itself is paired with food according to a partial reinforcement schedule, however, α on these trials will only rarely, if at all, decline to a low level. The effective salience of C will remain high, and the discrimination will remain difficult to solve.

These proposals, unfortunately, are of little help in understanding the results of our first experiment. Every pattern used in the first stage of that experiment contained elements from each of the three dimensions, so that all elements were individually and equally good as predictors for the outcome of a trial. The attentional modification to configural theory that has just been developed, therefore, predicts that all elements should be attended to equally. Because this prediction was not confirmed, the network shown in Figure 7 must be developed further so it can provide a comprehensive account of our results. One way this might be done is shown in Figure 8, which is derived from the exemplar-based network proposed by Kruschke (1992). For a somewhat different explanation of how configural information can influence attentional processes, see Buhusi and Schmajuk (1996).

The network in Figure 8 shows the eight configural units that will be formed during Stage 2 of Experiment 1. For the sake of convenience, the only connections shown are those that will be effective on a trial when the pattern containing green, black, and horizontal stripes is presented. The pattern is a signal for food, and brightness is the irrelevant dimension. The novel feature of the network is the addition of feedback paths from

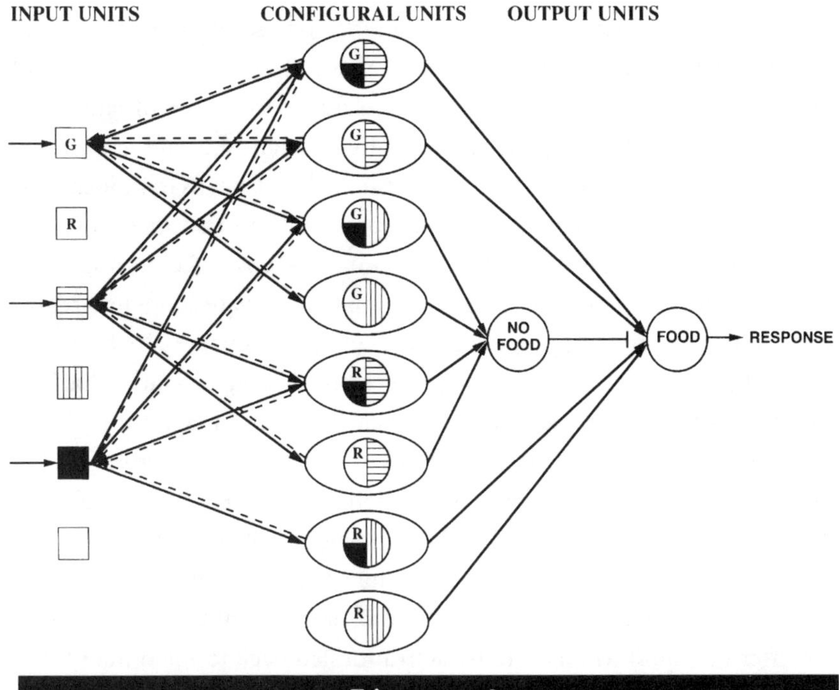

Figure 8

The connections that will be formed in a configural connectionist network during the second stage of Experiment 1.

the configural layer to the input layer, which are depicted by dashed lines. The purpose of these paths is to allow the extent to which a configural unit accurately predicts the outcome of a trial to influence the sensitivity of its input units.

Now consider what will happen when the pattern is presented to the network. The configural unit to which it corresponds will be activated fully by the three input units; other configural units will be activated quite strongly by two input units, some will be activated weakly by one input unit, and only one configural unit will remain inactive. Half of the configural units in the network correspond to patterns that signal food, and these units will excite the US center to an extent that is determined by their own level of activation. The remaining configural units correspond to patterns that were never followed by food; these configural units will inhibit the food center to a degree that is related to their level of activation.

In order for a change in attention to facilitate the rate at which a discrimination is solved, it needs to be sustained, or it needs to be increased to those stimuli that excite configural representations that make a strong contribution to performance of the appropriate CR. At the same time, attention should be reduced to those stimuli that activate configural representations that encourage performance of an inappropriate response. These changes in attention can be achieved by feeding activation back to the input units along each of the dashed lines. The magnitude of this activation should be related to the level to which each configural unit is excited. Furthermore, the value of the signal that is fed back along each dashed line should be positive if the configural unit predicts the correct outcome, and negative if it predicts the incorrect outcome. These principles ensure that input units for stimuli that are relevant to the solution of the discrimination will have more activation fed back to them than those for stimuli that are irrelevant to the discrimination.

To help clarify the preceding suggestion, consider the activation that the green input unit will receive from the top configural unit in Figure 8. We might assume that the amount of this activation will be +1, where the plus sign indicates that the unit signals the correct trial outcome and the value 1 derives from the fact that all inputs to the configural unit are active. In a similar way, the second configural unit will feed activation of magnitude +.66 to the green input unit, because two thirds of the inputs to this configural unit are active. The third and fourth configural units will feed back signals to the green input unit with values of –.66 and –.33. The sum of all four values is .66. Turning now to the black input unit, this will receive activation from the first, third, fifth, and seventh configural units with values of +1, –.66 –.66, and +.33, respectively, which have a net value of 0.

Thus, by adjusting the sensitivity of the input units on the basis of the activation they receive from configural units, it will be possible for the network to pay more effective attention to relevant than irrelevant stimuli.

Such a change will benefit the discrimination by increasing generalization among patterns that signal the same outcome and by reducing it among patterns that signal different outcomes.

In the discussion of Experiment 1, we raised the possibility that changes in attention may have been to entire dimensions rather than to specific stimuli. The proposals just made could readily accommodate this possibility by allowing activation from the configural units to influence all input units of a dimension, rather than a specific input unit.

CONCLUSION

The experiments described in this chapter show that, when pigeons are confronted with a conditional discrimination, two different attentional processes may influence the ease with which it is solved. One process results in more attention being paid to the stimuli that are relevant rather than irrelevant to solving the discrimination. This conclusion is consistent with the role that attention plays in discrimination learning that was described by Lawrence (1949), Mackintosh (1975), and Sutherland and Mackintosh (1971). The second process was shown to modify the disruptive influence of an irrelevant stimulus. If the attention paid to the irrelevant stimulus can be inferred from the extent to which its presence disrupted acquisition of the discrimination, our results imply that the rules specified by Pearce and Hall (1980) provide a good explanation of how attention to the incidental stimulus is determined.

Although we have shown how our findings can be incorporated into a configural theory of learning, the previous discussion has implications that extend beyond this theory. One implication is that animals have two different attentional systems that operate in different ways. The first is a rather general system that operates according to principles embodied in the Pearce and Hall (1980) theory; it needs only a single feedback loop, which transmits information about the extent to which a US can be regarded as surprising to all active input units on a trial. The second system is more complicated: it involves a number of parallel feedback loops and passes information that is harder to derive than in the first system; the changes in attention that take place on a trial can differ for different stimuli.

Once we accept that attention to a stimulus can be governed by two different processes, how they interact must be determined. For example, a natural prediction from the analysis relating to the network in Figure 7 is that the discrimination used for Experiment 1 will result in attention being paid equally to all stimuli. The results from that experiment, however, revealed that pigeons eventually paid more attention to some stimuli than to others. The changes in attention in Experiment 1 became evident during test sessions that followed 50 sessions of training. Perhaps the attentional process that was responsible for these changes works rather slowly. If this were the case, then the network shown in Figure 7 might be responsible for producing rapid changes in attention, which are then modified in a more leisurely manner by the network shown in Figure 8. On the other hand, the network shown in Figure 8 may come into operation only when animals are confronted with a difficult discrimination. These tentative suggestions will be difficult to test, unfortunately, unless a more efficient means than that used in Experiment 1 can be found to encourage animals to pay more attention to relevant than to irrelevant stimuli.

A common theme in several theories of attention is that the conditionability, or associability, of a stimulus is related to the amount of attention it receives (Mackintosh, 1975; Pearce & Hall, 1980). This feature does not extend to the connectionist network considered here. The modifications that have been proposed are effective by producing a change in the similarity of patterns that signal the occurrence or absence of a US—in other words, the changes in attention are assumed to be effective by altering the degree of generalization among configurations that are used in a discrimination task. If a shift in attention should effectively reduce the similarity of two patterns, the animal will find it easier to discriminate between them. For a brief discussion of how the network in Figure 6 might be modified to account for changes in conditionability, rather than discriminability, see Pearce (1994).

Throughout this discussion we have assumed that attentional changes are stimulus-specific. Such an assumption would certainly seem reasonable, given the results of the second set of experiments. The conclusion we drew from those experiments was that pigeons eventually paid more attention to dots of one color than another. By any reasonable use of the term *dimension,* it would seem that the stimuli for these experiments belonged to the same dimension, and thus the changes in attention must have been specific to values on that dimension. As noted earlier, however, the results from the first set of experiments are entirely consistent with the idea that the changes in attention were specific to entire dimensions of stimuli. Therefore, the two attentional processes that we have considered can perhaps be differentiated on the basis of whether they produce changes of attention to individual stimuli or to all stimuli that belong to a dimension. In any case, an important implication of our experiments is that more weight should be given to the idea that there are two separate attentional processes.

Much of the foregoing discussion is admittedly speculative; it is no doubt also possible to account for our findings within alternative theoretical frameworks. Quite apart from their implications for specific theories of associative learning, however, these experiments are important because they show that, during the course of an occasion-setting discrimination, there are changes in the attention that is paid to experimental stimuli. Moreover, these changes seem to be quite complex and beyond explanation by a single, simple theory. Any satisfactory account of occasion setting, no matter how it is expressed, must consider these attentional processes if it is to provide a comprehensive explanation for all the changes brought about by an occasion-setting task.

REFERENCES

Buhusi, C. V., & Schmajuk, N. A. (1996). Attention, configuration, and hippocampal function. *Hippocampus, 6,* 621–642.

George, D. N. (1998). *Attention and discrimination learning.* Unpublished doctoral dissertation, University of Wales. Cardiff.

Hall, G. (1991). *Perceptual and associative learning.* Oxford: Clarendon Press.

Hall, G., & Pearce, J. M. (1979). Latent inhibition of a CS during CS–US pairings. *Journal of Experimental Psychology: Animal Behavior Processes, 5,* 31–42.

Holland, P. C. (1985). The nature of conditioned inhibition in serial and simultaneous feature negative discriminations. In R. R. Miller & N. E. Spear (Eds.), *Information processing in animals: Conditioned inhibition* (pp. 267–297). Hillsdale, NJ: Erlbaum.

Kaye, H., & Pearce, J. M. (1984). The strength of the orienting response during Pavlovian conditioning. *Journal of Experimental Psychology: Animal Behavior Processes, 10,* 90–109.

Kruschke, J. K. (1992). ALCOVE: An exemplar-based connectionist model of category learning. *Psychological Review, 99,* 22–44.

Lawrence, D. H. (1949). Acquired distinctiveness of cues: I. Transfer between discriminations on the basis of familiarity with the stimulus. *Journal of Experimental Psychology, 39,* 770–784.

Mackintosh, N. J. (1975). A theory of attention: Variations in the associability of stimuli with reinforcement. *Psychological Review, 82,* 276–298.

Pearce, J. M. (1987). A model of stimulus generalization for Pavlovian conditioning. *Psychological Review, 94,* 61–73.

Pearce, J. M. (1994). Similarity and discrimination: A selective review and a connectionist model. *Psychological Review, 101,* 587–607.

Pearce, J. M., & Hall, G. (1980). A model for Pavlovian learning: Variations in the effectiveness of conditioned but not unconditioned stimuli. *Psychological Review, 87,* 532–552.

Pearce, J. M., Kaye, H., & Hall, G. (1982). Predictive accuracy and stimulus associability: Development of a model for Pavlovian learning. In M. L. Commons, R. J. Herrnstein, & A. R. Wagner (Eds.), *Quantitative analyses of behavior: Acquisition* (pp. 241–256). Cambridge, MA: Ballinger.

Pearce, J. M., & Redhead, E. S. (1993). The influence of an irrelevant stimulus on two discriminations. *Journal of Experimental Psychology: Animal Behavior Processes, 19,* 180–190.

Pullen, M. R., & Turney, T. H. (1977). Response modes in simultaneous and successive visual discriminations. *Animal Learning & Behavior, 5,* 73–77.

Rescorla, R. A. (1985). Conditioned inhibition and facilitation. In R. R. Miller & N. E. Spear (Eds.), *Information processing in animals: Conditioned inhibition* (pp. 299–326). Hillsdale, NJ: Erlbaum.

Rescorla, R. A. (1991). Separate reinforcement can enhance the effectiveness of modulators. *Journal of Experimental Psychology: Animal Behavior Processes, 17,* 259–269.

Rescorla, R. A., & Wagner, A. R. (1972). A theory of Pavlovian conditioning: Variations in the effectiveness of reinforcement and nonreinforcement. In A. H. Black & W. F. Prokasy (Eds.), *Classical conditioning II: Current research and theory* (pp. 64–99). New York: Appleton-Century-Crofts.

Siegel, S. (1967). Overtraining and transfer processes. *Journal of Comparative and Physiological Psychology, 64,* 471–477.

Siegel, S. (1969). Discrimination, overtraining and shift behavior. In R. M. Gilbert & N. S. Sutherland (Eds.), *Animal discrimination learning* (pp. 187–213). New York: Academic Press.

Sutherland, N. S., & Mackintosh, N. J. (1971). *Mechanisms of animal discrimination learning.* New York: Academic Press.

Swan, J. A., & Pearce, J. M. (1988). The orienting response as an index of stimulus associability in rats. *Journal of Experimental Psychology: Animal Behavior Processes, 14,* 292–301.

Wagner, A. R., & Brandon, S. E. (1989). Evolution of a structured connectionist model of Pavlovian conditioning (AESOP). In S. B. Klein & R. R. Mowrer (Eds.), *Contemporary learning theories: Pavlovian conditioning and the status of traditional learning theory* (pp. 149–189). Hillsdale, NJ: Erlbaum.

Wilson, P. N., Boumphrey, P., & Pearce, J. M. (1992). Restoration of the orienting response to a light by a change in its predictive accuracy. *Quarterly Journal of Experimental Psychology, 44B,* 17–36.

Wilson, P. N., & Pearce, J. M. (1989). A role for stimulus generalization in conditional discrimination learning. *Quarterly Journal of Experimental Psychology, 41B,* 243–273.

PART III

Formal Models

Skinner

organi

He used th

actions that

that are contr

(CS) a

was superse

ing and inst

controlled by

controlled by

relationship

lar action a

is often ne

now applied

informationa

though Skin

may no long

10

Conditioned Stimuli Are Occasion Setters

John W. Moore and June-Seek Choi

Skinner (1938) defined *occasion setters* (OSs) as stimuli that inform an organism about contingencies of reinforcement for operant behaviors. He used the term to stress the distinction between respondent behaviors—actions that are *elicited* by stimulation—and operant behaviors—actions that are *emitted.* Discriminative stimuli are OSs, but conditioned stimuli (CSs) are not. Skinner's dichotomy of respondent and operant behaviors was superseded by the distinction between classical (Pavlovian) conditioning and instrumental (operant) learning. The former encompasses actions controlled by stimulus-reinforcer contingencies, and the latter actions controlled by response-reinforcer contingencies. Because both types of relationships can be operating at the same time, classification of a particular action as being *either* a classically conditioned response *or* an operant is often next to impossible. Consequently, the term *occasion setting* is now applied to any situation in which it makes sense to separate the informational role of a stimulus from its capacity to trigger action. Although Skinner's distinction between respondent and operant behaviors may no longer be compelling or useful, the distinction between a stimulus that sets an occasion for reinforcement and one that triggers actions remains a valid one.

Occasion setting has become as much a part of classical Pavlovian conditioning as it has of operant learning. This chapter argues that CSs set the occasion for the *timing* of the reinforcer, the unconditioned stimulus (US). The actual triggers of action are neural representations of elapsed time. We will not be considering all instances of occasion setting in classical conditioning; instead, we shall develop a real-time model of Pavlovian reinforcement that makes testable predictions about conditioned response timing and integration. For concreteness, the model's predictions and neural implementation will focus on classical eyeblink conditioning.

Moore, Newman, and Glasgow (1969) investigated occasion setting in human eyeblink conditioning.[1] Occasion setters were tones or lights that were presented during intertrial intervals. In contemporary terminology, this task involved both positive and negative occasion setting. One OS (feature positive) signaled that the CS (target) would be paired with an airpuff US. Another OS (feature negative) signaled that the CS would not be paired with the airpuff. The CS was either a tone or light of 850-ms duration. The CS was paired with an airpuff US when preceded by one OS, the S^D or positive feature, but not when preceded by the other OS, the S^Δ or negative feature.

In some experiments, the OSs occupied the entire intertrial interval, typically 20 sec. In other experiments, the OSs were only 850 ms in duration, in order to control their timing with respect to the CS. In other experiments, the OSs for differential eyeblink conditioning also served as discriminative stimuli for an event-prediction task that was embedded within the eyeblink conditioning procedure.[2] In still other experiments, the presentations of the OS was contingent on an observing response by the subject. This task required that subjects depress a switch any time during the intertrial interval. This response produced the OS for the upcoming CS presentation.

[1] To our knowledge, this is the first study of occasion setting in classical conditioning.

[2] Such collateral tasks are commonly used in human eyeblink conditioning.

In keeping with subsequent studies with animals, Moore et al. (1969) found that appropriate differential conditioned responding in this occasion-setting paradigm was easiest to establish if the two OSs were of a different sensory modality than the CS. Differential responding was difficult to establish if all three stimuli were lights or tones.

Moore et al. also found that the timing of the intertrial OSs with respect to the CS had a powerful effect on differential responding. Occasion setters that preceded the CS by 5 seconds were more effective than those that preceded the CS by 15 seconds. Furthermore, subjects who could control the delivery of OSs (the observing response procedure) adjusted the timing of these cues to reduce the interval between their onset and that of the CS. This observation suggests that occasion setting is most efficient when the temporal separation between an OS and the target CS is minimal. Indeed, the best differential performance was achieved when the OSs and the CS were coextensive in time.

The dependence of occasion setting on the time interval between OSs and the CS may be related to the dependence of conditioning on the time interval between the CS and the US. In fact, the pertinent aspect of OS timing might be its predictive relationship to the US. Perhaps, then, OSs are simply CSs that are too temporally remote from the US to trigger action. This idea is supported by evidence that intertrial stimuli, such as tones, can control differentially conditioned responding, provided that their offsets occur near enough in time to the US to support conditioning (Liu & Moore, 1969).

CONDITIONED STIMULI AS OCCASION SETTERS

Like OSs, CSs provide information about the US. And like OSs, CSs do not trigger immediate action. Conditioned responses are typically delayed until the US is imminent.[3] This is illustrated in Figure 1, which shows the

[3]Most textbooks fail to mention this fact. They often portray CRs as being triggered by CS onset, in the same way that USs trigger URs. This is simply incorrect. Textbooks attribute temporally delayed CRs to *inhibition of delay*, a gradual process that involves the acquisition of inhibition during the earlier portions of the CS–US interval. Misleading portrayals of the development of CR timing and topography probably

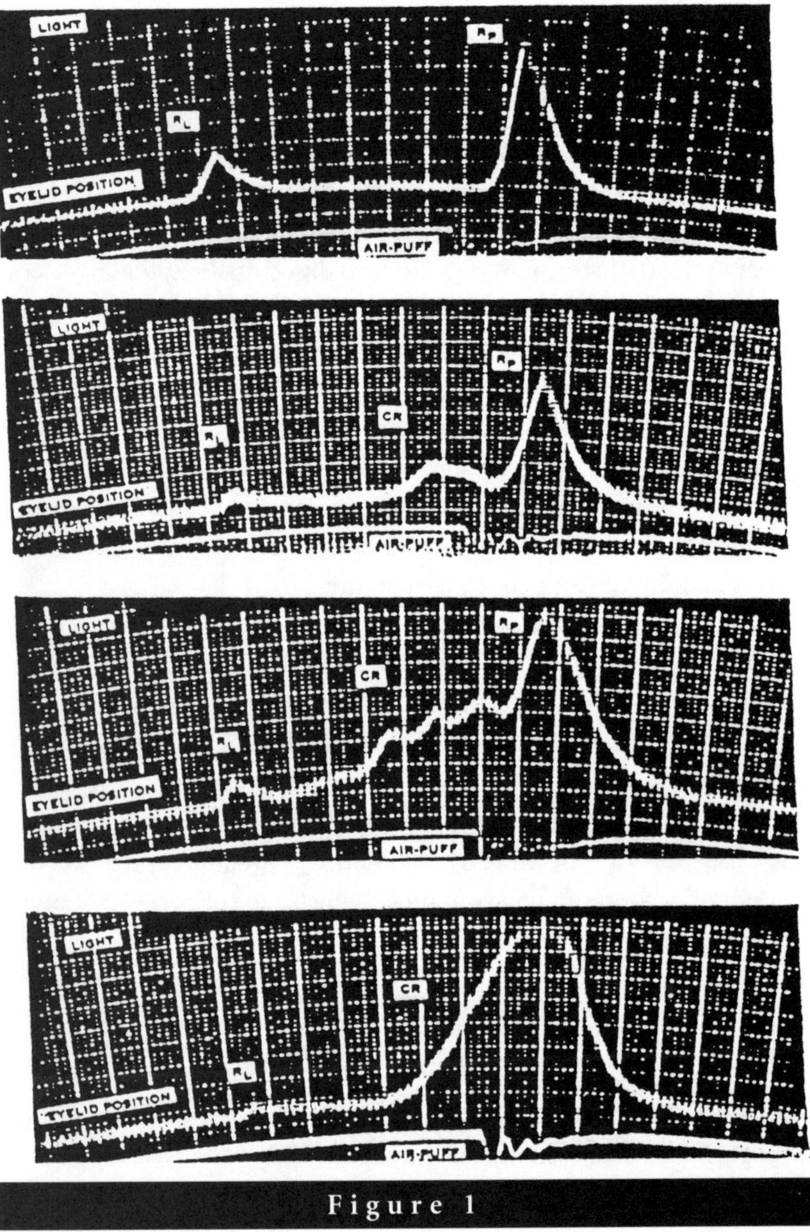

Figure 1

From top to bottom, four stages in the development of an eyeblink CR in a human subject. From Hilgard (1936). Reprinted with permission.

progressive stages in the development of human eyeblink CRs to a light CS and airpuff US (Hilgard, 1936). The delayed action of CSs was also noted by Pavlov (1960/1927). In describing the emergence of a salivation CR in dogs trained in a delay conditioning procedure, Pavlov observed that CRs begin to emerge at the temporal locus of the US. Latency decreases with training so that CRs begin to occur near the midpoint of the CS–US interval. The peak amplitude of the CR remains at the time of the US, however. With overtraining, CR latency increases and peak amplitude decreases, reflecting postasymptotic decrements in CR excitability that Pavlov attributed to *internal inhibition.*

If CS onset does not trigger action, what does? We suggest that the actual triggers for action are neural structures that encode elapsed time. These structures are activated by salient stimulus transients, such as CS onsets and offsets. This mechanism enables CSs to set the occasion for the timing of the US. Sutton and Barto (1990) devised a computational model of classical conditioning in neural networks that incorporates this timing structure—they referred to their model as the *Time-Derivative (TD) Model of Pavlovian Reinforcement* with a complete serial compound (CSC) representation of time. The timing structure of the TD model resembles that of Desmond and Moore's timing model (Desmond & Moore, 1988, 1991b; Moore & Desmond, 1992; Moore, Desmond, & Berthier, 1989). Because it can generate higher order conditioning and primacy effects, the TD model has supplanted the Desmond and Moore model (Moore & Choi, 1997).[4]

THE TD MODEL

The TD learning rule is given by the following equation:

$$\Delta V_i(t) = \beta[\lambda(t) + \gamma Y(t) - Y(t-1)] \times \alpha \overline{X}_i(t) \qquad (1)$$

originated with Pavlov's description of experiments in which the CS–US interval is gradually and progressively shifted from *simultaneous* to *long delay.*

[4] The TD model with the CSC representation of time has been applied to predictive timing in the dopaminergic reward system (Schultz, Dayan, & Montague, 1997).

where

$$Y(t) = \sum_j V_j(t)X_j(t) \tag{2}$$

$\overline{X}_i$ refers to eligibility for modification.

$$\overline{X}_i(t+1) = \overline{X}_i(t) + \delta[\overline{X}_i(t) - \overline{X}_i(t)] \tag{3}$$

α and β are rate parameters.

The learning rule reveals two reinforcement components. One component is contributed by the US, λ. The other component is contributed by the first time-derivative of output, Y.

$$\dot{Y} = \gamma Y(t) - Y(t-1) \tag{4}$$

A key feature of the TD model is the parameter γ ($0 < \gamma \leq 1$). γ is referred to as the *discount* parameter because $Y(t)$ is not known with certainty until after the fact—that is, $Y(t)$ must be estimated by using the connection weights computed on the previous time step, $Y(t) = \Sigma_j V_j(t-1) \times X_j(t)$. γ can be regarded as the penalty for using $V(t-1)$ as an estimate of $V(t)$.

The TD model overcomes the deficiencies of earlier models while retaining their ability to describe complex paradigms such as Kamin blocking and conditioned inhibition. In order for the TD model to encompass CR timing and topography, however, Sutton and Barto (1990) proposed that the elapsed time between the onset of a CS and the US be segmented into an ordered sequence of serial components. These serial components are for all intents and purposes the same as the time-tagged input elements of the Desmond and Moore model. The subscript i in the equations of the TD model refers to a single serial component.[5]

[5] By rights, $V_i(t)$ in Equation 1 should include additional subscripts. As with Desmond and Moore's (1988) model, one additional subscript would identify the source of the CS, for example, whether it arises from a light or a tone. The other additional subscript would specify whether an input element arises from CS onset or offset. These additional subscripts are suppressed in order to emphasize the fact that the subscript i is an index of elapsed time.

In order for the TD model to describe CR timing and topography in trace conditioning and in complex paradigms that involve multiple CSs, we have extended the CSC representation of a single CS to encompass situations in which more than one CS is acting at a time. Both CS onsets and offsets are assumed to trigger cascades of spreading activation. This spreading activation is mapped onto the serial components of the TD model. Each nominal CS, such as a tone and a light, initiates an independent cascade that sequentially activates the variables X_i in the model (i = 1, 2, 3, etc.). The duration of activation of a serial component need not be fixed or constant, but for simulation purposes we have assumed a temporal grain of 10 ms; hence, this is the assumed duration of activation of a serial component. When activated, $X_i = 1$; when inactivated (after 10 ms), X_i resets to a baseline of 0 as the next serial component, and X_{i+1} is activated. Although X_i is no longer active and therefore no longer contributes to Y, the output or response, its connection to the output, V_i, remains eligible for modification over succeeding time steps. Eligibility decays at a rate determined by δ, and, as mentioned earlier, just as a nominal CS initiates a cascade of activation among serial components, so too does its offset. The two cascades are assumed to operate independently and in parallel. There are limits on how long these cascades might last (i.e., on the number of sequentially activated elements in each cascade). The only requirement is that the cascades span the CS–US intervals that are employed in training.

The TD model with the CSC representation of time can simulate a variety of CR waveforms. Figure 2 shows simulated CRs with the TD model for a simple delay paradigm that involves one CS under variations of two parameters, γ and δ (λ held constant). Both parameters contribute to the latency and amplitude of CRs. These simulated CRs are realistic in that amplitude rises progressively to peak at the time of US onset, consistent with Figure 1. With two CSs, each trained with a different CS–US interval, the TD model predicts temporal integration, as depicted in Figure 3. Temporal integration also occurs in conditioned inhibition training, as illustrated in Figure 4.

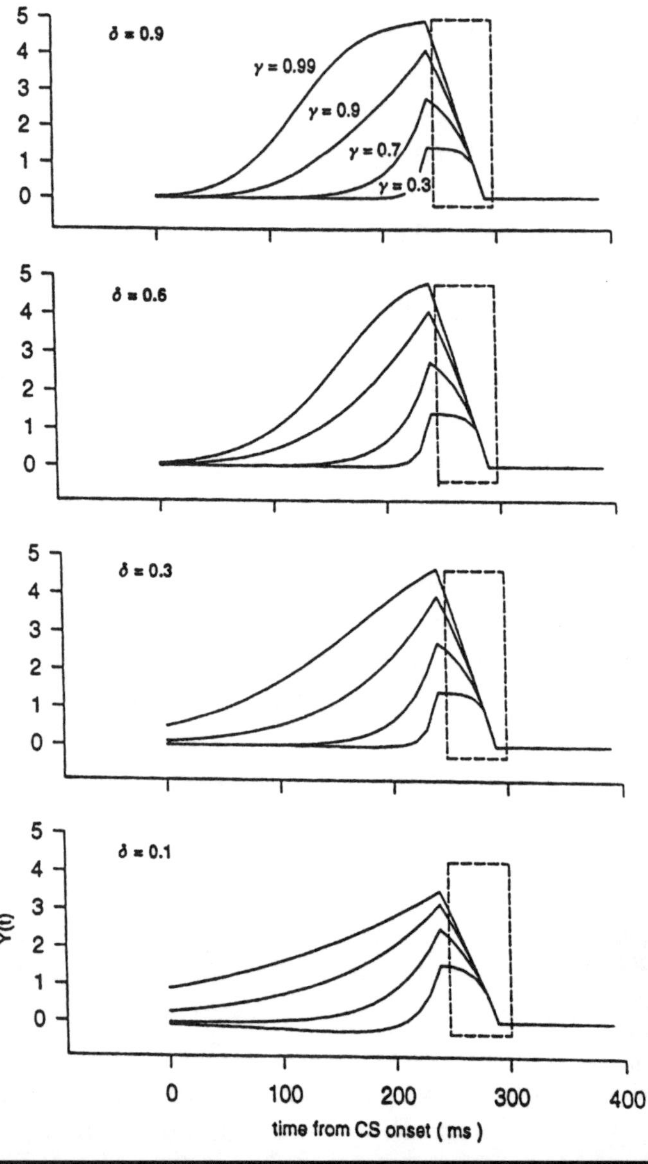

Figure 2

Simulated CRs, $Y(t)$, after 200 trials as a function of γ and δ. Time steps in this and other simulations are 10 ms, $\alpha = 0.05$, $\beta = 1.0$, and $\lambda = 1.0$. The rectangle in each panel indicates the duration (50 ms) and intensity of the US (scales in terms of $Y(t)$). Note that CR timing is determined primarily by the discount factor, γ.

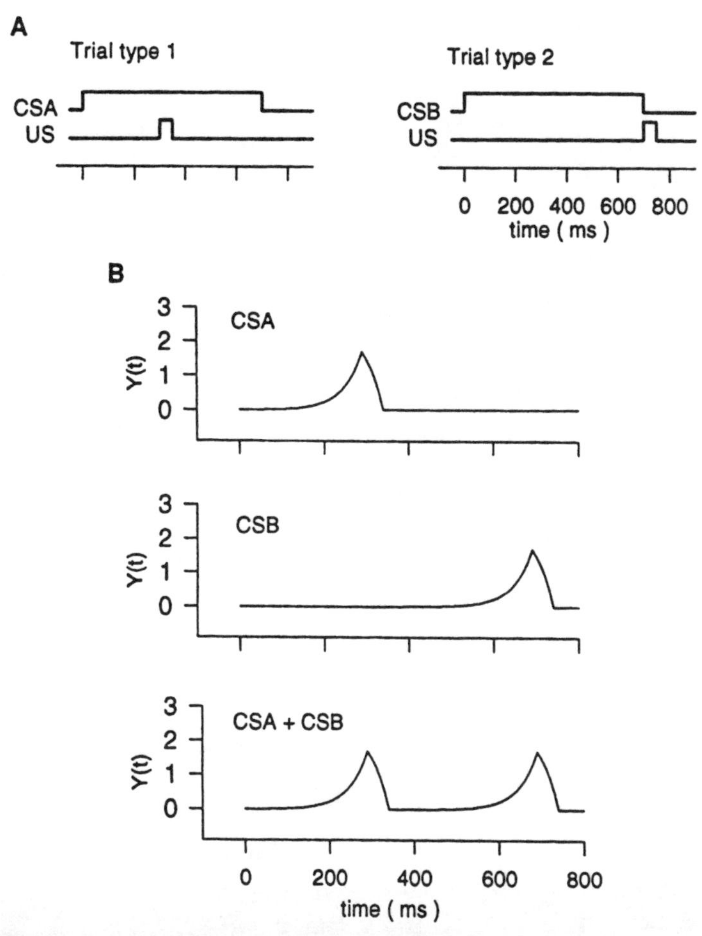

Figure 3

Simulated CRs showing temporal integration of training with two CSs, A and B, each trained with a different CS–US interval. (A) The two trial types: On Trial type 1, the CSA–US interval is 300 ms; on Trial type 2, the CSB–US interval is 700 ms. (B) CS-only probe trials to CSA *(top)*, CSB *(middle)*, and CSA + CSB *(bottom)*.

THE TD MODEL AND SECOND-ORDER CONDITIONING

Second-order conditioning in the TD model depends on the timing relationship between the primary CS (CSA) and the second-order CS (CSB).

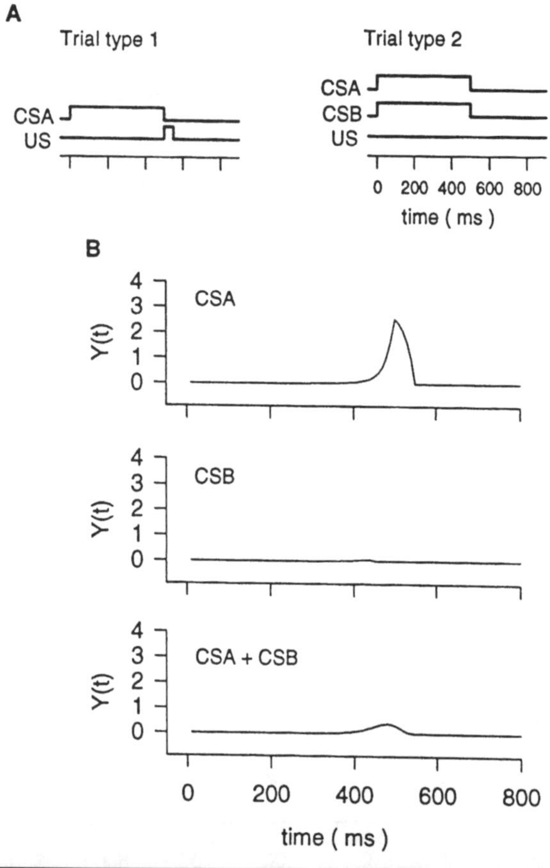

Figure 4

Simulated conditioned inhibition. (A) Two trial types: On Trial type 1, the CSA–US interval is 500 ms; on Trial type 2, CSA and CSB are coextensive in time, and the US is withheld. (B) CS-only probe trials to CSA *(top)*, CSB *(middle)*, and CSA + CSB *(bottom)*.

Figure 5 illustrates the results of a mixed-trial protocol in which CSA is paired with the US (Trial type 1) on half the trails and CSB is paired with CSA on the other trials (Trial type 2), after the procedure of Kehoe, Feyer, and Moses (1981). The figure shows asymptotic values of connection weights, *V (t)*, as functions of time from CS onset for CS-only probe trials with CSA *(left)* and CSB *(right)*. In Panel A, the CSB–CSA interval is 300 ms.

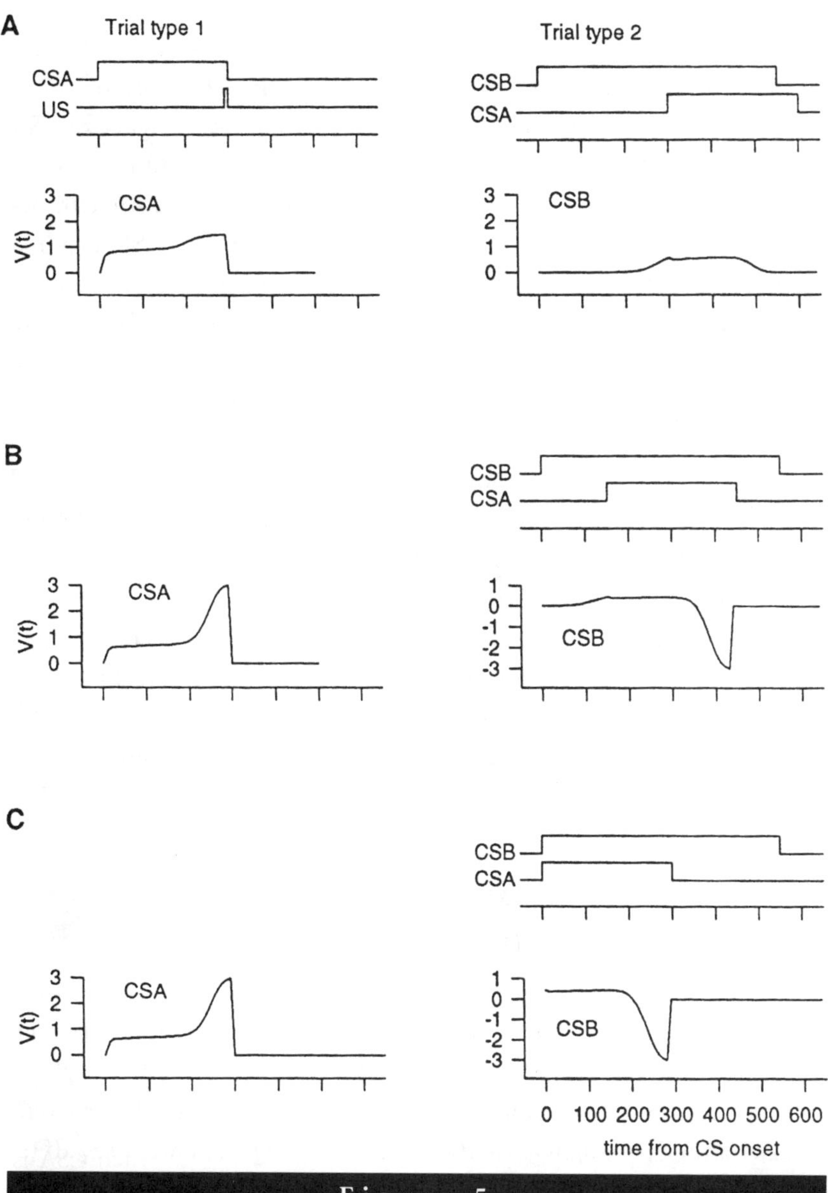

Figure 5

Simulated waveforms on CS-only probe trials showing that second-order conditioning depends on the CSB–CSA interval. Trial type 1: CSA–US interval = 290 ms. (A) Trial type 2: CSB–CSA interval = 300 ms. (B) CSB–CSA interval = 150 ms. (C) CSB–CSA internal = 0 ms.

In Panel B, the CSB–CSA interval is 150 ms. In Panel C, the CSB–CSA interval is 0 ms. The durations of CSA and CSB are held constant.

Panel A of Figure 5 shows that the largest connection weights for CSA occur at the time of the US, but that this peak is lower than in Panels B and C. This lower peak reflects competition for associative strength between CSA and CSB on Trial type 2. Panel A shows that CSB acquired positive connection weights that span the interval between 200 and 500 ms after its onset; Panel B shows that CSB acquired a lower level of positive weights than in Panel A, and these positive weights span the interval between 150 and 350 ms after its onset. These positive weights become negative, reaching a trough approximately 550 ms after CSB onset. Panel C shows that CSB acquired a lower level of positive weights than in Panel B, and these positive weights span the interval between 0 and 150 ms. These positive weights become negative thereafter, reaching a trough approximately 300 ms after CSB onset.

In sum, Figure 5 shows that both first- and second-order conditioning depend on the timing relationship between CSA and CSB. The figure also shows that conditioned inhibition (negative weights) can coexist with second-order excitation (positive weights) and that this inhibition is temporally specific.

THE TD MODEL AND MIXED CS–US INTERVALS

The TD model predicts the timing and amplitude of CR waveforms in complex training paradigms that involve temporal integration. The TD model can be applied to procedures that involve training with a single CS in which the CS–US interval varies randomly from trial to trial. We refer to this training paradigm as *conditioning under temporal uncertainty*. If the two CS–US intervals are sufficiently different, then rabbits learn to generate bimodal eyeblink CRs with amplitude peaks at the temporal loci of the two times of US occurrence (Hoehler & Leonard, 1976).

The temporal uncertainty paradigm differs from that employed by Millenson, Kehoe, and Gormezano (1977) in their seminal study of rabbit eyeblink conditioning[6] with a mixture of two CS–US intervals. In their procedure, the duration of the CS varies together with the CS–US interval. Consequently, CS offset provides a disambiguating cue about the timing of the US. Consistent with this interpretation, bimodal CRs are only observed on trials with a long CS duration; trials with a short CS duration yield unimodal CRs.

For example, in one experimental condition, Group P 1/2, the CS–US interval and CS duration was 200 ms on half the training trials and 700 ms on the remainder. Averaged CR waveforms of conditioned eyeblinks on CS-alone probe trials are shown in Figure 6; the results for Group P 1/2 appear in the middle panels. Notice that CS-alone probe trials of 700-ms duration *(right panel)* show two amplitude peaks, one at 200 ms and another at 700 ms. By contrast, CS-alone probe trials of 200-ms duration *(left panel)* show an amplitude peak at 200 ms, but the peak at 700 ms is suppressed.

The TD model can simulate the pattern of responding obtained by Millenson et al. (1977). Figure 7 shows the results of a simulation of CS-alone probe trials of 300 and 700 ms following simulated training with CS–US intervals of 300 and 700 ms. The simulated 700-ms probe *(right panel)* shows two amplitude peaks, as in Millenson et al. (1977). The second peak is larger than the first because the CS offset cascade, in becoming inhibitory, acquires the ability to block extinction of elements of the CS onset cascade that extend beyond the US. The inhibitory properties of the CS offset cascade is further revealed on 300-ms probes *(left panel).* On these trials, CS offset is synchronized with excitatory CS onset elements so that the amplitude peak at 700 ms is attenuated. In the TD model, elements of the CS offset cascade become inhibitory on training trials with the 300-ms CS–US interval because they are activated and not reinforced in the presence of activated elements of the CS onset cascade that extend beyond 300 ms. These onset elements become excitatory because they are reinforced on training trials with the 700-ms CS–US interval.

---

[6] Millenson et al. recorded the nictitating membrane response (NMR), a component of the defensive eyeblink. We refer to NMR conditioning as *eyeblink conditioning* for ease of exposition.

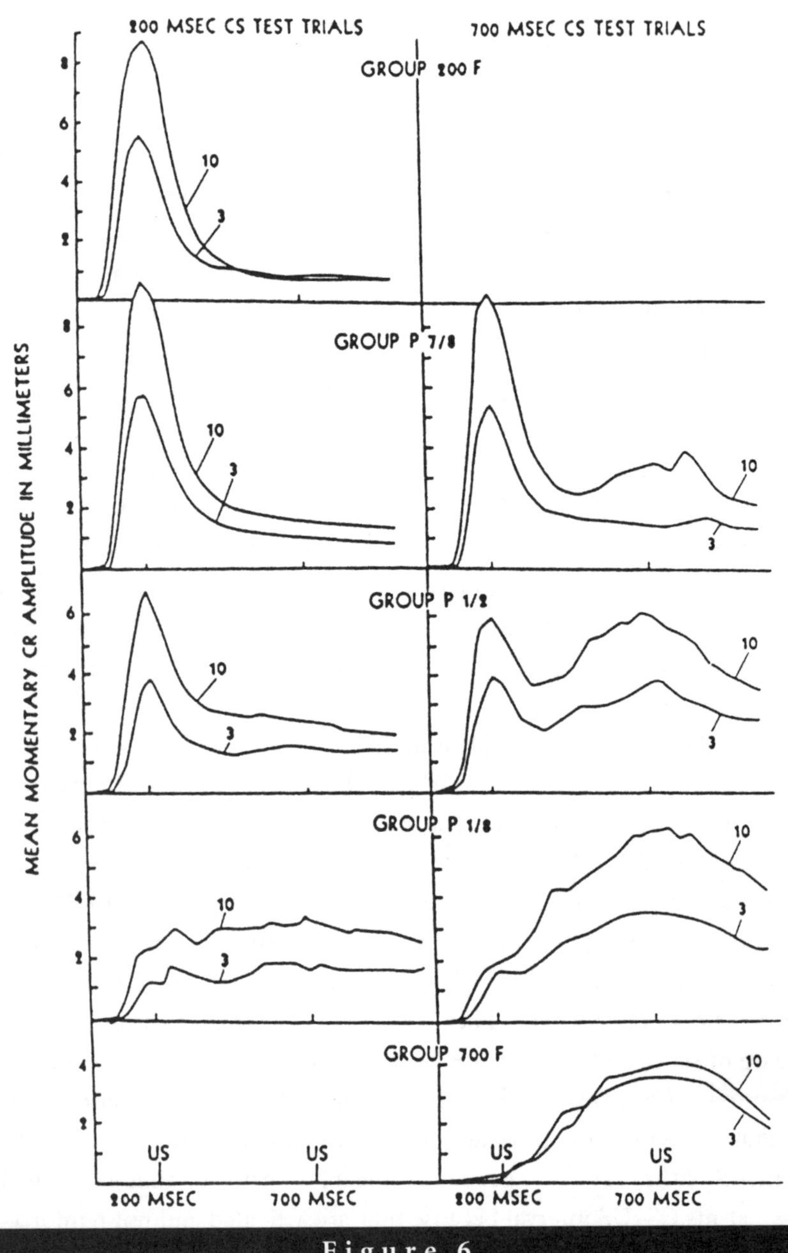

Figure 6

Experimental results of the Millenson et al. (1977) study. The waveforms represent group mean nictitating membrane movement for acquisition days 3 and 10 for long *(right side)* and short *(left side)* CS-alone probe trials. From "Classical Conditioning of the Rabbit's Nictitating Membrane Response Under Fixed and Mixed CS–US Intervals," by J. R. Millenson, E. J. Kehoe, & I. Gormezano, 1977, *Learning and Motivation, 8,* 351–366. Copyright 1977 by Academic Press. Reprinted with permission.

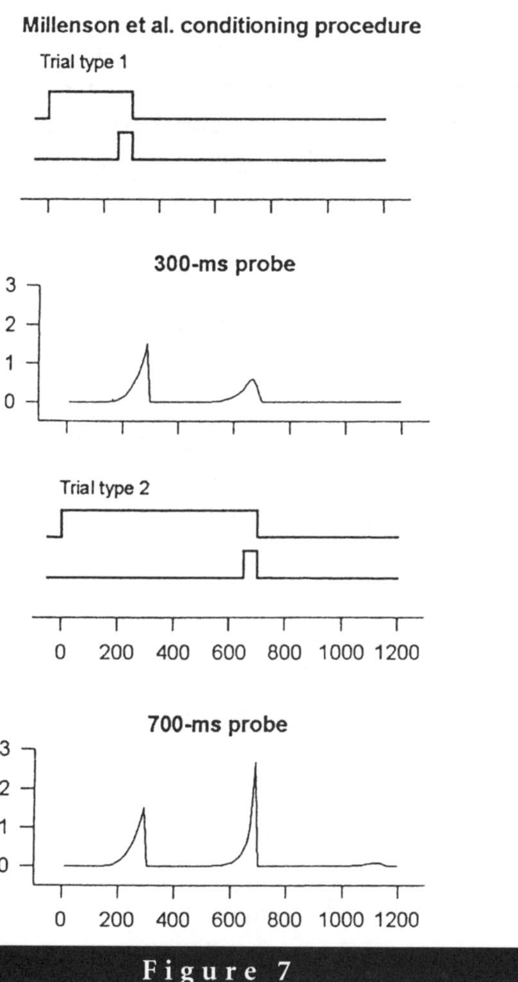

Figure 7

Simulated CRs for CS-alone probe trials following training with the Millenson et al. (1977) paradigm.

THE TD MODEL AND TEMPORAL UNCERTAINTY

Temporal uncertainty training differs from the Millenson et al. (1977) procedure in that all aspects of the CS remain constant, including its duration. Thus, CS offset does not necessarily signal the absence of the

US. In trace conditioning, for example, both CS onset and offset predict the US, and therefore CS offset does not acquire the inhibitory properties illustrated in Figures 6 and 7. It is possible, however, for the US to assume this role. Evidence presented later in this chapter suggests that the US can acquire inhibitory properties.

The inhibitory role of the US is illustrated by the bimodal CR shown in Figure 8, Panel A, which illustrates the results of simulated temporal uncertainty training with CS–US intervals of 300 and 700 ms and a constant duration CS of 300 ms. The protocol is a partial trace procedure because of the 400-ms trace interval between CS offset and the US on trials with the 700-ms CS–US interval. Because CS offset predicts the US on only half of the training trials, it is ambiguous with regard to US occurrences. The simulated CR in Panel A represents a single probe trial with the 300-ms CS. Notice that there are two amplitude peaks: The one at 700 ms is larger than the one at 300 ms because the simulation assumes that the US acquires inhibition during training in precisely the same way that CS offset acquires inhibition in the Millenson et al. (1977) procedure. Specifically, we assume that the US triggers a cascade of activation of time-tagged elements, just as CS onset does. These elements acquire inhibition during trials with the 300-ms CS–US interval because they are activated in the presence of excitatory CS onset and offset elements. The latter are excitatory by virtue of their association with the US on trials with the 700-ms CS–US interval. This inhibition effectively blocks extinction of associative value among elements of the CS onset on offset cascades that extend beyond 300 ms. This blocking of extinction increases the amplitude of the second peak.

In this simulation, we assume that the capacity of the US to trigger a timing cascade depends on the concurrent offset of the CS, otherwise the US cascade would not be engaged. For example, in Panel B, the CS duration is 800 ms. Because CS offset occurs after the longest CS–US interval, the US-triggered inhibitory cascade does not contribute to the second peak. Consequently, the two peaks have the same amplitude. There is no principled reason for the US not acquiring inhibition in the absence of a CS offset cascade—if it does, the second CR peak in Panel B would be larger

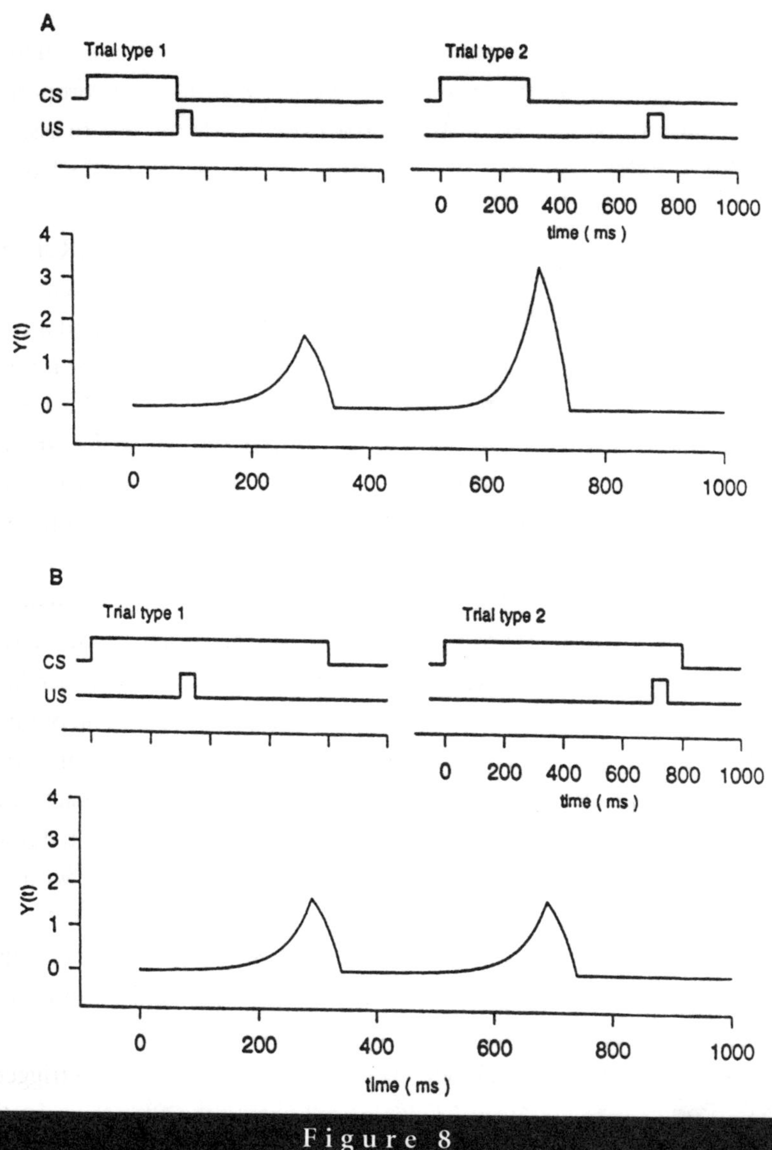

Figure 8

Simulated bimodal CRs following training with a random mix of two CS–US intervals. (A) Two types of training trials and a simulated bimodal CR waveform. The CS is 300 ms in duration. The CS–US interval is 300 ms on Trial type 1 and 700 ms on Trial type 2. Notice that the second CR peak is larger than the first. (B) Two types of training trials and a simulated CR waveform. The CS is 800 ms in duration. The CS–US intervals are the same as in A. Notice that the two CR peaks have the same amplitude.

than the first peak, as in Panel A. In sum, the simulations in Figure 8 assume that US-triggered cascades are only engaged in uncertainty paradigms that involve the partial trace procedure because of the ambiguous status of CS offset.

THE TD MODEL AND TEMPORALLY SPECIFIC BLOCKING

The temporal uncertainty paradigm can be extended to Kamin blocking. Although yet to be experimentally demonstrated, the TD model predicts that Kamin blocking is temporally specific. Temporally specific blocking implies that training with one CS interval will only block training specific to that CS–US interval. Temporally specific blocking is consistent with Miller's temporal encoding hypothesis, which predicts that forward conditioning blocks forward conditioning but blocks simultaneous and backward conditioning to lesser degrees (Barnet, Grahame, & Miller, 1993). The temporal encoding hypothesis simply states that temporal relationships between CSs and the US contribute to blocking. Temporal specificity refers to a CS's ability to block conditioning at a specific point in time.

Figure 9 summarizes the model's predictions of temporally specific blocking. Panel A indicates that the Stage 1 CS (CSA) is 800 ms in duration. The Stage 1 CS–US interval is 300 ms. In Stage 2, CSA is combined with CSB. On half of the Stage 2 trials, the compound CS (CSA + CSB) is trained with a CS–US interval of 300 ms (as in Stage 1). On the remaining Stage 2 trials, the CS–US interval is 700 ms. The two trial types are randomly mixed so that the learner cannot predict the timing of the US from one trial to the next. Panel B depicts simulated CRs to posttraining probe trials. Probes with the Stage 1 CS (CSA) show a large amplitude peak at 300 ms and a smaller peak at 700 ms. The larger peak reflects Stage 1 training at 300 ms, and the smaller peak reflects competition *(mutual overshadowing)* between CSA and CSB at 700 ms. Probes with CSB show a small amplitude peak at 300 ms and a second peak at 700 ms equal in size to the 700-ms peak to CSA. The small amplitude peak at 300 ms

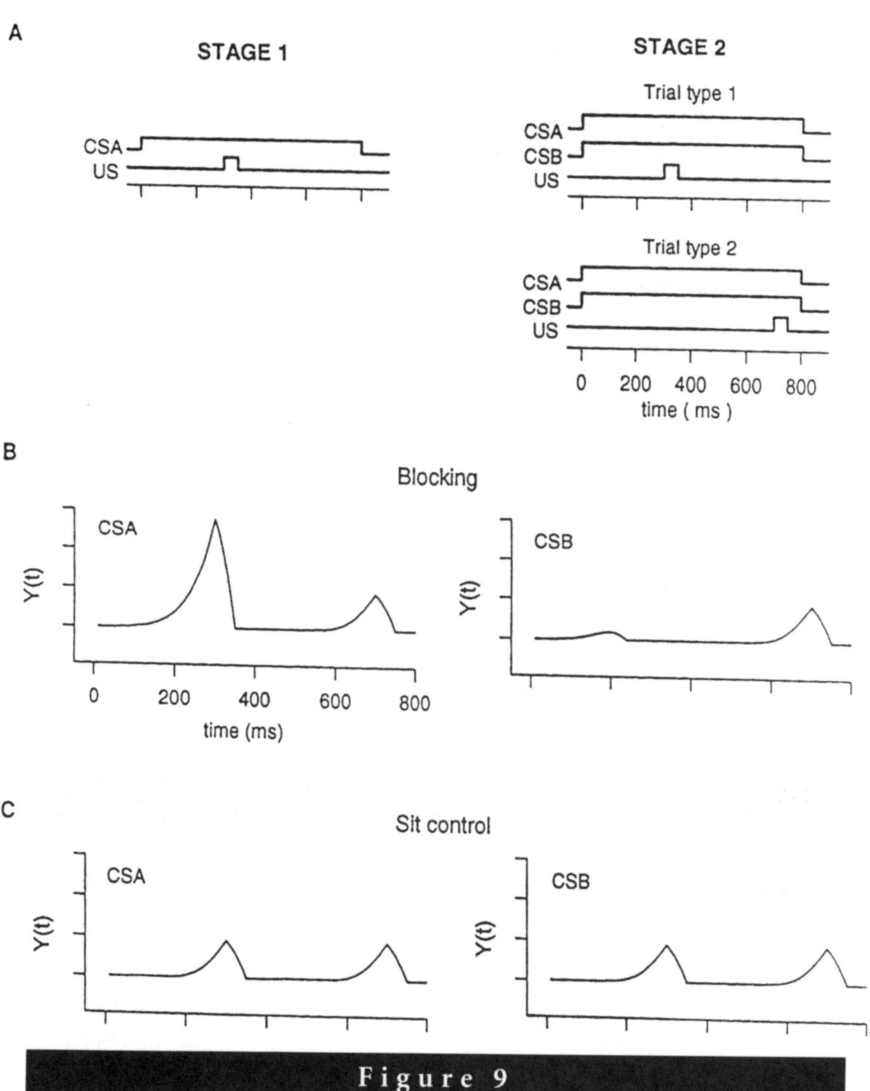

Figure 9

Simulated temporally specific blocking. (A) The training protocol. Stage 1: CSA is 800 ms in duration. The CS–US interval is 300 ms. Stage 2: CSA + CSB are 800 ms in duration. The CS–US interval is 300 ms on Trial type 1 and 700 ms on Trial type 2. The two trial types are randomly mixed in Stage 2. (B) Simulated CR waveforms after Stage 2 to CSA and CSB presented separately. Notice that temporally specific blocking is expressed as the small amplitude peak at 300 ms to CSB. (C) Simulated CR waveforms for a sit control procedure.

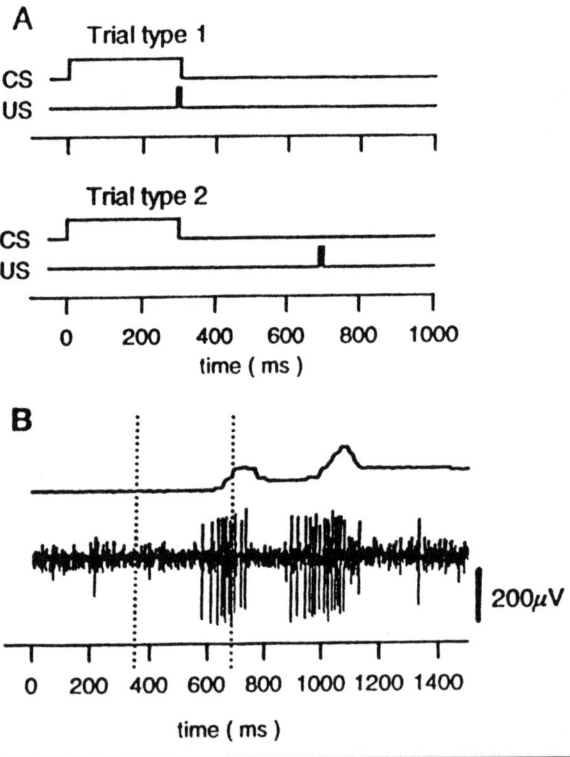

Figure 10

Firing patterns of an interpositus neuron related to bimodal CRs. (A) Two types of training trials: CS duration = 300 ms. CS–US intervals are 300 ms (Trial type 1) and 700 ms (Trial type 2). (B) A single CS-alone trial: top trace shows CR waveform; second trace shows neuronal response; vertical dotted lines mark CS onset and offset.

(*Figure 10 continued on next page*)

reflects temporally specific blocking by the Stage 1 CS (CSA). Temporally specific blocking is also evident from simulated posttraining probe trials for a control protocol consisting of Stage 2 training only; animals are assumed to sit in the training apparatus during Stage 1 without experiencing either CS or the US. Panel C shows that amplitude peaks for this sit control procedure have the same amplitude. This amplitude, which equals that of the 700-ms peak in the blocking procedure, reflects competition (mutual overshadowing) during compound training.

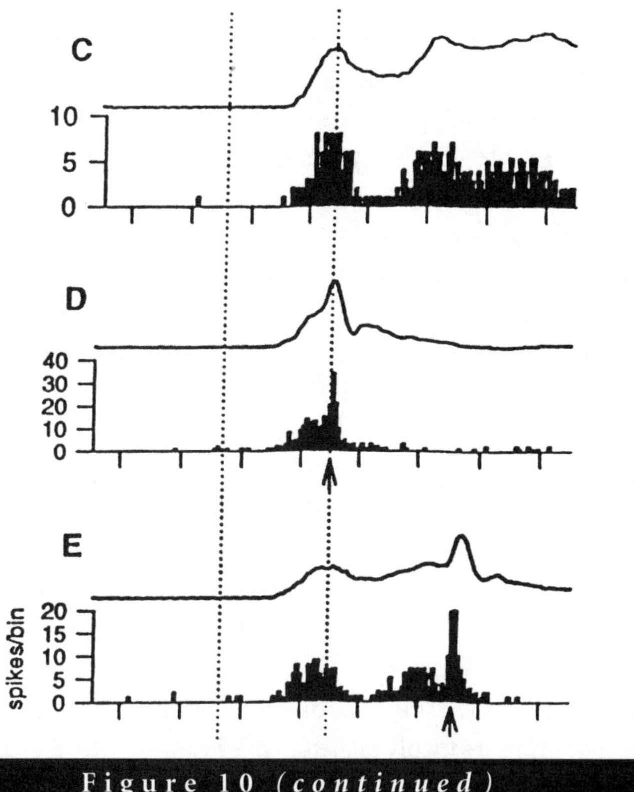

Figure 10 *(continued)*

(C) Average CR waveforms and spike histogram on probe trials ($n = 6$). (D) Average response waveform and spike histogram on Type 1 reinforced trials ($n = 11$). Arrows mark the US. (E) Average response waveform and spike histogram on Type 2 reinforced trials ($n = 8$).

TEMPORAL UNCERTAINTY TRAINING AND THE CEREBELLUM

How is experience with temporal uncertainty represented in the brain? Because the cerebellum is essential for eyeblink conditioning, we have been recording from single cerebellar neurons during postasymptotic stages of temporal uncertainty training (Choi & Moore, 1996). The question of interest is whether firing patterns of single neurons express the timing and amplitude of eyeblink CRs in a manner predicted by the TD model.

We employ the temporal uncertainty protocol shown in Figure 10,

Panel A (which is the same as Panel A in Figure 8). The CS is a 300-ms tone, and the US is a mild electric current applied to the periocular tissue of the right eye. Training consists of a random mixture of two trial types. On Trial type 1, the CS–US interval is 300 ms; on Trial type 2, the CS–US interval is 700 ms. After 20 daily sessions (80 trials per session with an average intertrial interval of 25 sec), rabbits are surgically prepared for microelectrode recording (Berthier & Moore, 1990). Training resumes following recovery to ensure that bimodal CRs are well-established. A microelectrode is then advanced through cerebellar cortex and into deep nucleus interpositus (IP). During recording, the two trial types that were employed in training continue to be presented, but there are also CS-alone probe trials.

Panel B of Figure 10 shows a single CS-alone probe trial (CS onset occurs at 350 ms). The top trace is a record of eyelid position as a function of time. Notice that there are two amplitude peaks and that they are located at the loci of the US. The second peak is larger than the first, in agreement with the TD model as shown in Figure 8, Panel A. The second trace shows the firing of an interpositus neuron on this trial. Notice that the rate and duration of firing are highly related to the two CR peaks. Panel C of Figure 10 shows the averaged CR topography (top trace) and spike histogram for all probe trials with this neuron.

Panels D and E of Figure 10 show averaged CR topographies and spike histograms for this neuron on reinforced trials (arrowheads mark the US). Panel D is interesting because it shows that the occurrence of the US cancels the second amplitude peak and terminates the CS-triggered spiking. This is an important observation, because it suggests that the US acts as a conditioned inhibitor. The US does not simply terminate all timing cascades, thereby accounting for the absence of the second amplitude peak on 300-ms probe trials, because this capacity develops progressively with training—that is, the US does not suppress the second peak until training is well advanced, as illustrated in Figure 11.

As discussed earlier in connection with Figure 8, the US appears to

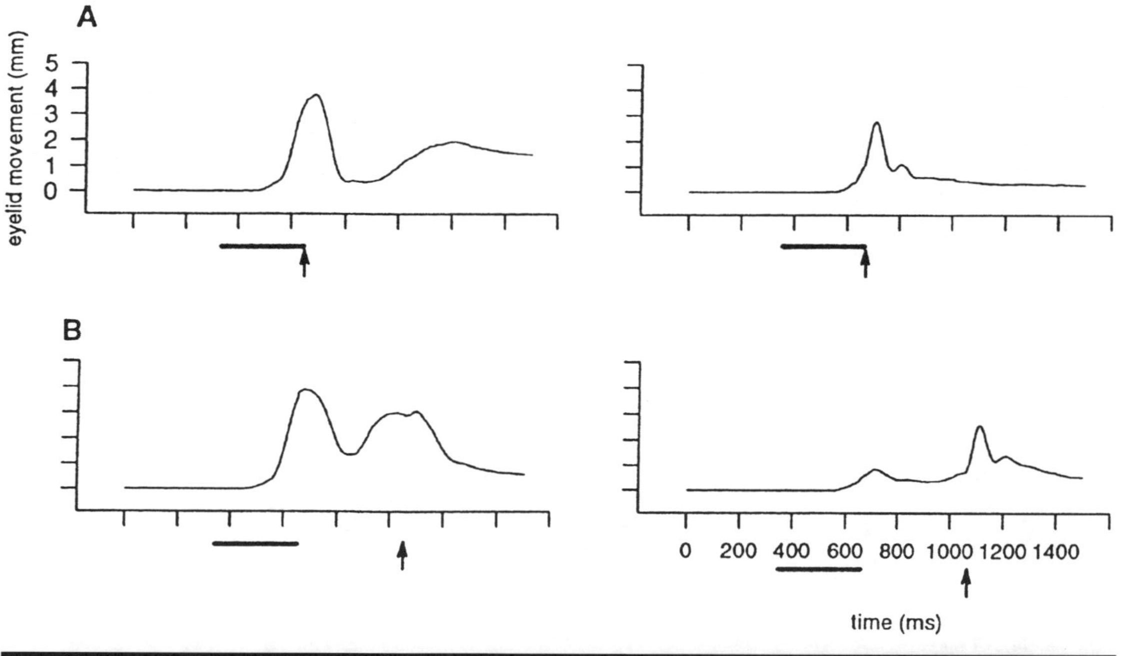

Figure 11

Apparent temporally specific conditioned inhibition by the US. The figure shows averaged eyeblink waveforms for a single rabbit. (A) Averaged waveforms for Type 1 trials (CS–US interval = 300 ms) of temporal uncertainty training on day 6 ($n = 49$), depicted on the left, and on day 31 ($n = 11$), depicted on the right. Notice that the second CR amplitude peak is present on day 6, but not on day 31. (B) Averaged waveforms for Type 2 trials (CS–US interval = 700 ms) of temporal uncertainty training on day 6 ($n = 37$), depicted on the left, and on day 31 ($n = 33$), depicted on the right.

initiate a cascade of activation of serial components that is never paired with the US. On training trials in which the US occurs at 300 ms (Trial type 1), the US-triggered cascade exists alongside two CS-triggered cascades, an onset cascade and an offset cascade. The CS-triggered cascades are paired with the US on Trial type 2 (700 ms CS–US interval), so they are excitatory. By contrast, because there is only one US per trial, the US-triggered cascade is never paired with the US. According to competitive learning rules, the cascade of serial components that is triggered by the US becomes a conditioned inhibitor and therefore acquires the ability to suppress CRs that might otherwise occur.

Because conditioned inhibition resembles extinction, the single-unit recording data that points to a conditioned inhibitory role of the US is consistent with evidence that the cerebellum is the locus of extinction, the gradual decline of the CR through repeated presentations of a CS without reinforcement: (a) Ramnani and Yeo (1996) showed that reversible inactivation of nucleus interpositus protects against extinction; (b) Perrett and Mauk (1995) showed that lesions of the vermis of the cerebellum interfere with extinction, just as lesions of hemispheral lobule VI of cerebellar cortex (HVI) interfere with CR acquisition and performance.

Furthermore, the expression of both excitation and inhibition within the same cerebellar neuron is an important discovery regarding the locus of action of conditioned inhibition (Blazis & Moore, 1991). In the mid-1970s it was commonplace to think of conditioned inhibition as being formed in one part of the brain, the prefrontal cortex, for example, and transported to centers that control conditioned responding. Neural network models that are based on adaptive neuron-like computing elements typically assume that both conditioned inhibition and conditioned excitation can be represented within single neurons. This is what appears to be going on within single neurons of the cerebellum. If this scenario is correct, it could have profound implications for our understanding of the computational power of single neurons and, by extension, the brain as a whole.

CEREBELLAR IMPLEMENTATION SCHEME

Our recording studies indicate that the full complexity of conditioned eyeblinks in a temporal uncertainty paradigm can be represented in the firing of single IP neurons. Furthermore, it is possible that this complexity is also captured in the activity of individual Purkinje cells (Moore & Choi, 1997), as suggested by theorists (e.g., Fiala, Grossberg, & Bullock, 1996; Moore et al. 1989). From this perspective, interpositus neurons execute motor programs by inverting signals that are generated by cerebellar Purkinje cells (Mauk & Donegan, 1997). We turn next to a consideration of how the TD model's learning rule might be implemented in cerebellar cortex.

TD learning can be implemented in the cerebellum by aligning known anatomical ingredients with elements of the learning rule. In TD learning, we assume that each computational time step after the onset or offset of a CS is represented by anatomically distinct inputs to the cerebellum. The onset or offset of a CS initiates a spreading pattern of activation among neurons that are tied to whatever sense modality is involved. This spreading of activation, possibly under entrainment from oscillators, engages pontine nuclear cells, the primary source of cerebellar mossy fibers, and their associated granule cells. Using stimulation of mossy fibers as a CS, Svensson, Ivarsson, and Hesslow (1997) showed that the timing of eyeblink CRs in decerebrate ferrets can be modulated by altering the intensity and frequency of the stimulus train. These results are consistent with the timing structure of the TD model. Therefore, timing elements should be regarded as ensembles that include pontine nuclear (PN) cells, mossy fibers (MFs), granule cells, parallel fibers (PFs), and influences from intrinsic cerebellar neurons such as Golgi (Go) cells. This may be why CR timing is disrupted by lesions of the cerebellar cortex (Perrett, Ruiz, & Mauk, 1993). Entrainment by oscillators might occur at the level of the pontine nuclei, because these are where the neural influences from the lemniscal systems, midbrain, and forebrain converge (Wells, Hardiman, & Yeo, 1989). Fine-grain temporal segmentation might occur locally within the cerebellum, as proposed by Bullock, Fiala, and Grossberg (1994). Coarse-grain temporal segmentation and coherence might occur globally with the participation of the hippocampus, as suggested by Grossberg and Merrill (1996).

The implementation relies on evidence from rabbit eyeblink conditioning that CR topography is formed in cerebellar cortex through converging contiguous action of parallel fiber and climbing fiber input to Purkinje cells. This action produces synaptic long-term depression (LTD). Chen and Thompson (1995) and Schreurs, Oh, and Alkon (1996) have demonstrated pairing-specific LTD of Purkinje cells in cerebellar slice preparations from rabbits by using parameters that support conditioning in intact animals. Consistent with the LTD hypothesis, Hesslow (1994) showed that stimulation of cerebellar cortex (HVI) inhibits eyeblink CRs in decerebrate cats. Mechanisms of LTD in the cerebellum have also been spelled out by other researchers (Hartell, 1996; Kim & Thompson, 1997; Schreurs, Tomsic, Gusev, & Alkon, 1997).

Figure 12 incorporates anatomical findings by Rosenfield and Moore (1995) that indicate the existence of projections to HVI from the red nucleus (RN) and spinal trigeminal nucleus (SpO). CS information ascends to granule cells in the cerebellar cortex (Larsell's lobule HVI) by way of mossy fibers that originate in the pontine nuclei. Information about the US ascends to cerebellar cortex by two routes, mossy fiber projections from the sensory trigeminal complex [spinal oralis (SpO) in the figure], and climbing fiber (CF) projections from the inferior olive (IO). A CR is generated within the deep cerebellar nucleus interpositus (IP), where the CR is formed by modulation from Purkinje cells (PCs). A full-blown CR is expressed as an increased rate of firing among IP neurons (e.g., Berthier, Barto, & Moore, 1991; Berthier & Moore, 1990). This activity is projected to the contralateral red nucleus (RN). From RN, activity is projected to motoneurons (MN) that innervate the peripheral musculature that controls the position and movements of the eyelids and eyeball (Desmond & Moore 1991a). The RN also projects to SpO, giving rise to CR-related activity among these neurons (Richards, Ricciardi, & Moore, 1991).

Figure 12 depicts an inhibitory projection from IP to IO. The conse-

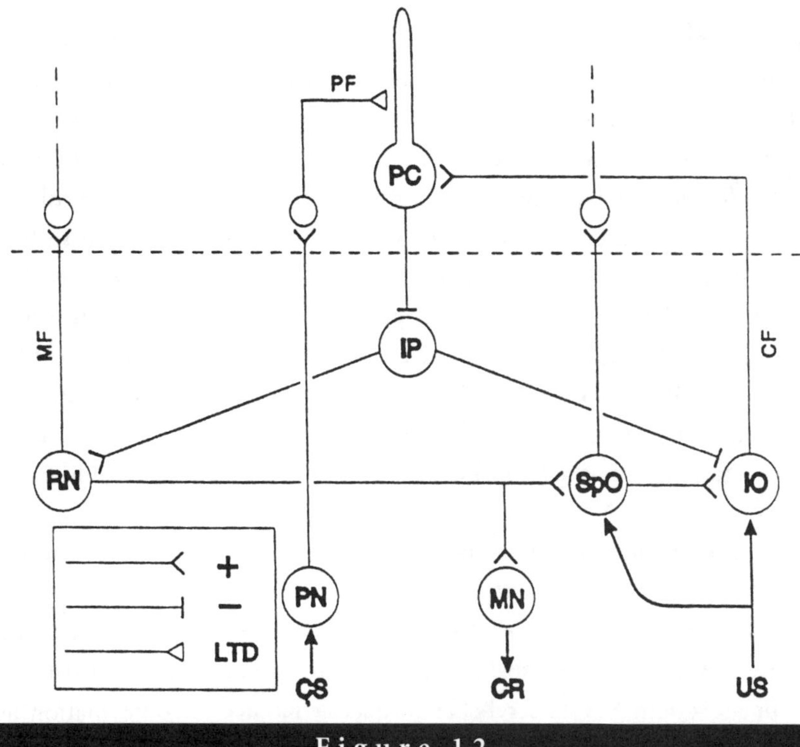

Figure 12

Cerebellar and brain stem circuits that underlie eyeblink conditioning, after Rosenfield and Moore (1995). MF = mossy fibers; PF = parallel fibers; PC = Purkinje cell; RN = red nucleus; IP = interpositus nucleus; SpO = spinal trigeminal nucleus pars oralis; CF = climbing fiber; IO = inferior olivary nucleus; PN = pontine nucleus; MN = motorneurons; LTD = long-term depression; CS = conditioned stimulus; CR = conditioned response; US = unconditioned stimulus.

quence of this arrangement is that olivary signals to PCs are suppressed when the CR representation within IP is robust enough to extend into time steps occupied by the UR. This anatomical feature suggests that climbing fibers are excited by the US only when the CR is weak or absent. This scenario has been supported by Sears and Steinmetz (1991), who showed that neural activity recording within IO diminishes during CR acquisition. In terms of the TD model, US presentations that do not trigger climbing fiber activity are tantamount to extinction trials. This feedback mechanism ensures that CRs are properly timed to just anticipate the US (Moore & Choi, 1997).

The TD learning rule is not a simple competitive rule because of the $\gamma Y(t)$ term in Equation 1. As noted earlier, the TD learning rule is implemented by a combination of two reinforcement components. The first is donated by the US and represented by λ in Equation 1. The implementation assumes that λ can be aligned with climbing-fiber activation of PCs, which functions to produce LTD among coactive parallel fiber (PF) synapses, as depicted in Figure 12. The second reinforcement component is donated by the $\dot{Y}(t)$ terms in the learning rule, $\gamma Y(t) - Y(t-1)$. This information is conveyed to HVI by the projection from RN and SpO shown in Figure 12.

Figure 13 shows circuit elements, not shown in Figure 12, for implementing the $\dot{Y}(t)$ component of the learning rule. These components include the projections to cerebellar cortex from the RN and SpO indicated in Figure 12. We hypothesize that the RN projection carries information (feedback) about $Y(t)$ to cerebellar cortex as efference copy. Parallel fibers project this information to PCs that have collaterals to a set of Golgi cells (Go). Because these projections are inhibitory (Ito, 1984), these PCs invert the efference signal from the RN. In addition, the interpositioning of the PCs between the RN and Golgi cells attenuates the signal and implements the TD model's discount factor, γ.

Because Golgi cells are inhibitory on granule cells, the effect of their inhibition by PCs that receive efference from the RN would be to disinhibit activity of granule cells. Because granule cells relay CS information from the PN to PCs that are involved in LTD and CR generation, disinhibition of granule cells by Golgi cells enhances the information flow from active CS components. Mathematically, the implementation assumes that the variables X_j in Equation 2 engage granule cells. Parallel fibers arising from these granule cells trigger output, and they affect connection weights that reside at LTD-PC synapses in relation to $\dot{Y}(t) \times X_j$.

Purkinje cells driven by projections from the RN would increase their firing rate so as to mimic the representation of the CR as it passes through

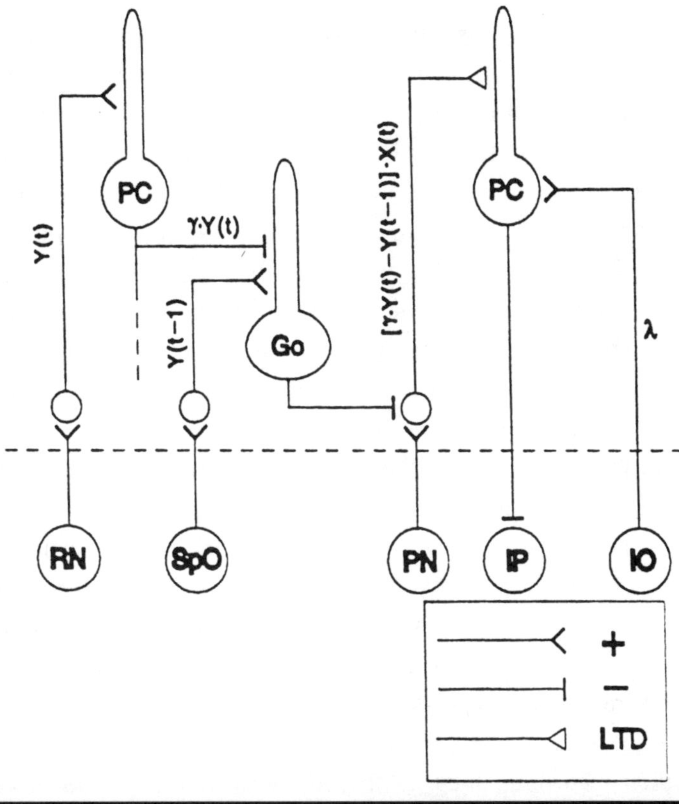

Figure 13

Neural circuits of the cerebellum that implement $\gamma Y(t)$ and other variables of the TD learning rule.

the RN en route to motorneurons and SpO. Berthier and Moore (1986) recorded from several HVI PCs with CR-related increases in firing. Because increases in firing during a CS is inconsistent with the LTD hypothesis of CR generation, these PCs serve some other function. One possibility is that they inhibit motor programs that are incompatible with CR generation. We suggest an additional function of these PCs, that of projecting inverted and discounted feedback efference from the RN to Golgi cells.

The implementation assumes that the Golgi cells that receive the inverted efference from the RN also receive a direct, noninverted, excitatory projection from SpO. This projection carries information about the CR at time $t - \Delta t$. Therefore, the Golgi cell in Figure 13 fires at a rate determined by the differential between two inputs: $\gamma Y(t)$ donated by the RN, and $Y(t - \Delta t)$ donated by SpO. Hence, Golgi cells act as $\dot{Y}(t)$ detectors. In terms of Equation 1, $Y(t)$ is transmitted to cerebellar granule cells by the RN, and $Y(t-1)$ is transmitted to granule cells from SpO. The RN input engages PCs that inhibit Golgi cells that are responsible for gating inputs from CSs to PCs; efference from SpO engages the same Golgi cells directly. Because Golgi cells are inhibitory on granule cells, the bigger the RN input relative to SpO input, the bigger the signal from the serial component CSs that are active at that time, be they from onset or offset cascades.

In this way, the Golgi cells that implement $\dot{Y}(t)$ reinforce and maintain the downregulated state of active PF–PC synapses. Parallel fiber–PC synapses that are activated by an input element are downregulated by the contiguous US-triggered activation of climbing fiber input from the inferior olive. As input elements earlier in the timing sequence become capable of evoking an output that anticipates the US, the downregulation of these synapses is maintained, and still earlier CS elements are recruited, by PFs carrying $\dot{Y} \times X_j$ to LTD–PCs, as indicated Figure 13.

In their recording study, Desmond and Moore (1991a) observed an average lead time of 36 ms between the initiation of CR-related firing in RN neurons and the peripherally observed CR. Richards et al. (1991) observed an average lead time of 20 ms in SpO neurons. The time difference in CR-related efference arising from the two structures is therefore on the order of 15–20 ms. This difference spans one 10-ms time step that is used in our simulations with the TD model. This temporal difference is consistent with a conduction velocity of 2 m/sec for the 10 mm trajectory of unmyelinated axons from the RN to rostral portions of SpO. The 10-ms grain also ensures good resolution of fast transients. The fastest transients in eyeblink conditioning occur during unconditioned responses (URs). At their fastest, the eyelids require 80 ms to close completely, with a peak velocity of 4 to 5 mm/20 ms.

Efference from SpO neurons that is recorded among HVI PCs would tend to lag behind the peripherally observed CR, especially if it arises from more caudal portions of the structure. Berthier and Moore (1986) observed a continuum of lead and lag times among PCs that increased their firing to the CS. Purkinje cells that receive projections from SpO (not shown in Figure 13) would be expected to increase their firing, but with a lag relative to those that receive projections from the RN. The proportion of CR-leading PCs observed by Berthier and Moore matched the number of CR-lagging PCs, which makes sense if the two populations reflect CR efference from two spatially separated sources, RN and SpO.

Figure 14 is an expanded version of Figure 13 that shows three sets of granule cells associated with three serial component CSs. These components might arise from CS onset or offset. The degree to which information from any of these serial CS components reaches the PCs to which they project is determined by Golgi cells firing in proportion to $\dot{Y}(t)$, as just described. Figure 2 shows that TD-simulated CRs tend to be positively accelerating (contingent on γ) up to the occurrence of the US, so $\dot{Y}(t)$ increases progressively over the CS–US interval. Therefore, those PF–PC synapses activated nearest the time of the climbing fiber signal from the US have the greatest impact in establishing and maintaining LTD. This mechanism ensures the appropriate form and timing of CRs (Katz & Steinmetz, 1997).

INTERPRETATIONS OF $\dot{Y}$: EFFERENCE OR AFFERENCE

Equation 1 emphasizes interpretations of $\dot{Y}$ as efference, but it is equally correct to interpret changes in associative values in terms of afference by substituting Equation 2 into Equation 1. Studies by Ramnani and Yeo (1996) suggest that the efference interpretation of $\dot{Y}$ is correct. These studies show that temporary inactivation of IP by muscimol prevents extinction of the CR—that is, CS-alone trials that would normally lead to a gradual elimination of the CR instead had no effect whatsoever. When tested after the muscimol blockade had been removed, the previously

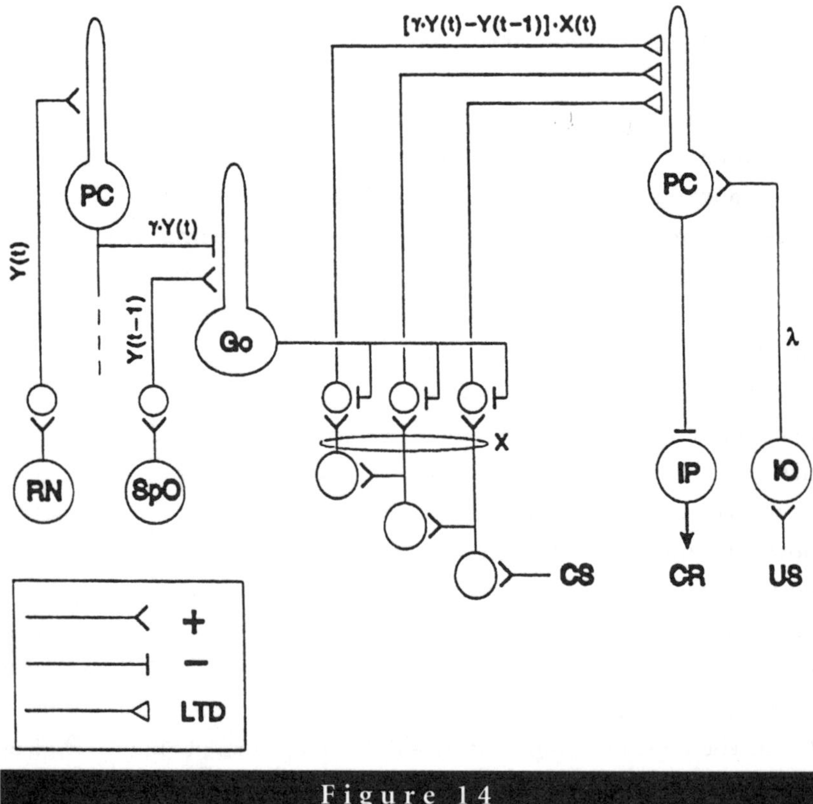

Figure 14

The complete TD implementation scheme showing three sequentially activated inputs, delimited by the ellipse marked by the symbol X.

established CR was at full strength but extinguished normally with continuing presentation of CS-alone trials. This finding is consistent with the efference interpretation of the TD implementation, because inactivation of IP eliminates the CR and therefore prevents efference from the RN and SpO from reaching the putative site of learning in HVI. In terms of Equation 1, connection weights cannot decrease if $Y(t)$ and $Y(t-1)$ are both equal to 0. If the afference interpretation were correct and efference plays no role in extinction, then inactivation of IP would not prevent extinction, because afference arises from PN and bypasses IP en route to HVI.

IMPLICATIONS OF THE IMPLEMENTATION

This implementation has several testable implications that are outlined as follows:

1. Some PCs decrease their firing rate in anticipation of CR peaks. These PCs express LTD; there are other PCs, however, perhaps the majority, that increase their rate of firing in relation to CR peaks, as reported by Berthier and Moore (1986). Some of these PCs express efference from the RN and SpO. Their function is to activate Golgi cells that modulate information flow through the granule cells. Another function would be to inhibit motor programs, such as eye-opening and saccadic movements, that could interfere with eyelid closure.

2. The implementation specifies that Golgi cells that modulate the flow of CS information in granule cells fire in relation to *changes* in eyelid position (i.e., they fire in relation to $\dot{Y}$). This property of Golgi cell firing patterns has been reported by van Kan, Gibson, and Houk (1993), in a study of monkey limb movements, and Edgley and Lidierth (1987), in a study of cat locomotion.

3. The implementation implies that reversible inactivation of the RN would prevent second-order conditioning. Although inactivation of the RN would cause a temporary interruption of information flow that results in a CR, however, it would not prevent learning of the primary association between components of the CS and the US. This association proceeds with little disruption because the pontine nuclei and the inferior olive can still convey CS and US information to the cerebellar cortex. Evidence for this proposition comes from a study of rabbit eyeblink conditioning by Clark and Lavond (1993), who demonstrated that inactivation of the RN by cooling did not prevent learning, because CR magnitude recovered on reactivation of the RN. Inactivation of the RN would, however, interrupt efference about the position of the eyelid at times t and $t - \Delta t$ from the RN and SpO. Thus, $\dot{Y}$ would not be available to cerebellar cortex. According to the TD model, $\dot{Y}$ allows for increments of predictive associations in the absence of the US, as would occur in second-order conditioning. This being the case, inactivation of the RN would interfere with

second-order conditioning. Animals trained with a mixture of first- and second-order conditioning (Kehoe et al., 1981) but with the RN inactivated would be expected to show first-order learning, as in the Clark and Lavond (1993) study, but little or no second-order learning. Figure 15 shows a simulation of the failure of second-order conditioning by down-regulation of the $Y(t)$ efference projection to HVI from the RN.

4. The implementation implies that lesions of the IP disrupt the pattern of firing of CR-related PCs, as reported by Katz and Steinmetz (1997). This disruption presumably occurs because IP lesions prevent error-correction feedback from IO, SpO, and the RN.

GENERALITY OF THE TD MODEL

Some readers might argue that the TD model is not appropriate for other varieties of conditioned responses because they do not express temporal specificity. Conditioned fear, for example, does not usually feature a temporal delay such as the one shown in Figure 1 and predicted by the model. Figure 2, however, shows that response latency is simply a matter a parameter setting, so short-latency CRs are not excluded by the model. This capacity of the model notwithstanding, Davis, Schlesinger, and Sorenson (1989) showed that conditioned fear is temporally specific. Autoshaping also reflects temporal specificity (Holland, Hamlin, & Parsons, 1997; Palya & Chu, 1996). We submit that temporal and sequential encoding lies at the heart of most, if not all, familiar forms of conditioning (Barnet, Cole, & Miller, 1997).

The TD model might be faulted because it does not explicitly provide a mechanism for the shape of CS–US interval functions. Long CS–US intervals are typically less effective than shorter, more “optimal” intervals, and mechanisms for simulating CS–US interval functions are inherent in the TD model; we have simply ignored this additional complexity in order to ease exposition. Typical CS–US interval functions can be generated by indexing the parameter α in Equation 1 with the i subscript, which designates the ordinal rank of sequential components that are activated by the

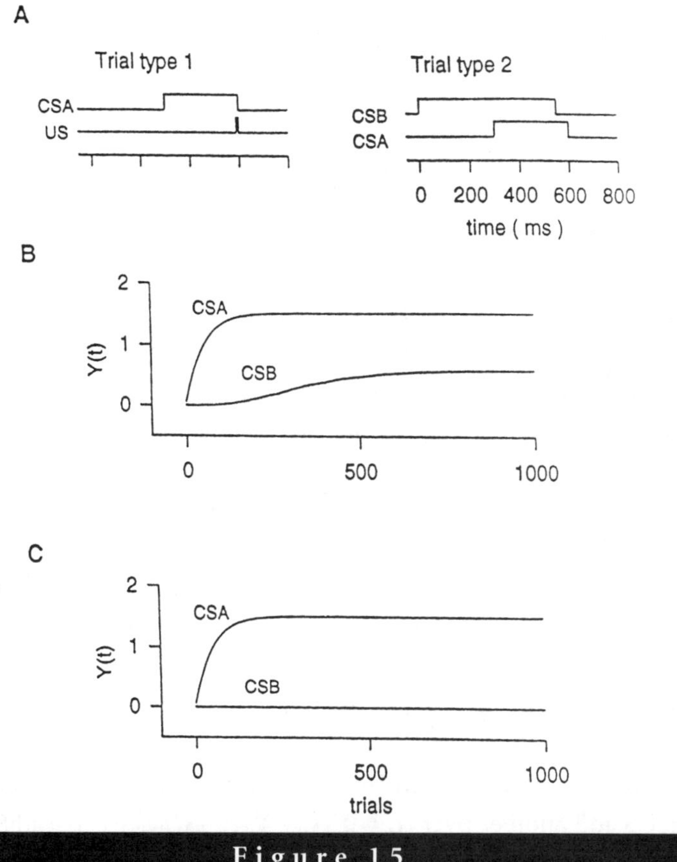

Figure 15

Simulated effect of RN inactivation on first- and second-order conditioning. (A) The training protocol. Trial type 1: CSA is 300 ms in duration, and the CS–US interval is 290 ms. Trial type 2: CSB is 550 ms in duration, and the CSB–CSA interval is 300 ms. The two trial types are randomly mixed, and each occurs 500 times. (B) Simulated peak CR amplitude ($Y(t)$) to CSA and CSB as a function of trials. Notice that $Y(t)$ to CSB increases with training, reflecting second-order conditioning. (C) With $\gamma = 0$ (equivalent to inactivation of the red nucleus), second-order conditioning does not occur.

CS (see Sutton & Barto, 1990, p. 523). CS–US interval functions can be customized by choosing appropriate α parameters.

The TD model might also be faulted because it does not generate increasing variability of timing parameters as the CS–US interval increases. This, too, is easy to implement, with appropriate additional assumptions about the structure and reliability of timing (Moore, Choi, & Brunzell, in press).

CONCLUSION

We have argued that CSs are occasion setters for the timing of reinforcing events, such as the US, in classical conditioning. We have described how Sutton and Barto's (1990) TD model of classical conditioning, with the complete serial compound representation of elapsed time, can generate appropriate CR waveforms in complex paradigms that involve temporal integration, including temporally specific summation and blocking, conditioned inhibition, second-order conditioning, and temporal uncertainty. We also suggest an implementation plan for TD learning within the cerebellum, which is the putative site of classical eyeblink conditioning. The implementation draws on neurobiological evidence regarding how LTD is established, reinforced, and maintained among cerebellar Purkinje cells that determine the timing and topography of CRs. The implementation incorporates recent anatomical findings, reviewed by Rosenfield and Moore (1995), that allow these Purkinje cells to receive the two components of the TD model's reinforcement operator, one component donated by the US and another by $\dot{Y}(t) = Y(t) - Y(t - \Delta t)$ as feedback efference. The implementation scheme lays the foundation for network simulations at the cellular level.

REFERENCES

Barnet, R. C., Cole, R. P., & Miller, R. R. (1997). Temporal integration in second-order conditioning and sensory preconditioning. *Animal Learning & Behavior, 25,* 221–233.

Barnet, R. C., Grahame, N. J., & Miller, R. R. (1993). Temporal encoding as a determinant of blocking. *Journal of Experimental Psychology: Animal Behavior Processes, 19,* 327–341.

Berthier, N. E., Barto, A. G., & Moore, J. W. (1991). Linear systems analysis of the relationship between firing of deep cerebellar neurons and the classically conditioned nictitating membrane response in rabbits. *Biological Cybernetics, 65,* 99–105.

Berthier, N. E., & Moore, J. W. (1986). Cerebellar Purkinje cell activity related to the classically conditioned nictitating membrane response. *Experimental Brain Research, 63,* 341–350.

Berthier, N. E., & Moore, J. W. (1990). Activity of deep cerebellar nuclear cells during classical conditioning of nictitating membrane extension in rabbits. *Experimental Brain Research, 83,* 44–54.

Blazis, D. E. J., & Moore, J. W. (1991). Conditioned inhibition of the nictitating membrane response in rabbits following hypothalamic and mesencephalic lesions. *Behavioural Brain Research, 46,* 71–81.

Bullock, D., Fiala, J. C., & Grossberg, S. (1994). A neural model of timed response learning in the cerebellum. *Neural Networks, 7,* 1101–1114.

Chen, C., & Thompson, R. F. (1995). Temporal specificity of long-term depression in parallel fiber-Purkinje synapses in rat cerebellar slice. *Learning and Memory, 2,* 185–198.

Choi, J-S, & Moore, J. W. (1996). Cerebellar single cell activity related to bimodal conditioned eyeblink responses. *Society for Neuroscience Abstracts, 22,* 1643.

Clark, R. E., & Lavond, D. G. (1993). Reversible lesions of the red nucleus during acquisition and retention of a classically conditioned behavior in rabbits. *Behavioral Neuroscience, 107,* 264–270.

Davis, M., Schlesinger, L. S., & Sorenson, C. A. (1989). Temporal specificity of fear conditioning: Effects of different conditioned stimulus-unconditioned intervals on the fear-potentiated startle effect. *Journal of Experimental Psychology: Animal Learning Processes, 15,* 295–310.

Desmond, J. E., & Moore, J. W. (1988). Adaptive timing in neural networks: The conditioned response. *Biological Cybernetics, 58,* 405–415.

Desmond, J. E., & Moore, J. W. (1991a). Activity of red nucleus neurons during the classically conditioned rabbit nictitating membrane response. *Neuroscience Research, 10,* 260–279.

Desmond, J. E., & Moore, J. W. (1991b). Altering the synchrony of stimulus trace processes: Tests of a neural-network model. *Biological Cybernetics, 65,* 161–169.

Edgley, S. A., & Lidierth, M. (1987). Discharges of cerebellar Golgi cells during locomotion in cats. *Journal of Physiology, London, 392,* 315–332.

Fiala, J. C., Grossberg, S., & Bullock, D. (1996). Metabotropic glutamate receptor activation in cerebellar Purkinje cells as substrate for adaptive timing of the classically conditioned eye-blink response. *Journal of Neuroscience, 16,* 3760–3774.

Grossberg, S., & Merrill, J. W. L. (1996). The hippocampus and cerebellum in adaptively timed learning, recognition, and movement. *Journal of Cognitive Neuroscience, 8,* 257–277.

Hartell, N. A. (1996). Strong activation of parallel fibers produces localized calcium transients and a form of LTD that spreads to distant synapses. *Neuron, 16,* 601–610.

Hesslow, G. (1994). Inhibition of classically conditioned eyeblink responses by stimulation of the cerebellar cortex in the cat. *Journal of Physiology, 476,* 245–256.

Hilgard, E. R. (1936). The nature of the conditioned response. I. The case for and against stimulus substitution. *Psychological Review, 43,* 366–385.

Hoehler, F. K., & Leonard, D. W. (1976). Double responding in classical nictitating membrane conditioning with single-CS dual ISI training. *Pavlovian Journal of Biological Science, 11,* 180–190.

Holland, P. C., Hamlin, P. A., & Parsons, P. A. (1997). Temporal specificity in serial feature-positive discrimination learning. *Journal of Experimental Psychology: Animal Behavior Processes, 23,* 95–109.

Ito, M. (1984). *The cerebellum and neural control.* New York: Raven Press.

Katz, D. B., & Steinmetz, J. E. (1997). Single-unit evidence for eye-blink conditioning in cerebellar cortex is altered, but not eliminated, by interpositus nucleus lesions. *Learning & Memory, 4,* 88–104.

Kehoe, E. J., Feyer, A. M., & Moses, J. L. (1981). Second-order conditioning of the rabbit's nictitating membrane response as a function of the CS2—CS1 and CS1—US intervals. *Animal Learning & Behavior, 9,* 304–315.

Kim, J. J., & Thompson, R. F. (1997). Cerebellar circuits and synaptic mechanisms involved in classical eyeblink conditioning. *Trends in Neuroscience, 20,* 177–181.

Liu, S. S., & Moore, J. W. (1969). Auditory differential conditioning of the rabbit nictitating membrane response: IV. Training based on stimulus offset and the effect of an intertrial tone. *Psychonomic Science, 15,* 128–129.

Mauk, M. D., & Donegan, N. H. (1997). A model of Pavlovian eyelid conditioning based on the synaptic organization of the cerebellum. *Learning and Memory, 4,* 130–158.

Millenson, J. R., Kehoe, E. J., & Gormezano, I. (1977). Classical conditioning of the rabbit's nictitating membrane response under fixed and mixed CS—US intervals. *Learning and Motivation, 8,* 351–366.

Moore, J. W., & Choi, J-S (1997). Conditioned response timing and integration in the cerebellum. *Learning and Memory, 4,* 116–129.

Moore, J. W., Choi, J-S, & Brunzell, D. H. (in press). Predictive timing under temporal uncertainty: The TD model of the conditioned response. In D. A. Rosenbaum & C. E. Collyer (Eds.), *Timing of Behavior: Neural, Computational, and Psychological Perspectives.* Cambridge, MA: MIT Press.

Moore, J. W., & Desmond, J. E. (1992). A cerebellar neural network implementation of a temporally adaptive conditioned response. In I. Gormezano & E. A. Wasserman (Eds.), *Learning and memory: The behavioral and biological substrates* (pp. 347–368). Hillsdale, NJ: Erlbaum.

Moore, J. W., Desmond, J. E., & Berthier, N. E. (1989). Adaptively timed conditioned responses and the cerebellum: A neural network approach. *Biological Cybernetics, 62,* 17–28.

Moore, J. W., Newman, F. L., & Glasgow, B. (1969). Intertrial cues as discriminative stimuli in human eyelid conditioning. *Journal of Experimental Psychology, 79,* 319–326.

Palya, W. L., & Chu, J. Y. M. (1996). Real-time dynamics in the interaction between trial stimuli and its temporal context. *Animal Learning & Behavior, 24,* 92–104.

Pavlov, I. P. (1960/1927). *Conditioned reflexes.* New York: Dover Publications.

Perrett, S. P., & Mauk, M. D. (1995). Extinction of conditioned eyelid responses requires the anterior lobe of cerebellar cortex. *Journal of Neuroscience, 15,* 2074–2080.

Perrett, S. P., Ruiz, B. P., & Mauk, M. D. (1993). Cerebellar cortex lesions disrupt learning-dependent timing of conditioned eyelid responses. *Journal of Neuroscience, 13,* 1708–1718.

Ramnani, N., & Yeo, C. H. (1996). Reversible inactivations of the cerebellum prevent the extinction of conditioned nictitating membrane responses in rabbits. *Journal of Physiology, 495,* 159–168.

Richards, W. G., Ricciardi, T. N., & Moore, J. W. (1991). Activity of spinal trigeminal pars oralis and adjacent reticular formation units during differential conditioning of the rabbit nictitating membrane response. *Behavioural Brain Research, 44,* 195–204.

Rosenfield, M. E., & Moore, J. W. (1995). Connections to cerebellar cortex (Larsell's HVI) in the rabbit: A WGA-HRP study with implications for classical eyeblink conditioning. *Behavioral Neuroscience, 109,* 1106–1118.

Schreurs, B. G., Oh, M. M., & Alkon, D. L. (1996). Pairing-specific long-term depression of Purkinje cell excitatory postsynaptic potentials results from a classical conditioning procedure in the rabbit cerebellar slice. *Journal of Neurophysiology, 75,* 1051–1060.

Schreurs, B. G., Tomsic, D., Gusev, P. A., & Alkon, D. L. (1997). Dendritic excitability microzones and occluded long-term depression after classical conditioning of the rabbit's nictitating membrane response. *Journal of Neurophysiology, 77,* 86–92.

Schultz, W. P., Dayan, P., & Montague, P. R. (1997). A neural substrate of prediction and reward. *Science, 275,* 1593–1599.

Sears, L. L., & Steinmetz, J. E. (1991). Dorsal accessory inferior olive activity diminishes during acquisition of the rabbit classically conditioned eyelid response. *Brain Research, 545,* 114–122.

Skinner, B. F. (1938). *The behavior of organisms.* New York: Appleton-Century-Crofts.

Sutton, R. S., & Barto, A. G. (1990). Time-derivative models of Pavlovian reinforcement. In M. Gabriel & J. Moore (Eds.), *Learning and computational neuroscience: Foundations of adaptive networks* (pp. 497–537). Cambridge, MA: MIT Press.

Svensson, P., Ivarsson, M., & Hesslow, G. (1997). Effect of varying the intensity and train frequency of cerebellar mossy fiber conditioned stimuli on the latency of conditioned eye-blink responses in decerebrate ferrets. *Learning & Memory, 4,* 105–115.

van Kan, P. L. E., Gibson, A. R., & Houk, J. C. (1993). Movement-related inputs to intermediate cerebellum of the monkey. *Journal of Neurophysiology, 69,* 74–94.

Wells, G. R., Hardiman, M. J., & Yeo, C. H. (1989). Visual projections to the pontine nuclei of the rabbit: Orthograde and retrograde tracing studies with WGA-HRP. *Journal of Comparative Neurology, 279,* 629–652.

11

A Temporally Sensitive Recurrent Network Model of Occasion Setting

James Zackheim, Catherine Myers, and Mark Gluck

The significance of external stimuli and the appropriate response to them is critically dependent on context. Contextual cues and their influence, however, can be seen as extending in time as well as space. For example, this applies to real-world tasks such as language comprehension, where the meaning of a word is disambiguated by the previous words, and also to well-defined classical conditioning experiments in the laboratory. Within the occasion-setting classical conditioning paradigm, stimulus relationships are arranged so that the appropriate response to a conditioned stimulus (CS; e.g., tone X) depends on whether an occasion setter or *feature* (e.g., light A) has been previously presented. In feature positive (FP) paradigms, the unconditioned stimulus (US) only accompanies X if it has been preceded by A. In effect, the previous occurrence of cue A disambiguates the meaning of cue X.

Just as a spatial phasic contextual cue need not be immediately juxtaposed to a conditioned stimulus (CS) in order to have significance, a pertinent punctate *contextual* cue need not be temporally synchronous with the CS. By studying the dependence of successful learning on the temporal relationships between cues, the temporal nature of stimulus processing can be clarified. Discovering the degree of temporal separation, or overlap, between cues that are necessary for successful associative learning can also help the study of neural and computational bases of classical conditioning by clarifying the limitations of the mechanisms at work. Empirical data from the occasion-setting paradigm, in which the temporal relationships between the occasion setter and the target cue are critical to determining performance, are thus key constraints on the modeling and understanding of stimulus processing and associative learning.

The occasion-setting paradigm allows a controlled analysis of how the temporal relationship between occasion setter and CS affects associative learning. The mechanisms by which temporally distinct cues interact in this or other paradigms are unknown. It has been proposed that the occasion setter (A) modulates the association between target and US (Holland, 1983). An alternative theory is that the occasion setter (OS) and the feature form a complex configuration that can be associated with a conditioned response that is distinct from the associations of either element alone (Pearce, 1987, 1994). These theories make substantially different claims about which elements in the OS–CS–US triad interact to subserve performance; consequently they would make different claims about the possible neural basis of associative learning. In this chapter we show that a generalized form of Gluck and Myers's (1993) model of hippocampal function in eyeblink conditioning, when extended to include recurrent connections, can (a) simulate the key empirical results from the existing literature, (b) suggest a resolution to the modulator versus configural stimulus debate, and (c) suggest a computational basis for the temporal sensitivity of some key empirical results. Furthermore, the model makes very few new assumptions over and above the Gluck and Myers model.

The occasion-setting paradigm is separated from other higher order conditioning paradigms by a key empirical result that also clarifies the temporal processing that subserves performance in several classical conditioning tasks (for example, trace conditioning): No significant association develops between the feature and the US. The absence of such an association, however, and hence the distinction between occasion setting and higher order conditioning, is sensitive to the temporal relationship between the CS and occasion setter. The onset of the feature presentation must precede the onset of the target in order to obtain the occasion-setting effect (Holland, 1986).

We propose that this temporal sensitivity is because of the temporal limitations of recurrent connections that feed back activity within the networks that subserve discrimination learning. Analysis of the computational impact of the recurrent connections suggests that both modulatory and configural processes may contribute to the task-solving within the occasion-setting paradigm. Recurrent activity can (a) allow association between current and reverberating activity that represents previous but now-terminated stimuli (a *configuration*), and (b) allow reverberations of activity derived from previous input to *modulate* the impact of current network input.

We have developed a recurrent real-time version of the Gluck and Myers (1993) model. The original model and the recurrent version have helped us to consider and model (a) the possible mechanisms by which context may act as an occasion setter, (b) the way in which phasic CSs can act as occasion setters, and (c) the computational mechanisms within the model that underlie the temporal sensitivity of that action. The simulation results presented here can be viewed as a natural extension of the principles at work in the 1993 model, which has been shown to successfully model the role of context as an occasion setter.

THE GLUCK AND MYERS (1993) MODEL

Gluck and Myers (1993) proposed a connectionist model of hippocampal function that was based largely on data from the classical eyeblink conditioning paradigm. This model of associative learning suggests how a distributed neural system, such as the hippocampus, could implement the computations needed to solve certain tasks, tasks that neuropsychological and lesion data suggest are hippocampal-dependent.

The hippocampal component of the hippocampal–cortical model is a three-layer feed-forward network that is based on the predictive autoencoder of Hinton (1989) (see Figure 1). Activation of some subset of the

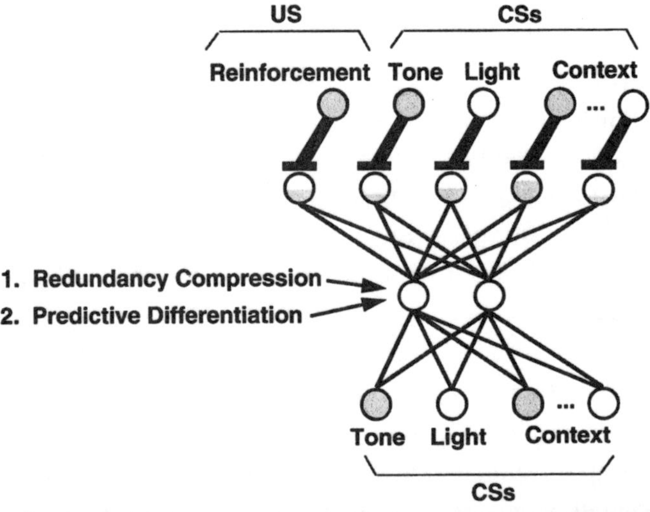

Figure 1

Schematic of the Gluck and Myers (1993) model. Stimulus presence is represented by node activity in the input (*bottom*) layer. Filled circles represent active nodes. The output layer is trained to reproduce the input and predict the US. Errors are then backpropagated through the network.

nodes in the input (first) layer represents (in binary) the presence or absence of certain stimuli and their context on a trial-by-trial basis. Node activation in the third layer is the output of the system. According to the learning rule of the network, the output should be a faithful reproduction of the input, with an additional node that has a value between 0 and 1; this value represents a prediction of the US. The hidden layer of the network is fully connected to all nodes of the output and input layers. Here the network forms an alternate adaptive representation of the inputs, which in many cases will better suit learning the correct US predictions and discriminations for a given task. The adaptability of this representation is ensured by the learning rule, which alters the strength of the connections between input and hidden, and hidden and output, layers. This rule calculates and then backpropagates the error of the output (the difference between the predicted value of the US and the actual value on that trial), adjusting the connections so that an identical or similar input, if presented again, will result in an output (prediction) that is closer to the desired value. This backpropagation rule is one general way to instantiate the computations that can be used to solve certain conditioning tasks; it does not make any specific claims regarding the neural basis of classical conditioning. The rule does have strong similarity to the Rescorla and Wagner (1972) algorithm, however, which has accurately captured much of the empirical data in the classical conditioning paradigm. This rule, in concert with the architecture of the network, forms adaptive, hidden representations according to two biases: redundancy compression and predictive differentiation. These biases can be thought of as making representations of stimuli more similar if they result in the same outcome, and more different if they result in different outcomes.

This network is connected, in the Gluck and Myers (1993) model, to a simpler cortical model with a more elementary learning rule. To learn a task, the cortical network, which mediates the final response (CR), must be trained by the values derived within the hippocampal hidden layer. The independent and codependent operation of these two components has accurately simulated a wide range of empirical data within the rabbit eyeblink paradigm (for example, latent inhibition and sensory preconditioning) and has generated novel predictions that are currently being tested (such as easy–hard discrimination transfer). One of the key features of this model is its flexibility; it has been extended to human category learning (Gluck, Oliver, & Myers, 1996) and also to include the effect of cholinergic tone on learning (Myers et al., 1996), which may have a significant human neuropsychological impact. The model has also been used to simulate the role of tonic context as an occasion setter (Myers & Gluck, 1994).

SIMULATIONS OF CONTEXT AS AN OCCASION SETTER: THE 1993 MODEL

Well-defined relationships between phasic stimuli (transient, with sudden onset and offset) result in learned associations between those stimuli. Well-defined relationships also usually exist between tonic (continuous and slow-changing, or unchanging) and phasic stimuli, and hence contextual cues can provide predictive information in much the same way as phasic cues. The similarity in terms of mode of action and representation between context and typical phasic cues has been debated. For the present purposes, however, one can simply state that contextual cues should and do act as occasion setters in conditional discrimination paradigms (Bouton & Swartzentruber, 1986).

Bouton and Swartzentruber (1986) and Bouton and Nelson (1994) have demonstrated the occasion-setting properties of context. Rats were trained to respond to a phasic cue (A) when in context X (AX+), but not to A when in context Y (AY–). This task can be solved in four ways: X can be become a conditioned excitor; a response can be learned to the configuration AX; Y can become a conditioned inhibitor; or X or Y can become occasion setters, forming no direct associations with the US but in some way modulating the learned relationship between A and the US. (This could occur through modulation of the A–US association or by some X-A-US configuration).

In order to demonstrate that contexts X, Y, or both act as occasion setters, the first three possibilities must be ruled out. In the first case, as shown in Figure 2, Panel A (simulated results), there is no response to X alone, so X cannot be a conditioned excitor. Second, Figure 2, Panel B shows the results of a transfer task following the initial AX+, AY– training, in which a new tonic cue (E) was presented and only rewarded in context X (EX+, X–). This task can be compared to another identical task in a new context, Z (EZ+, Z–). If learning is specific to the configuration AX, there should be no benefit of learning the new discrimination (with cue E) in context X rather than Z. Panel B of Figure 2 shows, however, that substantial transfer occurs to the EX+, E– discrimination. Third, a similar transfer task comparing EY+, Y– to EZ+, Z– can be used to establish whether Y is acting as a conditioned inhibitor (with A having a weaker positive association to the US). If Y is an inhibitor, the EY+ task should be harder to learn after the initial training than a new EZ+, Z– task. Figure 2, Panel C, shows no difference between the time taken to learn these tasks, however. The most plausible explanation for the data is the fourth one, that X, Y, or both are acting as contextual occasion setters, selectively

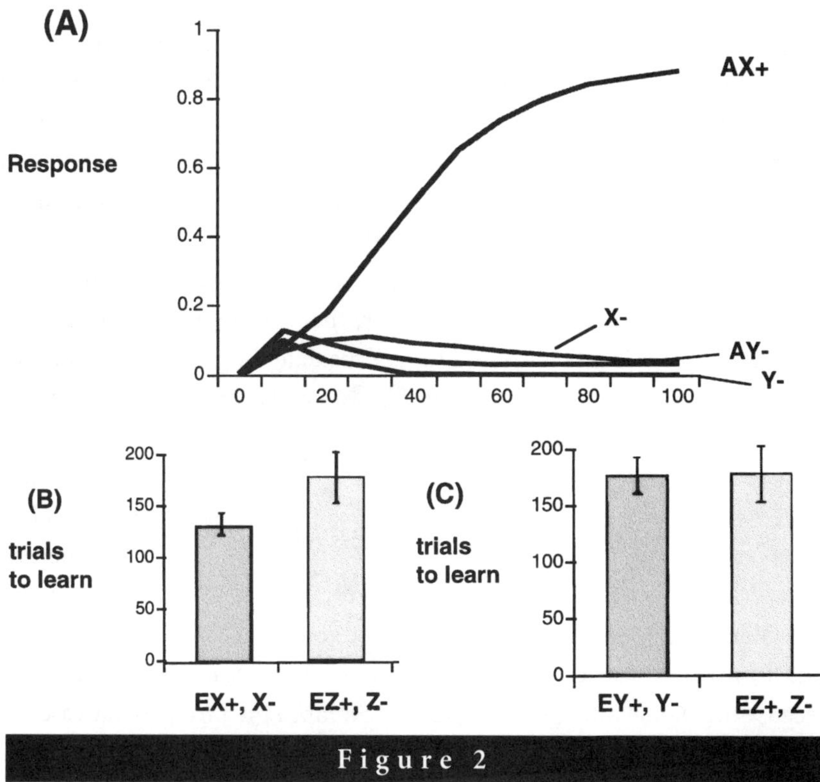

Figure 2

Occasion setting by contextual cues in the Gluck and Myers (1993) hippocampal–cortical model. (A) Conditional discrimination in which the correct response to A is determined by the context (X or Y). The lack of response to X–, AY–, and Y– indicates that performance is likely to be mediated by occasion setting and not the excitatory associations of X. (B) Responding is not a result of the configuration AX, because the context X facilitates the learning of a discrimination with a new cue, E. (C) Y is not acting as a conditioned inhibitor because there is no impairment seen when a discrimination is learned in context Y with a new cue, E, compared to a new neutral context, Z.

modulating the relationship between A and B and the US and thus allowing a representation of the conditional solution to the task.

Myers and Gluck (1994) have shown that their trial-level model of the hippocampal mediation of classical eyeblink conditioning can account for the occasion-setting properties of context. They demonstrate that their feed-forward network learns the discrimination and transfer tasks in the same way as described by Bouton and Swartzentruber (1986). One can therefore conclude that the Gluck and Myers model can account for the occasion-setting abilities of contextual cues, and insofar as the model is a simplified computational description of possible hippocampal function, it can clarify the mechanisms by which such higher order learning may occur. This model is limited in the temporal domain, however, because it is restricted to a static representation of intratrial events it therefore cannot address issues that relate to the occasion-setting properties of phasic cues. It does seem plausible to assert, however, that a minimally altered real-time version of this model should (a) encapsulate the performance of the trial level model; and (b) account for the cases in which a CS can, depending on intratrial temporal stimulus relationships, act as an occasion setter.

A RECURRENT GENERALIZATION OF THE 1993 MODEL

The Gluck and Myers (1993) model is not able to account for empirical data from tasks that are sensitive to intratrial temporal factors. This is because the model only receives and acts on input on a trial-by-trial basis. Occasion setting is well-known to be sensitive to these intratrial temporal factors: The onset of the occasion setter or feature must precede the onset of the target (CS). The 1993 model has therefore been extended in order to account for intratrial temporal sensitivity. Current results suggest that this model not only accounts for the central results in the occasion-setting literature but also exhibits a temporal sensitivity similar to that seen in the discrimination tasks. Moreover, the extended model accomplishes this without any qualitative changes from the 1993 model—that is, the computations of the original model that accounted for much of the empirical eyeblink conditioning data remain unchanged, and because of this the 1993 model can be viewed as a special case of the extended model. It should be noted, however, that rabbit eyeblink, pigeon autoshaping, and rat conditioning operate on substantially different time scales; simulations are unlikely to be quantitatively accurate when compared across paradigms, and correctly so, given the likelihood of differing but overlapping neural bases for such task performance.

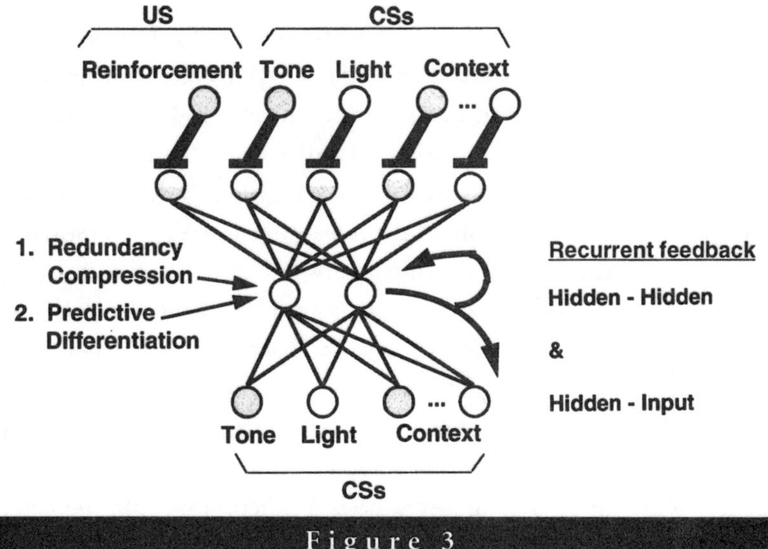

Figure 3

Schematic of the recurrent version of the Gluck and Myers model.

The primary extension of the 1993 model presented here is the addition of recurrent connections between layers of the network. Such architectures have been widely used for analyzing temporally dynamic data in many engineering applications (e.g., Maskara & Noetzel, 1993). Furthermore, parallel lines of research in our laboratory have investigated the computational significance of recurrent architectures for hippocampal–cerebellar interactions within classical conditioning tasks. In a model that describes the cerebellar basis of simple classical conditioning and the involvement of the hippocampus in solving more complex configural tasks, Gluck, Goren, Myers, and Thompson (1997) have shown that recurrent connections from the interpositus nucleus of the cerebellum can provide the circuitry necessary for producing well-timed and well-formed conditioned responding. Hence, a recurrent architecture should be expected to confer appropriate temporal sensitivity and resolution to the hippocampal component of the 1993 model.

The recurrent version of the Gluck and Myers model contains only two additions (see Figure 3). First, stimuli are presented to the input layer between 12 and 60 times per trial. For example, the continued presence of a stimulus for the first half of the trial is represented as a value of 1.0 (or any value above 0.0) at one or more of the input nodes during the first 6 of 12 trial bins. In this way, the relative timing of CS and US onset and offset can be modeled. Second, and in order to learn associations between stimuli that are distant in time within a trial, the new network contains two sets of recurrent connections—that is, the hidden layer has connections projecting forward to the output layer, spreading activation in that direction, but also back to itself and back to the input layer. These connections, like all others in the network, are complete (from every node to every other) and adaptively altered by the learning rule. Activity takes one time step (bin) to travel along the recurrent connections. Thus, the activity of the input layer at any time is a function of both the external input (stimuli) and the network's adaptive representation of the input from the previous time step; this is because the hidden layer contains the adaptive representations, and the connection has a one-time bin delay. In a similar manner, the hidden layer activity is a function of current and previous representations of stimuli—in this way information can be associated across time. Moreover, the nature of these recurrents and the learning rule (unchanged from the original model) will determine the extent to which input and activity at one time influence network activity at successive time steps. The architecture of the network ensures that, despite the limited temporal buffer, the influence of activity at any one point in time will have an exponentially decreasing influence at each of several subsequent points in time. This network is in fact a combination of Elman (1990) and Jordan (1986) networks, in that the recurrent connections provide the network with a buffer or memory that is equivalent to one time step. The Jordan network contained output-to-input recurrents, and the Elman network hidden-to-hidden recurrents.

Simulations have shown that, for a wide range of parameters, a dual set of recurrents is optimal. It has not been conclusively determined that both sets are necessary, but in all tested cases *in an occasion-setting paradigm* they were found to be superior to either set of recurrents alone. In other paradigms, such as simple trace conditioning, a single set of recurrents is often sufficient, depending on the trace interval.

NETWORK SIMULATION RESULTS: THE RECURRENT MODEL

Five separate experiments were run as simulations on our model. The stimulus protocol for each of the experiments is shown in the appendix (Figure 10). For each stimulus presentation within a given protocol, there were 10 context-only trials. Simulations of FP and FN discriminations, as well as tests of transfer, were performed. Furthermore, the effects of varying feature–target orthogonality (in terms of representation and amplitude) and the effect of varying feature–target presentation intervals were investigated. Finally, the ability of an occasion setter to transfer its efficacy to a new target was modeled. All simulations presented features and targets serially.

The model produces a US prediction that fluctuates with time. Thus, in order to present a trial-by-trial learning curve, the value of the US prediction for any one trial was considered to be the value of the US prediction at the time of US onset for that trial.

Ross and Holland (1981) showed that rats learn to respond selectively to serially presented, reinforced feature and target pairs. Simulation results shown in Figure 4 indicate that the model also learns this task, reliably predicting a US only when the feature–target pair is presented. Because the 1993 and hence the new model are based on eyeblink conditioning, however, there is no account of the response form of the CR. In fact, there is no CR—there is only a US prediction because the CR in eyeblink conditioning has only one form of expression, and hence the US prediction is an equivalent output. It should also be noted that the relative but not the absolute values of the interstimulus timing is preserved because of the strong bias toward rat discrimination learning and away from rabbit eyeblink conditioning in the empirical literature. Rabbit eyeblink conditioning operates on much smaller time scales. The network performance

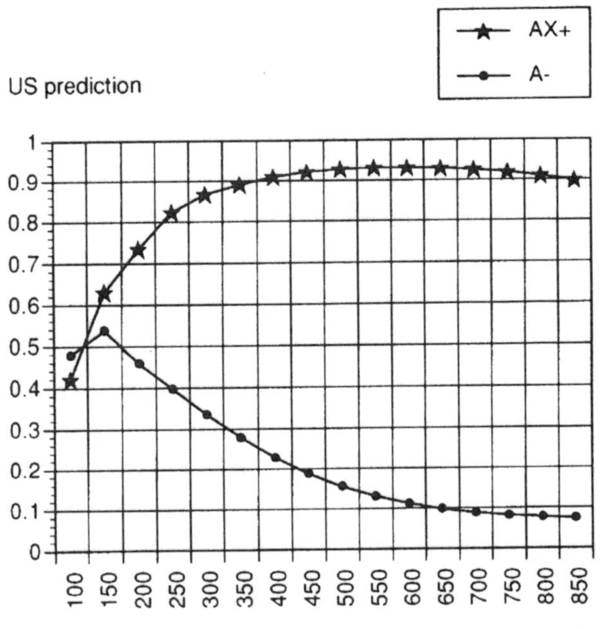

Figure 4

Feature-positive discrimination learning using the recurrent version of the Gluck and Myers model.

does not suffer from temporal scaling, however, and hence simulation results should be comparable to the rat literature. The topography of the networks' response within a given trial is shown in Figure 5. The value of the US prediction rises just before and peaks at the time of US arrival, as is typically seen in rabbit eyeblink conditioning experiments.

Because of the limited format for the expression of the learned response in the model, extinction tests were performed to ensure that the learned discrimination was truly based on the occasion-setting properties of the feature cue. If the feature is truly an occasion setter then extinction of the feature should not significantly alter its occasion setting properties. Two extinction procedures were adopted. First, all of the simulated experiments reported here were repeated with an additional block of feature extinction trials after discrimination reached asymptote. Extinction trials

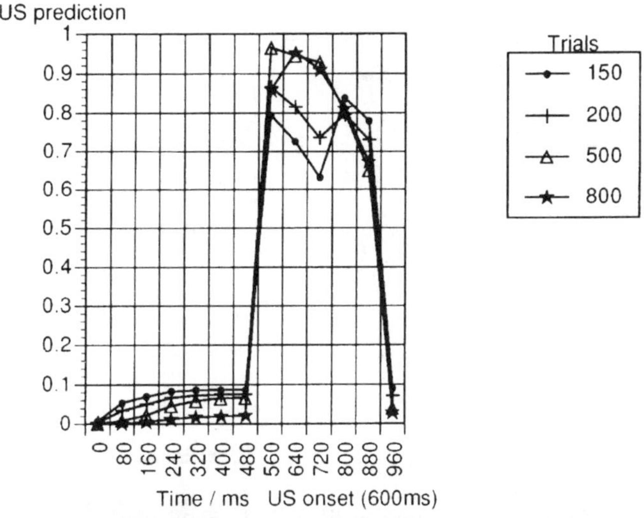

Figure 5

Development of the US prediction's topography.

were interleaved with continued discrimination training in a 1:1 ratio. The discrimination was unaffected by this procedure. However data from Holland (1989a) suggests that this procedure may in fact result in positive patterning rather than distinct feature-positive occasion setting and extinction. Thus, the feature-positive discrimination was again repeated using a block of 50 feature extinction-only trials after discrimination reached asymptote. Again, discrimination performance was unaffected, resulting in performance identical to that depicted in Figure 4.

Holland (1989b) has also shown that FN paradigms in the rat result in similar performance to that seen in the FP experiments. The model also performs well in an FN task (see Figure 6), although the 0.8 to 0.2 discrimination criterion is reached later (780 trials) than in the FP simulation. The response topography for the FN task is similar to that for the FP task shown in Figure 6.

A key result that characterizes the occasion-setting paradigm is the selectivity of transfer. Transfer experiments have a direct effect on theoretical issues regarding the occasion setter's mode of action. Two major find-

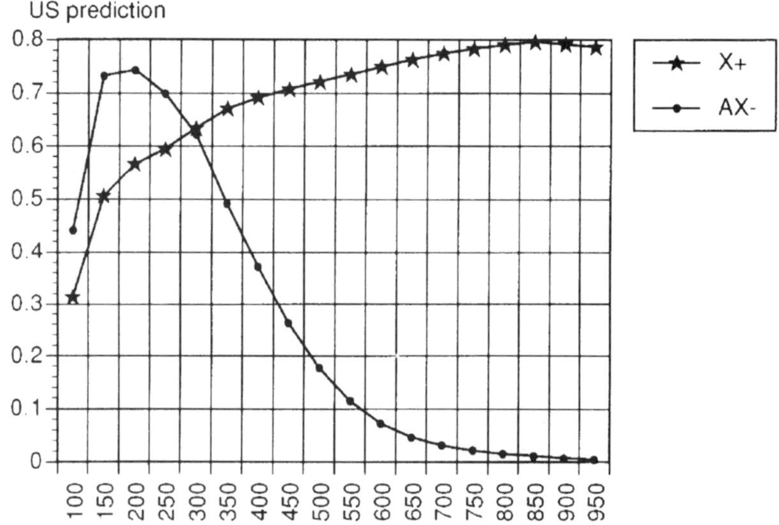

Figure 6

Feature-negative discrimination learning using the recurrent version of the Gluck and Myers model.

ings are that transfer of an occasion setters' efficacy, however this may occur, to a novel CS (not previously involved in an occasion-setting paradigm) is minimal. This suggests that occasion setters act in a target-specific manner. Transfer to other targets has been shown to occur, however, if the new target has been involved in an occasion-setting paradigm (Goddard & Holland, 1996; Holland, 1989a, 1989b; Holland & Lamarre, 1984). Our model was tested on a transfer task in which an occasion setter that had been paired with target X in an FP–FN task (AX+/BX–) was then paired with target Y in another AY+/BY– FP–FN task. Between these two training sessions, Y was trained in an occasion-setting paradigm (CY+, DY–). Although, in contrast to experimental results, initial responding to AY and BY was minimal, the AY+/BY– discrimination was eventually learned significantly faster than the initial AX+/BX– task (Figure 7). Control simulations (not shown) indicate that there is no reliable transfer effect when

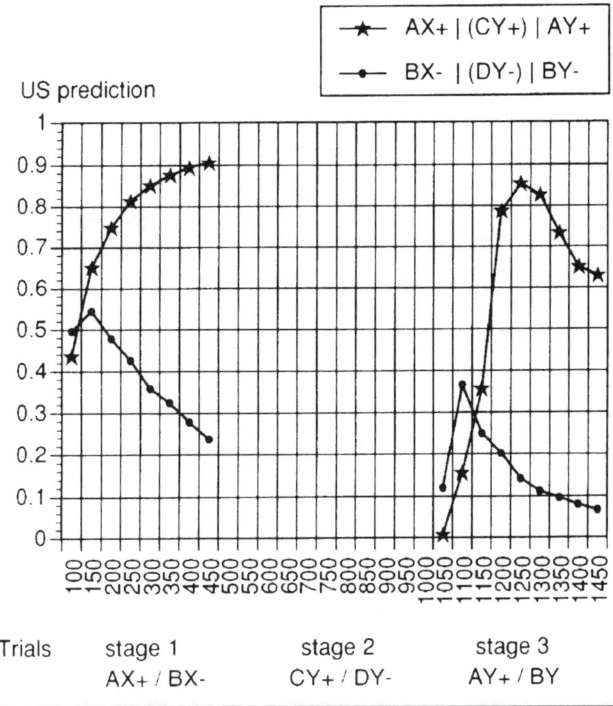

Figure 7

Transfer of occasion-setting efficacy.

Y has not been involved in an occasion-setting paradigm in the intermediate session.

The occasion-setting paradigm is of interest not only for the window it provides onto higher order and conditional learning, but also because of the sensitivity of the true occasion-setting result. Such sensitivity may help to clarify the neural basis of task performance by considering the types of computation and architecture that may confer this sensitivity. In this regard, it has been shown that increased similarity between target and feature slows discrimination learning (Lamarre & Holland, 1987). It is not obvious at first that this is the case in the model, because the discrimination to be learned does not involve partitioning target from feature per se. Simulations with our model (see Figure 8) have shown that orthogonal

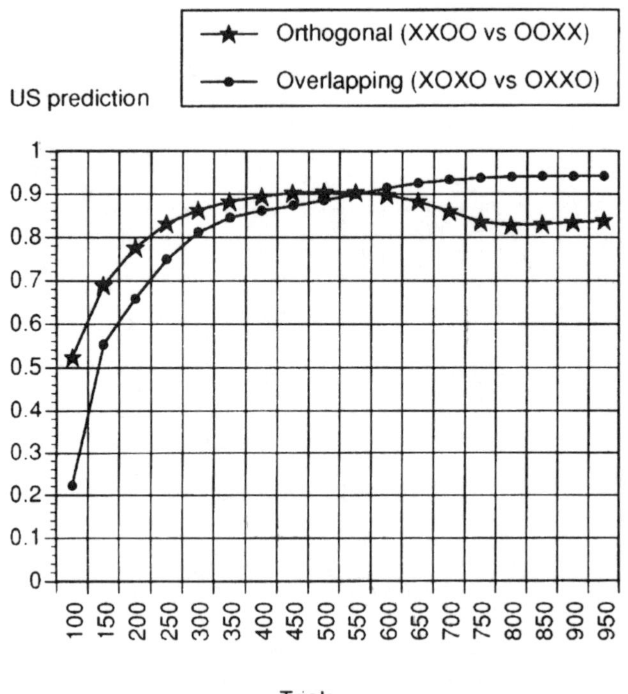

Figure 8

Orthogonality between the feature and the target speeds discrimination (AX+ only shown).

feature and target representations (1100 vs. 0011) result in faster discrimination learning than overlapping representations (1010 vs. 1100), however. This result suggests that the representational changes central to the Gluck and Myers (1993) model can also account for the processes that determine in part the efficacy of an occasion setter.

The efficacy of an occasion setter can be indexed by the difference between responding in US+ and US– trials (at the time of US onset). Previous work (Frey, 1970) suggests that the interstimulus interval (ISI, the time between CS and US onset) should influence this index of discrimination in occasion-setting and other paradigms. Furthermore, Holland (1986) has shown that the interval between feature and target onset and the gap between feature offset and target onset has a critical influence on the discrimination index. These results indicate that an attempt to extensively map the parameter space along these dimensions should reveal constraints that will clarify the computations that subserve occasion setting and also the divisions between different higher order conditioning paradigms. Exploring this parameter space with a model provides a strong test of the model itself and allows the model, once validated, to be used to manipulate conditions more flexibly and extensively than might be possible in the laboratory. In a first attempt at such an investigation, simulations were run with the recurrent model—the feature–target interval, as well as the intensities of the feature and target, were systematically varied. (This might be expected to have an impact similar to the orthogonality simulation.) Figure 9 shows a representation of the results. The plateau-like surface with steep sides suggests that there are intermediate values for the feature–target intensity ratio and for the gap and onset parameters that yield optimal occasion-set discrimination. Optimal occasion setting occurred when the intensity of the feature and target were similar and when there was a long gap between feature and target. Strong occasion setting can also be seen in a second region, where the gap is very short and the feature intensity slightly lower than that of the CS. It may be that this represents a discrete form of learning. This speculation could be further investigated using tests of selective transfer. In general, the nonuniformity of the plateau suggests a complex interaction between parameters that warrants a more extensive investigation, both within the model and in empirical studies.

CONCLUSION

The data presented in this chapter support the notion that the computational processes that define the Gluck and Myers (1993) model of hippocampus, when extended in time, account for the core empirical data in the occasion-setting paradigm. This extension involved a minimal number of changes; it is therefore plausible to interpret current results in terms of the computational underpinnings of the 1993 trial-level model. The 1993 model operated under two representational biases that adaptively influenced stimulus representations. These representations and the action of

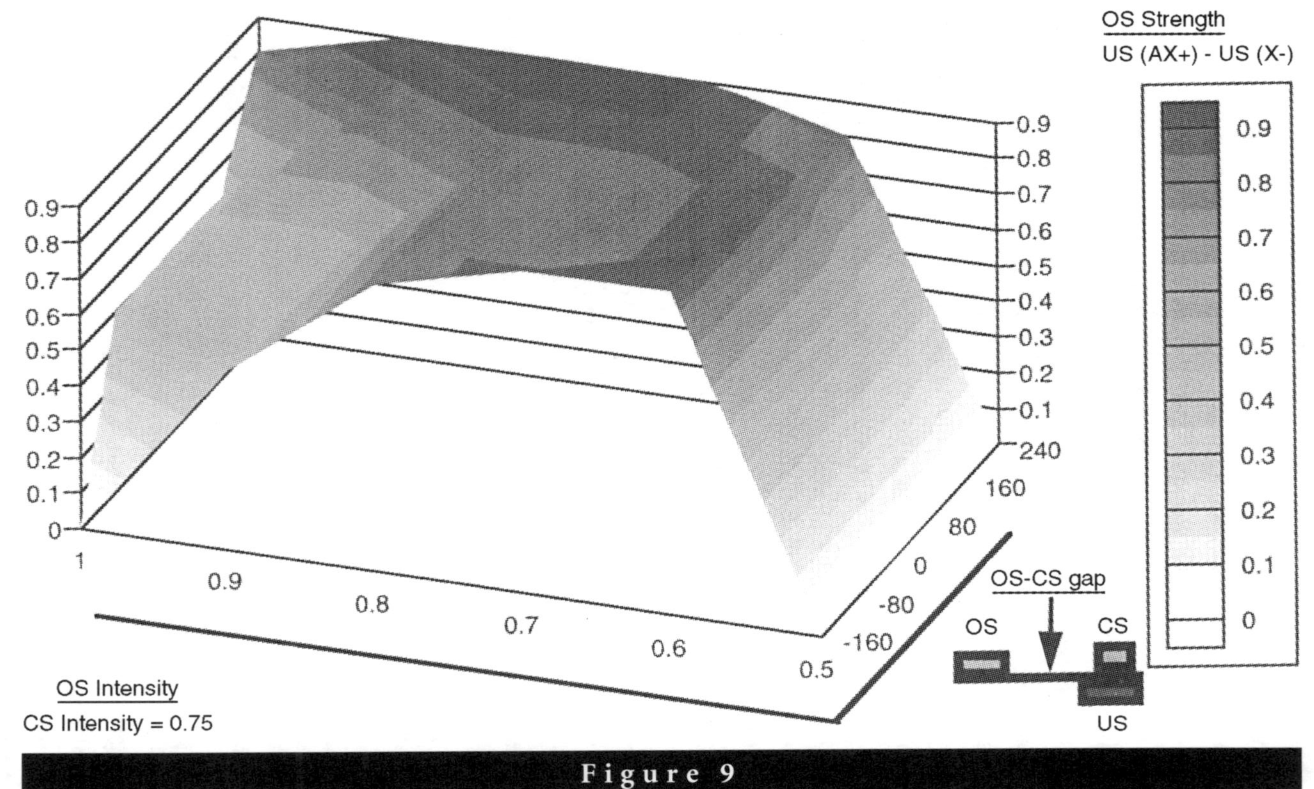

Figure 9

Representation of the temporal sensitivity of occasion setting in the recurrent model. The strength of occasion setting, indexed by the difference between AX+ and X– responding, is shown at each point along two dimensions that represent varying gaps between feature and target (stimulus length constant) and varying feature intensity.

the biases were static at the intratrial level but facilitated the associations between stimuli that are similar in terms of the outcome they predict. Hence, the 1993 model addresses issues that pertain not only to CS–US associations but to CS–CS associations—the associations that are critical in the occasion-setting paradigm.

In principle, the recurrent architecture of the extended model allows the adaptively altered hidden layer representations to associate and act on CSs that are distant in time; these recurrents only provide a buffer of one time step, however. As a result, the system is limited in its capacity to associate stimuli across long time spans. When the time span is sufficiently short, the representational processes of the 1993 model determine how CSs will interact and therefore the way in which the presence of one CS comes to influence the *meaning* or *significance* of the other.

The success of the 1993 model implies that hippocampal function can be considered in terms of adaptive representational processing. As a result, it is tempting to assume that the success of the extended model confines some part of the neural basis of occasion setting to the hippocampus. It has been demonstrated, however, that occasion setting still occurs after hippocampal lesion (Jarrard & Davidson, 1990). At this point it would be prudent to note that these models do not distinguish between the hippocampus proper (dentate gyrus and cornu ammonis) and the entorhinal, perirhinal, and parahippocampal cortices. The model as it stands does not make a specific neurobiological claim but a psychological and computational one: that certain representational processes as defined by the model's operation are capable of accurately describing several conditioning phenomena. Furthermore, within the rabbit eyeblink paradigm, a strong case can be made that the neural locus of these processes is hippocampal–entorhinal; a case of lesser strength can be made with regard to the rat paradigm. Multiple recurrents that are architecturally akin to those in the model do exist between hippocampus and entorhinal cortex, however, and experiments in hippocampal slice preparations have shown that activity does propagate through these recurrent loops several times per initial stimulation (Iijima et al., 1996).

In addition to any neurobiological conclusions that it may be tempting to infer, there are also conceptual conclusions that arise. Although not proven conclusively, the model, although within the occasion-setting paradigm, seems to work optimally with two sets of recurrent connections, from the hidden layer to itself and to the input layer. If these two sets of connections are indeed necessary, a possible resolution to the debate concerning the mode of action of occasion setters emerges. An occasion setter can be considered both a modulator of the target CS (and its association with the US) and part of a complex target–feature configuration. Recurrent connections between nodes within the hidden layer can be seen as bridging a temporal gap between two CSs that need to be associated and hence forms a configuration despite the offset of one stimulus before the onset of the other. Connections between nodes in the hidden layer and nodes in the input layer, on the other hand, influence the initial representation (before the action of biases) of incoming stimuli. This would be a way in which the biased representations of one stimulus can influence the network's interpretation of a forthcoming stimulus—that is, the occasion setter literally sets the occasion in the input layer. This forms an altered interpretation in the input and hidden layers that is adaptive in the sense that it is more likely to result in a correct prediction, because it has been placed in the appropriate *context.*

Thus it can be seen that adaptive stimulus representation of both occasion setters and CSs can act across a significant temporal span, and hence control the stimulus–stimulus interactions that mediate the occasion-setting phenomenon. The Gluck and Myers model now provides a strong platform from which to further investigate the temporal nature of stimulus representation and its physiological basis. Parallel lines of work already mentioned in this chapter have suggested some plausible anatomical and physiological bases for the computations that have been demonstrated to accurately capture empirical data. An approach with a finer temporal grain, as demonstrated here, can allow these more detailed investigations to make stronger contact with data that describe the temporal properties of neuronal ensembles in certain brain regions; as a result, the transition of our understanding of associative learning from the psychological to the neurobiological realm would be realized.

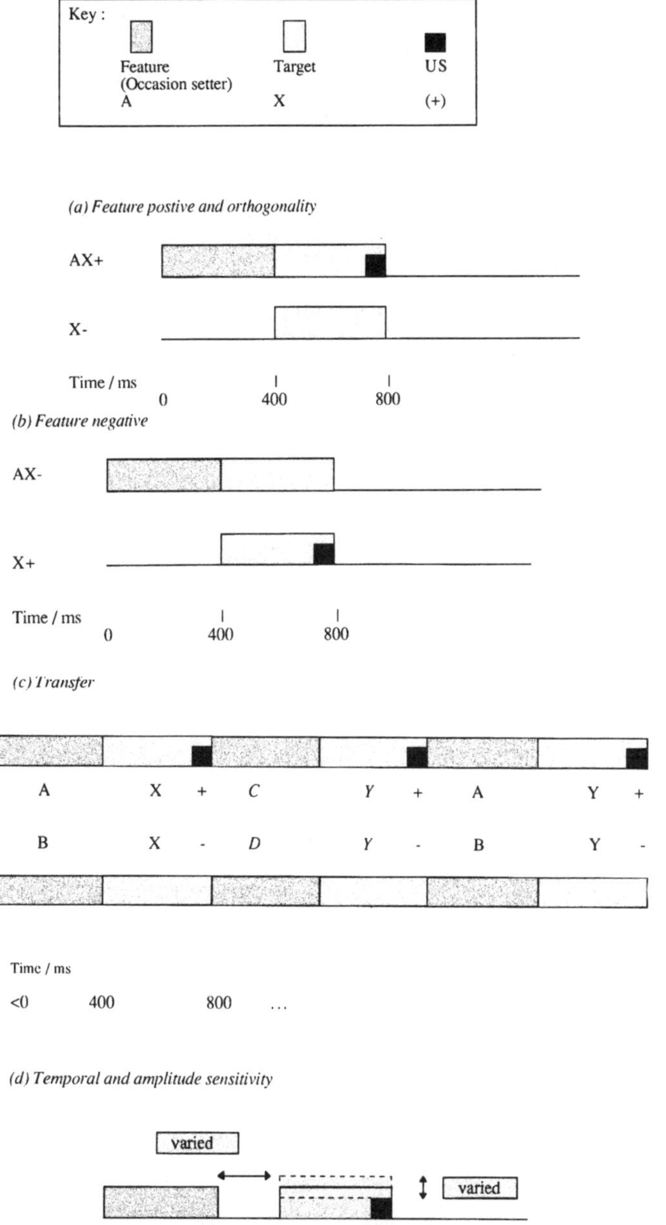

Figure 10

Stimulus protocol for network simulations.

APPENDIX

(a) Details of the network: Parameters as per Gluck and Myers (1993), except that:

B = 0.5 (US), 0.05 otherwise

No momentum

Bins per trial: 12 for all simulations presented

Recurrents: where

Ht = vector of hidden layer activity at time t, and

It = vector of input layer activity at time t:

$$f(x) = 1/(1 + e - x)$$

$$Ht + 1 = f((0.7 \times Ht) + (0.3 \times It + 1))$$

$$It + 1 = f((H \times H \times It)/5)$$

(b) All simulations began with 100 "trials" of network initialization—that is, presentation of the contextual cues alone.

The various simulated stimulus protocols are shown in Figure 10.

REFERENCES

Bouton, M. E., & Nelson, J. B. (1994). Context specificity of target versus feature inhibition in a feature negative discrimination. *Journal of Experimental Psychology: Animal Behavior Processes, 20,* 51–65.

Bouton, M. E., & Swartzentruber, D. (1986). Analysis of the associative and occasion setting properties of contexts participating in a Pavlovian discrimination. *Journal of Experimental Psychology: Animal Behavior Processes, 17,* 299–311.

Elman, J. L. (1990). Finding structure in time. *Cognitive Science 14*(2), 179–211.

Frey, P. W. (1970). Within-subject analysis of the CS–US interval in rabbit eyelid conditioning. *Learning and Motivation, 1,* 337–345.

Gluck, M. A., & Myers, C. E. (1993). Hippocampal mediation of stimulus representation: A computational theory. *Hippocampus 3*(4), 491–516.

Gluck, M. A., Oliver, L. M., & Myers, C. E. (1996). Late-training amnesic deficits in probabilistic category learning: A neurocomputational analysis. *Learning and Memory, 3*(4), 326–340.

Gluck, M. A., Goren, O. A., Myers, C. E., & Thompson, R. F. (1997). *A higher order recurrent network model of the cerebellar substrates of response timing in sensory-motor conditioning.* Manuscript submitted for publication.

Goddard, M. J., & Holland, P. C. (1996). Type of feature affects transfer in operant serial feature positive discriminations. *Animal Learning & Behavior, 24*(3), 266–276.

Hinton, G. E. (1989). Connectionist learning procedures. *Artificial Intelligence, 40,* 185–234.

Holland, P. C. (1983). Occasion setting in Pavlovian feature positive discriminations. In M. L. Commons, R. J. Herrnstein, & A. R. Wagner (Eds.), *Quantitative analyses of Pavlovian behavior: Discrimination processes* (Vol. 4, pp. 183–206). New York: Ballinger.

Holland, P. C. (1986). Temporal determinants of occasion setting in feature positive discriminations. *Animal Learning & Behavior, 14,* 111–120.

Holland, P. C. (1989a). Feature extinction enhances transfer of occasion setting. *Animal Learning & Behavior, 17,* 269–279.

Holland, P. C. (1989b). Transfer of negative occasion setting and conditioned inhibition across conditioned and unconditioned stimuli. *Journal of Experimental Psychology: Animal Behavior Processes, 15,* 311–328.

Holland, P. C., & Lamarre, J. (1984). Transfer of inhibition after serial and simultaneous feature negative discrimination training. *Learning and Motivation, 15,* 219–243.

Iijima, T., Witter, M., Ichikawa, M., Tominaga, T., Kajiwara, R., & Matsumoto, G. (1996). Entorhinal-hippocampal interactions revealed by real-time imaging. *Science 272,* 1176–1179.

Jarrard, L. E., & Davidson, T. L. (1990). Acquisition of concurrent conditional discriminations in rats with ibotenate lesions of hippocampus and of subiculum. *Psychobiology 18*(1), 68–73.

Jordan, M. I. (1986). The learning of representations for sequence performance. *Dissertation Abstracts International, 46*(12B, pt. 1), 4435. (University Microfilms No. 24-51887)

Lamarre, J., & Holland, P. C. (1987). Acquisition and transfer of serial feature negative discriminations. *Learning and Motivation, 18,* 319–342.

Maskara, A., & Noetzel, A. (1993). Sequence recognition with recurrent neural networks. *Connection Science: Journal of Neural Computing, Artificial Intelligence and Cognitive Research, 5*(2), 139–152.

Myers, C. E., & Gluck, M. A. (1994). Context, conditioning, and hippocampal representation in animal learning. *Behavioral Neuroscience, 108,* 835–847.

Myers, C. E., Ermita, B. R., Harris, K., Hasselmo, M., Solomon, P., & Gluck, M. A. (1996). A computational model of cholinergic disruption of septohippocampal activity in classical eyeblink conditioning. *Neurobiology of Learning and Memory, 66*(1), 51–66.

Pearce, J. M. (1987). A model for stimulus generalization in Pavlovian conditioning. *Psychological Review, 94,* 61–75.

Pearce, J. M. (1994). Similarity and discrimination: A selective review and a connectionist model. *Psychological Review, 101,* 587–607.

Rescorla, R. A., & Wagner, A. R. (1972). A theory of Pavlovian conditioning: Variations in the effectiveness of reinforcement and nonreinforcement. In A. H. Black & W. F. Prokasky (Eds.), *Classical conditioning II: Current research and theory.* New York: Appleton-Century-Crofts.

Ross, R. T., & Holland, P. C. (1981). Conditioning of simultaneous and serial feature positive discriminations. *Animal Learning & Behavior, 9,* 293–303.

12

Occasion Setting: Influences of Conditioned Emotional Responses and Configural Cues

Susan E. Brandon and Allan R. Wagner

The phenomenon of occasion setting as described by Ross and Holland (1981) and other early investigators (Holland, 1985; Jenkins, 1985; Rescorla, 1985) presented a clear challenge to all models of Pavlovian conditioning, including those that we otherwise had found to be useful (Rescorla & Wagner, 1972; Wagner, 1981). None of the available models could account for the fact that a conditioned stimulus (CS) could modulate the likelihood of some other CS eliciting a conditioned response (CR) without itself producing or inhibiting that CR.

Our first theoretical guess was that an elaboration on SOP (Mazur & Wagner, 1982; Wagner, 1981; Wagner & Donegan, 1989) that we referred to as *AESOP* (Wagner & Brandon, 1989) might be adequate. AESOP adopted a notion, emphasized by Konorski (1967), that unconditioned stimuli (USs) have separable representations of their affective versus their sensory/perceptual attributes and that, depending on the temporal arrangements during conditioning, some CSs may be more likely to be

This research was supported in part by National Science Foundation Grant BNS-9121094 to Allan R. Wagner.

associated with one or the other. Thus, it would be possible that experimental arrangements that produce occasion setting are ones in which target stimuli become associated with the sensory/perceptual attributes of the US and elicit a CR, whereas feature stimuli become associated with the emotive attributes of the US and control a conditioned emotive response (CER), acting to modulate, but not elicit, the CR.

There is now considerable evidence in support of AESOP—that is, that CRs and CERs are dissociatively controllable by different stimuli in Pavlovian training (Betts, Brandon, & Wagner, 1996; McNish, Betts, Brandon, & Wagner, 1996), and that CRs can be modulated by CERs (Brandon, Betts, & Wagner, 1994; Brandon & Wagner, 1991; Bombace, Brandon, & Wagner, 1991). However, the problem with AESOP as a view of occasion setting is that it does not predict a stimulus specificity that is sometimes observed. For example, in an instance where training is with A–X+, X– (A is a feature stimulus that is presented prior to the onset of a target stimulus X, and the US is paired with X only when it follows A), AESOP dictates that A should equally modulate a separately trained cue that has an equivalent history of reinforcement—for example, Y±. To the extent that the higher frequency or vigor of response to X following A is a function of modulation via the CER elicited by A, there should be comparable modulation of Y via the same CER. The literature presented in this volume and elsewhere (Bonardi, 1996; Bouton & Swartzentruber, 1986; Davidson & Rescorla, 1986; Holland, 1986b, 1989a, 1989d; Lamarre & Holland, 1987; Rescorla, 1985; Swartzentruber & Rescorla, 1994; Wilson & Pearce, 1990) indicate that this is not generally the case. In rabbit eyeblink conditions that we have frequently employed, A does modulate the response to Y, but less than it does the response to the original target cue X (Brandon & Wagner, 1991).

To account for such specificity, as well as the general modulating tendency of occasion setters, Brandon and Wagner (1991) and Wagner (1992) suggested the need to understand how configural cues might variably come to control conditioned responding in different circumstances. Wagner (1992) briefly outlined how a theoretical model that incorporates both the emotional modulation of AESOP and configural cues as *hidden units* can address some of the essential findings in occasion setting. In this chapter, we review representative data from our laboratory that convince us of the separate influences of emotional modulation and configural control in occasion setting, and show how the two factors can be simulated by a quantitative model that is more articulate than our earlier formulations (Brandon & Wagner, 1991; Wagner, 1992).

EXPERIMENTAL EVIDENCE

Our understanding of occasion setting is that it is said to occur when discrimination training with a combination of features and common cues—for example, so-called feature positive (FP), AX+, X–, feature negative (FN), X+, BX–, or full, AX+, BX– discrimination—leads to differential responding to X in the presence versus the absence of A and/or B, without differential responding to A and/or B in isolation. We supposed that this might come about in eyeblink conditioning if the durations of A and B were longer than those that support eyeblink conditioning and if the duration of X was short enough to support eyeblink conditioning.

Brandon and Wagner (1991, Experiment 1) reported a relevant experiment using rabbits and involving what we refer to here as A(X+), B(X–) training. A and B were two 30-sec auditory cues, and X was a 1050-ms light or vibrotactual stimulus, presented 5, 12, 17, 22, or 27 sec after the onset of A and B. When X occurred within the context of A, it was paired with a left paraorbital shock; when it occurred within the context of B, it was not. Stimulus A "set the occasion" for X to be followed by the US; Stimulus B "set the occasion" for X not to be followed by the US.

A(X+) and B(X–) trials were presented in a pseudo random order for a total of 280 trials each, across four training sessions. The last two training sessions also contained trials with another 1050-ms cue, Y, a vibrotactual or light stimulus, equally often presented with the US as without it, in the absence of any explicit auditory context. In this and all subsequent studies, the cues were counterbalanced: for half the subjects, A was a tone and B was a noise, and for the remaining subjects, this identification was reversed; for half of the subjects in each subgroup, X was the vibrotactual stimulus and Y was the light, and for the others, the reverse assignment was made.

The focus was on performance in the training condition, where X was presented within A and B, and in a test condition, where Y was similarly presented within A and B. The outcome was that, although the rabbits showed virtually no tendency to respond with eyelid closure to the onsets of A or B, or at any time during their presentation outside of those seconds when X or the US was present, they did show a greater likelihood and a greater amplitude of conditioned eyeblink to X within the context of A than to X within the context of B. Likewise, in testing, A and B similarly modulated response to Y: the frequency and amplitude of eyelid closure was greater to Y within A than within B. Figure 1 summarizes the results of this experiment in terms of the mean amplitude of eyelid closure to X within A and X within B, and the similar amplitude to Y within A, Y within B, and Y alone.

One of the ways that A and B might have controlled the response to X and to Y, other than through some inapparent summation effect, was through the differential control of conditioned emotional responses by A and B that might differentially modulate the CR (Wagner & Brandon, 1989). The notion of emotive modulation of conditioned responding is commonplace in the instrumental literature (Mowrer, 1947; Rescorla & Solomon, 1967; Spence, 1960) and has precedence in Pavlovian conditioning in the theorizing of Konorski (1967).

Evidence of Emotive Modulation

A substantial number of subsequent experiments from our laboratory supported the interpretation that differentially reinforced contextual stimuli like A and B differentially elicit a CER that then may modulate behavior. One expectation from this view is that the modulating effect of A and B should transfer to the Y cue used in testing. This was observed, as seen in Figure 1. Another expectation from this view is that A and B should have a similar modulating effect if they are differentially paired with reinforcement in the absence of a discrete X cue. We would assume that such

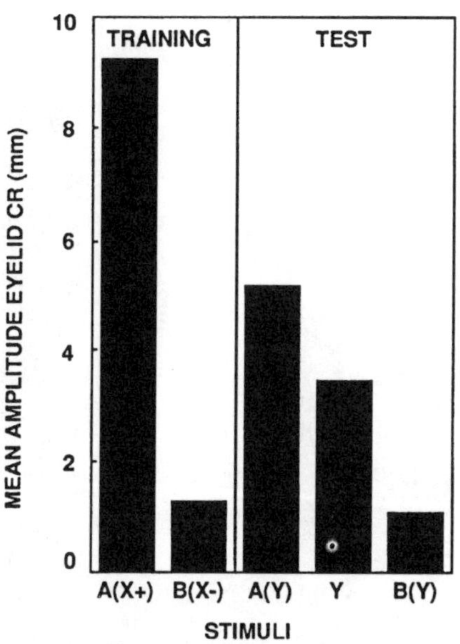

Figure 1

Mean amplitude eyelid conditioned responses (CRs) to a discrete conditioned stimulus, X, in the context of A [A(X+)] or [B(X–)], as during discrimination training, and to a transfer conditioned stimulus, Y, in the contexts of A [A(Y)], Y alone [Y], or B [B(Y)]. Reprinted with permission from Brandon & Wagner (1991, Experiment 1). Copyright 1991 by the American Psychological Association.

training would not support acquisition of a conditioned eyeblink, but would produce CER conditioning that could modulate an otherwise-provoked CR. In fact, theories of Pavlovian conditioning (e.g., Mackintosh, 1975; Pearce & Hall, 1980; Rescorla & Wagner, 1972; Wagner, 1981) would expect that such an arrangement would be better for CER conditioning than one that includes X, because X would not be in a position to block some of the conditioning to A and B. Brandon and Wagner (1991, Experiment 2) reported such an experiment. The parameters were deliberately selected so that they would be similar to those of the preceding experiment, except for the absence of X, including the separate training of Y and a final modulation test.

The results of the modulation test were essentially the same as those

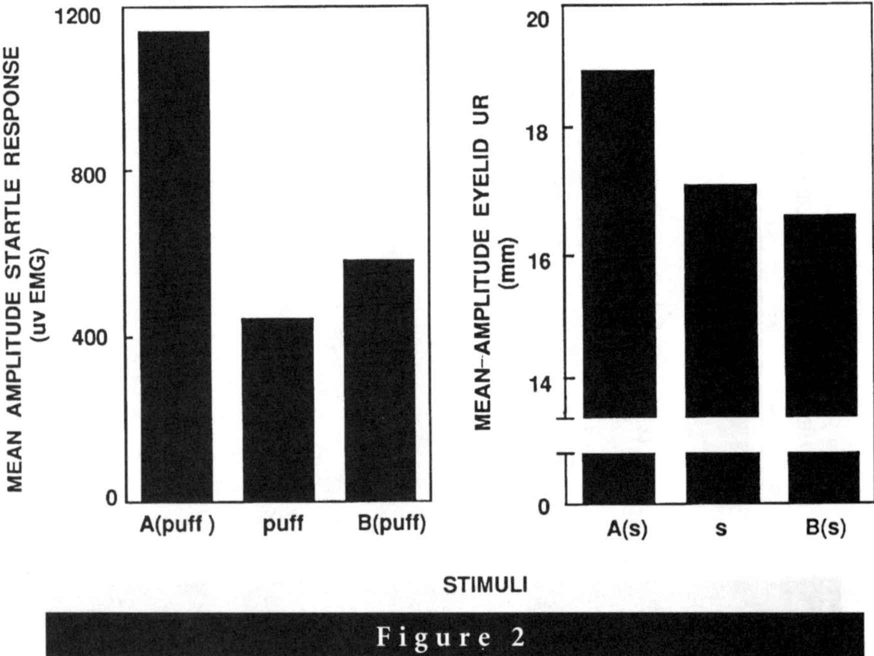

Figure 2

The left graph shows the mean amplitude startle response to an airpuff startle stimulus, delivered to the ear, in the context of A [A(puff)], alone [puff], or B [B(puff)]. The right graph shows the mean amplitude of eyeblink unconditioned responses (URs) at the time of application of an unconditioned paraorbital shock in the context of A [A(s)], alone [s], or B [B(s)]. Reprinted with permission from Brandon, Bombace, Falls, & Wagner (1991, Experiments 1 and 4). Copyright 1991 by the American Psychological Association.

of the previous experiment: the same outcome was obtained after simple A(+), B(−) training as in the "occasion setting" A(X+), B(X−) design. There were virtually no CRs to the A and B contexts, and the amplitude of the conditioned eyeblink response to Y was greater within A than within B.

If A and B had the effects shown by virtue of controlling a CER, one would expect A and B to modulate a variety of behaviors in addition to a conditioned eyelid closure. Figure 2 shows the results of two other modulation tests reported by Brandon, Bombace, Falls, and Wagner (1991). Following the same kind of A(+), B(−) training as indicated earlier, rabbits were tested with either a small airpuff to the ear, which elicited a startle response, or with a paraorbital shock, which elicited an unconditioned

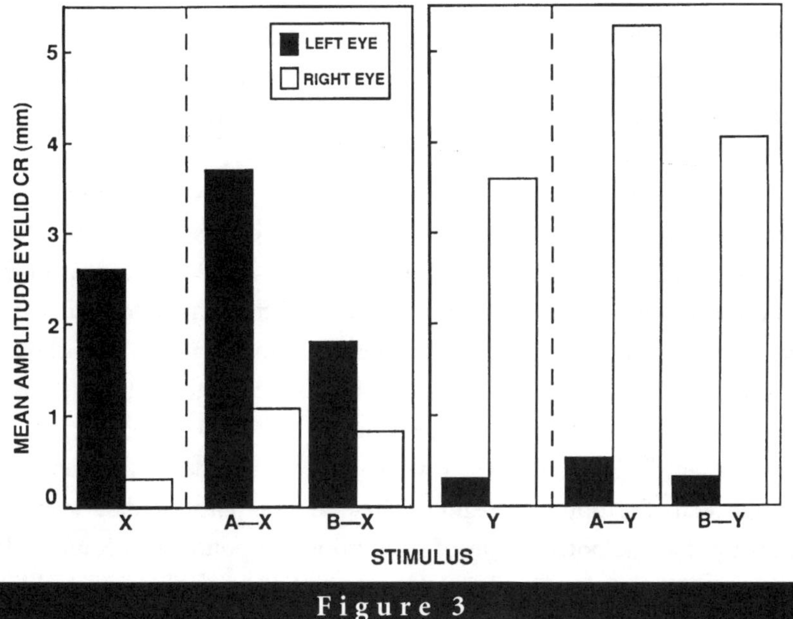

Figure 3

Mean amplitude left and right eyelid closure to X, trained with left paraorbital shock, to Y, trained with right pararobital shock, to X with A (A—X) and B (B—X), and to Y with A (A—Y) and B (B—Y). Note that A was trained with left paraorbital shock and B was nonreinforced. Redrawn with permission from Brandon, Betts, and Wagner (1994, Experiment 4). Copyright 1994 by the American Psychological Association.

eyeblink. The modulating properties of A and B appeared quite general in that they were found to differentially modulate the elicited startle response, as depicted in the left-hand graph of Figure 2 (cf. Davis, 1984) and the unconditioned eyelid response, as depicted in the right-hand graph of Figure 2 (cf. Weisz & LoTurco, 1988).

A further test for the generality of the CER reported by Brandon et al. (1994) took advantage of observations made in our laboratory that the rabbit can be trained to show discriminated, lateralized conditioned eyeblink responses. That is, if one CS is paired with a paraorbital shock to the left eye, and another, discriminably different CS is paired with a paraorbital shock to the right eye, the former will produce a left eyeblink CR, and the latter will produce a right eyeblink CR. Figure 3 depicts such discriminated, lateralized responding following training in which CS X was paired with a US to the left region, and CS Y was paired with a US to the right. As may be seen, when X was presented subjects closed their left eye more than their right, but when Y was presented, they closed their right eye more than their left.

The question of interest addressed in Figure 3 was what the responding would be like if X and Y were presented within contexts A and B, where A also was reinforced on the left side, and B was nonreinforced, as in the previous studies. As may be seen, A and B differentially facilitated the eyelid response that was previously acquired to both X and Y. Importantly, A, which had been paired with a paraorbital shock to the left eye, showed no greater tendency to increase eyeblink CRs to X, which had been paired with the same US, than it did to Y, which had been trained with a paraorbital shock to the opposite region. These are the clearest data available showing that the potentiation of conditioned responding to X and Y by A versus B is not due simply to the summation of conditioned eyeblink tendencies. They support the view that such potentiation is due to a general, CER-like process.

Thus, by several independent tests, it appears that A and B elicited differential emotive responses, which then modulated a variety of conditioned and unconditioned behaviors. We took data like these as sufficient evidence to implicate emotive modulation in the differential responding seen in the occasion-setting experiment of Brandon and Wagner (1991, Experiment 1), and perhaps in the studies of others.

Evidence of Control by Configural Cues

No one who has followed the occasion-setting literature would suppose that emotive modulation can provide a comprehensive account of the phenomenon. The fact is that the degree of generality of the modulation seen in our rabbit eyeblink studies has not commonly been observed in studies of occasion setting using other preparations (Bonardi, 1996; Bouton & Swartzentruber, 1986; Davidson & Rescorla, 1986; Holland, 1986b, 1989a, 1989d; Lamarre & Holland, 1987; Rescorla, 1985; Swartzentruber & Rescorla, 1994; Wilson & Pearce, 1990). Indeed, although it is now recognized that a feature often will show behavioral control with a target

CS that has been trained with a different feature (Davidson & Rescorla, 1986; Holland, 1986a, 1989a, 1995; Lamarre & Holland, 1987; Rescorla, 1986b, Wilson & Pearce, 1989, 1990), such transfer of control is typically incomplete. In addition, even in the Brandon and Wagner (1991) studies (see Figure 1), there was clear indication that A(X+), B(X–) discriminative training leads A and B to have greater control over responding to X than over responding to a separately trained CS, Y.

One way to account for such a difference is to postulate that, when occasion setting occurs, there is likely to be substantial control by configural cues. It is common to assume (e.g., Hull, 1943, 1945; Jenkins, 1985; Pearce, 1987; Rescorla & Wagner, 1972; Spence, 1936) that the conjoint presentation of A and X results in a configural cue, ax, and the conjoint presentation of B and X results in a configural cue, bx, in addition to the elemental cues. We also would expect that, if resolution of an A(X), B(X) discrimination were dependent on such cues, there would be little generalization of discriminative responding to A(Y) or B(Y), which involved similar A and B elements but different, that is, ay and by, configural cues.

The challenge, of course, is in understanding why configural cues might gain more control in studies that produce occasion setting than in other circumstances of compound discrimination training (Detke, 1991; Holland, 1984, 1986b, 1989a, 1989d; Holland & Lamarre, 1984; Lamarre & Holland, 1987; Rescorla, 1985, 1989; Ross & Holland, 1981; but see Rescorla, 1985, 1989). Wagner (1992) proposed an account in which the configural cues are *hidden units* (cf. Schmajuk & Buhusi, 1997; Schmajuk, Lamoureux, & Holland, 1998).

The available data that are perhaps most suggestive of control by configural cues are those in which, following original discrimination learning with features and targets, the correlation of the feature with the US is reversed either in isolation or in conjunction with another target (Holland, 1984, 1989b, 1989c, 1989d; Rescorla, 1985; 1986a; 1991). For example, after A(X+), B(X–) discrimination training, subjects are shifted to A(Y–), B(Y+). What has been characteristic in the studies of occasion setting mentioned earlier is that the differential response to A(X+) and B(X–) survived the A(Y–), B(Y+) reversal. And, it is important that this happens more robustly in cases of serial or successive ordering of the features and target than when the compounds involve simultaneous stimuli (Holland, 1989b, 1989d; Rescorla, 1985, 1986a). It appears as though the control by configural cues, which would not be altered by the intervening A(Y–), B(Y+) training, is greater in serial or successive compounds than in simultaneous compounds.

An experiment by Bahçekapili, Brandon, and Wagner (1997, Experiment 1B) was designed in an attempt to replicate, with the rabbit eyeblink preparation, just such effects, as reported by Holland (1989b, 1989d) with an appetitive task using rats, and by Rescorla (1985, 1986a) with an appetitive task using pigeons. The design of the experiment involved two groups. For Group Successive, A and B were 10-sec auditory stimuli, and X, a 1050-ms tactile or visual stimulus, coterminated with A and B. In A, X was reinforced; in B, X was not reinforced. For Group Simultaneous, the same A, B, and X stimuli were presented in simultaneous arrangements: each 1050-ms in duration. It should be noted that the 10-sec features in the Successive group were shorter than the 30-sec contexts used in the experiments described earlier (Brandon & Wagner, 1991). However, the 10-sec CS–US interval is still considerably longer than those that support eyelid conditioning (e.g., Smith, Coleman, & Gormezano, 1969) and produced no CRs to A and B prior to the presentation of X.

After ten sessions with the A, B, and X stimuli as described for the two groups, Y, a 1050-ms visual or tactile stimulus (as in the previous experiments), was substituted for X, and the reinforcement contingencies for A and B were reversed—that is, for three sessions, the subjects of Group Successive were trained with A—Y–, B—Y+, and the subjects of Group Simultaneous were trained with AY–, BY+. Finally, all animals were given a single test session with the several compounds: first, 10 trials each with A—Y– and B—Y+ for Group Successive animals, AY– and BY+ for Group Simultaneous animals, and then 20 trials each with the original compounds A—X+, B—X–, and AX+, BX–, respectively.

Figure 4 shows the outcome of initial training with A, B, and X, and the results of the final test session for the two groups. Performance in the reversal sessions is not shown because the outcome is adequately repre-

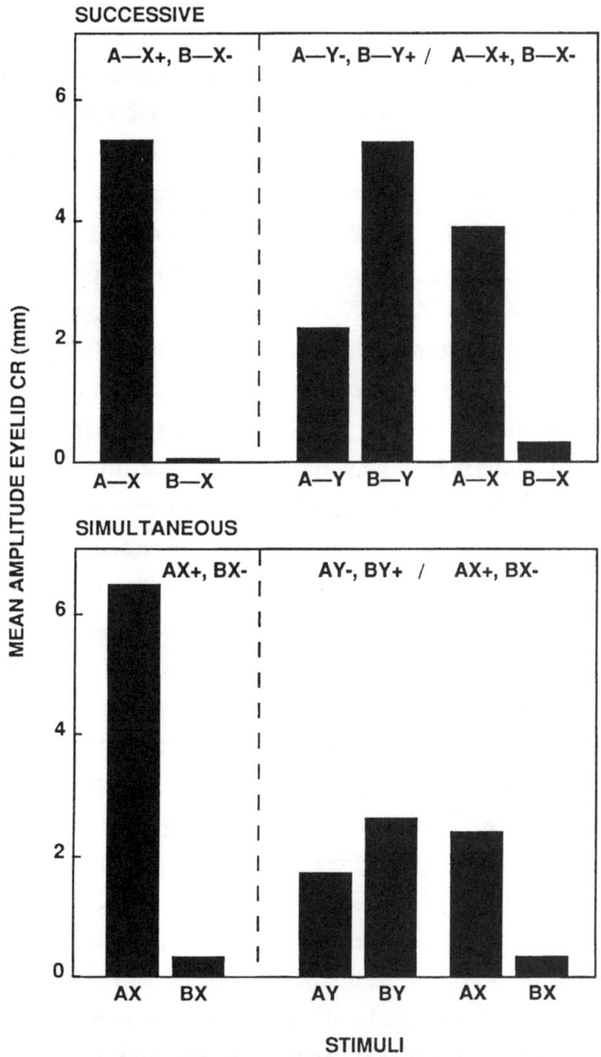

Figure 4

The left panel of the top graph shows mean amplitude eyelid closure CRs to X in successive training with A—X+, B—X–, averaged across a single session. The right panel shows mean amplitude eyelid CRs to Y, averaged across 10 trials of training with A—Y–, B—Y+, and to X, averaged across a subsequent 20 trials of training with A—X+, B—X–. The bottom graph shows the same for animals trained with a simultaneous arrangement of the same cues, in the same sessions. Data from Bahçekapili, Brandon, and Wagner (1997, Experiment 1B).

sented by performance in the test session. The data are the mean peak response amplitudes to X or Y on training and test trials prior to the time of presentation of the US. As shown, both the Successive and Simultaneous animals acquired the original discrimination, and at comparable levels. In the test sessions, however, the Successive animals showed both better learning of the reversal discrimination and less loss of the original discrimination than did the Simultaneous animals. The Successive animals rather readily acquired the A—Y, B—Y discrimination while maintaining the A—X, B—X discrimination. The Simultaneous animals barely acquired the AY, BY discrimination and were more disrupted, relative to their original performance, in the original problem. In summary, the data were similar to those reported by others in the occasion-setting literature, showing that discriminative behavior developed with a sequential arrangement of cues is peculiarly resistant to degradation by reinforcement of the negative feature, nonreinforcement of the positive feature, or both (Holland, 1989b, 1989d; Rescorla, 1985; 1986a). This would be expected if, with a successive arrangement of cues, discriminative behavior is strongly controlled by configural cues unique to the compounds.

Bahçekapili et al. (1997) reported a second experiment that was designed to comment on the nature of these putative configural cues. Rabbits were trained with two problems concurrently: A—X+, B—X–, C—Y+, D—Y–, where the temporal arrangement of cues was the same as that for the successive group of the preceding experiment: A, B, C, and D, all auditory stimuli, were 10-sec in duration, and X and Y were 1050-ms vibrotactual or light stimuli that coterminated with the 10-sec contexts. X in A was paired with paraorbital shock, X in B was not; similarly, Y in C was paired with paraorbital shock, and Y in D was not.

Several kinds of tests followed acquisition of discriminative performance in the original A—X+, B—X–, C—Y+, D—Y– problems. First, explicit tests were conducted with the *original order/original configuration* of cues, where X and Y were presented following A or B, and C or D, respectively, as in training. Second, X and Y were presented in the alternate contexts, resulting in tests with A—Y, B—Y, C—X, and D—X. This is labeled as *original order/shifted configuration,* because whereas A, B, C, and

D preceded the targets X and Y as in training, all of the configurations involved novel conjunctions of stimuli. Third, in the *shifted order/original configuration* tests, X and Y were presented with their training contexts, but the order of feature and target was reversed: now X and Y were 10 sec in duration, and A and B, or C and D, respectively, were 1050-ms in duration and presented 9 sec later. The last test condition shifted both order and cue configuration, that is, it maintained neither the original order nor the original configurations.

The outcome of the tests under the several conditions is shown in Figure 5. There were no differences between the test results for the different parallel stimulus combinations in each condition, so the data were pooled, as shown, across X and Y, in combination with A or C and B or D. The measure is the amplitude of eyeblink during the 1-sec terminal stimulus when the indicated configurations were present.

Performance in the original order/original configuration test showed that A and B effectively controlled differential responding to X, and C and D likewise controlled differential responding to Y. The original order/shifted configuration test showed significantly greater response to X and Y when they were presented in the presumably emotive contexts A and C than when they were presented in the presumably neutral contexts B and D, even though the compounds were novel. It is quite clear, however, that differential responding was degraded in comparison to that controlled by the original configuration of stimuli. The substantial discriminative performance in the original order/shifted configuration test may be because of the common emotive advantage of A and C over B and D; that the performance is less than with the original configuration can be understood as resulting from differential associative loadings of the configural cues, for example, ax versus ay.

There was also a reliable discrimination in the shifted order/original configuration test, but not in the shifted order/shifted configuration test. This difference may be especially informative concerning the nature of the putative configurations. Even when the order of features and targets was reversed with respect to the original training conditions, there was reliable evidence that performance in the tests was superior when the

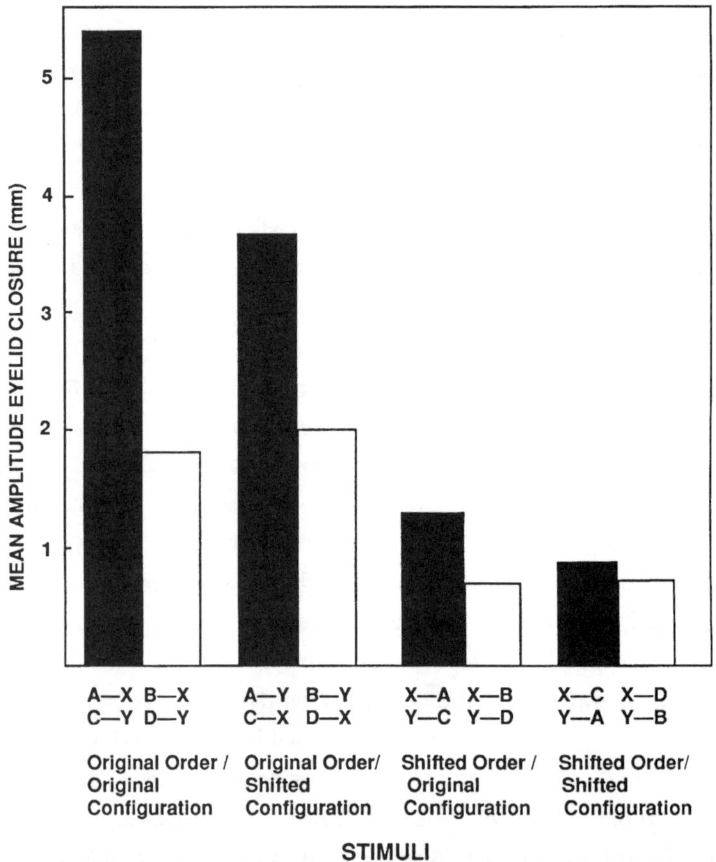

Figure 5

Mean amplitude eyelid closure to the 1-sec terminal stimulus for each of the tests indicated, following successive A—X+, B—X–, C—Y+, D—Y– training. The data are collapsed across X and Y, A and C, and B and D. Data from Bahçekapili, Brandon, and Wagner (1997, Experiment 2).

compounds included the original configurations of stimuli rather than novel combinations.

We were obliged to conclude that there is some control, in the A(X+), B(X–) discrimination problem, not only by emotive responses elicited by A and B, but also by cues that are formed by the conjunction of explicit CSs. It needs to be pointed out that the transfer that we observed in the shifted order/original configuration condition had not been observed in similar shifts in order of feature and targets in the FP discrimination learning conducted by Holland (1992) and Rescorla (1985). These previous studies differed from ours in many respects, including appetitive learning in rats and pigeons versus aversive conditioning in rabbits. Our guess, however, is that the critical difference lies in our use of successive compounds in which the feature and target overlap, versus Holland's and Rescorla's use of serial compounds in which the features terminated before the target. This supposition, which obviously needs to be tested, has influenced how we have chosen to characterize configural cues in our model, to which we now turn.

THE MODELS

The data just described encouraged us to elaborate on a model of Pavlovian conditioning, SOP, that we have otherwise found useful (Wagner, 1981; Wagner & Donegan, 1989). Figure 6 is drawn to suggest the essential characteristics of SOP to which the elaborations remain faithful. It is assumed that each stimulus, including CSs and USs, is represented, as depicted, by an initial and a secondary node. Each node is conceived to be formed from a large but finite set of elements. The stochastic principles of the model stipulate how some proportion of the initial elements will be activated in each moment that a stimulus is presented, and how these will, over time, activate an increasing proportion of the corresponding secondary elements, which will recurrently inhibit the initial elements before themselves decaying to inactivity.

It is assumed that conditioning occurs because the secondary, adaptive node that is unconditionally activated by a US can also come to be activated by CSs. The rules for excitatory and inhibitory learning are shown in Figure 6: There is an increase in the excitatory linkage between any CS and US, $\Delta V+$, according to the momentary products of the proportion of the initial elements representing the CS and the proportion of the initial elements representing the US that are concurrently active. Likewise, there is an increase in the inhibitory links between the CS and the US, $\Delta V-$,

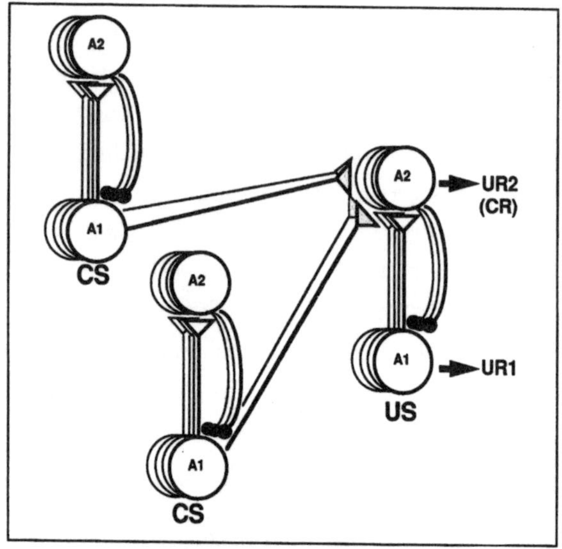

SOP Learning Rules:

$$\Delta V^{+}_{CSi\text{-}USj} = L^{+} \sum^{t} (p_{A1,csi} \times p_{A1,usj})$$

$$\Delta V^{-}_{CSi\text{-}USj} = L^{-} \sum^{t} (p_{A1,csi} \times p_{A1,usj})$$

$$\Delta V_{CSi\text{-}USj} = \Delta V^{+}_{CSi\text{-}USj} - \Delta V^{-}_{CSi\text{-}USj}$$

CR-Generation Rule:

$$CR_{usj,t1} = f(p_{A2usj,t1})$$

$$= f\left[\sum_{i=1}^{n} (p_{A1csi,t1} \times V_{CSi\text{-}USj})(1 - p_{A2usj,t-1}) + p_{A2usj,t-1}(1 - p_{d2})\right],$$

$$\text{where } 0 \leq \Sigma(p_{A1csi} \times V_{CSi\text{-}USj}) \leq 1.$$

Figure 6

A brief characterization of SOP as a connectionist network, and rules of the model for learning and response-generation. Redrawn from data of Wagner (1997).

according to the momentary products of the proportion of the initial elements representing the CS and the proportion of the adaptive, secondary elements representing the US that are concurrently active. The algebraic combination of the two determines the net associative change in any episode of time. Also shown in Figure 6 is the computational rule for generation of the conditioned response. The CR is a function of the activation of the adaptive node of the US by the constellation of CSs, which is determined by the degree of activation of the associated CSs and the level of associative strength that each CS has with the US.

To illustrate how emotive modulation and behavioral control by configural cues, appropriate to the phenomena of occasion setting, can be integrated into SOP, first we will describe the modification of SOP that we think is useful in addressing emotive modulation, and then add to that model the modifications that we suppose to be suggested by the apparent control by configural cues.

AESOP

The essential modification of SOP that we have assumed (Wagner & Brandon, 1989) to allow for conditioned emotive modulation of Pavlovian, discrete CRs is characterized in the diagram of Figure 7. In this view, representation of the US is not unitary but taken to involve multiple theoretical nodes that (a) code for dissociable components of the stimulus, (b) have differential consequences in behavior, and (c) can have their separate connections with CS nodes independently modified. Because the theory assumes that stimulus coding involves theoretically separable *emotive* as well as *sensory* components (Dickinson, 1980; Konorski, 1967; Mackintosh, 1983), it was referred to as *AESOP*, an acronym for "affective extension of SOP" (Wagner & Brandon, 1989). The diagram is meant to suggest how a CS, conditioned to an aversive US, will come to elicit a CER that then will modulate the processing of concurrent CSs and their associated outputs (here, a CR that reflects processing in a sensory/perceptual US–associated node), according to the modulation rule stated.

The model assumes a single parametric difference in the operating characteristics of the US-emotive and US-sensory nodes: the decay parameters associated with the primary and secondary activity states, pd_1 and pd_2, respectively, are assumed to be smaller for the US-emotive than for the US-sensory nodes. Thus, processing of the emotive aspect of a US is more protracted than processing of the sensory/perceptual aspect of that same US. Many interesting consequences follow from this assumption.

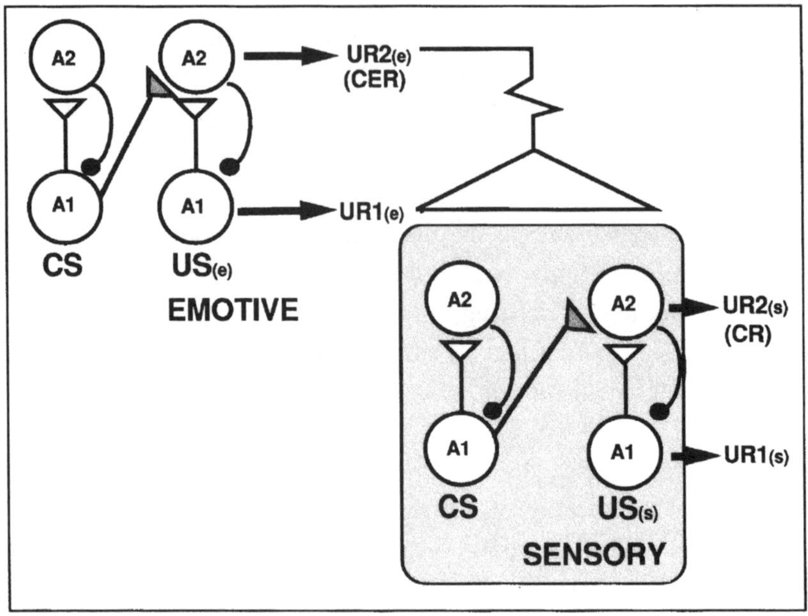

AESOP Modulation Rule:

$$p_{1,i} = p_{0,i}(1+kp_{A2,e}), \quad 0 \leq p_1 \leq 1$$

Figure 7

A brief characterization of AESOP as a connectionist network, and the rule for modulation by a conditioned emotive response. Redrawn from data of Wagner (1992).

Here the important consequence, in keeping with a considerable body of literature (Gormezano & Moore, 1969; Kamin, 1965; Vandercar & Schneiderman, 1967), is that emotive conditioning occurs at considerably longer CS–US intervals than does conditioning of discrete responses, such as eyeblinks.

The modulation rule shown in Figure 7 expresses a presumed manner in which conditioned activity in the emotive representation can influence the conditioned and unconditioned response to a wide range of stimuli. We assume that the parameters that express the efficacy with which a stimulus provokes its initial node to activity, p_1, is an increasing function of the prevailing conditioned emotive state that is represented by the US_e parameter, $p_{A2,e}$. By this assumption, CRs are increased in amplitude by prevailing CERs because the initiating CS is increased in effective intensity. Likewise, the UR to a US is increased in amplitude by prevailing CERs because the US is increased in effective intensity. This interpretation is one of several that could equally explain the available data on CR and UR modulation. We make it based on the findings of Gewirtz, Brandon, and Wagner (1998), which show that persisting associative learning, as well as the immediate performance of an eyeblink CR, is modulated by the CER state that prevails during training. This would follow, theoretically, if the CER increased the effective intensity of the CS and US during training.

Two sets of simulations using the AESOP model are shown in Figures 8 and 9.[1] The top part of Figure 8 describes the temporal relationship of cues in an A(Y), B(Y) test following training with A(+), B(−), Y± as in the experiment of Brandon and Wagner (1991, Experiment 2), which was described earlier. The simulation graphs depict theoretical processes on two nonreinforced test trials, each trial occupying 400 processing *moments*. The top simulation graph shows activity changes in the nodes representing the primary excitatory states of the CSs, that is, $CS_{A,A1}$, $CS_{B,A1}$, and $CS_{Y,A1}$. The middle graph shows the associatively generated processing in the

[1] The rules for nodal activation and associative change were otherwise as specified for SOP (Wagner, 1981, 1997; Wagner & Donegan, 1989), with modification for emotive modulation and configural associative change as described in the text.

The same parameters were used for each simulation shown in the chapter. These are $p1_{USe} = .60$, $p1_{USs} = .60$, $p1_{CSs} = .10$; $pd_{1USe} = .0001$, $pd_{2USe} = .00002$; $p1d_{USs} = .10$, $pd2_{USs} = .02$; $pd1_{CS} = .10$; $pd2_{CS} = .02$; $L+ = .001$, $L- = .0002$, $k = 10$, $T = 0.06$. The duration of a feature stimulus (e.g., A or B) for the simulations shown in Figures 8 and 9 was 300 calculation *moments,* and the duration of a target stimulus (e.g., X or Y) for the same simulations was 10 calculation moments. The US duration was in all instances 1 calculation moment. In recognition of a presumed difference in salience between elemental and configural cues, there were assumed to be five elemental cues representing A, B, or X, for each of the configural cues representing the conjunctions, e.g., of A and X.

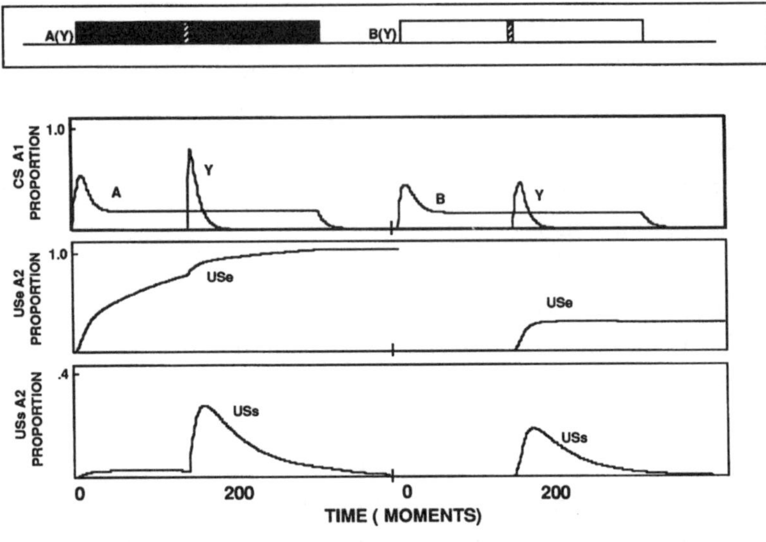

Figure 8

The top of the figure depicts the arrangement of cues for test trials with A(Y) and B(Y) following A(X+), B(X−), Y± training (as in Brandon & Wagner, 1991, Experiment 2). Each simulation is across 400 theoretical *moments.* As shown, the durations of A and B are 300 moments each; Y is 10 moments and occurs 140 moments after the onsets of A and B. The first graph shows activity in CS_A, CS_B, and CS_Y nodes produced by the presentation of Y within A and B; the second shows associatively generated activity in US-emotive (USe) nodes, and the third shows associatively generated activity in US-sensory (USs) nodes. Note that the scales on the ordinates differ. The model assumes that activity in the USs nodes represents the CR. More details regarding parameters are provided in footnote 1.

US-emotive nodes, USe_{A2}. The bottom graph shows the associatively generated processing in the US-sensory nodes, USs_{A2}, which is taken by the model to generate CRs.[2]

Application of the learning rules of *AESOP* to the A(+), B(−) training events, as depicted in Figure 8, results in little more excitatory than inhibitory sensory conditioning accruing to CS_A. In contrast, the emotive condi-

[2] We have not attempted to formulate an exact mapping function of CR on USs_{A2} here, but it is interesting that the simulations show some small USs_{A2} to A alone whereas our data show no CRs to such a stimulus, suggesting that USs_{A2} may have been present but below threshold for CR evocation in our experiments.

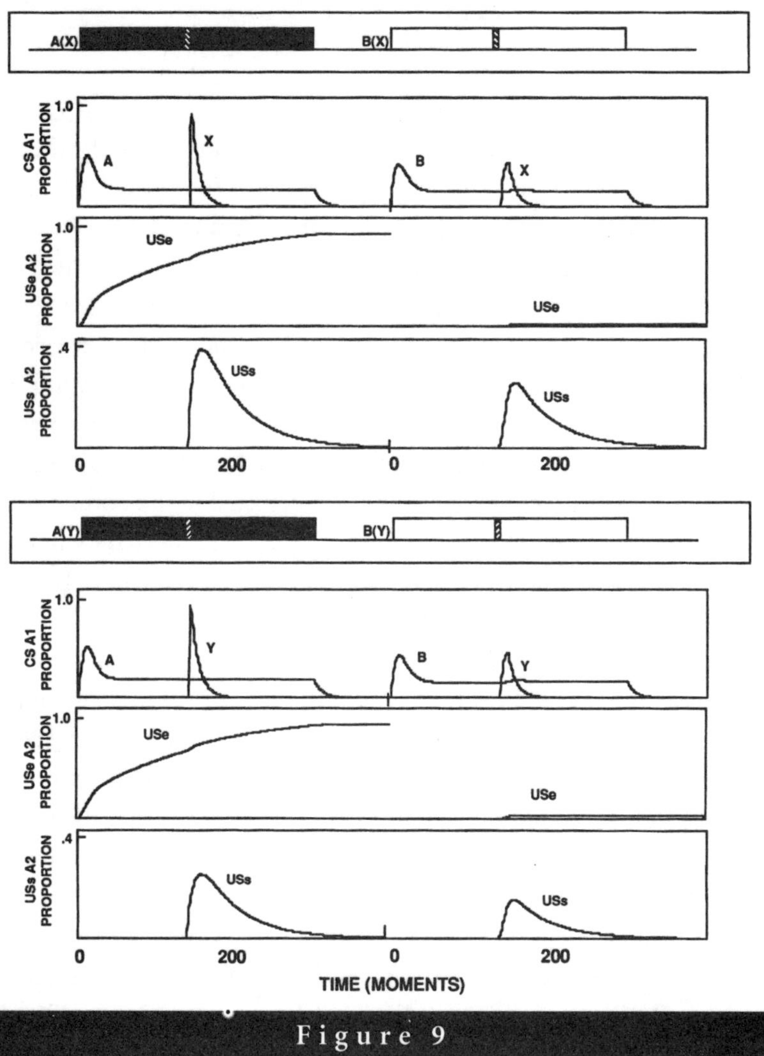

Figure 9

The top of the figure shows simulations of test trials with X placed within Context A or Context B, following training with A(X+), B(X–), and Y± (as in Brandon & Wagner, 1991, Experiment 1). As shown, the duration of A and B is 300 moments, the duration of X and Y is 10 moments, and X and Y begin at moment 140. The next three graphs show patterns of activity in CS, US-Emotive (USe) nodes, and US-Sensory (USs) nodes on a single nonreinforced test trial. Note that the scales on the ordinates differ. The bottom of the figure shows simulations of test trials with Y placed within Context A or Context B, following training with A(X+), B(X–), and Y± (also as in Brandon & Wagner, 1991, Experiment 1). As shown, the duration of A and B again is 300 moments, the duration of Y is 10 moments, and Y begins at moment 140. The next three graphs show patterns of activity in CS, USe nodes, and USs nodes on a single nonreinforced test trial. Note that the scales on the ordinates differ. More details regarding parameters are provided in footnote 1.

tioning to CS_A is substantially more excitatory than inhibitory (because the slower-to-decay USe_{A1} and USe_{A2} processing affords relatively greater concurrent processing of $CS_{A,A1}$ with the USe_{A1} than the USe_{A2} processing states). Thus, on the test trials depicted in Figure 8, there is little tendency for CS_A to elicit USs_{A2}, which would produce a CR, but considerable tendency to evoke USe_{A2}, in other words, a substantial CER. The consequences of the CER seen in Figure 8 are (a) an enhancement of $CS_{A,A1}$ relative to $CS_{B,A1}$, and (b) a greater $CS_{Y,A1}$ when Y is presented within A relative to when it is presented within B. The resulting greater USs_{A2} activated by the conjunction of A(Y) than by the conjunction of B(Y) is depicted in the bottom graph. For the simulations of USs_{A2}, as in the eyeblink CRs reported by Brandon and Wagner (1991), there is a greater response to Y in A than in B.

Of particular interest is what the model does in an occasion-setting training situation, where X is reinforced in the context of A and nonreinforced in the context of B. Simulations of this are similar in many respects to those offered in Figure 8 and are depicted in Figure 9. CS nodal activation comes to be enhanced in CS_A, relative to CS_B and therefore so is the conditioned responding. An important difference is that the emotive conditioning to the contexts A and B is not as great as when A and B were differentially reinforced alone, because of the blocking action of X.

The predicted modulatory effects of A and B produced by A(X+), B(X−) training, as revealed by subsequent nonreinforced test presentations of A(X) and B(X), as well as of A(Y) and B(Y), as in Brandon and Wagner (1991, Experiment 1), are shown in Figure 9. What should be noted is that, although the overall level of responding is somewhat less for Y than for X, the direct nodal activation produced by both X and Y is greater in A than in B. This is because of the differential emotive tendencies controlled by the two cues that result in greater USe_{A2} in A than in B, which then affects CS processing via proportional increase in p1 values for the CS nodes. The result is a greater sensory processing of the US, in other words, a greater USs_{A2}, to A(X) than to B(X) (top graphs), and to A(Y) than to B(Y) (bottom graphs).

Figure 9 illustrates both how the model succeeds and how it fails. It succeeds in indicating appropriate discriminative performance in the A(X), B(X) problem and in showing transfer of the emotive modulating properties to the test with an independently trained Y. The model fails in suggesting that the transfer to Y should be such that the A(Y), B(Y) discrimination is comparable to the A(X), B(X) discrimination. As shown in our own data (see Figure 1), as well as that from other laboratories (Bonardi, 1996; Bouton & Swartzentruber, 1986; Davidson & Rescorla, 1986; Holland, 1986b, 1989a, 1989d; Lamarre & Holland, 1987; Rescorla, 1985; Swartzentruber & Rescorla, 1994; Wilson & Pearce, 1990), such equivalence is not generally found.

AESOP With Hidden Units

The other half of our theoretical story, written in large part because the transfer of modulation is typically incomplete, is the elaboration on SOP that incorporates configural representations as hidden units. SOP, like the Rescorla–Wagner model (Rescorla & Wagner, 1972), is *elementistic* in its general approach to stimulus representation. Again, like the Rescorla–Wagner model, however, it assumes the existence of configural elements, that is, elements that are present when and only when a compound of two or more elements is presented. The elaboration that we think is useful does not change the general conception but does presume that the nodes that represent conjunction of components depend on the activity of component nodes and are what are often called *hidden units* in connectionist models (Kehoe, 1988; Rummelhart & McClelland, 1986).

Figure 10 is meant to suggest what is involved. It is presumed that CS units—for example, CS A and CS X—have direct modifiable connections with the adaptive unit of the US, as well as indirect modifiable connections, through configural units—here, a_o, a_x, x_a, and x_o. The configural units are activated only when there is a specified conjunction of activity states in two or more elemental units: the *hidden units rules* for activation of the configural units depicted are specified in the figure.

Presentation of CS A results in activation of the adaptive node of the US through its direct connection with that node, as well as activation of

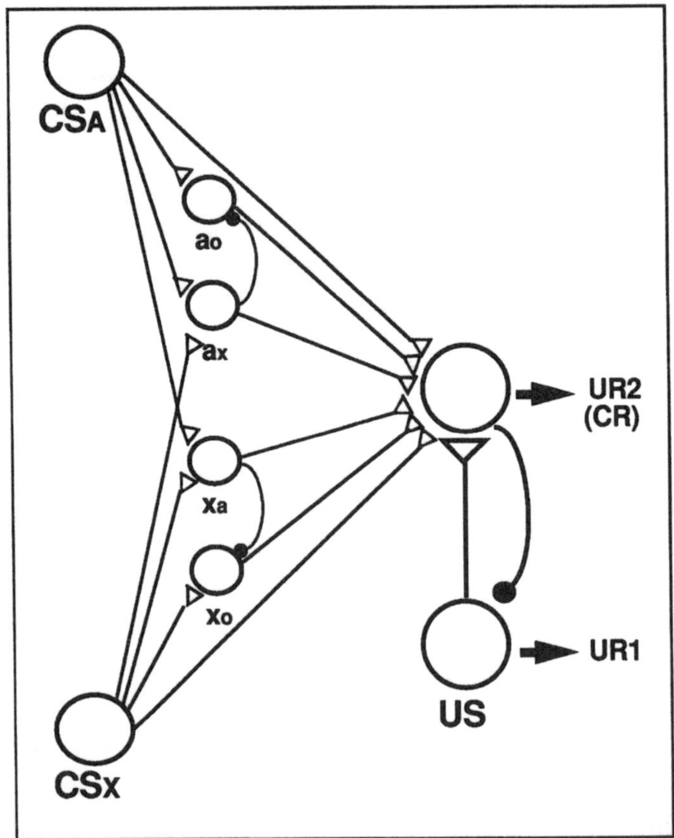

Hidden Unit Rule:

$$p_{1,ao} = k \text{ when } (p_{1,a} > 0 \cap p_{A1,x} < T), \text{ else } 0.$$
$$p_{1,ax} = k \text{ when } (p_{1,a} > 0 \cap p_{A1,x} \geq T), \text{ else } 0.$$
$$p_{1,xa} = k \text{ when } (p_{1,x} > 0 \cap p_{A1,a} \geq T), \text{ else } 0.$$
$$p_{1,xo} = k \text{ when } (p_{1,x} > 0 \cap p_{A1,a} < T), \text{ else } 0.$$

Figure 10

A brief characterization of SOP with hidden units, and the rules for activation of the hidden units a_x, a_o, x_a, and x_o. Redrawn from data of Wagner (1992).

the configural unit, a_o, in the absence of inhibition by a_x—that is, when the A1 units representing X are *below* some threshold value, T ($p_{A1,x} < T$). If, however, CS X also is activated so that its A1 units are *above* some threshold T ($p_{A1,x} \geq T$), the configural unit a_x is activated, which then inhibits the a_o configural unit. Corresponding rules apply for activation of x_o and x_a. Why the particular rules displayed here were chosen, among other possibilities, will be discussed later.

Simulation of nodal activity across time following A—X+, B—X– training with successive compounds, as in the experiments of Bahçekapili et al. (1997), is shown in Figure 11.[3] It is assumed that X occurred 9 sec after the onset of 10-sec features A and B, and that both trials are nonreinforced. The top simulation graph depicts activity in the first-order, elemental units representing A, B, and X; the second graph depicts activity in the second-order, hidden units, which include a_o, a_x, and x_a on A—X trials, and b_o, b_x, and x_b on B—X trials.

The changes in emotive associative loadings that accrued across training, to produce the activity in the US-emotive node depicted in the third graph of Figure 11, had the effect of changing the activity dynamics in the CS nodes, both elemental and hidden. This is most easily seen in the way that nodes representing CSs X, a_x, and x_a are more active on the A—X trial than are the nodes representing CSs X, b_x and x_b on the B—X trial. As in the case of the simple AESOP model, this enhancement is because B inhibits the emotive reaction and A fails to enhance it. The result is a greater emotive response by the conjunction of cues produced by A—X than by B—X. The fourth graph in Figure 11 shows activity in the sensory/perceptual US node in a test trial with A—X and B—X. The discriminative conditioned response is clear.

What is different in this simulation as compared to the *AESOP* simulation in Figure 9 is that the configural nodes that are dynamically dependent on the conjunction of A and X activity and B and X activity compete

[3]The simulation parameters for Figures 11 and 12 are the same as those for Figures 8 and 9, except that for Figures 11 and 12 the features were 100 moments in duration. In Figure 13, the successive arrangement was simulated with 100-moment feature durations, and the simultaneous arrangement was simulated with 10-moment feature durations.

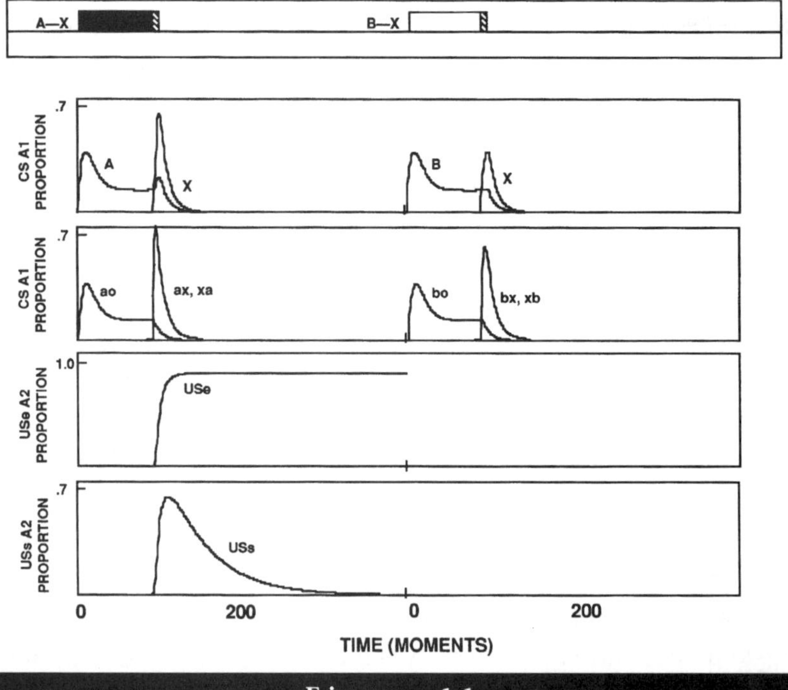

Figure 11

Simulations of test trials with A—X, B—X following training with A—X+, B—X− (as in Bahçekapili, Brandon, & Wagner, 1997, Experiment 2). As shown, the duration of A and B is 100 moments, the duration of X is 10 moments, and X begins at moment 90. The first two graphs show patterns of activity in elemental unit CSs and hidden-unit CSs, respectively; the third graph shows activity in USe, and the last graph shows activity in USs nodes. Note that the scales on the ordinates differ. More details regarding parameters are provided in footnote 1.

successfully with the elemental and configural nodes that are dynamically dependent on the activity of A and B alone to gain differential associative strength. We show this first by its consequences, by simulating the previously reported experiment (Bahçekapili et al., 1997, Experiment 2), in which training was with two sets of features and two targets, that is, A—X+, B—X− and C—Y+, D—Y−, and tests were made with the original stimulus arrangements or with shifts in the stimulus combination, their order, or both. Figure 12 presents the simulation results for the several

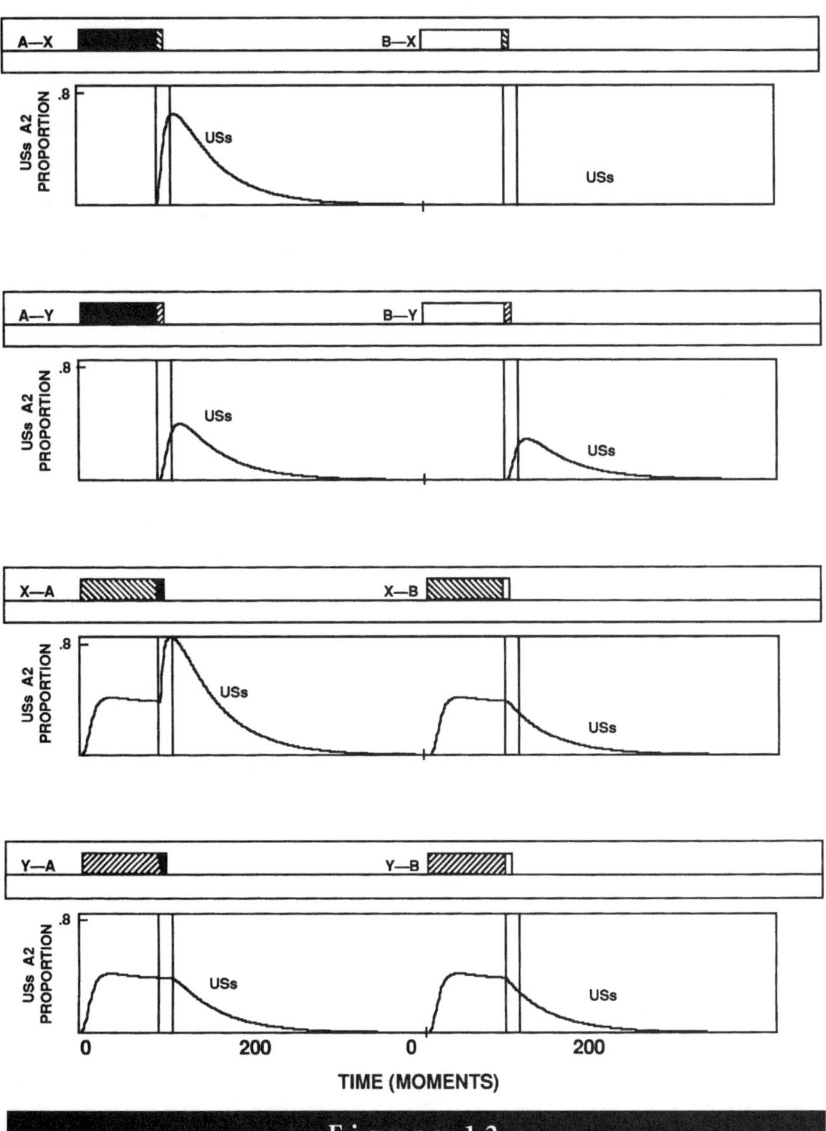

Figure 12

Simulations of test trials with X and Y following A—X+, B—X–, C—Y+, D—Y– training. The four graphs depict processing in the US-sensory (USs) node in the "original order/original configuration," "original order/shifted configuration," "shifted order/original configuration," and "shifted order/shifted configuration" tests as described in the text. The parallel lines indicate where the conditioned response would be assessed.

types of tests conducted. The parallel lines on each graph indicate where the conditioned response would be assessed. As for other simulations of test trials, these were without US presentation so that the conditioned response is not obscured by the unconditioned response. In the top graph, USs_{A2} in the original training situation indicates a good discrimination between X in the presence of A versus X in the presence of B. The model predicts this to the extent that the behavior is a function of differential emotive modulation of response-eliciting tendencies to X, by A versus B, and of the differential associative loadings of the configural stimuli generated by A—X versus B—X. In the second graph, the Y target from the C—Y+, D—Y− alternate problem is tested in the presence of A and B. The discriminative behavior is still apparent, as it should be as a result of differential emotive modulation of the response-eliciting tendencies of Y by A and B. The predicted discriminative performance is not as good as with the training compounds, however, reflecting the fact that some portion of the original discrimination was carried by the differential emotive and/or sensory/perceptual loadings that accrued to the configural cues occasioned by A—X and B—X but not by A—Y and B—Y.

The third graph depicts the conditioned USe_{A2} activity expected when the features and targets involved the training stimuli but in the reverse temporal order. Here, X precedes A by 9 sec, and the two terminate together; similarly, X precedes B by 9 sec, and B and X terminate together. In this case, the model expects a response to the onset of X on both X—A and X—B trials. Although not evident from the summary data shown in Figure 5, this was observed in the experimental data (see Bahçekapili et al., 1997, Experiment 2). The question was whether the CR-generating US nodal activity would be reprovoked by the addition of A and B: As may be seen, it is on X—A trials and not on X—B trials. That the discrimination that is present in this case is a function of the contribution of the configural cues a_x, x_a, b_x, and x_b that survive the shift in order is apparent from the simulations in the bottom graph, where both the temporal order and feature/target relationships were reversed.

Without the configural cues that formed the original discrimination, negligible discriminative responding is predicted.[4]

A hallmark of occasion setting is that the phenomena involved are more apparent in serial or successive stimulus arrangement than with simultaneous compounds. And Bahçekapili et al. (1997, Experiment 1B) demonstrated that apparent configural control appropriately varied between simultaneous and successive discriminations. AESOP with hidden units accurately predicts that control acquired by configural units should be greater in the case of the successive presentation of cues in training than in the case of the simultaneous presentation of cues in training. This is because although the relative salience (i.e., degree of activation) of the configural cues is somewhat greater in the simultaneous than in the successive arrangement, the configural cues are in a better position, relative to the features, to compete for associative strength in the successive compounds. Thus, not only should more of the original A—X, B—X discrimination depend on control by configural cues, but the reversal of reinforcement contingencies for A and B should be less disruptive for the successively than simultaneously trained subjects.

Figure 13 summarizes the results of a simulation of Bahçekapili et al. (1997, Experiment 1B). Depicted in the top graph is the well-trained performance in successive A—X, B—X test trials following successive A—X+, B—X training. Depicted in the second graph is similar well-trained performance in simultaneous AX, BX test trials following simultaneous AX+, BX– training. As can be seen, the discrimination is very good in both instances. What is different, however, is the associative loadings underlying the discrimination in the two cases. The bar graph in Figure 13 shows the associative strengths, Vs, summed across the designated

[4] Again, a response-mapping function is called for. As noted, the experimental data indicated that the animals blinked to the X and Y cues when they were presented, but the frequency decayed sharply across the 9-sec interval, until the onset of A. Also, the observed frequency of responding on X—A and X—B trials was less than that to the terminal X cue on A—X trials, and the frequency of responding on Y—A and Y—B trials was less than that to the terminal Y cue on A—Y trials. In the simulations, the activity state assumed to be generating the CR (USs_{A2}) is not sufficiently decayed in the interval between the onset of X and the onset of A or B, so that the peak of the function generated by the configual cues, a_x and x_a, are larger than they would be had the function decayed to 0.

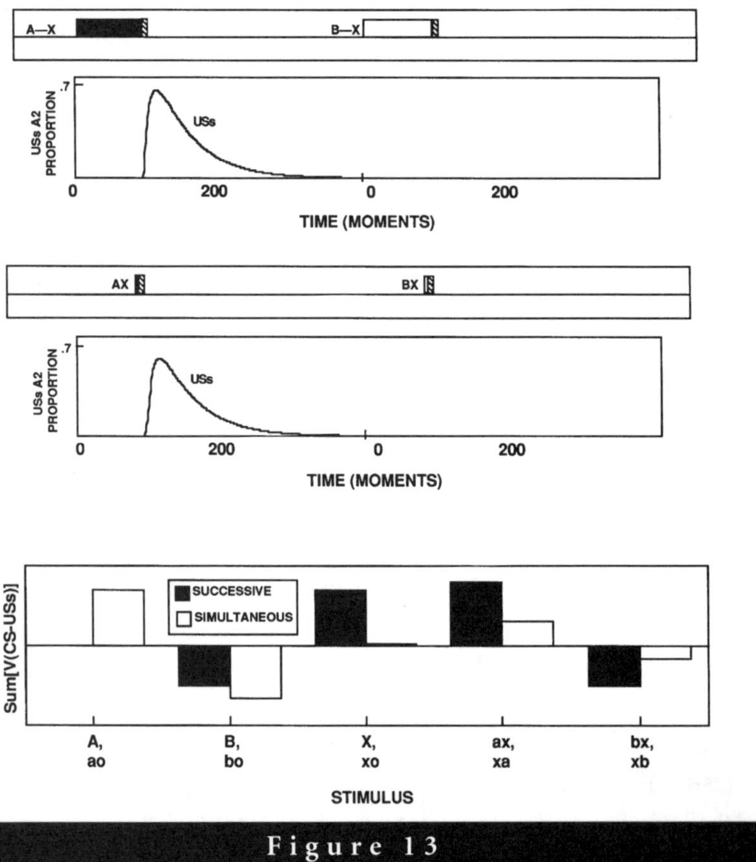

Figure 13

The top graphs show test trials with a 10-moment X coterminating with a 100-moment A and B, and with AX and BX in a simultaneous arrangement where A, B, and X were each 10 moments. For each, activity in the US-sensory/perceptual (USs) node is indicated. The bar graph indicates the associative strength accrued across training with the successive, A—X+, B—X– or simultaneous, AX+, BX– arrangement, for the elemental units a, b, and x, and for the configural units a_x and x_a (ax), and b_x and x_b (bx).

elemental units and their configural units. For both arrangements there was a high level of associative strength to X. For the simultaneous arrangement, the elements (A and a_o versus B and b_o) acquired considerable differential excitatory and inhibitory strength, and the configural cues (a_x and x_a versus b_x and x_b) less. For the successive arrangement, the elemental cues acquired less differential strength, whereas the configural cues acquired more.

DISCUSSION

Like other real-time models of conditioning that have been adapted to deal with facts of occasion setting (Gluck & Myers, 1994; Moore & Choi, chapter 10, this volume; Schmajuk et al., 1998; Lamoreux, Buhusi, & Schmajuk, chapter 13, this volume; Zackheim, Myers, & Gluck, chapter 11, this volume), our approach accounts for various aspects of occasion setting with theoretical machinery that is consistent with associative theory, rather than assuming that the processes involved in occasion setting are beyond the reach of conventional theories. Of course, whether the elaborated model proposed here adequately captures all of the important characteristics of occasion setting remains to be determined. There are some advantages of the model that we believe are worthy of note.

AESOP

We otherwise have described in some detail what we believe to be some of the advantages of the AESOP model (Wagner & Brandon, 1989). The model allows us to offer an account of aspects of Pavlovian conditioning besides occasion setting that have been especially challenging. For example, the distinction between an emotive and a sensory/perceptual representation provoked by a US gives us a way of understanding how a shift in quality of a US from pretraining to compound training in a blocking experiment leads to different blocking effects, depending on the response measure used (Betts et al., 1996; Stickney & Donahoe, 1983). Similarly, the assumption that the emotive and sensory/perceptual nodes activated by a US differ in their decay parameters, pd1 and pd2, allow us to account for observed differences in CS–US interval functions for behavioral measures that reflect sensory conditioning (e.g., the conditioned eyeblink response) versus those that reflect emotive conditioning (e.g., the CER; e.g., Schneiderman, 1972). From this reasoning we also can derive how the same CS might appear excitatory on one response measure and inhibitory on another under certain conditions (McNish et al., 1997; Tait & Saladin, 1986).

AESOP is equally advantaged by the implication of its assumed emotive-modulatory processes. We have suggested in this chapter how the modulation works and how it affects occasion setting. Among the various mechanisms by which modulation of a Pavlovian skeletal response might occur through a CER, we assume that the CER increases the effective salience of ongoing stimulus events—that is, the SOP parameter, p1, assumed to increase with increasing stimulus intensity or salience, is, in AESOP, assumed to be increased proportionately to the degree of activation of the CER, by the rule depicted in Figure 7. As pointed out earlier, this rule for modulation was favored by data that indicated that contexts trained like the stimuli A and B can modulate not only the performance of an otherwise-elicited eyeblink response, but also its acquisition. In our model, this observation naturally invites the assumption that the modulation impacts on the stimulus side of the CS–US processing. This assumption is consistent with neuroanatomical analyses of other fear-potentiated behaviors, most notably the auditory evoked startle response in the rat (Davis, 1986). Of course, there is the possibility that a CER facilitates response output as well. To limit the modulation for the present to the parameter p1 is simply a matter of parsimony.

AESOP With Hidden Units

There are several aspects of the hidden unit model that we judge to be important. First, of course, as has been emphasized, the model treats configural representations as *hidden units* that are dependent on the activity of first-order units. This is called for if one thinks that configural representation can occur when component stimuli are separated in time. It is also a way of accounting for how configural representation enters into the control of behavior in serial FP or FN discrimination, where the features are presented and removed before the occurrence of the target, as has been commonly reported in the occasion-setting literature.

We also have assumed that there is a hidden unit that is activated by the configuration of x-alone, without concurrent activity in an A or B node, and that this activation of x_o is inhibited by the activation of x_a or x_b, dependent on concurrent activity in the first-order A or B nodes. This is reminiscent of Hull's notion of *afferent neural interaction* (Hull, 1943, 1945). We employ a componential version, however: There are first-order nodes, which are excited by a stimulus, that are immune to whatever else is in the environment. There are also second-order nodes, which are dependent on a stimulus, that are in turn dependent on what other representations are active. When we say that one second-order node represents *x-alone,* we of course need mean no more than *x in the experimental environment in the absence of A or B activity.* A theoretical advantage of this conception is that it allows for external inhibition (Pavlov, 1927), in other words, for a generalization decrement when training with A and then testing with AX, as well as when training AX and then testing X. Our componential version of SOP is a measured acknowledgment of configural cues, as these are witnessed in biconditional discriminations and serial FP or FN discriminations, but are not the most salient controllers of behavior (Savaadra, 1975).

It follows from the componential conception that there are two potential representations for each two-component configuration. For example, the configuration of A and X is assumed to involve an a_x hidden unit (that inhibits a_o, which would be active if X's nodes were not active), and an x_a hidden unit (that inhibits x_o, which would be active if A's nodes were not active). Our treatment thereby predicts different outcomes of shifting the order of feature and target if the original discrimination is one in which the two components overlap, as in the data of Bahçekapili et al. (1997, Experiment 2, described earlier), than if the original discrimination involves a serial presentation in which the two components do not overlap, as in the experiments described by Holland (1992) and Rescorla (1985). In the successive arrangement of an A—X+, B—X– discrimination, where features overlap with the target, both a_x and x_a will be activated on reinforced trials to gain excitatory strength, and both b_x and x_b will be activated on nonreinforced trials to gain inhibitory strength. Furthermore, on test trials with X—A and X—B, the same hidden units will be activated to produce differential responding. In contrast, in the serial arrangement of an A→X+, B→X– discrimination, only x_a will be activated on the reinforced trials, and only x_b will be activated on the nonreinforced trials, to gain differential associative strength. On test trials with X→A and X→B, neither of these hidden units will be activated, but a_x and b_x will be, neither of which have acquired associative strength.

That occasion setting involves something beyond simple CR elicitation by elemental CSs has nowhere been more obvious than in the groundbreaking studies of Ross and Holland (1981). They exploited the fact that rats exhibit different forms of conditioned responding to auditory and visual stimuli paired with the receipt of food. They found that rats trained with an FP sequence of light, followed by tone reinforced versus tone nonreinforced, gave tone-characteristic CRs to the compound, whereas animals trained with a sequence of tone followed by light reinforced, versus light nonreinforced, gave light-characteristic CRs. Our model, like other existing abstract theories, does not specify why different CSs, such as a light versus a tone, might provoke different CRs (Holland, 1977). Thus, we claim it as no great success for the model that we can account for any fact of occasion setting relating to this phenomenon. We can note, however, that if there is a distinction made in the theory between an a_x hidden unit and an x_a hidden unit, it is not unreasonable to suppose that the CR observed to the former might have a different form (e.g., be more A-like) than that observed to the latter (which might be more X-like). This allows the theory to at least be reconcilable with a substantial literature that shows that, in serial discrimination learning, the CR frequently reflects the qualitative nature of the target rather than of the feature.

CONCLUSION

The two elaborations of SOP described in this chapter, one to include modulation of a CR through emotive processes and the other to include control by configural stimuli, reflect our view that occasion setting may be a relatively overdetermined phenomenon (Wagner, 1992). These two processes may variously contribute to occasion setting, depending on the particulars of the conditioning procedures—for example, whether the reinforcer is appetitive or aversive. They at least offer a clue to sorting out some of the variations in occasion setting that are observed with different conditioning preparations and in different laboratories.

REFERENCES

Bahçekapili, H. G., Brandon, S. E., & Wagner, A. R. (1997). *Emotive modulation and stimulus configuration in "occasion setting" in rabbit eyeblink conditioning.* Unpublished manuscript.

Betts, S. L., Brandon, S. E., & Wagner, A. R. (1996). Dissociation of the blocking of conditioned eyeblink and conditioned fear following a shift in US locus. *Animal Learning & Behavior, 24,* 459–470.

Bombace, J. C., Brandon, S. E., & Wagner, A. R. (1991). Modulation of a discrete conditioned eyeblink response via an emotive Pavlovian conditioned stimulus trained with hindleg shock. *Journal of Experimental Psychology: Animal Behavior Processes, 17,* 323–333.

Bonardi, C. (1996). Transfer of occasion setting: The role of generalization decrement. *Animal Learning & Behavior, 24,* 277–289.

Bouton, M. E., & Swartzentruber, D. (1986). Analysis of the associative and occasion-setting properties of contexts participating in a Pavlovian discrimination. *Journal of Experimental Psychology: Animal Behavior Processes, 12,* 333–350.

Brandon, S. E., Betts, S. L., & Wagner, A. R. (1994). Discriminated, lateralized, eyeblink conditioning in the rabbit: An experimental context for separating specific and general associative influences. *Journal of Experimental Psychology: Animal Behavior Processes, 20,* 292–307.

Brandon, S. E., Bombace, J. C., Falls, W. T., & Wagner, A. R. (1991). Modulation of unconditioned defensive reflexes via an emotive Pavlovian conditioned stimulus. *Journal of Experimental Psychology: Animal Behavior Processes, 17,* 312–322.

Brandon, S. E., & Wagner, A. R. (1991). Modulation of a discrete Pavlovian conditioned reflex by a putative emotive Pavlovian conditioned stimulus. *Journal of Experimental Psychology: Animal Behavior Processes, 17,* 299–311.

Davidson, T. L., & Rescorla, R. A. (1986). Transfer of facilitation in the rat. *Animal Learning & Behavior, 14,* 380–386.

Davis, M. (1984). The mammalian startle response. In R. C. Eaton (Ed.), *Neural mechanisms of startle behavior* (pp. 287–351). New York: Plenum Press.

Davis, M. (1986). Pharmacological and anatomical analysis of fear conditioning using the potentiated startle paradigm. *Behavioral Neuroscience, 100,* 808–818.

Detke, M. J. (1991). Extinction of sequential conditioned inhibition. *Animal Learning & Behavior, 14,* 380–354.

Dickinson, A. (1980). *Contemporary animal learning theory.* New York: Cambridge University Press.

Gewirtz, J. C., Brandon, S. E., & Wagner, A. R. (1998). Modulation of the acquisition of the rabbit eyeblink conditioned response by conditioned contextual stimuli. *Journal of Experimental Psychology: Animal Behavior Processes, 24,* 106–117.

Gluck, M. A., & Myers, C. E. (1994). Context, conditioning, and hippocampal representation in animal learning. *Behavioral Neuroscience, 108,* 835–847.

Gormezano, I., & Moore, J. W. (1969). Classical conditioning. In M. H. Marx (Ed.), *Learning: Processes* (pp. 121–203). Toronto: Collier-Macmillan Ltd.

Holland, P. C. (1977). Conditioned stimulus as a determinant of the form of the Pavlovian conditioned response. *Journal of Experimental Psychology: Animal Behavior Processes, 3,* 77–104.

Holland, P. C. (1984). Differential effects of reinforcement of an inhibitory feature after serial and simultaneous feature negative discrimination training. *Journal of Experimental Psychology: Animal Behavior Processes, 10,* 461–475.

Holland, P. C. (1985). The nature of conditioned inhibition in serial and simultaneous feature negative discriminations. In R. R. Miller & N. E. Spear (Eds.), *Information processing in animals: Conditioned inhibition* (pp. 267–297). Hillsdale, NJ: Erlbaum.

Holland, P. C. (1986a). Temporal determinants of occasion setting in feature positive discriminations. *Animal Learning & Behavior, 14,* 111–120.

Holland, P. C. (1986b). Transfer after serial feature positive discrimination training. *Learning and Motivation, 17,* 243–268.

Holland, P. C. (1989a). Acquisition and transfer of conditional discrimination performance. *Journal of Experimental Psychology: Animal Behavior Processes, 15,* 154–165.

Holland, P. C. (1989b). Feature extinction enhances transfer of occasion setting. *Animal Learning & Behavior, 17,* 269–279.

Holland, P. C. (1989c). Occasion setting with simultaneous compounds in rats. *Journal of Experimental Psychology: Animal Behavior Processes, 3,* 183–193.

Holland, P. C. (1989d). Transfer of negative occasion setting and conditioned inhibition across conditioned and unconditioned stimuli. *Journal of Experimental Psychology: Animal Behavior Processes, 15,* 311–328.

Holland, P. C. (1992). Occasion setting in Pavlovian conditioning. In D. Medin (Ed.), *The psychology of learning and motivation* (Vol. 28, pp. 69–125). New York: Academic Press.

Holland, P. C. (1995). Transfer of occasion setting across stimulus and response in operant feature positive discriminations. *Learning and Motivation, 26,* 239–263.

Holland, P. C., & Lamarre, J. (1984). Transfer of inhibition after serial and simultaneous feature negative discrimination training. *Learning and Motivation, 15,* 219–243.

Hull, C. L. (1943). *Principles of behavior.* New York: Appleton-Century-Crofts.

Hull, C. L. (1945). The discrimination of stimulus configuration and the hypothesis of afferent neural interaction. *Psychological Review, 52,* 133–142.

Jenkins, H. M. (1985). Conditioned inhibition of key pecking in the pigeon. In R. R. Miller & N. E. Spear (Eds.), *Information processing in animals: Conditioned inhibition* (pp. 327–353). Hillsdale, NJ: Erlbaum.

Kamin, L. J. (1965). Temporal and intensity characteristics of the conditioned stimulus. In W. F. Prokasy (Ed.), *Classical conditioning* (pp. 118–147). New York: Academic Press.

Kehoe, E. J. (1988). A layered network model of associative learning: Learning to learn and configuration. *Psychological Review, 95,* 411–433.

Konorski, J. (1967). *Integrative activity of the brain: An interdisciplinary approach.* Chicago: University of Chicago Press.

Lamarre, J., & Holland, P. C. (1987). Acquisition and transfer of serial feature negative discriminations. *Learning and Motivation, 18,* 319–342.

Mackintosh, N. J. (1975). A theory of attention: Variations in the associability of stimuli with reinforcement. *Psychological Review, 82,* 276–298.

Mackintosh, N. J. (1983). *Conditioning and associative learning.* New York: Oxford University Press.

Mazur, J. E., & Wagner, A. R. (1982). An episodic model of associative learning. In

M. Commons, R. Herrnstein, & A. R. Wagner (Eds.), *Quantitative analyses of behavior: Acquisition* (Vol. 3, pp. 3–39). Cambridge, MA: Ballinger.

McNish, K., Betts, S. L., Brandon, S. E., & Wagner, A. R. (1997). Divergence of measures of conditioned eyeblink and conditioned fear in backward Pavlovian training. *Animal Learning & Behavior, 25,* 43–52.

Mowrer, O. H. (1947). On the dual nature of learning—A reinterpretation of "conditioning" and "problem-solving." *Harvard Educational Review, 17,* 102–148.

Pavlov, I. P. (1927). *Conditioned reflexes.* Oxford: Oxford University Press.

Pearce, J. M. (1987). A model for stimulus generalization in Pavlovian conditioning. *Psychological Review, 94,* 61–75.

Pearce, J. M., & Hall, G. (1980). A model for Pavlovian learning: Variations in the effectiveness of conditioned but not unconditioned stimuli. *Psychological Review, 87,* 532–552.

Rescorla, R. A. (1985). Inhibition and facilitation. In R. R. Miller & N. E. Spear (Eds.), *Information processing in animals: Conditioned inhibition* (pp. 299–326). Hillsdale, NJ: Erlbaum.

Rescorla, R. A. (1986a). Extinction of facilitation. *Journal of Experimental Psychology: Animal Behavior Processes, 12,* 16–24.

Rescorla, R. A. (1986b). Facilitation and excitation. *Journal of Experimental Psychology: Animal Behavior Processes, 12,* 325–332.

Rescorla, R. A. (1989). Simultaneous and sequential conditioned inhibition in autoshaping. *Quarterly Journal of Experimental Psychology, 41B,* 275–286.

Rescorla, R. A. (1991). Separate reinforcement can enhance the effectiveness of modulators. *Journal of Experimental Psychology: Animal Behavior Processes, 17,* 259–269.

Rescorla, R. A., & Solomon, R. L. (1967). Two-process learning theory: Relationships between Pavlovian conditioning and instrumental learning. *Psychological Review, 74,* 151–182.

Rescorla, R. A., & Wagner, A. R. (1972). A theory of Pavlovian conditioning: Variations in the effectiveness of reinforcement and nonreinforcement. In A. H. Black & W. F. Prokasy (Eds.), *Classical conditioning II* (pp. 64–99). New York: Appleton-Century-Crofts.

Ross, R. T., & Holland, P. C. (1981). Conditioning of simultaneous and serial feature-positive discriminations. *Animal Learning & Behavior, 9,* 292–303.

Rumelhart, D. E., & McClelland, J. L. (1986). *Parallel distributed processing: Explorations in the microstructures of cognition, Vol. 1.* Cambridge, MA: MIT Press.

Savaadra, M. A. (1975). Pavlovian compound conditioning in the rabbit. *Learning and Motivation, 6,* 314–326.

Schmajuk, N. A., & Buhusi, C. V. (1997). Stimulus configuration, occasion setting, and the hippocampus. *Behavioral Neuroscience, 111,* 1–24.

Schmajuk, N. A., Lamoureux, J. A., & Holland, P. C. (1998). Occasion setting: A neural network approach. *Psychological Review, 105,* 3–32.

Schneiderman, N. (1972). Response system divergencies in aversive classical conditioning. In A. H. Black & W. F. Prokasy (Eds.), *Classical conditioning II: Current theory and research* (pp. 313–376). New York: Appleton-Century-Crofts.

Smith, M. C., Coleman, S. R., & Gormezano, I. (1969). Classical conditioning of the rabbit's nictitating membrane response at backward, simultaneous, and forward CS-US intervals. *Journal of Comparative and Physiological Psychology, 69,* 226–231.

Spence, K. (1936). The nature of discrimination learning in animals. *Psychological Review, 43,* 427–449.

Spence, K. W. (1960). *Behavior theory and learning.* Englewood Cliffs, NJ: Prentice-Hall.

Stickney, K. J., & Donahoe, J. W. (1983). Attenuation of blocking by a change in US locus. *Animal Learning & Behavior, 11,* 60–66.

Swartzentruber, D., & Rescorla, R. A. (1994). Modulation of trained and extinguished stimuli by facilitators and inhibitors. *Animal Learning & Behavior, 22,* 309–316.

Tait, R. W., & Saladin, M. E. (1986). Concurrent development of excitatory and inhibitory associations during backward conditioning. *Animal Learning & Behavior, 14,* 133–137.

Vandercar, D. H., & Schneiderman, N. (1967). Interstimulus interval functions in different response systems during classical discrimination conditioning of rabbits. *Psychonomic Science, 9,* 9–10.

Wagner, A. R. (1981). SOP: A model of automatic memory processing in animal behavior. In N. E. Spear & R. R. Miller (Eds.), *Information processing in animals: Memory mechanisms* (pp. 5–47). Hillsdale, NJ: Erlbaum.

Wagner, A. R. (1992, July). Some complexities anticipated by *AESOP* and other dual-representation theories. In H. Kimmel (Chair), *Pavlovian conditioning with complex stimuli.* Symposium conducted at the XXV International Congress of Psychology, Brussels, Belgium.

Wagner, A. R. (1997). *A network model version of SOP.* Unpublished manuscript.

Wagner, A. R., & Brandon, S. E. (1989). Evolution of a structured connectionist model of Pavlovian conditioning (ÆSOP). In S. B. Klein & R. R. Mowrer (Eds.), *Contemporary learning theories: Pavlovian conditioning and the status of traditional learning theory* (pp. 149–189). Hillsdale, NJ: Erlbaum.

Wagner, A. R., & Donegan, N. H. (1989). Some relationships between a computational model (SOP) and a neural circuit for Pavlovian (rabbit eyeblink) conditioning. In R. D. Hawkins & G. H. Bower (Eds.), *The psychology of learning and motivation, Vol. 22: Computational models of learning in simple neural systems.* Orlando, FL: Academic Press.

Weisz, D. J., & LoTurco, J. L. (1988). Reflex facilitation of the nictitating membrane response remains after cerebellar lesions. *Behavioral Neuroscience, 104,* 21–27.

Wilson, P. N., & Pearce, J. M. (1989). A role for stimulus generalization in conditional discrimination learning. *Quarterly Journal of Experimental Psychology, 41B,* 243–273.

Wilson, P. N., & Pearce, J. M. (1990). Selective transfer of responding in conditional discriminations. *Quarterly Journal of Experimental Psychology, 42B,* 41–58.

13

A Real-Time Theory of Pavlovian Conditioning: Simple Stimuli and Occasion Setters

Jeffrey A. Lamoureux, Catalin V. Buhusi, and Nestor A. Schmajuk

In their classic article, Rescorla and Wagner (1972) indicated that the impetus for their new theoretical model was not new data that clearly disconfirmed existing theories but the accumulation of a pattern of data that appeared to invite a more integrated account. The salient pattern of data that the authors referred to was a set of observations involving Pavlovian conditioning with compound conditioned stimuli (CSs). The central notion of the theory was that organisms only learn when the actual value of the unconditioned stimulus (US) differs from its expected value. By proposing the novel principle that this expected value of the US is computed as a linear combination of the associative strength of all active CSs, the effect of reinforcement or nonreinforcement on the associative strength of a CS depends on the existing associative strength, not only of that CS, but also of other CSs that are concurrently present.

Recognizing the limitations of verbal formulations to make specific predictions, Rescorla and Wagner proposed to formalize the central notion of their theory by modifying Hull's (1943) account of the growth of habit strength (stimulus–response associations) as described by Bush and Mosteller's (1955) linear operator. In the Rescorla–Wagner (RW) model, variations in the strength of the CS–US association, $V_{i,US}$, are given by

$$\Delta V_{i,US} = \alpha_i \beta_{US} (\lambda_{US} - B_{US}), \qquad (1)$$

where α_i represents the salience of CS_i, β_{US} represents the learning rate parameter corresponding to the US, and B_{US} is the linear combination of the prediction of the US by all active CSs. B_{US} is given by

$$B_{US} = \Sigma_j V_{j,US}. \qquad (2)$$

By Equation 1, CSs compete to gain association with the US. The conditioned response (CR) was assumed to be proportional to B_{US}.

The RW model correctly described many Pavlovian conditioning phenomena, such as acquisition and extinction of conditioned excitation, conditioned inhibition, overshadowing and blocking, overprediction, and contingency effects. The success of the model in making specific, correct predictions inaugurated the modern era of experimental psychology.

Despite its significant achievements, the RW model was unable to describe several aspects of classical conditioning, including (a) the effects of temporal parameters, such as stimulus duration or interstimulus intervals; and (b) Pavlovian paradigms whose solution require a nonlinear combination of the prediction of the US by all active CSs, such as negative patterning.

A REAL-TIME MODEL OF PAVLOVIAN CONDITIONING

Schmajuk and DiCarlo (1992) proposed a real-time network that described both the effects of temporal parameters on classical conditioning as well as nonlinear classical conditioning paradigms. Like the RW model, one central notion of the Schmajuk–DiCarlo (SD) theory is that organisms

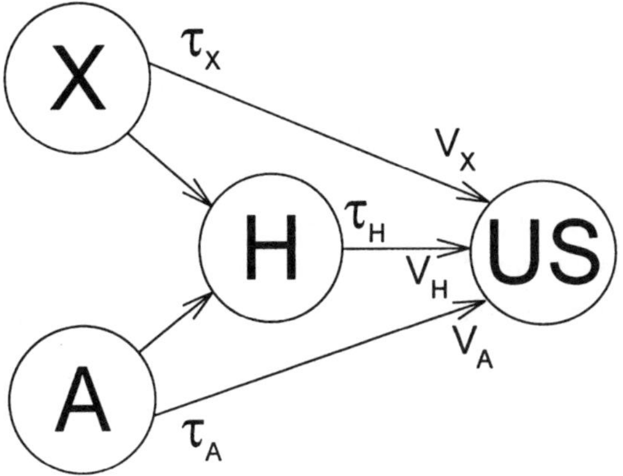

Figure 1

The Schmajuk–DiCarlo (SD) model for a single response system. Simplified diagram of the SD network, which incorporates a layer of hidden units (H) capable of describing stimulus configuration. τ_X and τ_A = short-term memories of X and A, τ_H = short-term memory of H, V_X = X–US association, V_A = A–US association, V_H = H–US associations, US = unconditioned stimulus.

only learn when the actual value of the US differs from its expected value. A second notion is that CSs generate short-term memory traces that can become associated with the US, thereby describing trace conditioning. A third notion is that the expected value of the US is computed on a linear combination of the associative strength of all active CSs, plus the associative strength of configurations of those active CSs.

Figure 1 offers a simplified diagram of the network. It consists of one input layer, one hidden-unit layer, and one output layer (although the complete formal model incorporates two output layers; see Schmajuk & DiCarlo, 1992). Conditioned stimuli, X and A, activate short-term memory traces, τ_X and τ_A, which increase when the stimuli are active and otherwise decrease. The context, CX, which is not shown in Figure 1, activates a short-term memory trace, τ_{CX}, which increases when the animal is placed in that CX and otherwise decreases. These traces form direct associations, V_X, V_A, V_{CX}, with the output layer. In addition, the traces form associations, VH_{ij}, with the hidden-unit layer, simplified and represented singly by H in Figure 1. The hidden units form associations, V_j, with the output layer. The output activities of the hidden-unit layer are assumed to code configural stimuli whose traces are denoted by τ_{Hj}.

Changes in the associations between τ_{CSi} or τ_{Hi} and the US, V_i, are controlled by a simple delta rule that minimizes the output error, US–B_{US}, between the actual value of the US and its aggregate prediction, B_{US},

$$\Delta V_i = K\ \tau_i\ (US - B_{US}), \qquad (3)$$

where τ_i represents either τ_{CSi} or τ_{Hi} and B_{US} is the linear combination of the predictions of the US by all active τ_{CSi} and τ_{CNi}

$$B_{US} = \Sigma_i\ V_i\ \tau_{CSi} + \Sigma_j\ V_j\ \tau_{Hj}. \qquad (4)$$

Although the individual CS–US associations can be positive or negative, B_{US} can be assumed to adopt values between 0 and 1. Interestingly, under this assumption, the model correctly describes results showing that the presentation of a neutral CS with a conditioned inhibitor does not yield a conditioned excitor, and that nonreinforced presentations of a conditioned inhibitor do not extinguish its inhibitory association with the US. The CR output of the system is proportional to B_{US}. Equations 3 and 4 in the SD model correspond to Equations 1 and 2 in the RW model.

Two more equations are added in the SD model to describe the changes in the association between τ_{CSi} and hidden unit j, VH_{ij}, which is proportional to

$$\Delta VH_{ij} = K\ \tau_{CSi}\ \tau_{Hj}\ V_j\ (US - B_{US}), \qquad (5)$$

where the output activity of hidden unit j is given by

$$\tau_{Hj} = S(\Sigma_i\ VH_{ij}\ \tau_{CSi}), \qquad (6)$$

S being a nonlinear sigmoid function. Associations between τ_{CSi} and hidden unit j increase in proportion to the magnitude of τ_{CSi}, the effect of hidden unit j on the output, τ_{Hj} V_j, and the difference between the desired output US and the actual output B_{US}. This procedure used to compute the associations between τ_{CSi} and hidden unit j, VH_{ij}, is similar to backpropagation (see Rumelhart, Hinton, & Williams, 1986; Werbos, 1987).

Equation 5 specifies how stimulus configuration is achieved by adjusting τ_i-hidden unit associations, VH_{ij}. A configural stimulus has traditionally been defined as a stimulus that is active when its component stimuli are active together (e.g., CS_1 and CS_2) and that can acquire excitatory or inhibitory associations with the US (e.g., Kehoe, 1988; Pearce, 1987; Rescorla, 1973; Rescorla & Wagner, 1972, p. 86). In the SD model, by contrast, configuring is accomplished by training hidden units that may respond to various combinations of stimuli (e.g., CS_1 and not CS_2), and each one may acquire excitatory or inhibitory associations with the output units. In other words, whereas hidden units may come to respond to the concurrent excitatory input from multiple stimuli, as in the classic view of configuration (Rescorla, 1973), CSs may also develop associations with hidden units that are inhibitory in nature. For example, a hidden unit may be activated by presentation of the CX or one or more CSs, but the addition of another CS may actually inhibit or attenuate the activation of that node.

Learning in the Hidden Units and Learning in the Output Units

Although Equations 3 and 5 are very similar, learning in the output units and in the hidden units show important differences. According to Equation 3, when the US is present ($US > B_{US}$), V_i increases proportionally to the magnitude of τ_i and to the ($US - B_{US}$) difference. When the US is absent ($US < B_{US}$), V_i decreases proportionally to the magnitude of τ_i and to B_{US}. The asymptotic value of V_i is therefore the result of a dynamic equilibrium in which increments in V_i, during the periods when $US > B_{US}$, balance the decrements in V_i during the periods when $US < B_{US}$.

Consequently, V_i will be large for short CS–US interstimulus intervals because τ_i is large at the time of the US presentation (large acquisition) and small when the US is absent (little extinction); but V_i will be small for long CS–US interstimulus intervals because τ_i is small at the time of the US presentation (small acquisition) and large when the US is absent (large extinction). By contrast, according to Equation 5, on a reinforced trial, CS–H associations increase in proportion to the magnitudes of τ_{CSi} and τ_{Hj}, and to the (US–B) difference. When the US is absent, CS–H associations decrease in proportion to the magnitudes of τ_{CSi} and τ_{Hj}, and to B. CS–H associations will therefore be large even for long CS–US interstimulus intervals because, even if τ_i is small at the time of the US presentation (little acquisition), τ_{Hj} is small when the US is absent (little extinction). In sum, the difference in the way CS–US and CS–H associations are computed explains why, even though a CS might not be able to establish strong direct CS–US associations (by Equation 3), it still can establish strong CS–H associations with the hidden units (by Equation 5).

Another important difference between Equations 3 and 5 is that, when τ_{Hj} changes because a new stimulus activates the hidden unit, the effective values of the constants change, thereby modifying the rate at which ΔVH_{ij} is computed.

A Model for Multiple Pavlovian Conditioned Responses

The SD model (as well as all other extant conditioning models) assumes that all inputs activate essentially the same CR, that is, that the form of the CR is determined by the choice of US. Much investigation of occasion setting, however, has exploited the fact that the form of the CR is sometimes determined not only by the US but also by the nature of the CS. Holland (1977) found that rats exhibited very different CR forms during visual (e.g., rear behavior) and auditory (e.g., head jerk behavior) signals for food. Consequently, in order to more completely describe conditioned behavior in general and to address the outcomes of experiments in occasion setting in particular, Schmajuk, Lamoureux, and Holland (1998) extended the SD model to describe multiple response systems.

In the SD model for multiple response systems (the Schmajuk-Lamoureux–Holland, or SLH, model), associations computed by the network shown in Figure 1 are organized to generate not only aggregate prediction B and the CR, but also responses that are specific to the modality of the CS. For example, if the model is trained on a feature-positive (FP) discrimination in which X is a visual stimulus and A is an auditory stimulus, the network generates response levels for both rearing (CR_X responses) and head jerking (CR_A responses). Specifically, each stimulus (a) excites its own response system (e.g., CR_A for A) through direct associations; (b) equally excites or inhibits both CR_X and CR_A response systems indirectly through associations with configural, hidden units; and (c) inhibits both CR_X and CR_A through direct associations. In simple mathematical terms, one response system generates $CR_A = \tau_{CSA}\ [V_{CSA}]^+ + \Sigma_j\ \tau_{Hj}\ V_{Hj} + I$, whereas the other response system generates $CR_X = \tau_{CSX}\ [V_{CSX}]^+ + \Sigma_j\ \tau_{Hj}\ V_{Hj} + I$. The term $I = \tau_{CSA}\ [V_{CSA}]^- + \tau_{CSX}\ [V_{CSX}]^-$ is the output of a system that provides inhibition to both response systems, where $[V_{CSA}]^+$ indicates values of $V_{CSA} > 0$, and $[V_{CSA}]^-$ indicates values of $V_{CSA} < 0$. In short, CR_A and CR_X result from simply reorganizing the values of τ_{CSA}, V_{CSA}, τ_{CSX}, V_{CSX}, and V_{Hj} computed for the single response system.

WHAT IS AN OCCASION SETTER?

As suggested by Rescorla and Wagner (1972), the impetus for a new theoretical model is the accumulation of a pattern of data that appears to invite a more integrated theoretical account. Such a pattern of data that currently begs for a new theoretical account is a set of observations involving Pavlovian conditioning in which CSs seem to act as simple CSs or as occasion setters. Depending on factors that influence the strength of its association with the US (i.e., the CS's intensity, duration, and the CS–US interval), as well as the requirements of the task at hand, a CS acts as a simple CS, evoking CRs characteristic of its own modality, or as an occasion setter, apparently modulating the association between the target and the US.

In the framework of the SLH model, Schmajuk et al. (1998) assumed that a stimulus performs as a simple CS when it acts on a response system through its direct excitatory or inhibitory associations and as an occasion setter when it acts on a response system through its configural associations (by way of the hidden unit layer). Although a CS's simple and configural representations compete to gain association with the US, a CS can act as both a simple CS and an occasion setter at the same time. Furthermore, these roles can be completely antithetical: A CS can simultaneously behave as an excitatory simple CS and as an inhibitory occasion setter because of the dual independent paths through which the CS can become associated with the US.

Because the SLH model assumes that different stimuli excite their own response systems (i.e., CR_A for A, CR_X for X) through direct associations, percentages of rearing or head jerk behaviors without the other behavior are considered a measure of the simple (excitatory) CS role of tone A and light X, respectively. Notice that these specific behaviors might be attenuated by the simple (inhibitory) CS role of other CSs, the (inhibitory) occasion-setting role of this same CS, or the (inhibitory) occasion-setting role of other CSs. Furthermore, because the model assumes that stimuli equally excite or inhibit both CR_X and CR_A response systems indirectly through associations with configural hidden units, percentages of rearing or head jerk behaviors in the presence of the other behavior can be considered a measure of the occasion-setting roles of tone A and light X, respectively (see Holland & Block, 1983).

WHEN DOES A CS BEHAVE AS AN OCCASION SETTER?

Having provided explicit definitions for simple CSs and occasion setters, this section illustrates, through computer simulations, how the model determines the situations in which a CS behaves as a simple CS or as an occasion setter. We analyze performance in (a) a simultaneous FP discrimination with a feature and target that are equal in salience, (b) a simultaneous FP discrimination with a feature that is weaker than a relatively salient target, (c) a serial FP discrimination, and (d) a conditional contextual discrimination.

We will demonstrate that, when direct and indirect CS–US associations are combined in the SLH real-time network, the same competitive rule that governs phenomena that involve training with compound stimuli—such as blocking, overshadowing, or conditioned inhibition—dictates the *role* of a CS—a simple CS or an occasion setter—as indicated by response form data.

Simultaneous FP Discrimination

Ross and Holland (1981, Experiment 1) observed the responding of rats in simultaneous (XA+/A–) FP discriminations. As shown in the upper panel of Figure 2, the form of the CR acquired to the XA compound was characteristic of the predictive X feature (CR_X). Consequently, Ross and Holland concluded that responding in simultaneous FP discrimination procedures was entirely the result of feature–US associations. The lower panel of Figure 2 shows a computer simulation of responding to the XA compound stimulus in the test phase in Ross and Holland's study. As in the empirical data, the model generated mostly CR_X responses during XA presentations—that is, responding of a form appropriate to the X feature CS.

Figure 3 illustrates the real-time values of X, A, the US, and the hidden units H during reinforced and nonreinforced trials in a simultaneous FP discrimination. The feature X and target A generate short-term memory traces that grow after X and A onset and decay to zero after X and A termination. Hidden unit H is active on A trials only. According to the SLH model, in a reinforced trial, X–US and A–US associations increase in proportion to the shaded area under each trace and decrease in proportion to the clear area under the curve. When X and A are presented together on a reinforced trial, they compete for association with the US. Furthermore, A is also presented in isolation on nonreinforced target-alone trials, during which the A–US associations decrease in proportion to the whole area under the memory trace curve. The result is that X–US associations become very strong, whereas A–US associations remain relatively weak. Thus, FP discrimination is achieved because XA presentations result in strong CRs that are based on X–US associations, but A presentations result in weak CRs.

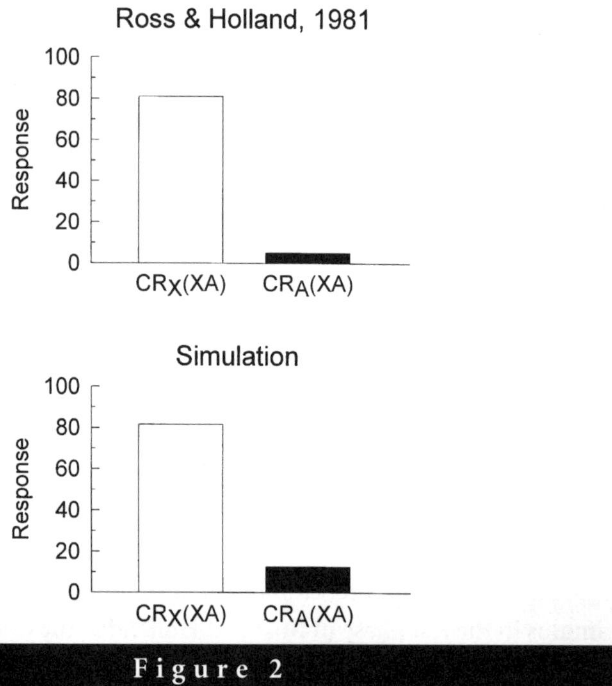

Figure 2

Response form (CR_X and CR_A) during simultaneous feature-positive (FP) discriminations. (*Top panel*) CR_X and CR_A responding of rats trained in simultaneous FP discriminations. The bars indicate the percentage of behavior that was CR_X (open bar) or CR_A (solid bar) on XA compound trials. Data are from Ross and Holland (1981). (*Lower panel*, simulation) Peak CR_X (open bar) and CR_A (solid bar) on an XA test trial after 30 training trials (15 XA+ trials alternated with 15 A– trials). Reprinted with permission from Schmajuk, Lamoureux, & Holland (1998). Copyright 1998 by the American Psychological Association.

Figure 4 shows a computer simulation of the acquisition of a simultaneous FP discrimination when X and A have similar intensities. The top panel of Figure 4 shows CR_X and CR_A responding to XA and A during acquisition. At the beginning of training, CR_X responding to the XA compound and CR_A responding to A are similar. With increasing number of trials, CR_X responding to the XA compound increases, CR_A responding to A decreases, and the discrimination is achieved. The lower panel of Figure 4 shows that the US prediction generated by X increases over trials, whereas the prediction of the US by A remains relatively weak. The US prediction generated by the collection of all hidden units H ($\Sigma_j \tau_{Hj} V_j$) remains close

SIMULTANEOUS

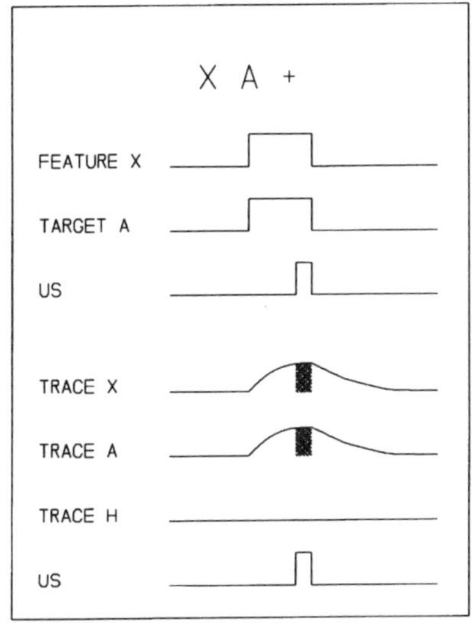

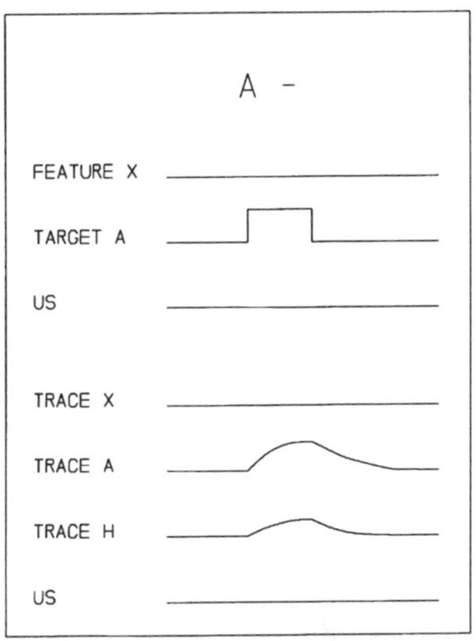

Figure 3

Simultaneous feature-positive discrimination. Real-time representations of X and A, their traces, and of the US on an XA+ and an A– trial. Adapted with permission from Schmajuk et al., 1998. Copyright 1998 by the American Psychological Association.

to zero. Thus, in a simultaneous FP discrimination with X and A of comparable salience, X acts as a simple CS because it controls behavior through strong direct associations with the US, whereas the hidden units play little role.

Figure 5 summarizes the model's solution for a simultaneous FP discrimination. Whereas X acts as a simple CS because it acquires strong direct associations with the US, A acquires weak ones. Because direct associations of A and X with the US determine the response form, CR_A or CR_X, the model generates mostly CR_X responses during compound XA presentations.

Simultaneous FP Discrimination and Target Intensity

Holland (1989a) examined the acquisition of simultaneous FP (XA+/A–) discriminations in Pavlovian procedures as a function of the relative inten-

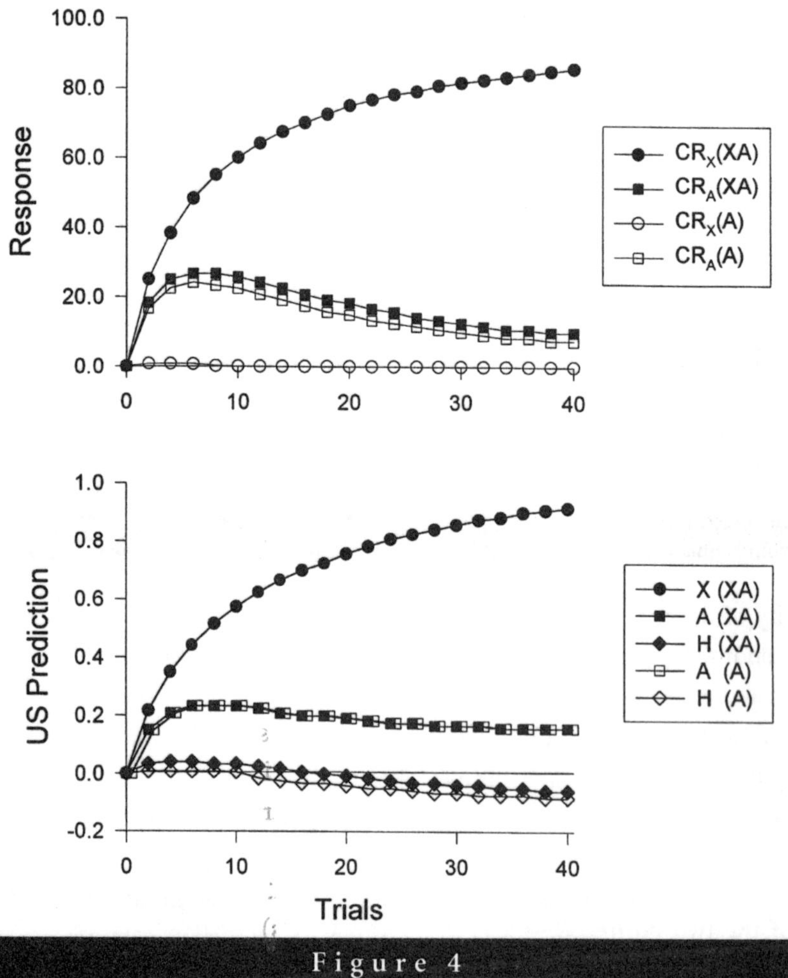

Figure 4

Acquisition of simultaneous feature-positive discrimination (simulation). (*Top panel*) CR_X (XA) = feature-appropriate responses during XA trials, CR_A (XA) = target-appropriate responses during XA trials, CR_X (A) = feature-appropriate responses during A trials CR_A (A) = target-appropriate responses during A trials. (*Lower panel*) X (XA) = US prediction by X during XA trials, A (XA) = US prediction by A during XA trials, H (XA) = US prediction by all the hidden units during XA trials, A (A) = US prediction by A during A trials, H (A) = US prediction by all the hidden units during A trials. Reprinted with permission from Schmajuk et al. (1998). Copyright 1998 by the American Psychological Association.

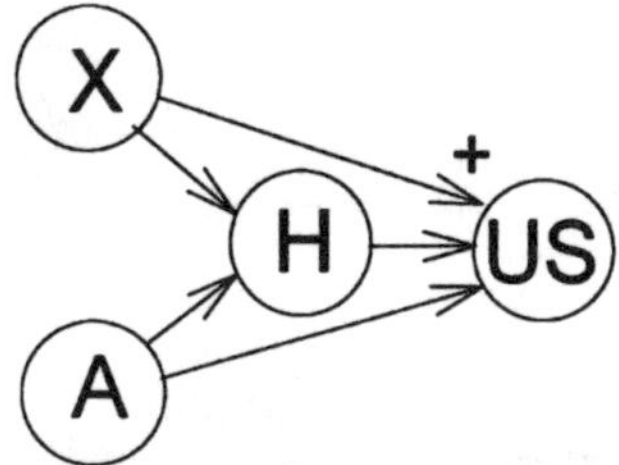

Figure 5

Simultaneous feature-positive discrimination. Simplified diagram of the network. When A and X are of similar intensities, X acquires a direct excitatory association with the US. Neither A nor the hidden units acquire strong associations with the US. Associative strengths are represented by plus or minus signs placed next to the arrows that connect the nodes. Only significant associative strengths are indicated. Reprinted with permission from Schmajuk et al. (1998). Copyright 1998 by the American Psychological Association.

sity of the feature and target stimuli. The upper panel of Figure 6 shows response form data on XA trials in which the target cue was either relatively weak or relatively strong with respect to the feature stimulus. As we saw earlier with cues of similar intensity, an FP discrimination in which the X cue is more intense than the A target results in conditioned responding of the form CR_X (Figure 6, upper panel, left bars). Interestingly, however, when a normal X is trained with a relatively weak A target, the response on XA trials is a mix of CR_X and CR_A, the latter being the predominant of the two (Figure 6, upper panel, right bars). These data suggest that when A was of relatively low intensity, X–US associations were formed, but if A was a very salient stimulus, X came to modulate the action of A.

The lower panel of Figure 6 shows responses generated on XA test trials in simulations of Holland's (1989a) experiment. Notice that the model correctly generates predominantly CR_X responding when the discrimination involves a weak target (left bars), and—also in agreement with experimental data—CR_A is stronger than CR_X when a relatively strong A is used. In the framework of the model, X–US and A–US associations

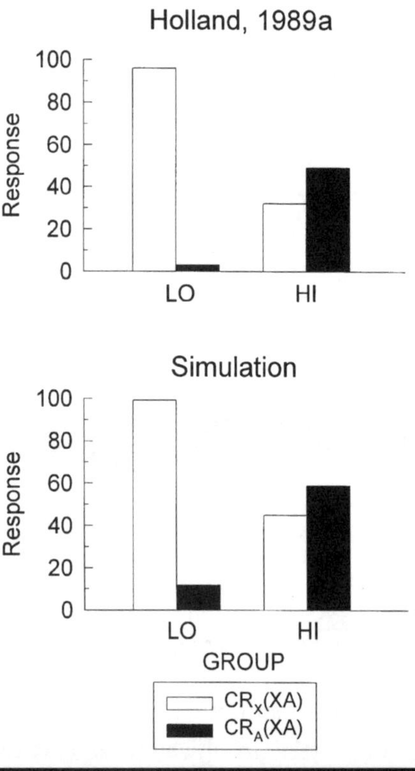

Figure 6

Simultaneous feature-positive (FP) discrimination with a high-intensity target. (*Top panel*) $CR_A(XA)$ (solid bars) and $CR_X(XA)$ (open bars) responding after simultaneous FP training with either a low-intensity (LO) or high-intensity (HI) auditory A cue. Data are from Holland (1989a). (*Lower panel,* simulation), Peak $CR_A(XA)$ and $CR_X(XA)$ after 30 training trials (15 XA+ trials alternated with 15 A– trials) with X salience .95 and A salience .3 (LO), or after 250 training trials (125 XA+ trials alternated with 125 A– trials) with X salience .3 and A salience .95 (HI). Reprinted with permission from Schmajuk et al. (1998). Copyright 1998 by the American Psychological Association.

increase with increasing intensities of A and X. When X is less intense than A, the A–US associations block X–US associations. Because A is not a good predictor of the occurrence of US, and X, which is a perfect predictor, cannot accrue an appreciable association with the US because of the blocking by A, the discrimination is solved by occasion setting—in other words, the hidden units are engaged to compensate for the overprediction of the

SIMULTANEOUS

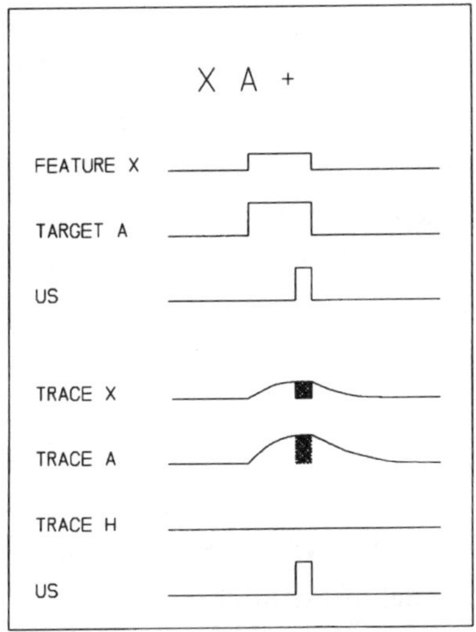

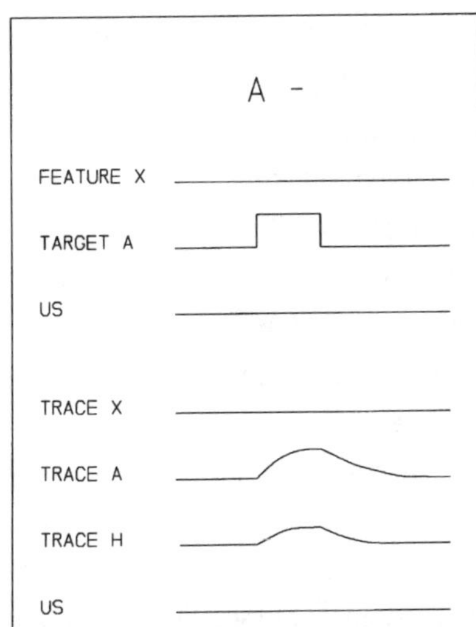

Figure 7

Simultaneous feature-positive discrimination with a high-intensity target. Real-time representations of X and A, their traces, and of the US on an XA+ and an A– trial. Adapted with permission from Schmajuk et al. (1998). Copyright 1998 by the American Psychological Association.

US (by direct A–US associations) on A-alone trials, which establishes an inhibitory H–US association. Thus, A–US associations activate CR_A, but CR_A is inhibited by the hidden units in the absence of X.

Figure 7 illustrates the real-time values of X, A, H, and the US during simultaneous FP discrimination training trials with a strong target. Feature X and target A generate short-term memory traces that grow after X and A onset and decay to zero after X and A terminate; but notice that the weak X stimulus generates a trace whose peak is much lower than that of target A. As before, hidden unit H is activated on A trials only. According to the SLH model, on a reinforced trial, X–US and A–US associations increase in proportion to the shaded area under each trace and decrease in proportion to the clear area under the curve. Although, during a nonreinforced trial, both X–US and A–US associations decrease in proportion to the whole area under the curves that represent their respective memory traces, X–US associations will eventually become weaker than A–US associations. This happens because the overshadowing of X by the more salient A cue on reinforced trials outweighs the greater amount of extinction observed with the A cue—in other words, because the constants that are associated with increases in CS–US change are greater than those that are associated with decreases in associative strength, the relative differences in the shaded areas under the curve are exaggerated, and the net effect is that the A stimulus gains relatively more association than it has extinguished.

A computer simulation of the acquisition of a simultaneous FP discrimination when A is more salient than X, shown in Figure 8, presents a picture that is quite different from that observed when CSs are of equivalent intensities (see Figure 4). The top panel of Figure 8 shows CR_X and CR_A responding to XA and A. At the beginning of training, CR_A responding to the XA compound and CR_A responding to A are similar. With increasing number of trials, CR_X and CR_A responding to the XA compound increase, CR_A responding to A decreases, and the discrimination is achieved. In contrast to the simulations shown in Figure 4, however, CR_X responding to the XA compound first increases and then decreases, and by trial 250 the dominant response to the XA compound is CR_A. Interestingly, the experimental data reported by Holland (1989c, Figure 5) show all of these patterns, although the model slightly overpredicts CR_A responding on A-alone trials.

The lower panel of Figure 8 shows that the US prediction generated by both X and A increase over trials. Importantly, the US prediction generated by the collection of all hidden units H becomes inhibitory, and this inhibition is expressed more strongly on A trials than on XA trials (i.e., the hidden units are more active on A trials than on XA trials). The discrimination is therefore achieved (stronger CR_A responding on XA trials than on A trials) because the same US prediction is generated by A on XA and A trials, whereas the hidden units generate stronger inhibition on A than on XA trials. Thus, feature X acts as an occasion setter because it acts on the A response system through its configural associations.

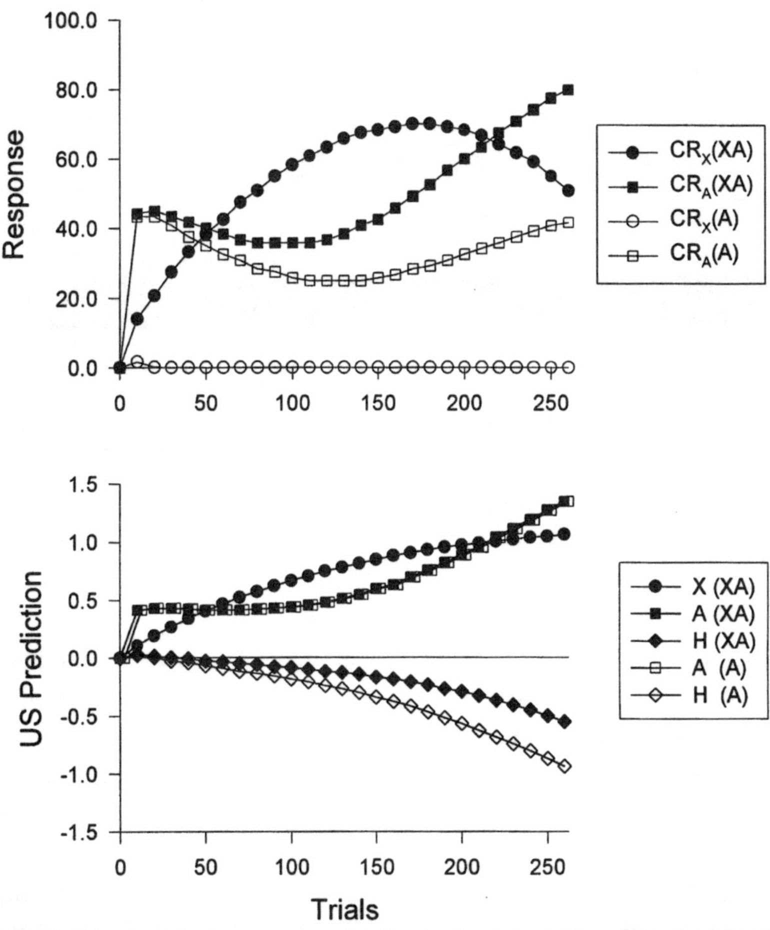

Figure 8

Acquisition of simultaneous feature-positive discrimination with a high-intensity target (simulation). (*Top panel*) CR_X (XA) = feature-appropriate responses during XA trials, CR_A (XA) = target-appropriate responses during XA trials, CR_X (A) = feature-appropriate responses during A trials, CR_A (A) = target-appropriate responses during A trials. (*Lower panel*) X (XA) = US prediction by X during XA trials, A (XA) = US prediction by A during XA trials, H (XA) = US prediction by all the hidden units during XA trials, A (A) = US prediction by A during A trials, H (A) = US prediction by all the hidden units during A trials. Reprinted with permission from Schmajuk et al. (1998). Copyright 1998 by the American Psychological Association.

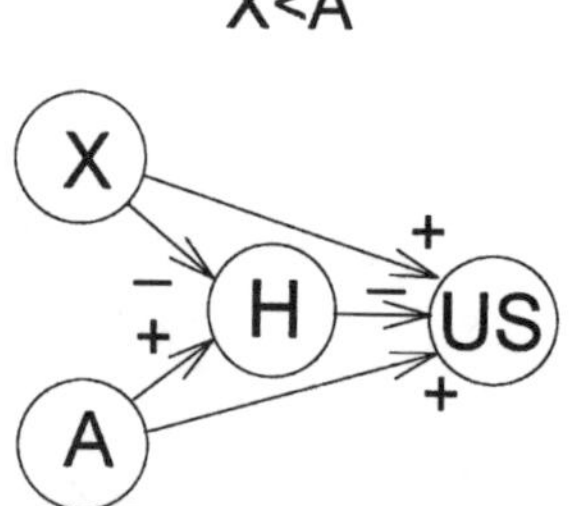

Figure 9

Simultaneous feature-positive discrimination with a high-intensity target. Simplified diagram of the neural network. When A intensity is relatively high compared to X, X acquires a direct excitatory association with the US and an inhibitory association with the hidden units (H). A acquires an excitatory association with the US and an excitatory association with the hidden units (H). The hidden units acquire an inhibitory association with the US. Associative strengths are represented by plus or minus signs placed next to the arrows that connect the nodes. Only significant associative strengths are indicated. Reprinted with permission from Schmajuk et al. (1998). Copyright 1998 by the American Psychological Association.

Figure 9 summarizes the model's solutions for the case of simultaneous FP discriminations with X less salient than A. In this case, X and A acquire strong direct associations with the US. On A-alone trials, A also activates the hidden units, which then inhibit the US prediction and therefore reduce the display of responding on A-alone trials on the basis of the A–US association. On XA trials, however, X attenuates the inhibition that is normally exerted by the hidden units (see Figure 8, lower panel), thus enabling the performance of both CR_A and CR_X. X therefore acts both as a simple CS, because of its strong direct excitatory association with the US, and as an occasion setter, because of its inhibitory associations with the hidden units.

Serial FP Discrimination

Compared to their findings with simultaneous compounds in FP discriminations, Ross and Holland (1981) observed quite different patterns of behavior when the X feature preceded the A target on compound trials.

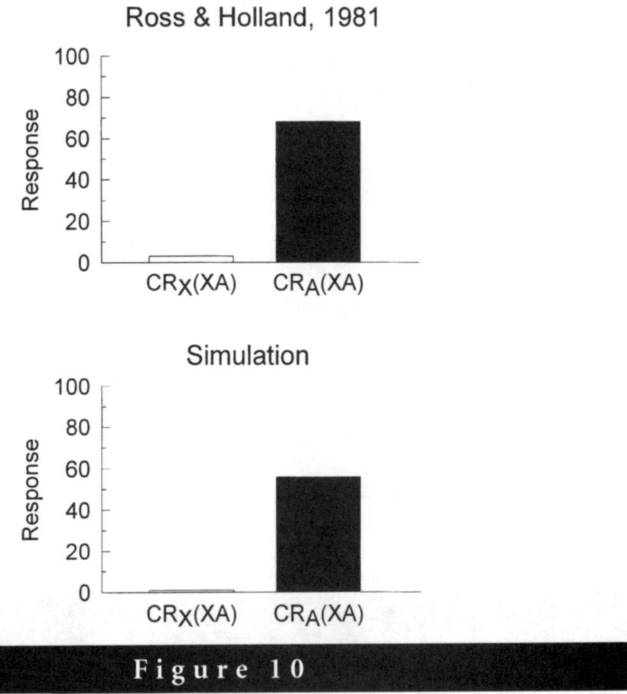

Figure 10

Response form (CR_X and CR_A) during serial feature-positive (FP) discriminations. (*Top panel*) CR_X and CR_A responding of rats trained in serial FP discriminations. The bars indicate the percentage of behavior that was CR_X (open bar) or CR_A (solid bar) on X→A compound trials. Data are from Ross and Holland (1981). (*Lower panel,* simulation) Peak CR_X (open bar) and CR_A (solid bar) on X→A test trials after 60 training trials (30 X→A+ trials alternated with 30 A− trials). Compare with Figure 2. Reprinted with permission from Schmajuk et al. (1998). Copyright 1998 by the American Psychological Association.

When a feature→empty interval→target (X→A) serial compound was reinforced and separate presentations of the target (A) were nonreinforced, the rats exhibited substantial behavior appropriate to the target (i.e., CR_A) during A on compound trials (see Figure 10, top panel), but not on A-alone trials. Thus, the target cues controlled behavior that was characteristic of target–US associations. Because responding to the target occurred only on serial compound trials, Ross and Holland suggested that the feature set the occasion for the occurrence of responding on the basis of target–US associations.

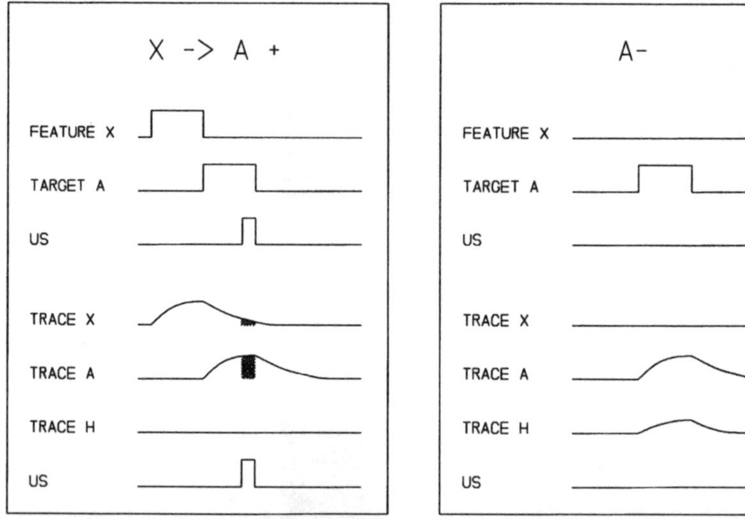

Figure 11

Serial feature-positive discrimination. Real-time representations of X and A, their traces, and of the US on an X→A+ and an A− trial. Adapted with permission from Schmajuk et al. (1998). Copyright 1998 by the American Psychological Association.

The lower panel of Figure 10 shows a simulation of the test results of Ross and Holland's (1981, Experiment 2) study. In agreement with the experimental data *(top panel),* the model generated mostly CR_A responding during X→A trials. Thus, the model captures the essence of Ross and Holland's response form distinction: Whereas with simultaneous presentation of the feature and target cues in training the response form was appropriate to the feature (see Figure 2), with serial feature–target arrangements the response form was appropriate to the target.

Figure 11 illustrates the real-time values of stimuli, including the hidden units, during reinforced and nonreinforced trials in a serial FP discrimination. According to the SLH model (see Equation 3), on a reinforced trial the X–US and A–US associations increase in proportion to the shaded area under each trace and decrease in proportion to the clear area under the curve. Because the X feature temporally precedes presentation of the A target and the US on a compound trial, the proportional increase in the association between X and the US (i.e., shaded area) is very small. Therefore, during reinforced X→A trials, X–US associations grow less than A–US associations.

Figure 12 shows a computer simulation of the acquisition of a serial FP discrimination. The top panel of the figure shows CR_X and CR_A responding to XA and A training trials. As the number of trials increases, CR_A responding to the XA compound increases, CR_A responding to A decreases, and the discrimination is achieved. The lower panel of Figure 12 shows that the US prediction generated by X ($\tau_X V_X$) increases only slightly because it is temporally remote from the US, whereas the US prediction generated by A ($\tau_A V_A$) increases substantially because it is contiguous with the US. Because the US is overpredicted by the A–US associations on A's nonreinforced trials, the system trains its hidden units in order to reduce the output error by generating a strong inhibition on the output on A trials. Over the course of training, the expression of this inhibition is differentiated on compound and target-alone trials: A relatively weak inhibitory output is generated on compound trials, whereas strong inhibition is generated on A-alone trials. Thus, the US predictions that are generated by the collection of all hidden units H ($\Sigma_j V_j \tau_{Hj}$) become increasingly negative, being more inhibitory on A trials than on XA trials.

Figure 13 shows a simplified depiction of the associative structure that is established in the network after 100 serial discrimination trials. Because of their different temporal relations with the US (see Figure 11), A accrues strong A–US associations, but X accrues only weak X–US associations. Because the form of responding is determined by the direct associations of X and A with the US, responding on X→A presentations involves mostly CR_A responses (see Figure 10). Furthermore, responding on A-alone trials is small because it is strongly inhibited by the hidden units (which are activated by A), and responding on X→A presentations is large because the inhibitory influence of the hidden units is ameliorated by the inhibitory action of X on the hidden units.

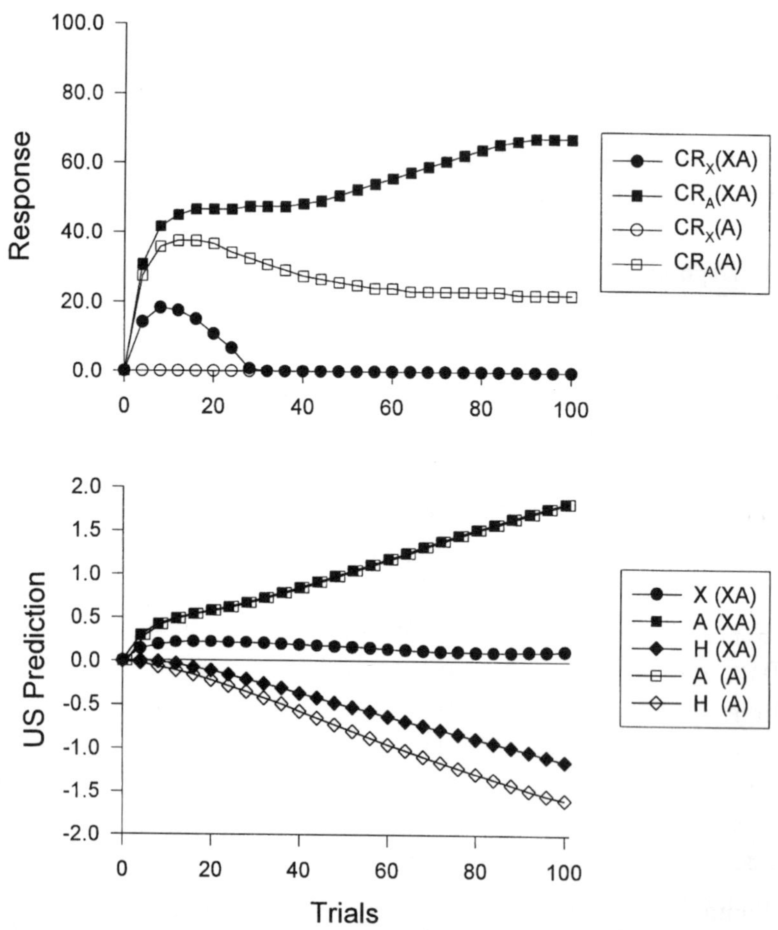

Figure 12

Acquisition of serial feature-positive discrimination (simulation). (*Top panel*) CR_X (XA) = feature-appropriate responses during X→A trials, CR_A (XA) = target-appropriate responses during X→A trials, CR_X (A) = feature-appropriate responses during A trials, CR_A (A) = target-appropriate responses during A trials. (*Lower panel*) X (XA) = US prediction by X during X→A trials, A (XA) = US prediction by A during X→A trials, H (XA) = US prediction by all the hidden units during X→A trials, A (A) = US prediction by A during A trials, H (A) = US prediction by all the hidden units during A trials. Reprinted with permission from Schmajuk et al. (1998). Copyright 1998 by the American Psychological Association.

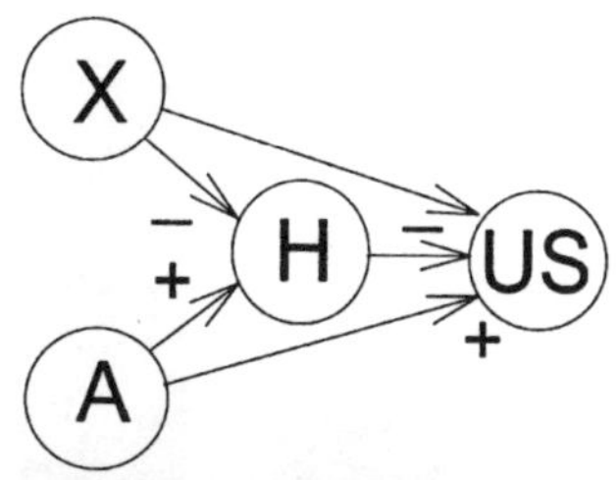

Figure 13

Serial feature-positive discrimination. Simplified diagram of the network. X acquires an inhibitory association with the hidden units (H). A acquires an excitatory association with the US and an excitatory association with the hidden units (H). The hidden units acquire an inhibitory association with the US. Associative strengths are represented by plus or minus signs placed next to the arrows that connect the nodes. Only significant associative strengths are indicated. Reprinted with permission from Schmajuk et al. (1998). Copyright 1998 by the American Psychological Association.

Conditional Contextual Discrimination

Just as in the case of simultaneous feature-positive (FP) or feature-negative (FN) discriminations with the target more salient than the feature or serial FP or FN discriminations, in conditional contextual discriminations, in which a CS is reinforced in one context and nonreinforced in another, the contexts seem to act as occasion setters—in other words, the contexts control responding through their configural associations but not through their direct associations.

Bouton and Swartzentruber (1986) studied a conditional contextual discrimination by administering a tone CS and a shock US during sessions in Context 1, and the CS alone in Context 2. After the discrimination was learned, neither context showed any reliable evidence of direct excitatory or inhibitory association with the US, and nonreinforced exposure to Context 1 alone did not reduce responding to the CS in that context. Figure 14 *(top panel)* shows more conditioned suppression to the CS in Context 1 than in Context 2 (Bouton & Swartzentruber, 1986, Experiment 1).

The lower panel of Figure 14 shows that suppression to A is large in

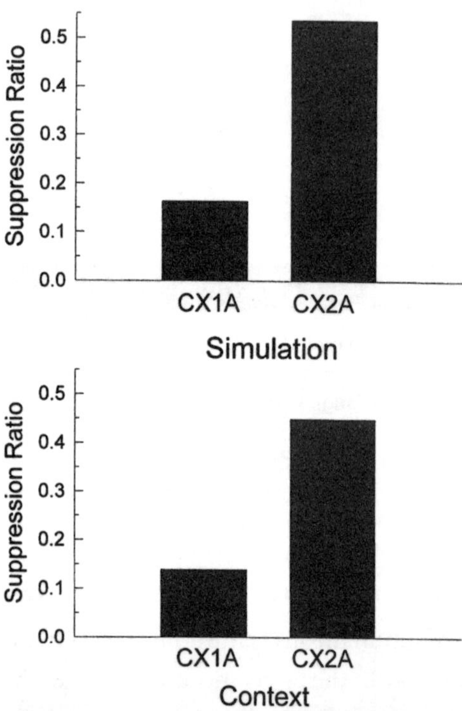

Figure 14

Conditional contextual discrimination. (*Top panel*) Suppression ratios to the CS in Context 1 (CX1A) and Context 2 (CX2A). Data are from Bouton and Swartzentruber (1986). (*Lower panel*, simulation): Suppression ratios to the CS in Context 1 (CX1A) and Context 2 (CX2A) after 300 training trials (150 A+ trials in Context 1 alternated with 150 A– trials in Context 2). Suppression ratio was computed by $(L-CR_A)/(L + (L-CR_A))$, where L (L = 64) represents the baseline rate of lever pressing as a percentage of the maximum CR_A. Reprinted with permission from Schmajuk et al. (1998). Copyright 1998 by the American Psychological Association.

Context 1 and small in Context 2. These simulated results are in agreement with Bouton and Swartzentruber's (1986) data.

Figure 15 illustrates the real-time values of CX1, CX2, A, H, and the US during a reinforced CX1:A+ trial *(left panel)* and a nonreinforced CX2:A– trial *(right panel)* in a conditional contextual discrimination. Ac-

CONTEXTUAL

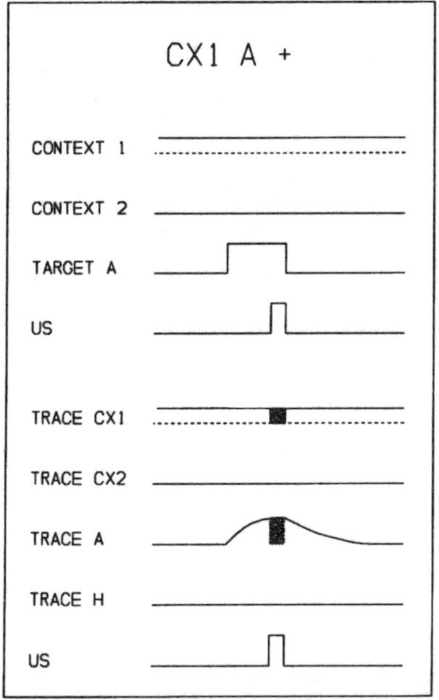

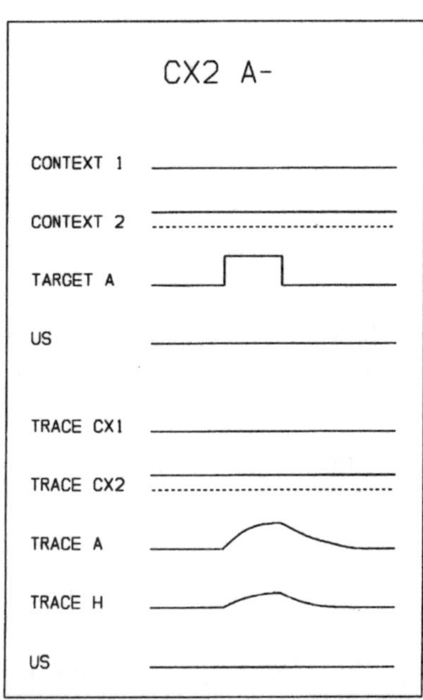

Figure 15

Conditional contextual discrimination. Real-time representations of CX1, CX2, and A, their traces, and of the US on a CX1 A+ and a CX2 A– trial. Adapted with permission from Schmajuk et al. (1998). Copyright 1998 by the American Psychological Association.

According to the SLH model, on reinforced trials the association between any stimulus input—including the hidden units H—and the US increases in proportion to only the shaded area under the curves that represent the activation of each stimulus node. In contrast, stimulus–US associations decrease proportionally to the clear area under the memory trace curves. As the left panel of Figure 15 shows, both CX1 and Target A are able to accrue excitatory associations with the US on CX1:A+ trials. The fact that CX1 is a tonic stimulus that undergoes extinction throughout the entire course of the trial, however, results in an overshadowing of CX1 by A—in other words, A accrues a relatively strong direct association with the US over trials, whereas the CX1–US association remains relatively weak.

The right panel shows that both CX2 and A, as well as the hidden units H, undergo extinction during nonreinforced CX2:A– trials.

Figure 16 shows the computer simulation of the acquisition of a conditional contextual discrimination. The top panel shows CR_A responding to CS_A in Context 1 and Context 2. At the beginning of training, CR_A responding is similar in both contexts. With increasing number of trials, CR_A responding decreases in Context 2, increases in Context 1, and the discrimination is achieved. The lower panel of Figure 16 shows that the US predictions generated by the contexts show little change ($\tau_{CX} V_{CX}$) and that the US prediction generated by A ($\tau_A V_A$) increases over trials. The US predictions generated by the collection of all hidden units H ($\Sigma_j V_j \tau_{Hj}$) first increase and then decrease, being more inhibitory on trials in Context 2 than on those in Context 1.

Figure 17 shows a simplified depiction of the network where CX_1 and CX_2 represent, respectively, Contexts 1 and 2; A represents the CS; and H represents the hidden-unit layer. Whereas A accrues strong A–US associations because of its temporal proximity to the US, the contexts accrue only weak direct associations with the US because they are present for most of the time in the absence of the US. The discrimination is therefore acquired because hidden units H exert a stronger inhibition on the US prediction during A presentations in Context 2 than during A presentations in Context 1. Both contexts acquire an almost negligible association with the US.

This section demonstrates that, when direct and indirect CS–US associations are combined in a real-time network, the same rule that Rescorla and Wagner introduced to describe phenomena that involve training with compound stimuli dictate the *role* of a CS. On the basis of this competitive rule, a feature acts as a simple CS (through its direct associations with the US) or an occasion setter (through its indirect associations with the US by way of the hidden units) depending on the strength of its direct association with the US, as determined by its intensity (in the case of simultaneous discriminations), the interstimulus interval (in the case of serial discriminations), or its duration (in the case of conditional contextual discriminations).

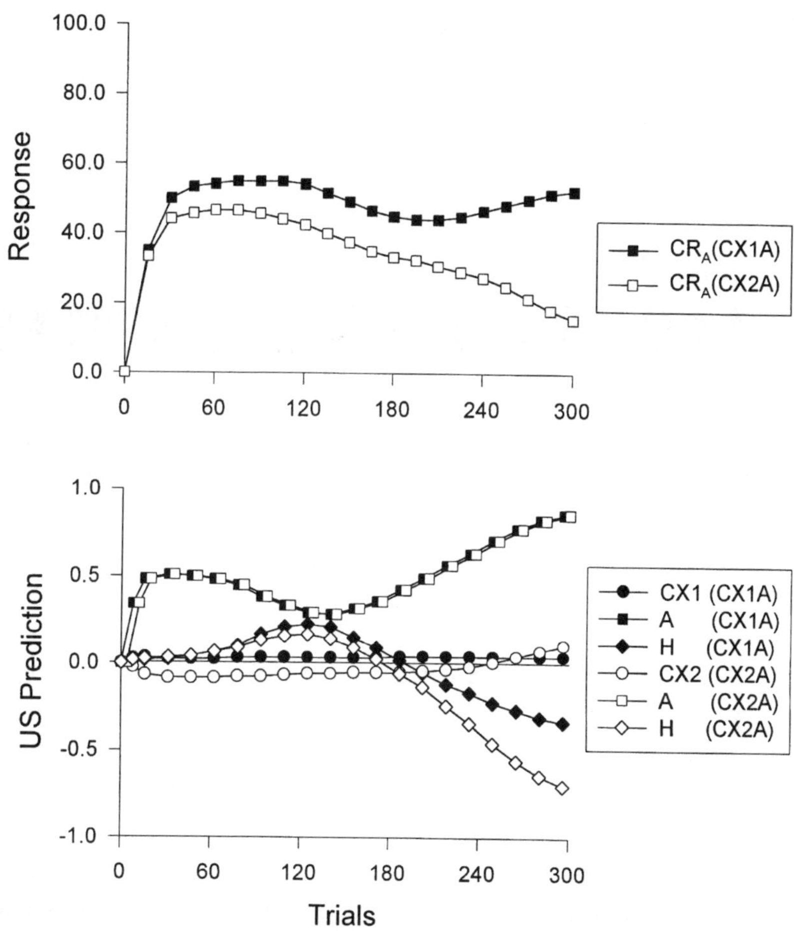

Figure 16

Acquisition of a conditional contextual discrimination (simulation). (*Top panel*) CR_A (CX1A) = responding in Context 1 during A+ trials, CR_A (CX2A) = responding in Context 2 during A– trials. (*Lower panel*) CX1(CX1A) = US prediction by CX1 during A trials, A (CX1A) = US prediction by A during A trials in Context 1, H (CX1A) = US prediction by all the hidden units during A trials in Context 1, CX2(CX2A) = US prediction by CX2 during A trials in Context 2, A(CX2A) = US prediction by A during A trials in Context 2, H(CX2A) = US prediction by all the hidden units during A trials in Context 2. Reprinted with permission from Schmajuk et al. (1998). Copyright 1998 by the American Psychological Association.

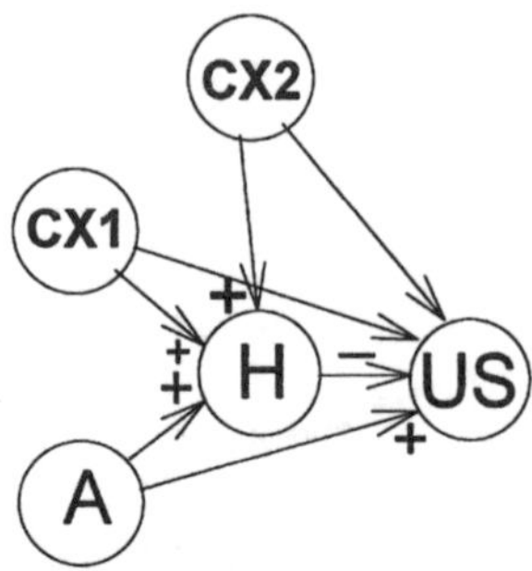

Figure 17

Conditional contextual discrimination. Simplified diagram of the network. CX1 acquires an excitatory association with the hidden units (H), CX2 acquires a stronger excitatory association with the hidden units (H), A acquires an excitatory association with the US and an excitatory association with the hidden units (H). The hidden units acquire an inhibitory association with the US. Associative strengths are represented by plus or minus signs placed next to the arrows that connect the nodes. Only significant associative strengths are indicated. Adapted with permission from Schmajuk et al. (1998). Copyright 1998 by the American Psychological Association.

The simulations show in detail three situations in which the model arrived at a similar associative solution to a discrimination problem. Perhaps the most interesting aspect common to all three, which unifies the paradigms and results in the similar solutions, is that the cue that best predicts the occurrence of the US (the X feature or the CX1 context) is a stimulus that is overshadowed by an A target that is relatively more salient. In one case, the X feature was weaker than A because of relative physical intensity. Similarly, when X preceded A in time in a serial discrimination, the memory trace of X had decayed and was thus relatively weak at the time the US was presented; in this case the A cue once again overshadowed X's ability to gain an association with the US. In the last case, CX1 suffered not only from having a trace that was relatively weak with regard to the A target, but also experienced substantial extinction during its presentation over the intertrial interval. In other words, in the framework of these simulations, a context is like a weak feature stimulus that also receives extra extinction training.

It is interesting to notice the similarity between the diagrams shown in Figures 13 and 17 with Bouton and Nelson's approach. Bouton and Nelson (1994) suggested that discrimination learning produces a combination of direct and indirect associative links among the CSs, the context, and the US. A control element, which gates the action of the associations formed between the CSs and the US, is established, and both the CSs and the contextual cues form associations with that control element. Consequently, some associations are only effective when the control element is jointly activated by the CSs and the contextual cues. Bouton and Nelson (1994) proposed that different conditioning procedures might encourage the encoding of one type of link over the other (e.g., direct connections with the US versus indirect connections with the control element), although they have not proposed explicit rules.

WHY IS AN OCCASION SETTER IMPERVIOUS TO EXTINCTION?

The previous section illustrated the conditions under which a CS may act as a simple CS (through its direct associations with the US), as an occasion setter (through its indirect associations with the US), or as a combination of both. According to the model, manipulations that change only CS–US direct connections should affect the simple properties of the CS, but not its occasion-setting properties. Similarly, a number of experiments have shown that manipulations that alter direct associations between occasion setters and the US leave the features' modulatory properties largely unaffected. For example, Holland (1989b) showed that repeated nonreinforced presentations of FP feature X resulted in extinction of the X–US association, as observed by a loss in CR_X responding on both X-alone and XA compound trials. In one experiment the FP discrimination was trained with a simultaneous XA compound, whereas in another the XA compound was presented serially. Interestingly, CR_A responding on compound trials, which is assumed to be indicative of occasion setting and not simple feature conditioning, was unaffected in the serially trained discrimination.

With the network model for multiple response systems, we have obtained simulations that correctly describe the various effects of feature extinction on responding to the X feature and the XA compound. According to the model, the effect of X extinction training is limited to decreases in the direct X–US associations involved in simple conditioning (see Figure 5). This results from the fact that, although presentation of X-alone on extinction trials fully activates τ_X, by contrast it does not result in activation of the hidden units (τ_H). Therefore, X–H or H–US associations involved in occasion setting are only minimally modified (see Figure 13).

Because simultaneous FP discriminations are solved by the model almost completely by direct X–US associations, the effect of X extinction is dramatic—it abolishes CR_X responding on both X and XA test trials. As Figure 4 illustrates, the level of CR_A on all trials, which would be indicative of occasion setting and generated through indirect H–US associations, was minimal to begin with. By contrast, compound responding for serial FP discriminations was mostly of the form CR_A (see Figure 12), generated not by X–US associations but by A–US associations that are attenuated by the inhibitory H–US associations. Because X–H and H–US associations are only minimally affected by X extinction, very little decrement was observed in XA compound responding after extinction.

WHY DOES A FEATURE TRANSFER ITS OCCASION-SETTING PROPERTIES TO OTHER TARGETS?

The previous sections demonstrated that the model captures the gist of two basic empirical distinctions between simple conditioning and occasion setting: response form and resistance to extinction. In addition to these basic differences, simple CSs and occasion setters also differ in the way they control responding when combined with other CSs and occasion setters. According to the model, whereas a simple CS can linearly combine its CS–US associations with the CS–US associations of other CSs, an occasion setter combines its CS–configural associations with the CS–configural associations of other occasion setters and the CS–US associations of simple CSs that follow more complicated, nonlinear rules.

The result of combining CSs and occasion setters with other CSs has been studied in transfer experiments. For example, if a feature X previously trained in a simultaneous FP discrimination is paired with a trained-then-extinguished CS, B, the simple CS–US associations of the feature will immediately generate responses on XB trials (Holland, 1986a). This result is easily explained in terms of the direct connections accrued by X during acquisition of the discrimination that can be added to any potential target (see Figure 5). By contrast, as shown in Figure 18 *(top panel),* if a feature X previously trained in a serial FP discrimination is paired with a trained-then-extinguished CS, B, the occasion-setting properties of the feature might (Davidson & Rescorla, 1986; Jarrard & Davidson, 1991) or might not (Holland, 1986a) generate responses on XB trials. These conflicting results are explained in terms of whether the complete associative structure that is necessary for an occasion setter to exert its influence on the target–US associations is present (see Figure 9). According to the model, this depends on the salience of the context.

As shown in Figure 9, the mechanism by which an occasion setter increases responding to other stimuli is by inhibiting an inhibitory H–US association that is activated by excitatory target CS–H associations, and thus allowing a direct target–US excitatory association to be expressed. Therefore, transfer will be observed only if a potential transfer target possesses these two associations (X–H and CS–H) with the output layer. According to the model, in the case of a trained-then-extinguished CS, this depends on the salience of the context (see Figure 18, *bottom panel).*

Figure 19 shows the training and extinction phases of a computer simulation for an experiment on transfer to a trained-then-extinguished cue. The top panel shows CR_A (the target is assumed to be an auditory cue), as well as the prediction of the US by the direct CS–US association (CS), and by the hidden units (H). In this simulation, context salience is low. Over training trials, CR_A first increases and then decreases as the CS is presented without reinforcement. More importantly, note that this response results from changes that occur almost exclusively in the direct CS–US associations: The direct prediction of the US increases during conditioning and then is decremented during extinction, whereas the pre-

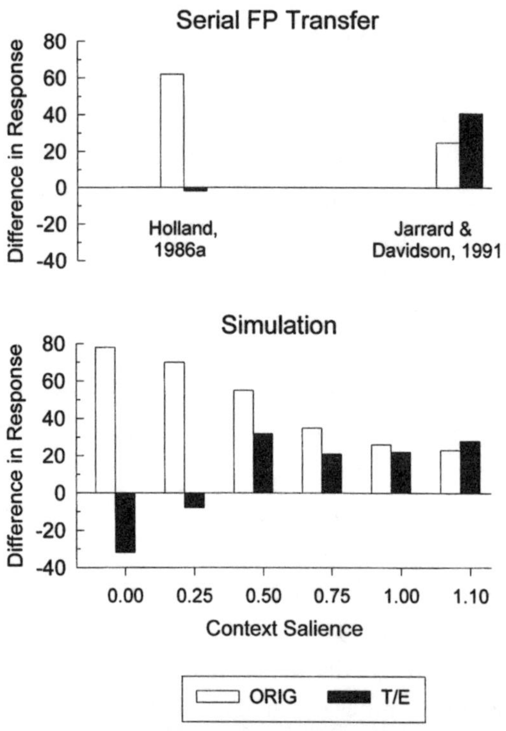

Figure 18

Serial feature-positive (FP) discrimination. Transfer to a trained and extinguished CS in different contexts. (*Top panel*) Differences in CR_A responding between X→A and A trials (open bars) and between X→B and B trials (solid bars) after serial FP training with X and A, and training and extinguishing B. Data are from Holland (1986a) and Jarrard and Davidson (1991). (*Lower panel,* simulations) Differences between peak CR_A(X→A) and CR_A(A) (open bars) and between peak CR_A(X→B) and CR_A(B) (solid bars) after 38 X→A+ trials alternated with 38 A– trials, followed by 6 B+ trials and 3 B– trials for different values of context salience. Reprinted with permission from Schmajuk et al. (1998). Copyright 1998 by the American Psychological Association.

diction of the US by the hidden units remains largely unchanged. By contrast, the bottom panel of Figure 19 depicts a simulation in which the conditioned response is a result of changes in both the direct and configural associations. In this simulation, the salience of the context is high. Although CR_A increases and then decreases in a fashion similar to the previous simulation, the relative contributions of the configural and direct

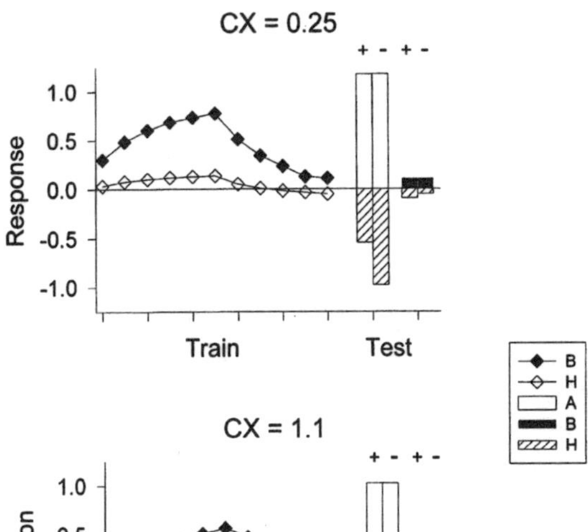

Figure 19

Training and extinction of a cue in salient and nonsalient contexts. (*Top panel*) In a nonsalient context, B first acquires a strong direct association with the US, but this association decreases during extinction. Transfer will not be observed. (*Bottom panel*) In a salient context, B first acquires a strong direct association with the US, but this association does not decrease during extinction. Instead, B and the CX acquire strong excitatory associations with the hidden units (H). The hidden units acquire an inhibitory association with the US. Transfer will be observed. Associative strengths are represented by plus or minus signs placed next to the arrows that connect the nodes. Only significant associative strengths are indicated.

associations have been altered. During conditioning, the increase in CR_A is based largely on a direct CS–US association. During extinction, however, the decrease in responding is a result of both a decrement in the direct excitatory association as well as establishment of an *inhibitory* association between the hidden units and the US. This inhibitory association is excited by activation of the transfer CS input unit (not represented in the figure).

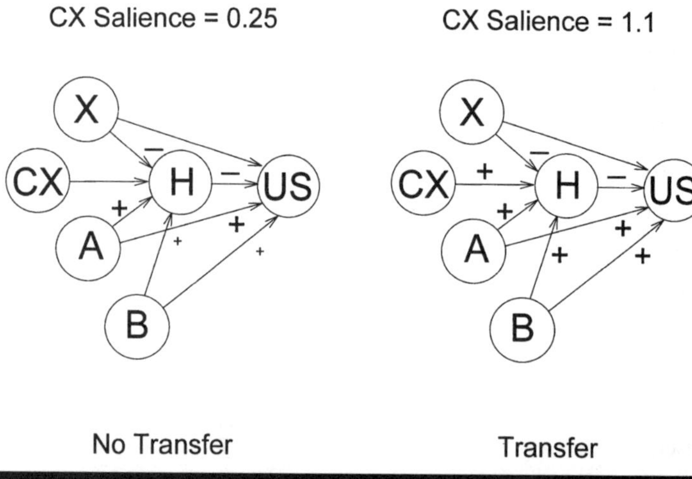

Figure 20

Transfer to a trained and extinguished cue. Simplified diagrams of the model including the context (CX). (*Left panel*) In a nonsalient context, X acquires an inhibitory association with the hidden units (H), CX acquires a weak excitatory association with the hidden units (H), A acquires an excitatory association with the US and an excitatory association with the hidden units (H), and B acquires a weak excitatory association with the US. The hidden units acquire an inhibitory association with the US. No transfer is observed. (*Right panel*) In a salient context, CX acquires a strong excitatory association with the hidden units (H), and B acquires a strong excitatory association with the US. Transfer is observed. Associative strengths are represented by plus or minus signs placed next to the arrows that connect the nodes. Only significant associative strengths are indicated.

The result of these differing associative structures after extinction training is that one CS trained in salient context possesses the associative structure necessary to support transfer with an occasion setter, whereas the other trained in relatively weak context does not (see Figure 20). This implication was confirmed with simulations of transfer tests in which an occasion setter enhanced responding to the former cue, but not the latter (see Schmajuk et al., 1998). The accuracy of this theoretical account remains to be verified in future empirical studies.

WHY MULTIPLE REPRESENTATIONS OF A CS ARE NEEDED

As mentioned earlier, in the SLH model a stimulus performs as a simple CS when it acts on a response system through its direct excitatory or inhibitory associations, and as an occasion setter when it acts on a response system through its configural associations (by way of the hidden unit layer). In other words, a CS is assumed to have two distinct representations, a simple one and a configural one. Some theories and models of classical conditioning assume, as the SLH model does, that CSs have multiple representations, and that these different representations underlie the different CS roles. By contrast, other models assume only one type of representation. Models that include both simple and configural representations include those of Bouton (1994), Kehoe (1988), Schmajuk and DiCarlo (1992), and Wagner (1992). Models that include only configural representations include those of Gluck and Myers (1993) and Pearce (1987, 1994). Finally, the Moore and Choi (chapter 10, this volume) model includes simple CS and temporally active representations.

Some experimental data seem to favor the multiple representation view: (a) response form, (b) compound conditioning, (c) extinction and renewal effects, and (d) some neurophysiological studies.

Response Form

Data indicating that different CSs generate different CRs (Holland, 1977) require information about the specific CS to be preserved when the CS enters an associative relationship with the US. Also, Holland and Block (1983) showed that animals trained in positive patterning showed a mixed CR different from the CRs that were generated by each individual component.

Compound Conditioning

In compound conditioning, two or more stimuli are presented together in the presence of the US. Kehoe (1986) explored the relation between configuration and summation by comparing the responding to a CS1–CS2 compound and its components, CS1 and CS2, under different proportions of reinforced presentations of CS1–CS2, CS1, and CS2. He found that responding to each component, CS1 and CS2, decreased with increasing proportion of CS1–CS2 presentations. Kehoe suggested that the result supports the notion that CS1–CS2, CS1, and CS2 have separate representations that compete to establish associations with the US. Responding to the CS1–CS2 compound is approximately proportional to the sum of the responding to CS1 and CS2 after a high proportion of reinforced presentations of CS1 and CS2, but much larger than the sum of responding to CS1 and CS2 after a high proportion of reinforced presentations of the CS1–CS2 compound.

Extinction and Renewal

When the context is salient, the SLH model accounts for extinction as the consequence of the CS's configural associations canceling the action of the CS direct associations, but leaving them intact. This view is similar to Domjan and Burkhard's (1986) view that extinction is not simply a passive decrease in the CS–US association but instead involves the active inhibition of responding, and to Bouton's (1994) suggestion that acquisition and extinction are mediated by separate, context-controlled mechanisms. The interaction between CS direct and configural associations also allows our model to describe the renewal phenomenon, in which the CS generates a CR when, after undergoing extinction in one context, it is tested in another context. In the case of renewal, excitatory CS–US associations are preserved as inhibitory contextual configural associations are formed. Return to the original training context reduces the contribution of those inhibitory configural associations, resulting in the reemergence of responding.

Neurophysiological Evidence

Gallagher, Graham, and Holland (1990) reported that neurotoxic lesions of the central nucleus (CN) of the amygdala impair acquisition of conditioned orienting responses to light (rearing) and conditioned orienting responses to tone (startle) in a simple discrimination paradigm. LeDoux (1992) described how information about auditory CSs reaches the amygdala. The CS is first relayed through auditory pathways to the medial geniculate body (MGB) of the thalamus, and from there to the lateral nucleus (LN) of the amygdala through two parallel pathways. One pathway involves a direct projection from the medial division of the MGB and the posterior intralaminar nucleus (PIN) to the lateral amygdala; the other pathway includes a projection from the ventral and medial divisions of the MGB and the PIN to the auditory cortex, to the perirhinal cortex, and to the lateral amygdala. Whereas the direct pathway is capable of establishing "quick and dirty" connections, the cortical system is needed for discriminatory functions. On the basis of these data, Schmajuk and Buhusi (1997) conjectured that, whereas direct connections in the model correspond to direct thalamic–amygdalar pathways, indirect pathways in the model correspond to indirect thalamic–cortical–amygdalar pathways.

Interestingly, direct thalamic–amygdalar and indirect thalamic–cortical–amygdalar pathways might underlie Domjan and Burkhard's (1986) and Bouton's (1994) separate mechanisms for acquisition and extinction. Evidence favoring this view come from Teich et al.'s (1989) study reporting that lesions of the auditory cortex impair the extinction of differential heart rate Pavlovian conditioning to tones in rabbits. Whereas auditory cortex lesions did not impair acquisition of differential conditioning, they did hinder extinction of responding to CS+.

In sum, the idea that a CS gives rise to multiple representations—one that simply maintains a short-term memory of the CS, one that becomes combined with the representations of other CSs, and a set of representations that are active at different times following the CS onset—seems to receive support from both behavioral and neurophysiological data. Understanding how these representations interact among themselves and with the US appear to be central to our understanding of classical conditioning phenomena.

DISCUSSION

Schmajuk and DiCarlo (1992) offered a real-time, single-response neural network that successfully describes many classical conditioning paradigms. In the network, a CS can establish direct, simple associations and indirect, configural associations with the US, all of which operate in accordance with the Rescorla and Wagner (1972) rule. Schmajuk, Lamoureux, and Holland (1998) extended this theory to include (a) multiple response systems that establish associations with simple and configural stimuli to control different responses (e.g., eyeblink, headjerk, rearing), (b) a system that provides both stimulus configuration and generalization to the different response systems, and (c) a system that provides inhibition to the different response systems.

The SLH model offers a precise description of the different roles that a CS can play in classical conditioning. A CS acts as a simple CS through its direct, simple associations with the US or as an occasion setter through indirect, configural associations with the US. As a result of their own excitatory or inhibitory associations with the output (US) units, hidden units that correspond to stimulus configurations join the action of direct excitatory and inhibitory associations of simple CSs with the US. Importantly, hidden-unit action does not reflect a special process or function. Connections between the hidden units and the output units are not qualitatively different from direct connections between input and output units and are both controlled by a Rescorla and Wagner (1972) rule.

Once the roles of simple CS and occasion setter are defined in the context of the model, the model describes the principal differences in response form, extinction and counterconditioning effects, and transfer following serial and simultaneous FP discrimination training. Exhibit 1 summarizes these findings and translates some empirical questions into theoretical questions in the context of the model. For instance, the question of when a CS behaves as an occasion setter becomes the issue of what type of connections, as shown by the response form, the features establish with the US. The question of the effect of extinction and counterconditioning on discrimination performance becomes the issue of how the connec-

Exhibit 1

Occasion Setting: Simulations Obtained With the SLH Model

When does the feature (or CS) behave as an occasion setter?

- Simultaneous feature-positive (FP) discrimination
- Simultaneous FP discrimination with a strong target
- Simultaneous feature-negative (FN) discrimination
- Serial FP discrimination
- Serial FN discrimination
- Conditional contextual discrimination

What is the effect on the discrimination of extinction and counterconditioning of the feature?

- Simultaneous FP discriminations and extinction
- Simultaneous FN discrimination and counterconditioning
- Serial FP discrimination and extinction
- Serial FN discrimination and counterconditioning

How are the features combined with the targets?

- Simultaneous FP discrimination
- Simultaneous FN discrimination
- Serial FP transfer to a trained and extinguished cue
- Serial FP within-category transfer
- Serial FN within-category transfer

tions established by the features are affected by reinforced or nonreinforced presentations of the features. Finally, the question of transfer effects becomes the issue of how the associative powers of the features are combined with the associative powers of the targets.

Besides the phenomena enumerated in Exhibit 1, the model correctly describes the effects of pretraining to A, X, and X and A (e.g., Rescorla, 1986). In addition, the model qualitatively addresses how temporal factors, such as (a) feature–target (X–A) and X–US intervals; (b) X–A, X–US, and A–US intervals; (c) termination asynchrony; and (d) relation of within- and between-trial time intervals affect the nature of FP discriminations (see Holland, 1986b, 1992).

Interestingly, Schmajuk and Buhusi (1997) demonstrated through computer simulations—under the assumptions that (a) nonselective lesions of the hippocampal formation impair both competition (Equation 3) and configuration (Equation 5), and (b) selective lesions of the hippocampus proper impair only stimulus configuration (Equation 5)—how the model describes the effects of selective and nonselective hippocampal lesions on paradigms in which stimuli act as occasion setters.

In conclusion, a real-time network that assumes that (a) organisms only learn when the actual value of the US differs from its expected value, (b) CSs generate short-term memory traces that can become associated with the US, and (c) the expected value of the US is computed on a linear combination of the associative strength of all active CSs plus the associative strength of configurations of those active CSs, seems to provide an integrated account for complex patterns of experimental data.

REFERENCES

Bouton, M. E. (1994). Conditioning, remembering, and forgetting. *Journal of Experimental Psychology: Animal Behavior Processes, 20*(3), 219–231.

Bouton, M. E., & Nelson, J. B. (1994). Context-specificity of target versus feature inhibition in a feature-negative discrimination. *Journal of Experimental Psychology: Animal Behavior Processes,* 20(3), 51–65.

Bouton, M. E., & Swartzentruber, D. (1986). Analysis of the associative and occasion-setting properties of contexts participating in a Pavlovian discrimination. *Journal of Experimental Psychology: Animal Behavior Processes, 12,* 333–350.

Bush, R. R., & Mosteller, F. (1955). *Stochastic models for learning.* New York: Wiley.

Davidson, T. L., & Rescorla, R. A. (1986) Transfer of facilitation in the rat. *Animal Learning & Behavior, 14,* 380–386.

Domjan, M., & Burkhard, B. (1986). *The principles of learning and behavior* (2nd ed.). Monterey, CA: Brooks/Cole.

Gallagher, P. C., Graham, P. W., & Holland, P. C. (1990). The amygdala central nucleus and appetitive Pavlovian conditioning: Lesions impair one class of conditioned behavior. *The Journal of Neuroscience, 10,* 1906–1911.

Gluck, M. A., & Myers, C. E. (1993). Hippocampal mediation of stimulus representation: A computational theory. *Hippocampus, 3,* 491–516.

Holland, P. C. (1977). Conditioned stimulus as a determinant of the form of the Pavlovian conditioned response. *Journal of Experimental Psychology: Animal Behavior Processes, 3,* 77–104.

Holland, P. C. (1986a). Transfer after serial feature positive discrimination training. *Learning and Motivation, 17,* 243–268.

Holland, P. C. (1986b). Temporal determinants of occasion setting in feature positive discriminations. *Animal Learning & Behavior, 14,* 111–120.

Holland, P. C. (1989a). Occasion setting with simultaneous compounds in rats. *Journal of Experimental Psychology: Animal Behavior Processes, 15,* 183–193.

Holland, P. C. (1989b). Feature extinction enhances transfer of occasion setting. *Animal Learning & Behavior, 17,* 269–279.

Holland, P. C. (1989c). Acquisition and transfer of conditional discrimination performance. *Journal of Experimental Psychology: Animal Behavior Processes, 15,* 154–165.

Holland, P. C. (1992). Occasion setting in Pavlovian conditioning. In D. L. Medin (Ed.), *The psychology of learning and motivation* (Vol. 28, pp. 69–125). New York: Academic Press.

Holland, P. C., & Block, H. (1983). Evidence for a unique cue in positive patterning. *Bulletin of the Psychonomic Society, 21*(4), 297–300.

Hull, C. L. (1943). *Principles of behavior.* New York: Appleton-Century-Crofts.

Jarrard, L. E., & Davidson, T. L. (1991). On the hippocampus and learned conditional responding: Effects of aspiration versus ibotenate lesions. *Hippocampus, 1,* 103–113.

Kehoe, E. J. (1986). Summation and configuration in conditioning of the rabbit's nictitating membrane response to compound stimuli. *Journal of Experimental Psychology: Animal Behavior Processes, 12,* 186–195.

Kehoe, E. J. (1988). A layered network model of associative learning: Learning to learn and configuration. *Psychological Bulletin, 95,* 411–422.

LeDoux, J. E. (1992). Emotion and the amygdala. In J. Aggleton (Ed.), *The amygdala: Neurobiological aspects of emotion, memory, and mental dysfunction* (pp. 339–351). New York: Wiley-Liss.

Pearce, J. M. (1987). A model for stimulus generalization in Pavlovian conditioning. *Psychological Review, 94,* 61–75.

Pearce, J. M. (1994). Similarity and discrimination: A selective review and a connectionist model. *Psychological Review, 101,* 587–607.

Rescorla, R. A. (1973). Evidence of a "unique stimulus" account of configural conditioning. *Journal of Comparative and Physiological Psychology, 85,* 331–338.

Rescorla, R. A. (1986). Facilitation and excitation. *Journal of Experimental Psychology: Animal Behavior Processes, 12,* 325–332.

Rescorla, R. A., & Wagner, A. R. (1972). A theory of Pavlovian conditioning: Variations in the effectiveness of reinforcement and nonreinforcement. In A. H. Black & W. F. Prokasy (Eds.), *Classical conditioning II* (pp. 64–99). New York: Appleton-Century-Crofts.

Ross, R. T., & Holland, P. C. (1981). Conditioning of simultaneous and serial feature-positive discriminations. *Animal Learning & Behavior, 9,* 293–303.

Rumelhart, D. E., Hinton, G. E., & Williams, G. E. (1986). Learning internal representations by error propagation. In D. E. Rumelhart & J. L. McClelland (Eds.), *Parallel distributed processing: Explorations in the microstructure of cognition, Vol 1: Foundations.* Cambridge, MA: Bradford Books, MIT Press.

Schmajuk, N. A., & Buhusi, C. (1997). Stimulus configuration, occasion setting, and the hippocampus. *Behavioral Neuroscience,* 111, 235–258.

Schmajuk, N. A., & DiCarlo, J. J. (1992). Stimulus configuration, classical conditioning, and the hippocampus. *Psychological Review, 99,* 268–305.

Schmajuk, N. A., Lamoureux, J. A., & Holland, P. C. (1998). Occasion setting: A neural network approach. *Psychological Review, 105,* 3–32.

Teich, A. H., McCabe, P. M., Gentile, C. C., Schneiderman, L. S., Winters, R. W., Linkowsky, D. R., & Schneiderman, N. (1989). Auditory cortex lesions prevent the extinction of Pavlovian differential heart rate conditioning to tonal stimuli in rabbits. *Brain Research, 480,* 210–218.

Wagner, A. R. (1993). Some complexities anticipated by ÆSOP and other dual-representation theories [abstract]. In H. Kimmel (Chair), Symposium on Pavlovian Conditioning with Complex Stimuli, XXV International Congress of Psychology (1992), *Psychologia, 36,* 101–102.

Werbos, P. (1987, March/April). Building and understanding adaptive systems: A statistical/numerical approach to factory automation and brain research. *IEEE Transactions SMC,* 1–4.

Author Index

Italicized page numbers refer to listings in the reference sections; *n* following a page number indicates listings in a note.

Subject Index

n following a page number indicates a note.

About the Editors

Nestor A. Schmajuk graduated from the University of Buenos Aires and became an Associate Professor of Biomedical Engineering in Argentina. In 1986, he obtained a doctorate in psychology from the University of Massachusetts and became a postdoctoral fellow at the Center for Adaptive Systems at Boston University. From 1988 until 1993 he was an assistant professor of psychology at Northwestern University. In 1992 he obtained a fellowship from the Royal Society (London) to develop models of the neurophysiological basis of latent inhibition. In 1993 he moved to Duke University where he is an Associate Professor of Psychology.

He has developed neural network models of classical conditioning, operant conditioning, animal communication, spatial learning, and cognitive mapping. Using these neural networks he has described the consequences of hippocampal, cortical, and cerebellar lesions, as well as the effects of the administration of dopaminergic and cholinergic drugs, in different learning and cognitive tasks. His book *Animal Learning and Cognition: A Neural Network Approach* was recently published by Cambridge University Press.

Most recently, he has applied neural network models to the description of occasion setting and the effect of hippocampal lesions on this phenomenon.

Peter C. Holland received his undergraduate degree from Michigan State University in 1972, and his doctorate from Yale University in 1976. From 1976 to 1985 he served on the faculty of the University of Pittsburgh. In 1986 he moved to Duke University, where he is now James B. Duke Professor of Psychology: Experimental.

He has published extensively on occasion setting, determinants of the form of Pavlovian appetitively conditioned responses, and functional aspects of event representation in conditioning. Most of his recent research, conducted in collaboration with Dr. Michela Gallagher of Johns Hopkins University, has examined brain systems for changes in attention in conditioning.